Rules of Evidence
A PRACTICAL APPROACH

SECOND EDITION

Michael Gulycz
Mary Ann Kelly
Doug Cochran

 emond ▪ Toronto, Canada ▪ 2016

Emond Montgomery Publications Limited
60 Shaftesbury Avenue
Toronto ON M4T 1A3
http://www.emond.ca/highered

Printed in Canada.
Reprinted February 2022.

We acknowledge the financial support of the Government of Canada.
Nous reconnaissons l'appui financier du gouvernement du Canada.

Canadä

Emond Montgomery Publications has no responsibility for the persistence or accuracy of URLs for external or third-party Internet websites referred to in this publication, and does not guarantee that any content on such websites is, or will remain, accurate or appropriate.

Managing editor, development: Kelly Dickson
Developmental editor: Heather Gough
Director, editorial and production: Jim Lyons
Production editor: Laura Bast
Copy editor: Francine Geraci
Proofreader: Lila Campbell
Permissions editor: Lisa Brant
Indexer: Paula Pike
Cover and text designer: Tara Wells
Typesetter: Shani Sohn
Cover image: Forance/Shutterstock

Library and Archives Canada Cataloguing in Publication

Cochran, Doug, 1950--
[Rules of evidence]
    Rules of evidence : a practical approach / Michael Gulycz, Mary Ann Kelly, Doug Cochran. 2nd edition.

Revision of: Cochran, Doug, 1950-. Rules of evidence.
Includes bibliographical references and index.
ISBN 978-1-55239-480-9 (paperback)

    1. Evidence (Law) Canada. I. Gulycz, Michael, 1958-, author II. Kelly, Mary Ann, 1948-, author III. Title. IV. Title: Rules of evidence.

KE8440.C62 2016   347.71'06   C2015-907401-0   KF8935.ZA2C62 2016

To my students at Seneca College, who remind me that
teaching is also a learning experience.

—*Mary Ann Kelly*

For Veronica, who has always encouraged and supported me.

—*Mike Gulycz*

Contents

PART I

BASIC CONCEPTS AND FUNDAMENTAL PRINCIPLES

7 The Principled Exception to the Hearsay Rule 111

8 Character Evidence 125

PART III

EVIDENCE AND THE CHARTER

Preface

Evidence law is different from most other types of law. Rather than substantive and procedural matters, it focuses on the information that will be made available to the court to help the trier of fact answer the question, "What happened in this case?" While this question can never be answered with absolute certainty—the trier of fact cannot travel back in time to witness events as they actually occurred—the main object of evidence law is to provide the trier of fact with as much reliable information as possible in order to make the best possible decision. If the information that is given to the trier of fact is not reliable, the resulting decision is unlikely to reflect what actually happened. Therefore, much of evidence law seeks to determine the reliability of information presented in a court proceeding.

Many observers have commented that evidence law is essentially a system of complex rules and principles that govern what information is deemed reliable and can therefore be heard by the trier of fact. But evidence law is much more than this. It demands analysis of a fact situation and application of the "rules" in a logically sequenced manner to arrive at a correct decision. Sometimes there may be more than one correct decision. This is the reason evidence law is part science and part art. There are rules, but there is also sufficient flexibility in their application to permit an effective advocate to present the best case for his or her client.

The object of this book is to give the legal professional a practical approach to analyzing and applying the rules in order to represent a client effectively before a court or tribunal. We have tried to achieve this goal by sequencing the material to provide a working template for the practitioner.

The introductory chapters present basic background about the justice system in order to show how evidence law fits into the "big picture." The latter chapters deal with methods of presenting evidence in proceedings.

The middle part of the text explains the threshold tests that apply in determining the information that may be considered by the trier of fact. In Chapter 4, Fundamental Principles, we state that the first question is always, "Is the proposed evidence material and relevant?" If it is not, it is generally not admitted. If it is, the process of examining the relevant and material evidence continues in order to determine whether it is sufficiently reliable to be introduced into the proceeding.

We then move on to the examination of the rules for excluding evidence that meets the threshold tests of materiality and relevance, yet may otherwise be viewed as unreliable. Chapters 5 through 7 deal with the hearsay rule and its various exceptions. The other major exclusionary rules are dealt with in Chapters 8 through 10. Part III of the text then looks at the impact of the *Canadian Charter of Rights and Freedoms* on evidence law, including the confession rule. One notable feature here is an explanation of the interaction of the common law with the Charter right to silence.

The first edition of this text was published in 2008. Much has happened in law since then. The most obvious changes involve the Charter and how the courts use it in relation to the law of evidence. For example, in *R v Grant* and subsequent decisions, the Supreme Court of Canada has completely overhauled the approach to remedies available under section 24(2) of the Charter (exclusion of evidence whose admission "would bring the administration of justice into disrepute"). The law on self-incrimination and the right to silence has also experienced material changes since the first edition was published. While the most obvious changes relate to the interpretation and application of the Charter, every exclusionary rule has been touched in some way by the forces of change. For example, recent amendments to the *Canada Evidence Act* have changed the manner in which one spouse can be compelled as a witness against the other spouse.

This new edition also contains updated information on DNA testing, which has identified serious miscarriages of justice in which innocent people were imprisoned for crimes they did not commit, as well as the dangers associated with placing too much reliance on expert evidence.

Our intent was to preserve the character and straightforward presentation that made the original text a success. We believe we have accomplished this goal. But we have also sought to enhance the presentation of the material. For example, most chapters now contain Case in Point features that illustrate how courts apply evidentiary principles.

We hope that you will find this revised edition of *Rules of Evidence: A Practical Approach* a useful tool in preparing for a career as a legal professional.

PART I

Basic Concepts and Fundamental Principles

Who's Who in the Courtroom

1

LEARNING OUTCOMES

After completing this chapter, you should be able to:

▪ Demonstrate an understanding of the adversarial system and the role evidence plays in that system.

▪ Demonstrate an understanding of the roles of the judge and jury and the division of their responsibilities.

▪ Demonstrate an understanding of the function of the voir dire and the charge to the jury in the trial process.

Introduction

In this book, we will examine the rules of evidence and their practical application in a courtroom or administrative tribunal. The role of evidence is to assist the trier of fact in determining the truth in a fair manner. Evidence is about proof of facts, and while that may seem simple at first glance, the principles and rules about the admission and exclusion of evidence in a legal proceeding can be quite complex.

The text is divided into four parts. The first deals with fundamental principles and the legal tests applied to determine whether a particular piece of information meets the basic test for admissibility. The second part deals with the rules about excluding potential evidence from a proceeding. Next we discuss the role of the *Canadian Charter of Rights and Freedoms* and its substantial impact on evidence law. Finally, after we have examined the rules and principles, we look at how evidence is presented in a proceeding.

In this chapter, we take an overview of the criminal and civil (non-criminal) processes in the Canadian legal system and examine how the two processes work within the adversarial system, which is used in Canadian courts to try to reach the truth. We discuss the roles of the decision-makers and the role of evidence in that adversarial system.

Overview of the Criminal and Civil Litigation Processes

The criminal and civil litigation processes are similar in a number of respects. Each starts with a specific court document commencing the action. In a criminal trial, the document is called an information. It is usually laid by a police officer but, in some circumstances, may be laid by a private person. The information outlines the offences that the person charged has allegedly committed. In a civil (that is, non-criminal) process, the person starting the case, usually called the plaintiff, issues a document required by the rules of court. (The name of this document may differ according to province, court level, or type of case. It is often called a writ or a statement of claim.) In this document, the plaintiff outlines the wrong that she feels was done to her by the opposite party, usually called the defendant, and sets out how she is asking the court to correct that wrong. In both criminal and civil matters, various pre-trial steps are taken. Most often, these steps are designed to ensure that there will be a fair hearing of the issues. In civil cases, these steps ensure that all parties have an opportunity to discover the evidence that is available both for and against their position, as well as to explore alternatives to a full trial on the issues.

On television and in the movies, court cases are often won when one side surprises the other with a major witness or a major piece of documentary or physical evidence right in the courtroom. While this might make for good drama, it does not reflect the real-life litigation process in Canadian courts. In both criminal and civil cases, there are specific requirements to share evidence before the trial begins. The sharing of evidence is called **disclosure** in the criminal process and **discovery** in the civil process.

In a criminal or quasi-criminal proceeding, the prosecution has an absolute duty to disclose the full evidence against the accused person to the defence, but the defence is not required to disclose the basis for its case or the evidence supporting its position. This difference is due to the fact that an individual, charged with an offence, is not usually on an equal footing with the government prosecuting the case. The government has huge resources to investigate and obtain evidence that is not normally available to individuals unless they are very wealthy. Therefore, to try to ensure fairness and a relatively level playing field, the Crown prosecution must disclose its full case so that the accused person has an opportunity to prepare a proper defence to the charges.

The sharing of evidence, besides attempting to provide fairness, is also designed to streamline the trial process and, where possible, avoid trial entirely by permitting all parties to evaluate what their chances might be in a trial. By assessing the case that the opposing side will present in court, each party can weigh the advantages and disadvantages of continuing on a litigious path. In a criminal matter, after reviewing all of the Crown's evidence against him, an accused may want to offer a guilty plea if the Crown is willing to reduce the charge or agree to a lesser sentence in exchange. This is commonly referred to as a plea bargain or a plea arrangement and is a central process in the criminal justice system. In a civil matter, settlement may be a safer and more economical route than the very expensive and uncertain road of litigation.

disclosure
the requirement that the Crown produce to the defence, before the trial begins, all the evidence that has been gathered in a criminal case

discovery
the process in a non-criminal case through which every party to the case has an opportunity to examine the evidence

The Litigation Process

The following chart compares and contrasts the major steps involved in the criminal and civil litigation processes.

Criminal	Civil
Process commenced by an information.	Process commenced by a specified court document, often called a writ or statement of claim.
Pre-trial process to ensure full disclosure to the accused of the Crown's case.	Pre-trial process to ensure that each side has full opportunity to discover the evidence that the other side has at its disposal.
Selection of mode of trial. (For most serious offences, the accused can choose trial by judge alone or trial by judge and jury.)	Selection of mode of trial. (In the superior civil court in the provinces, either party usually can choose trial by judge or trial by judge and jury.)
Trial commences with the Crown presenting evidence first, usually by having its witnesses testify. The Crown's questioning of its witnesses is known as direct examination or examination-in-chief. The defence then has an opportunity to ask questions or "cross-examine" the witnesses.	Trial commences with the plaintiff presenting evidence first, usually by having its witnesses testify. The plaintiff's questioning of its witnesses is known as direct examination or as examination-in-chief. The defence then has an opportunity to ask questions or "cross-examine" the witnesses.

Criminal	Civil
Evidentiary issues that arise before or during the trial may be dealt with in pre-trial motions or in a voir dire.	Evidentiary issues that arise before the trial may be dealt with in pre-trial motions, but evidentiary issues may arise during the course of the trial as well and are dealt with as they arise.
The Crown continues to call evidence until it has presented all of its evidence. The Crown then closes its case.	The plaintiff continues to call evidence until it has presented all of its evidence. The plaintiff then closes its case.
If the defence believes that the Crown has not met its burden of proof (that is, proof beyond a reasonable doubt), the defence may decide not to call any evidence but to make an application to the judge for a directed verdict of acquittal. If the application is successful, the accused will be formally acquitted of the charges.	If the defence believes that the plaintiff has not met its burden of proof (that is, proof on the balance of probabilities), the defence may decide not to call any evidence but to bring a motion for non-suit and argue that the case against the defendant has not been made and there is nothing to answer or defend against. If the motion is successful, the case will be dismissed.
If there is no motion for a directed verdict or such a motion is unsuccessful, the defence counsel who chooses to present evidence then calls its first witness and so on until the defence has presented all of its evidence.	If there is no motion for a directed verdict or such a motion is unsuccessful, the defence calls its first witness and so on until it has presented all of its evidence.
Once the Crown and the defence have presented their evidence, the Crown may be entitled to call reply or rebuttal evidence.	Once the plaintiff and the defendant have presented their evidence, the plaintiff may have an opportunity to call reply or rebuttal evidence.
Both the Crown and the defence now have a chance to argue their case or to state to the trier of fact (judge or jury, if there is one) why they should "find" in their favour (that is, give them what they are asking for). It is at this stage that counsel argue that the evidence that has been presented supports the outcome they are seeking. This stage of the proceedings is called submissions.	Both the plaintiff and the defendant now have a chance to argue their case to the trier of fact (judge or jury, if there is one), showing why they should "find" in their favour (that is, give them what they are asking for). It is at this stage that counsel argue that the evidence that has been presented supports the outcome they are seeking. This stage of the proceedings is called submissions.
The trier of fact (judge or jury, if there is one) then considers the evidence and submissions and makes a decision (renders a verdict). This involves a finding that the accused is guilty or not guilty of the offence he is charged with. If the accused is found not guilty, the judge discharges the accused, who is then free to go on with his life. If the accused is found guilty, the judge initiates the sentencing process.	The trier of fact (judge or jury, if there is one) then considers the evidence and submissions and makes a decision. This involves a determination of liability—that is, has the defendant caused a wrong to the plaintiff that has resulted in her suffering damages? If the defendant is found liable, the trier of fact awards compensation to the plaintiff in a set amount of dollars.

The Adversarial System

In Canada, as in most other countries whose legal system is based on the British common law system, the judicial process is adversarial. In theory, each party in the **adversarial system** is represented by a skilled advocate (often referred to as counsel, if a lawyer, or as an agent, if a paralegal), knowledgeable in the law, who presents the party's case in the best possible light, within the permitted ethical rules. The case is presented before an impartial, unbiased judge who remains relatively passive during the proceedings.

> **adversarial system**
> judicial process in which parties present evidence before an impartial decision-maker, who then makes a decision in the case

The premise of the adversarial system is that when each party presents and argues its case in the most favourable light, and has an opportunity to vigorously challenge the opposing party's case through cross-examination before an impartial judge, the truth can be approached or reached more often than not.

While the adversarial system has profoundly shaped common law legal thinking, other fact-finding systems exist. The one we may be most familiar with is the inquisitorial system, also known as the scientific process, used in most civil law jurisdictions such as Quebec and France. This system involves an investigation directed at finding the truth. The fact-finder may use various avenues to resolve the problem she faces—for example, whether the accused person committed the assault or which of the parties in a civil case broke the business contract between them. This fact-finder is an active participant who seeks out the truth by investigating and questioning the facts as they are presented.

Impartial Decision-Makers in the Adversarial System

Judges in the adversarial system do not take an active part in the search for truth. In the Canadian system, the judge does not extensively question witnesses or make other investigations into finding the "truth." In fact, too much comment, expression of opinion, or active questioning of witnesses by a judge can be the basis for a successful appeal and a new trial. In legal terms, too much participation in the hearing can result in a finding by an appeal court that there has been "a reasonable apprehension of bias" on the part of the decision-maker, even if there is no actual bias—a perception of bias by a reasonable person is enough.

In our system, a judge who engages in questioning or challenging the evidence, or making comments in relation to it, is more likely to influence or to be seen to influence the outcome of the judicial process through any bias she may hold or be perceived as holding. This may be particularly important in a trial involving a jury. A judge who makes comments or asks questions of a witness may be seen as influencing the jury's decision. However, even in a non-jury trial, questioning of witnesses, making comments, or expressing opinions can lead to a reasonable apprehension of bias on the part of a judge. It is said that a judge who "descends into the arena … is liable to have his vision clouded by the dust of conflict" (see *Yuill v Yuill*, [1945] 1 All ER 183 at 189 (CA), per Lord Green). That is, a judge who takes too active a role risks losing the objectivity we so prize in a decision-maker.

On the other hand, the passivity of the decision-maker can also be reviewed by a higher court if the trial judge acted in a manner that favoured, or appeared to favour, one party over another. This does not mean that the judge cannot participate in the proceedings in any way—in some circumstances, it is important for the judge to take a more active role. In cases where a witness has some frailty due, for example, to age, lack of legal representation, or limited knowledge of English, a judge often must take a role in ensuring that the witness can effectively communicate her evidence. In fact, a judge who does not intervene to facilitate testimony in such circumstances may be subject to criticism by the higher courts. The main concern is that the judge not engage in behaviour that actually aids one side to the disadvantage of the other or prevents an accused from mounting a proper defence to the charges he faces, or is perceived as doing so.

CASE IN POINT

Provincial Court Judge Removed from Case for Acting Like Counsel

R v Musselman (2004), 25 CR (6th) 295 (Ont Sup Ct J)

An Ontario Provincial Court judge was prohibited from hearing an impaired driving case when it came up for trial again because he appeared to be wearing two hats, Crown and judge, in the matter. On reviewing his conduct, the Court of Appeal noted that the judge had "become an advocate in his own cause in the forum reserved for disputes he is to decide impartially in a process of calm and detached deliberation." The judge did not disguise his distaste for those who represent impaired drivers and for the law that the court must apply in these cases. The judge's descent into the arena was particularly strongly demonstrated when he

sent a series of emails to Crown counsel who would deal with any appeal of his decision, inquiring whether an appeal had been commenced and whether they would like his "thoughts on it" to assist them. The judge also crossed the line with some comments in *obiter dicta* which were critical of an appeal court judge. In prohibiting the judge from hearing the case, the Court of Appeal stated that "an atmosphere has been created where it appears that the trial judge has matters of his own reputation and integrity in mind when approaching these cases, rather than the dispassionate adjudication of the underlying cases."

By opting for the adversarial system, we have chosen to temper the quest for truth with other values, such as limiting the power of the state to prosecute individuals and emphasizing the appearance of fairness and impartiality. Some would argue that the latter maintains the high regard in which the system of justice is held, an essential ingredient in any system of justice in a democracy.

However, there are criticisms of the adversarial system. The nature of the adversarial system implies that only one party can be a winner. If each side is partially right, then a process that affords only a win–lose resolution contains, by definition, some injustice. Trials are not the only system for resolution of legal disputes in our society, but they remain the main vehicle of last resort. Some parties will include a clause in a contract requiring them to resolve disputes through arbitration, but this process looks very much like litigation by trial. Its main advantage is speedier decision-making, thus allowing the parties to go on with their lives. With the speedier decisions can also come monetary savings, but since the arbitration system is largely private, the savings are not assured.

How Evidence Fits into the Adversarial System

The rules of evidence that we apply today were developed over a considerable period of time in an effort to ensure that there was a fair and equitable process in place for resolving legal disputes. In the early stages of development, fairness and equity were not always prime considerations; the original process was more about protecting royalty and other highly placed persons from having their power (property and ability to tax) eroded. Many disputes were settled by trial by ordeal and trial by battle—that is, the legality of a claim (say, to ownership of land) was determined by how strong, skilled, or lucky a claimant was. But as the concept of democracy took root, fairness and equity became more important goals of the judicial process, and the principles of natural justice evolved in keeping with the political evolution.

Philosophically, the Age of Reason contributed the thinking that a system of justice should be rational. Trial by ordeal and other crude approaches to justice gave way to more rational concepts such as relevance and materiality, which were developed to ensure that the decision-maker would consider valid or useful information in coming to its conclusions in a dispute. Think of the expression "garbage in—garbage out": essentially, a decision-maker cannot make a good decision when considering unhelpful, confusing, or useless information. The primary function of evidence law is to ensure that useful or valuable information is placed before decision-makers. It is a vehicle for transmission of information to the decision-makers, and, as with any vehicle, we must ensure that it provides a safe and reliable conveyance. Just as the adversarial system of justice has evolved to its present form over a thousand or more years, the use and abuse of evidence law has likewise evolved over time, and we should not assume that there is nothing to improve upon. We should also keep in mind that an evidentiary system that worked well at one point in our history may become outmoded, awkward, and unsatisfactory at a later time.

Division of Responsibilities in the Adversarial System

In a trial, two types of decisions must be made: the facts must be decided and the law that applies must be determined. The decision-maker may be a judge sitting alone or it may be a judge and jury hearing the case. A very important aspect of this latter situation is the division of their responsibilities.

When a judge sits alone, without a jury, she fulfills both decision-making roles. In other words, she is both the **trier of fact** and the **trier of law**. When there is a judge and jury, the judge is the trier of law and the jury is the trier of fact. The responsibility of the judge in a jury trial is to make all the decisions that require legal training. She controls the process to ensure that all parties are treated fairly and that the rules, including the rules of evidence, are complied with. The parties to the dispute cannot be relied upon to present only valid information that will help the decision-maker come to a just conclusion, because at least one of the parties would prefer simply that the conclusion was favourable to him, whether or not it was just. Thus, the judge determines whether information that one side wishes to present to the jury in the form of evidence will be admitted before the jury. This means the judge can control whether the jury gets to see or hear this information. This role is like that of a gatekeeper,

trier of fact
person in a trial who assesses the evidence and renders a verdict; in a jury trial, the jury

trier of law
person in a trial who controls the trial process, determines the admissibility of evidence, and instructs the trier of fact on the applicable law; in a jury trial, the judge

someone who protects a group from harmful intrusions. In this instance, the harmful intrusion is the admission of information that will potentially damage the fact-finding process, or that will make it harder or impossible for the jury to do its job properly.

Perspective and Relevancy

One particularly egregious example of how perspective can cloud a determination of relevancy is the case of Frank Joseph Paul. He was a New Brunswick Mi'kmaq who froze to death on the streets of Vancouver after having been taken from police custody and dumped drunk and wet in an alleyway in freezing weather. Paul's treatment was in fact consistent with the common police practice in some parts of Canada of taking intoxicated people, particularly intoxicated Aboriginal people, and dumping them in areas where the police won't have to deal with them.

In reviewing the matter, Crown counsel determined that no charges should be laid against the police, saying, "Given the available evidence, the Crown is unable to establish that any police officer failed to perform a duty upon them in such a manner that demonstrated a marked departure from the conduct of a reasonably prudent person *or that it was objectively foreseeable that the conduct of the officers in failing to provide a more adequate shelter for Mr. Paul endangered his life or was likely to cause permanent damage to his health.*" How it is not foreseeable that dumping a severely intoxicated person in an alley in freezing weather would at the very least endanger his health is unclear. There were police records and a police surveillance video showing the police dragging Mr. Paul into the elevator, dripping wet, a short time before depositing him into the alley.

Mr. Paul's death led to calls for a public inquiry. Those advocating for an inquiry questioned whether the Crown's assessment of available evidence or application of the standard of objective foreseeability and reasonable prudence is impartial, or whether it reflects the Crown's close relationship to the police.

In 2007, as a result of revelations that jail guard Greg Firlotte, who was present the night Paul was dumped in the alleyway, was not even spoken to in the police investigation of the incident, the BC attorney general announced that an inquiry would be held.

The gatekeeper lets in the desirable information and keeps out the mischief-making information. Desirable evidence is information that will assist the trier of fact in coming to a fair determination of the issues on the basis of the facts before them. As we will see when examining the other roles of evidence law, the gatekeeper may keep information from the trier of fact that might be helpful in terms of fact-finding but is undesirable for other reasons. These reasons include the maintenance of societal values that are considered more important than the proper resolution of one particular dispute.

The jury, where there is one, has the duty of determining what information they accept and what weight they assign to that information. As the trier of fact, the jury has exclusive authority over issues involving credibility and reliability of the evidence, once it has been admitted. The jury is also responsible for rendering a verdict on the issues—that is, making a finding of guilty or not guilty in a criminal matter, and determining whether the plaintiff or the defendant has proven his or her claims in a civil matter. In a jury trial, the roles of judge and jury must be carefully segregated to ensure that the process is fair. If a judge erodes the jury's independence by directing their conclusions on the facts, the decision in the case may be appealed by the losing party.

Where a judge is sitting without a jury, the judge must play a dual role of trier of law and trier of fact. Thus, the judge will consider certain evidence as required by law and will not consider information he has heard but not admitted into evidence. To illustrate the judge's position, consider an example: An accused person has confessed to an offence. The defence lawyer argues that the confession should not be admitted into evidence for a number of alleged violations of the *Canadian Charter of Rights and Freedoms*. The defence asks the judge to rule the confession inadmissible. Obviously, the judge must hear that there was a confession before he can rule on whether or not it is admissible as evidence. If the judge determines that the confession is not admissible, then he will not consider the confession in any way in determining the guilt of the accused.

However, when there is a jury, it is the responsibility of the judge, in his gatekeeper role, to ensure that jurors hear only admissible evidence so that they are not swayed by information that they are not permitted to consider. The thinking is that a judge, because of his legal training, can more easily separate admissible evidence from inadmissible information.

Roles in the Courtroom

The following chart summarizes the division of responsibilities in the courtroom.

Trier of Law (always the judge)	Trier of Fact (judge or jury)
• Controls the process in the courtroom	• Weighs all admissible evidence
• Determines the admissibility of individual pieces of proposed evidence	• Assesses the credibility and reliability of witnesses and evidence
• Instructs the trier of fact on the law that applies	• Renders a verdict

Voir Dire

A **voir dire** is an examination that is designed to determine the admissibility of a proposed piece of evidence. The expression, which found its way into the English common law system through the Norman influence, literally means "to speak the truth." It is a process that can be used with information such as a confession where the Crown is obliged to prove that the statement is voluntary, or with any other evidence where the two parties are in disagreement about its admissibility. It is sometimes said that a voir dire is a trial within a trial.

The process used to keep information from being wrongly considered by a jury is to exclude the jury from hearing information in dispute until the judge determines

voir dire
mini-trial, or trial within a trial, that is designed to determine the admissibility of evidence in the absence of the trier of fact

whether the information is admissible as evidence. The judge declares a voir dire and the jury is sent out of the room while the parties argue the issue. Counsel then present arguments to the judge as to whether the disputed information should be admissible. If the judge determines that it is not admissible, the jury returns and never hears any of it. If the judge determines that it is admissible, the jury returns and the information is repeated in front of the jury, as evidence. Where the judge is sitting alone and has heard the proposed evidence on a voir dire but excluded it, she must forget what she has heard, or "disabuse herself of the evidence," and not consider it in her decision. If a judge does consider information that did not properly become evidence, the decision may be appealed for this error.

We have seen that the admission and consideration of evidence are roles that are handled by two separate bodies, the trier of law and trier of fact, even where the two are contained within one physical body—the judge. We also know that it is an error for the trier of fact to consider information that is not properly before it. Because the legally trained trier of law determines what information is seen and therefore can be considered by the trier of fact, the system has a built-in protection from improper or dangerous assumptions or conclusions that can result when the trier of fact considers prejudicial information in reaching its decision in a case.

Charge to the Jury

In a jury trial, once all the evidence has been presented by all parties, counsel for each side will make submissions and attempt to persuade the jury to accept its version of the facts. The judge then gives the jury very precise instructions about the law that must be applied to the facts of the case. In a criminal trial, the judge gives a summary of the facts the Crown must prove in order to establish the guilt of the accused. The judge must also explain all defences that are reasonably available to the accused, even if a particular defence was not raised by the accused during the trial. In a civil trial, the judge outlines the issues the plaintiff must establish and the defences available to the defendant. Jury instructions may be very lengthy in some cases, taking several days or longer. The jurors are then instructed on their duties once they begin deliberations. This process is called the **charge to the jury**.

charge to the jury
judge's instructions to the jury, before the jury begins deliberations, regarding the applicable law, the standard of proof, and the available defences

Many US jurisdictions have standardized jury instructions and have "refined" them so that they are much simpler and shorter than Canadian jury instructions. The Canadian Judicial Council has created model jury instructions for criminal matters to assist judges in giving instructions in order to reduce errors that lead to appeals and possible case dismissals and to make the trial system more efficient.

The Supreme Court of Canada has restated the elements that must be addressed in the charge to the jury as follows (see *R v Daley*, 2007 SCC 53 at para 29):

1. instruction on the relevant legal issues, including the charges faced by the accused;
2. an explanation of the theories of each side;
3. a review of the salient facts that support the theories and case of each side;
4. a review of the evidence relating to the law;

5. a direction informing the jury that they are the masters of the facts and it is for them to make the factual determinations;

6. instruction about the burden of proof and presumption of innocence;

7. the possible verdicts open to the jury; and

8. the requirements of unanimity for reaching a verdict.

According to the judgment in another Supreme Court case (see *R v Osolin*, [1993] 4 SCR 595 at 683):

The jury system has in general functioned exceptionally well. Its importance has been recognized in s. 11(f) of the *Charter*. One of the reasons it has functioned so very well is that trial judges have been able to direct the minds of jurors to the essential elements of the offence and to those defences which are applicable. That process should be maintained. The charge to the jury must be directed to the essential elements of the crime with which the accused is charged and defences to it. Speculative defences that are unfounded should not be presented to the jury. To do so would be wrong, confusing, and unnecessarily lengthen jury trials.

Because the charge to the jury is so important, it is often the subject of an appeal. One party or the other may take the view that the jury has come to an improper conclusion owing to errors in the judge's charge.

Just Not Getting the Point

A jury in British Columbia was hearing the case of a man charged with stealing a horse. After hearing all the evidence and the judge's instructions, the jury went off to deliberate. The jurors returned with their verdict: Not guilty, but the accused had to return the horse. When the judge patiently explained that they could not come up with such a verdict because it was contradictory, the jurors dutifully returned to the jury room for further deliberations. They returned with their new verdict: Guilty, but the accused could keep the horse.

Source: Peter V MacDonald, *Court Jesters: Canada's Lawyers and Judges Take the Stand to Relate Their Funniest Stories* (Don Mills, Ont: Stoddart, 1985).

Commentary on the Jury System

The jury system developed in England under Henry II in 1166 with the appointment of 12 free men who would resolve civil disputes over land and taxes. Criminal matters were still dealt with by way of trial by ordeal or trial by battle at this time. In the 13th century, the jury system began to be applied to criminal matters. Initially, the jury was an "informed jury," meaning that they either had knowledge of the parties and the facts beyond what they heard in court, or were charged with conducting an investigation of the facts on their own. Oath helpers, or witnesses who commented on how reliable or believable other witnesses were, were commonly called upon to bolster the credibility of the parties themselves. By the 16th century, the concept of an informed jury was replaced by the principle that the jury should be independent and impartial, and thus not "informed" in the sense of having any foreknowledge of the parties. Decisions were to be based solely on the information that was legitimately placed before them. This established the importance of evidence law, which attempted to ensure that reliable evidence made its way into the courtroom and prejudicial and unreliable evidence was excluded. Witnesses testified under oath. These rules were all positive influences in the search for truth and justice.

The separation of the roles of judge and jury was solidified in 1670 in the trial of the Quaker William Penn. Penn was charged with unlawful assembly under the *Conventicle Act*, which had been passed by Parliament to shore up the position of the Church of England and suppress religious dissent. Thousands of Quakers were imprisoned for their beliefs. Penn challenged this oppression by organizing a public meeting on August 14, 1670. The Lord Mayor had him arrested, and at his trial Penn made an eloquent defence of liberty:

> [I]f these ancient and fundamental laws, which relate to liberty and property, and which are not limited to particular persuasions in matters of religion, must not be indispensably maintained and observed, who then can say that he has a right to the coat on his back? Certainly our liberties are to be openly invaded, our wives to be ravished, our children slaved, our families ruined, and our estates led away in triumph by every sturdy beggar and malicious informer—as their trophies but our forfeits for conscience's sake.

Penn and his co-defendants were acquitted by the jury, but this displeased the Lord Mayor, who fined the jurors and imprisoned them in Newgate Prison to encourage them to alter their verdict. The jury seemed to have listened to Penn's comments about liberty, for they declined to change the verdict. After two months in the terrible conditions of the prison, the jurors were set free by the Court of Common Pleas. The outcome of this episode was that the highest court in England affirmed that juries must not be coerced to come to a particular verdict or punished if they disagreed with the court. Thus was born one of the more important features of our democratic system: the concept of jury independence. As for William Penn, he later left England for the United States, where he was so influential that the state of Pennsylvania was named after him.

In most serious criminal matters and many civil trials in courts of superior jurisdiction, a litigant can choose a trial by jury. Most criminal matters empanel a 12-member jury, just like the free men of yore. In civil matters, depending on the province, the jury may consist of fewer than 12 jurors; 8 is not uncommon. Failure to reach a unanimous decision results in a hung jury, and the accused must be tried again by a new jury.

Suggestions for Reforming the Jury System

It has been suggested that the jury system should be reformed and that jury sizes could be reduced and majority verdicts be allowed. A majority verdict would eliminate the need for a unanimous verdict. However, a disadvantage of this reform is that it could result in more wrongful convictions. Academics suggest that a more cautious and reasoned approach be taken to the problem presented by jury trials and jury instructions. It would certainly be easier to obtain convictions without unanimity, but Canada already has a scandalous level of wrongful convictions. If we reduced the size of a criminal jury to ten and required only a majority for a verdict, then six jurors in favour of conviction and four against could send a person to jail for life. Contrast that with the scenario of *Twelve Angry Men*, a play and then a movie made in the 1950s but still relevant today, in which one obstinate juror forces the jury to weigh the evidence and test its credibility and reliability, thus avoiding wrongfully convicting a teenaged boy. If prosecutors can obtain "quick and dirty" verdicts from juries, then the dangers of a miscarriage of justice skyrocket.

Still, one can appreciate the frustration of professionals in the criminal justice system, who see so much time and energy go into prosecuting a case only to have a jury not resolve the issue and a mistrial result. Consideration could be given to implementing, on at least a test basis, some of the following modifications:

- Require pre-trial training of jurors in a workshop setting to prepare them for the task.
- Shorten and simplify standard jury instructions.
- Give judges more freedom to set aside an unreasonable verdict from a jury (subject to appeal of the judge's decision).

CHAPTER SUMMARY

In the adversarial system, there are similarities and differences between the criminal and the civil litigation processes. The adversarial system is the approach to fact-finding that is used in the Canadian judicial system and in the other systems with their roots in the British common law tradition. The adversarial process has evolved to temper the quest for truth with other values, including limiting the power of the state to prosecute individuals and emphasizing the appearance of fairness and impartiality. The rules of evidence that are applied today developed over a considerable period of time in an effort to ensure that the process for resolving legal disputes is fair and equitable.

There are two primary decisions to be made at trial. The first is what the facts of a particular case are and the second is how the law applies to those facts. The role of the jury is to determine the facts, and the role of the judge is to apply the law. When the judge sits alone, without a jury, he fulfills both decision-making roles.

The judge also acts as a gatekeeper to ensure that only the evidence that will assist in a fair determination of the issues is admitted. The voir dire is the process of "a trial within a trial" to determine what information may properly be admitted into evidence. At the end of the trial, the judge gives a charge to the jury, instructing them on the application of the law to the facts of the case.

Suggestions for reforming the jury system in Canada have been proposed, but they are not without their problems.

KEY TERMS

adversarial system, 7
charge to the jury, 12
disclosure, 5
discovery, 5
trier of fact, 9
trier of law, 9
voir dire, 11

REFERENCES

Canadian Charter of Rights and Freedoms, Part I of the *Constitution Act, 1982*, being Schedule B to the *Canada Act 1982* (UK), 1982, c 11.

Daley, R v, 2007 SCC 53.

Osolin, R v, [1993] 4 SCR 595.

Yuill v Yuill, [1945] 1 All ER 183 (CA).

REVIEW QUESTIONS

1. What are the major differences between the civil and the criminal justice systems? What are the similarities?

2. Describe the major features of the adversarial system.

3. Describe the differences between the role of the judge and the role of the jury in the trial process.

4. What is meant by the term "trier of fact"? Who performs this function in a trial?

5. What do we mean when we say that the judge is the "gatekeeper" for the admission of evidence?

6. What is the role of a voir dire in the trial process?

7. What is the purpose of the charge to the jury?

DISCUSSION QUESTIONS

1. Do you think the adversarial approach to court proceedings is one that tends to render a just determination of the case? What other approaches might be considered?

2. The following suggestions have been made for improving the jury system:

   a. Require pre-trial training of jurors in a workshop setting to prepare them for the task.

   b. Shorten and simplify standard jury instructions.

   c. Give judges more freedom to set aside an unreasonable verdict from a jury (subject to appeal of the judge's decision).

   What effect do you think each of these suggestions might have if implemented? Can you think of any other suggestions?

Evidence in the Decision-Making Process

2

LEARNING OUTCOMES

After completing this chapter, you should be able to:

- Explain the role of evidence in the court process.

- Understand the part that judicial discretion plays in the application of evidence law in a proceeding.

- Explain the effect that the admission or exclusion of evidence has on a proceeding.

- Identify the sources of evidence law.

- Understand how evidence is dealt with in administrative tribunals.

- Identify the evidentiary issues that may arise on appeals.

- Distinguish the use of evidence in criminal and civil cases from its use in alternative dispute resolution mechanisms and military justice proceedings.

Introduction

In this chapter, we look at the role that evidence law plays in the courtroom. We learn that it has a twofold role in that it lays out the principles for finding the truth in a fair manner, and it helps to ensure that the decision-making process is not overwhelmed by facts that would do nothing but extend the time needed to decide a matter. The judge uses her discretion to ensure that the two aspects of the admission of evidence are met. In small claims and military courts, and in non-courtroom decision-making proceedings such as administrative tribunals and alternative dispute resolution, the rules of evidence may be applied differently, or in many cases less strictly, owing to the nature of those proceedings.

The Role of Evidence Law

The primary purpose of a legal proceeding is to resolve the dispute between the parties according to the law. Legal disputes involve both issues of fact and issues of law. Whether the matter involves a court case or an administrative hearing, or some other comparable proceeding, a decision must be made as to which version of the facts is the most credible and how the law applies to those facts. In most cases, the decision-maker who determines the facts then also applies the law. However, as we saw in Chapter 1, in court proceedings involving a jury, it is the jury that decides on the facts and the judge who decides on the applicable law. The jury is the "trier of fact" and the judge is the "trier of law." If there is no jury, the judge or other adjudicator is both the trier of fact and the trier of law.

The role of evidence law in a proceeding is twofold. First, it establishes a set of principles that operate to exclude facts that may not be helpful to the trier of fact as well as facts that may be downright harmful in the fair determination of the case. Second, the rules of evidence function to limit the sheer volume of information put before the trier of fact so that legal proceedings are kept to a reasonable length and therefore manageable within our system of justice. For example, consider the case of a car buyer suing a vendor who sold her a used car in poor condition. In his defence, the vendor might want to ask all his friends to testify that he is an upstanding, honest person. The vendor has a lot of friends, so calling them all as witnesses would take a couple of days. No court would permit all this evidence to be called. In fact, even one witness of this sort may be irrelevant, because the issue is the condition of the car and the contractual terms relating to its sale—not the character of the defendant (see Chapter 8 for further discussion of character evidence).

In other words, the rules of evidence are meant to provide an orderly method of determining which facts may actually be considered by the trier of fact in deciding the case, keeping in mind the fundamental principle of fairness. However, in any discussion of what is fair, there may be competing interests and concerns. As a result, the application of evidence law is a balancing act, and in order to understand how the law is applied, this struggle for balance must be kept in mind. For example, in a criminal trial, if the police have gathered evidence in a manner that contravenes the Charter rights of the accused, the evidence may not be admissible. The evidence might be very helpful to the trier of fact in deciding the guilt of the accused, but there is a higher consideration to be taken into account by the court, and that is the right of all persons to be protected from illegal interference by police.

Judicial Discretion

Although we refer to the "rules of evidence," in practice these so-called rules are often more flexible than other rules one encounters in the law. Because the legal dispute-hearing process is an attempt to find the truth, or as close an approximation of the truth as possible, and at the same time must be fair and efficient, judges have a considerable amount of discretion when applying the rules. This discretion allows judges to balance competing considerations.

Beginning in the 1990s, developments in evidence law have widened the scope of **judicial discretion**. Now, each case is examined on its own basis to determine the best application of the evidentiary principles within the context of that case. This approach involves an examination of the policy that gave rise to the rule in the first place to determine whether that policy is achieved by the application of the rule in the case at hand. In this way, the rules of evidence support the finding of truth, the concept of fairness, and the promotion of efficiency in the judicial system, rather than directing or driving the proceedings by stringent and automatic application. This method of applying the rules is often referred to as the **principled approach**, and it has changed the face of evidence law over the last several decades. It is crucial in the principled approach to have a solid understanding of the policy behind an evidentiary rule to determine whether application of the rule will actually promote that policy in a particular case.

The bottom line is that although we have "rules" in evidence law, they may be applied differently in different cases in order to achieve the underlying principle of justice for which the rules were developed. In this way, judicial discretion plays a major role in the application of evidence law.

judicial discretion
a judge's freedom to apply rules or decide issues in the context of a case

principled approach
method of applying rules of evidence by reference to the policy underlying the rules

Admission and Exclusion of Evidence

Admissible evidence is evidence that may be considered by the trier of fact in determining the issue that it has been asked to decide. **Excluded evidence** is evidence that cannot be considered by the trier of fact. It is important to remember that just because evidence is excluded does not mean that it is not heard by the trier of fact.

If a judge is hearing the case without a jury, she must actually hear the evidence before she can rule whether or not it is admissible. For example, in a murder trial, if the defence wants to call evidence that the deceased victim told his mother that he was a drug dealer, it must first establish that the evidence is relevant. Because this information involves a statement made by one person to another, it is, on the face of it, **hearsay evidence**. It will not be admitted into evidence unless it fits within one of the exceptions to the rule that makes hearsay generally inadmissible. But how can the judge possibly determine these issues if she does not hear the statement itself? She cannot. Therefore, she will hear the statement and the legal arguments the

admissible evidence
evidence that may be considered by the trier of fact

excluded evidence
evidence that cannot be considered by the trier of fact

hearsay evidence
evidence given by a witness that is based on information received from others rather than personal knowledge; generally considered inadmissible

parties want to make about the admission or exclusion of the statement, and then decide on its admissibility. If she rules that the statement is admissible, she may consider it in deciding whether or not the accused is guilty of the charge against him. However, if the judge rules that the evidence is inadmissible, she must not consider it in deciding the case.

Things get more complicated when the trial involves a jury. Judges, with their legal training and experience, are considered to have the ability to ignore or disregard information they have already heard, but jurors are not expected to possess such a skill. Therefore, every effort is made to keep the jury from hearing any evidence until a judge has determined whether it is admissible. If the evidence is ruled inadmissible, the jury does not hear it. In fact, if the jury inadvertently hears a piece of excluded evidence, the result can be a mistrial. In the event of a mistrial, the trial has to be started all over again from the beginning with a new judge and jury, or with a judge alone.

The process of determining the admissibility of evidence usually starts with one of the parties objecting to the admission of a particular piece of evidence that the other side wants to introduce. Whenever possible, the judge sends the jury out of the courtroom and then conducts a voir dire. As you will recall from Chapter 1, a voir dire is a trial within a trial. The issue on the voir dire is the admissibility of the evidence in dispute. All parties make their legal arguments before the judge, and she renders her decision. If the judge rules that the evidence is admissible, the trial resumes and the evidence is introduced. If the judge rules that the evidence should be excluded, the trial resumes and the jury is not aware that there is information that they have not been permitted to hear. Even when there is no jury, the portion of the trial in which the judge rules on the admissibility of evidence is still referred to as a voir dire, and the same rules apply to admissibility even though the judge has heard or seen the evidence.

Despite a judge's best efforts to keep inadmissible evidence away from the jury through voir dire, sometimes a witness will just blurt out evidence that the jury cannot help but hear. If that happens, and the evidence is ruled inadmissible, the judge will instruct the jurors that they must disregard the witness's remark and not consider it in any way during their deliberations.

Voir Dire

The expression "voir dire" found its way into the English common law system following the Norman invasion and conquest of England in 1066. For a period of time, the language of the courts in England was Norman French. Many of the expressions of that time remain part of the legal language in court systems that are based on English common law.

A voir dire is designed to determine the admissibility of a proposed piece of evidence. It can be used with information such as a confession where the Crown is obliged to prove that the statement is voluntary, or with any other evidence where the two parties are in disagreement about its admissibility. It is important to remember that the judge does not determine the truth of the evidence, only its admissibility. Determining the truth of the evidence is the exclusive domain of the trier of fact.

Sources of Evidence Law

Common Law

Most evidence law is common law. The vast majority of the rules of evidence used today in Canadian courtrooms have their roots in judge-made law, some of which dates back centuries to the earliest courts in England. But that does not mean that the rules have not been updated. In fact, over the last 30 years or so, the Supreme Court of Canada has made major changes in the common law of evidence. As discussed earlier, the court has moved away from a rigid application of the rules of evidence to an approach that examines the policy behind the rule and considers how best to apply the rule to achieve that policy in the case at hand. This principled approach has had a profound effect on many of the long-standing common law rules of evidence, most notably hearsay. We will look at these changes as we go along.

Statute Law

Statute law also plays an important role in evidence law. The federal government and each of the common law provinces and territories in Canada have an evidence act. (Note that Quebec is a civil law province and does not have an evidence act, though it does have rules and regulations regarding the use of evidence in court and tribunal hearings. See the appendix to this chapter for a complete list of evidence acts in Canada.) The federal act applies to court proceedings conducted in relation to federal legislation—for example, the *Criminal Code* and the *Divorce Act*. The provincial/territorial statutes apply to proceedings conducted under provincial/territorial legislation.

All the evidence acts are very similar in approach. In some instances, they codify various aspects of the common law of evidence. In other instances, they alter or add to common law rules. For example, the common law has established that business records that meet a court-established test are excepted from the hearsay rule. Most of the evidence acts in Canada also deal with business records as a hearsay exception but they have added variations to the common law rule.[1]

In addition to the various evidence acts, there are individual statutes that have specific evidentiary requirements for particular proceedings under that statute, as well as rules of procedure in each province that dictate the process for civil cases at various court levels.

Evidence in Small Claims Court

The purpose of small claims courts is to provide a speedier, less costly, and easier process to deal with civil cases involving smaller amounts of money. The upper financial limit on a small claims court varies from province to province but because no major sums are involved, the courts have been set up to deal with cases as expeditiously as possible from both a time and a financial perspective. Although the parties in these courts may have legal representation, they often represent themselves, and because of that, the rules of the small claims court may permit judges in these courts to exercise more discretion in deciding the admissibility of some types of evidence.

For example, in Ontario, Small Claims Court judges may admit any relevant evidence, even if the evidence would not be admitted in a higher court or in a criminal or quasi-criminal court. However, the court may not give the same weight or importance to such evidence as it would to evidence admitted according to the more formal rules. While written witness statements might be admissible, if there is a witness present in the courtroom to testify and be cross-examined, the court may give the evidence of that witness more importance than that of the written statement of another witness with contradictory evidence, who is not present.

There are never juries in small claims courts, and judges may have the discretion to admit evidence such as hearsay that might not be strictly admissible in higher or criminal courts. We will examine the rules around hearsay in depth later in the text (see Chapter 5 through Chapter 7) but essentially, hearsay is second-hand evidence. A witness in court wants to repeat what someone else told him or wrote down in a document when the person who made the original statement is not in court to give sworn evidence and be cross-examined by the opposing party. Second-hand evidence may not be as reliable as other evidence because it cannot be fully tested in court in the usual manner.

The rules of evidence, generally speaking, do not permit hearsay to be admitted unless certain exceptions apply in a particular case. In small claims court cases, the judge often has discretion to admit hearsay evidence that might not meet the test for admissibility. Non-legally trained litigants are not expected to know and follow the complicated rules of evidence. The issue for the court is how much weight or importance to give to evidence that might not meet the general rules of evidence. Courts will give more weight to first-hand evidence that can be tested properly in court.

Parties cannot count on judicial discretion always to admit otherwise inadmissible evidence. Therefore, it is best to follow the rules of evidence as much as possible. This advice applies particularly to legally trained representatives, who are not likely to be given the same latitude as self-represented litigants.

It is important to remember that, just as in all non-criminal cases, the standard of proof in small claims court is "on the balance of probabilities," and the plaintiff or applicant has the burden of proving his or her case to that standard. The burden and standard of proof will be further discussed in Chapter 3.

Evidence in Appellate Courts

In the adversarial system of justice, decisions of trial courts may be appealed to a higher court, and many are. For the sake of certainty, time limits have been established within which a party who does not like the outcome of a case must commence an appeal. It may even be possible to appeal the appeal, so to speak, and take the issue to "the highest court in the land." Although many litigants would like to go "all the way" with their appeals, few cases fit the condition of being of national importance that is required for an appeal to the Supreme Court of Canada. There is no right to appeal to the Supreme Court. The court determines what cases it will hear on appeal and usually chooses only cases that involve a major point of law, a legal issue that will affect a large number of people, or some other matter of significance.

The judge or judges hearing an appeal are generally restricted to considering whether the decision-maker in the initial case ("the first instance") applied the law correctly or whether a reasonable decision-maker *could* have come to that decision on the basis of the admissible evidence. Thus, it is vital for litigants to have the necessary evidence admitted at the trial level; otherwise, they may be stuck with an unfortunate outcome simply because the appeal court cannot say the decision-maker got it wrong on the basis of the evidence admitted at trial. In addition, appeal courts claim that they will not second-guess the decision-maker in the trial, partly out of respect for the other decision-maker, but largely for fear of opening the floodgates if they send a message that a litigant can get a "second kick at the can" through an appeal. On rare occasions, an appeal court will admit new evidence, but usually not when the evidence was available to a litigant who neglected to present it at trial. Appeals are not opportunities to second-guess trial strategies and relitigate the issues.

In the case of *R v Lévesque* (2000 SCC 47, [2000] 2 SCR 487), the Supreme Court of Canada revisited and reaffirmed the test for the admission of fresh or new evidence on appeals:

(1) The evidence should generally not be admitted if, by due diligence, it could have been adduced at trial provided that this general principle will not be applied as strictly in a criminal case as in civil cases: see *McMartin v. The Queen*.

(2) The evidence must be relevant in the sense that it bears upon a decisive or potentially decisive issue in the trial.

(3) The evidence must be credible in the sense that it is reasonably capable of belief, and

(4) It must be such that if believed it could reasonably, when taken with the other evidence adduced at trial, be expected to have affected the result.

As a rule of law, lower courts are bound to follow the decisions of higher courts, including their rulings on matters regarding the admissibility of evidence.

CASE IN POINT

Fresh Evidence on Appeal

Law Society of Upper Canada v James William Sinclair, 2006 ONLSAP 0002

A lawyer was appealing the decision of the Law Society of Upper Canada to disbar him and take away his licence to practice law. The reason for the disbarment was that he had misappropriated three million dollars of his clients' money to use in a land deal. At the appeal, he wanted to introduce new evidence that had not been introduced at his original disciplinary hearing.

Much of the fresh evidence that the lawyer wanted to have admitted on the appeal related to events that occurred prior to the date of the first hearing and disbarment. The Appeal Panel ruled that this evidence did not meet the test for admissibility as fresh evidence on appeal because it was or could have been available at the original hearing if due diligence had been exercised. The evidence related to the sale of the lawyer's practice, the fact that he was being sued, and how those factors affected his ability to pay restitution to the clients from whom he had misappropriated the money. The practice was already for sale, and the litigation had begun at the time of the hearing. The failure to introduce that evidence at that time was a strategic choice made by the lawyer.

The remainder of the supposed fresh evidence related to the lawyer's claim that he tried to deal with the development land in such a way that would benefit the victimized clients. However, the lawyer chose not to give evidence at the initial disciplinary hearing, and he did not offer any explanation for the misappropriation.

The Appeal Panel stated:

What occurred at Mr. Sinclair's hearing is cast in stone, except to the extent that he can demonstrate that there is fresh evidence that qualifies for admission before this Appeal Panel, under the principles set out in *Lévesque*.

The Appeal Panel found that the test in *Lévesque* was not met because all the evidence that was supposedly fresh was, or would have been, available at the hearing but was not introduced, largely because the lawyer was arguing throughout the original hearing that his clients lent him the money. The disbarment was confirmed on the appeal.

Evidence in Administrative Tribunals

Over the last few decades, governments in Canada at both the federal and the provincial/territorial levels have enacted numerous pieces of legislation regulating the interaction between individuals and the government and governmental bodies. This area of government regulation is administered by an array of agencies, boards, and commissions that have their own decision-making bodies, collectively referred to as **administrative tribunals**. Tribunals deal with a wide variety of issues, including labour relations, workers' compensation, immigration and refugee claims, and property zoning. In fact, Canada has embraced administrative tribunals as a way of resolving disputes more than have most democracies in the world. Among the better-known tribunals are the Labour Relations Board, the Workers' Compensation Appeal Board, and the Canadian Radio-television and Telecommunications Commission.

Administrative tribunals (often referred to as "quasi-judicial" bodies) are like courts in the sense that they are established to pass judgment in circumstances where there is a dispute. One of their major purposes is to ensure a fair and just determination of a regulatory dispute in a timely and cost-efficient manner. Tribunals tend to be adversarial, and individuals who appear before them often have lawyers to assist in presenting their case. Take the example of a person whose social assistance benefits have been cut off. The statute that governs social assistance payments typically allows a decision to deny benefits to be appealed. The person who has been cut off would file a notice of appeal with the appeal board, which would then arrange a hearing. The person appearing before the appeal board ("the appellant") would present her evidence and arguments as to why she is entitled to benefits. The appeal board would then "exercise its discretion" and either agree with the appellant, allowing the appeal and restoring the benefits, or disagree with the appellant, denying the appeal and thus upholding the decision of the social assistance agency to cut off benefits.

The body of law known as administrative law deals with the rules and procedures for proper decision-making in the tribunal hearing process, and it has developed over the last half-century. Although tribunals themselves are created by statute, most of the main principles of administrative law are common law, made by judges who were reviewing tribunal decisions.

administrative tribunals decision-making bodies, similar to courts, that rule on regulatory disputes

Relaxation of Rules of Evidence in Administrative Tribunal Hearings

The rules of evidence in administrative hearings are much more relaxed than they are in civil or criminal court cases. There are a number of reasons for this difference in approach.

First, there is less danger in administrative tribunals of "faulty" evidence misleading the decision-maker. Administrative tribunals are usually run by people who have distinguished themselves as experts in their field—workers' compensation, labour relations, property tax levies, or whatever the specific area the tribunal is set up to administer. Of course, judges are also experts in areas of law, but in both civil and criminal matters, the parties often have a right to choose trial by jury. In a jury trial, the decision-makers are laypersons, who are much less sophisticated than judges in their knowledge of the law and in their ability to discount or "forget" evidence that should not be considered in their decision. Strict rules of evidence are enforced to ensure that a jury hears only the evidence that the expert judge decides is admissible.

A second reason that the rules of evidence for administrative tribunals are more relaxed than they are for courts is that tribunal hearings are meant to deal with issues more expeditiously and less formally than court proceedings. In addition, while administrative tribunals deal with important matters such as whether a worker can retain his job or whether a person will succeed with her refugee claim, they do not deal with matters where the personal liberty of an individual is at stake.

Another reason for the relaxed approach to the admission of evidence before administrative tribunals is that while their decisions may be reviewed by a court, courts have generally taken a "hands-off" approach to tribunal decisions. Therefore, the admission or rejection of evidence by tribunals is not closely scrutinized. Given the specialized nature of administrative tribunals, courts often defer to their findings on the basis that it is better to have such decisions made and enforced close to the source of the issue, by the tribunals themselves.

Rules of Evidence in Tribunals

The fact that the rules of evidence for administrative tribunals are more relaxed than they would be in a courtroom does not mean that there are no rules of evidence at all. Most provincial tribunals are generally governed by a statute, such as Ontario's *Statutory Powers Procedures Act* (SPPA). Statutes such as this often set out the rules of evidence for the tribunals that fall under the jurisdiction of the statute and may give the tribunal power to make additional rules governing its proceedings, including rules about the admissibility of evidence.

For example, section 15 of the Ontario SPPA provides as follows:

What is admissible in evidence at a hearing
   15(1) Subject to subsections (2) and (3), a tribunal may admit as evidence at a hearing, whether or not given or proven under oath or affirmation or admissible as evidence in a court,
      (a) any oral testimony; and
      (b) any document or other thing,
relevant to the subject-matter of the proceeding and may act on such evidence, but the tribunal may exclude anything unduly repetitious.

What is inadmissible in evidence at a hearing
   (2) Nothing is admissible in evidence at a hearing,
      (a) that would be inadmissible in a court by reason of any privilege under the law of evidence; or

(b) that is inadmissible by the statute under which the proceeding arises or any other statute.

Conflicts

(3) Nothing in subsection (1) overrides the provisions of any Act expressly limiting the extent to or purposes for which any oral testimony, documents or things may be admitted or used in evidence in any proceeding.

In addition to these subsections, section 25 of the SPPA gives authority to Ontario tribunals to create rules to provide specific direction in relation to their proceedings. These tribunal-specific rules may contain requirements regarding evidence. Many tribunals have comprehensive rules that deal with notice requirements, disclosure of evidence, disclosure and use of expert evidence, summonsing witnesses, and evidence at trial. These rules can be found on the individual websites of the provincial tribunals, and anyone appearing before a tribunal should ensure that they are familiar with them.

Tribunals governed by federal law, such as the Immigration and Refugee Board, or the Canadian Human Rights Tribunal, very often have regulations created under their governing statutes, and these rules may contain specific evidentiary requirements pertaining to that tribunal. Once again, practitioners before these tribunals must ensure that they understand the rules, not only in relation to the submission of their own evidence but also to know when an opposing party may not be following them.

Judicial Review of Administrative Tribunal Decisions

There are two circumstances where a court will overrule an administrative tribunal: where the tribunal exceeds its legislated jurisdiction, and where it denies the applicant natural justice.

Jurisdiction

Tribunals are creatures of statutes; their powers derive from that legislation. A tribunal may make a decision only as permitted by the statute that created it. Any other decision is not within its jurisdiction, or the scope or limit of its authority. For example, a human rights tribunal could not order Air Canada to improve its meal service. Such an order is not within the power of a human rights tribunal and would certainly not be upheld by a court because it would be a clear breach of the tribunal's decision-making authority.

Natural Justice

natural justice
fundamental legal principle entitling a person to a fair and unbiased hearing

Natural justice is one of the fundamental legal principles applied in administrative law. Basically, natural justice entitles a person who may be affected by a decision of government or a governmental agency to a hearing conducted in a fair and unbiased manner. This includes the right to present evidence. It would not be fair if a person were presented with evidence and not permitted to respond to it, or had "secret" evidence used against him. A person who has been dealt with by an administrative tribunal should be able to ascertain the factual basis of the tribunal's determination and to know that the process was a fair one.

Natural justice balances two aims: to provide flexibility in the admission of evidence, and to carefully consider the weight to be given the evidence that is admitted. The search for truth in the administrative hearing process is balanced against fairness to the parties. As a society, we reject a situation in which a person can be treated unfairly by government or be denied rights that any person should be able to count on from a quasi-judicial body.

CASE IN POINT

Procedural Fairness and Oral Hearings

Black v Advisory Council for the Order of Canada, 2012 FC 1234

Conrad Black was a multi-millionaire owner of a major media corporation that, at one time, published newspapers around the globe, including in Canada, the United States, the United Kingdom, and Israel. He was appointed an Officer of the Order of Canada in 1990. The Order of Canada is an award in recognition of the highest levels of achievement and service to humanity at large, to Canada, or to the recipient's community, group, or field of activity. At the time of his appointment to the Order, Mr. Black was a Canadian citizen, although he later renounced that citizenship in order to be made a peer in Britain.

Mr. Black was convicted in the United States of the criminal offences of fraud and obstruction of justice; he spent a number of years in jail there. Upon completion of his sentence and his return to Canada, he was advised in 2011 by the council that makes appointments to the Order of Canada that consideration was being given to the termination of his appointment to the Order. The policy of the Order permits termination for a number of reasons, including conviction for a criminal offence. Mr. Black was invited to make written submissions to the council, which he did at length several times, but he wanted an oral hearing. When he was told that the council would not be holding an oral hearing, Mr. Black brought an application to the Federal Court of Canada for judicial review on the basis that the council's refusal to grant an oral hearing before making its decision was a denial of procedural fairness. The court ruled that procedural fairness is not breached if a party was given full opportunity to participate in the process in writing.

The court said (at para 85):

> In short, Mr. Black has failed to demonstrate that an oral hearing is necessary to ensure that his arguments are dealt with fairly or that written submissions do not and cannot provide him a reasonable opportunity to participate effectively in the process leading to the Council's recommendation to the Governor General. Mr. Black has been advised that the Council will consider five U.S. decisions concerning his convictions in making its recommendation, and that he may file any written representations or other written material necessary in support of his position. Should the Council be unable to resolve any concerns when it considers these submissions, it could solicit additional information from Mr. Black. All of this to say that Mr. Black will have ample opportunity to present his side of the story and to make sure that the Council is well aware of his views before deciding on its recommendation. Finally, and contrary to his assertion, credibility is not the key factor or the primary consideration for the Council in assessing whether it should recommend the termination of his appointment to the Order. For all of these reasons, I believe that Mr. Black's right to procedural fairness has not been breached by the Council's decision not to hold an oral hearing.

Although courts generally defer to the decisions of administrative tribunals, they will intervene when a party has been denied natural justice, including in the admission or rejection of evidence. Some enabling legislation attempts to limit or eliminate the courts' ability to review the decisions of administrative tribunals. These provisions are known as "privative clauses," implying that what goes on in the tribunal is private and not to be interfered with. Courts do tend to respect tribunals, if only to protect themselves from the flood of litigation that would occur if they did not, but they are more likely to review and modify or overturn a tribunal's decision when the tribunal acted in a particularly cavalier or outlandish way. A decision can be so unreasonable as to exceed the tribunal's jurisdiction, and such decisions may be interfered with if they are "patently unreasonable." In reviewing a tribunal decision, the applicant can complain that the tribunal made an error of law or simply an error of fact. Errors of fact are much less likely to be interfered with because even if the judge hearing the review had a different view of the evidence, the discretion of the tribunal would still be respected.

Questions of law that would require intervention by a reviewing court include

- where the tribunal exceeds its legislated jurisdiction and
- where an adjudicator exceeds his discretion.

Questions of fact, which are less likely to be overturned on review, include

- the weight given to certain pieces of evidence,
- assessments of credibility of witnesses, and
- balancing competing interests in complying with the tribunal's mandate.

While the formal rules of evidence do not constrain administrative tribunals from admitting evidence, they do assist tribunal members in determining the weight to give particular kinds of evidence on the basis of its reliability. Even where an appeal court determines that evidence was wrongly admitted, the court will not interfere with the outcome of the tribunal hearing unless it can be shown that admission of the evidence affected the outcome from the tribunal.

Like courts, tribunals are responsible for managing the evidence that is before them. In that respect, tribunals can limit the number of witnesses or determine that certain kinds of witnesses are not necessary. Because tribunal members have the expertise to understand the central issues between the parties, they are in the best position to determine what evidence will be relevant to their determination. A tribunal cannot refuse to permit a party to cross-examine a witness, although it has the same powers as a judge to limit the cross-examination if it is irrelevant or argumentative. If a tribunal were to deny a party the right to cross-examine, then any assessments of credibility by the tribunal would be suspect because the party did not have the opportunity to test the witness's credibility. Tribunal members can also play a part in questioning a witness, particularly where a party presenting evidence is not represented by counsel and may not have a clear grasp of the subtleties involved in proving his case. If a tribunal member does partake in the questioning process, she must be careful not to "descend into the arena" and take an adversarial position in relation to one of the parties. Tribunal members must be careful to show favour to no one. The point is to be fair to all and to show no bias.

One danger that is particularly problematic for tribunal members is their familiarity with the issues, the parties, and counsel. While tribunal members may be chosen for their experience and expertise in a particular field, knowing too much can cause them to base their decisions on information that is "known" to them but not in evidence. Tribunals often have access to legal opinions, can review the record or pleadings in a matter, and will hear submissions in the course of their handling of the application. None of this is evidence as such, and their decision must clearly be based on the admissible evidence in the proceeding, not on these other sources of information. Tribunal members can also become biased in favour of or against parties who frequently appear before them, and they may be inclined to discount approaches or submissions from counsel whom they have learned to distrust. However, even if a particular counsel may have attempted to "put one over on" tribunal members in the past, it is the client of counsel who is before the tribunal, and he or she deserves to start with a clean slate.

Alternative Dispute Resolution Mechanisms

Not all civil matters are resolved through court or tribunal processes. There are alternative dispute resolution mechanisms available to litigants, including arbitration and mediation. Criminal matters are generally tried through the courts, but there are mechanisms that permit Crown attorneys to divert minor charges from the trial system. In addition, alternative sentencing mechanisms may be used in appropriate cases, such as those involving Aboriginal people. There has been an increase in the use of the process of "diversion" and, in youth matters, "extrajudicial sanctions." Both of these measures circumvent the court process and are advantageous for the accused because, in some circumstances, they allow the accused to avoid a criminal record.

Arbitration

Arbitration is not bound by the rules of evidence under which courts operate, but because it is an adversarial system, it tends to take a somewhat formal approach to litigation, including its approach to admissibility of evidence. While evidence that would not be admissible in some courts may come before an arbitrator, individuals who are legally trained are less likely to give such evidence any weight, thus defeating any advantage of relaxed rules of evidence.

Mediation

Mediation is also an alternative to litigation through the courts. Although it is growing in popularity, it remains a fringe approach. The main advantage of mediation is that no result is imposed on the parties; instead, an attempted resolution is facilitated by a neutral, experienced, third-party moderator. This means, however, that a mediation may not necessarily conclude in a resolution of the matter. An additional drawback is that the mediation process cannot even begin without the cooperation of both parties.

In some instances, one party can require a mediation, for example, by serving the other party with a notice to mediate. In practical terms, however, because it requires agreement, the process cannot be successful without genuine participation by both parties. Mediation can also be an extra cost if the two sides cannot resolve their dispute. This may be hard to accept when a party willing to mediate feels that the other side is not genuinely trying to reach agreement. In addition, mediation does not work well where there is a power imbalance. When one side, which may be entirely wrong in its position, has enormous funds to spend on litigation, mediation will often result in the well-heeled litigant taking baby steps in compromise and expecting or demanding that the financially strapped opponent take giant steps to bridge the gap in their positions.

Mediations tend to be very relaxed in their evidentiary requirements. They often feel more like informal discussions than legal proceedings. Mediations are almost always "without prejudice," which means that information disclosed in mediation cannot be used in any subsequent trials. This approach encourages each party to be freer in its comments and to acknowledge the strong points in its adversary's position. When a party acknowledges some weaknesses in its own position and some strengths in its opponent's, a resolution prior to trial often appears much more appealing. Both plaintiffs and defendants can use the mediation process to "test-drive" their positions and to assess how well the other side will stand up to litigation in the courts. While statements in mediation cannot be disclosed ("attract privilege from disclosure") in court proceedings, parties are not prevented from exploiting new information to shore up their case prior to trial by exploring avenues they had not thought of and by revising their questioning approach and other evidentiary strategies.

Military Justice

Military justice in Canada is unique and separate from the civilian criminal justice system. The Supreme Court of Canada has endorsed a separate system that would not meet the standards required of civilian courts. There are systemic obstacles to the application of civilian principles of fairness in a military context. Social organization in the military is built on unquestioned adherence to commands from superiors. Thus, a higher-ranking officer's word by definition carries greater weight than that of a lower-ranking officer.

The rules of evidence are very relaxed in the summary trial process used by the Canadian military. A commanding officer is free to accept any evidence he or she thinks is appropriate. In this process, the accused has no right to counsel, and unsworn hearsay statements can be admitted as evidence. In the much more formal **court martial** process, which can be chosen by an accused and is sometimes mandated, the same rules of evidence used for civilians apply. The election of the court martial process comes with considerable risk because the penalties are much harsher than in civilian courts. For example, a sentence of five years is served in its entirety—no time off is granted for good behaviour.

Some offences, such as murder and crimes against children, must be tried in civilian courts, not military courts.

court martial
formal military justice process in which civilian rules of evidence apply

CHAPTER SUMMARY

Evidence law has two purposes. The first is to eliminate information that would not be helpful to the trier of fact in coming to a fair and just determination of the facts, and the second is to reduce the sheer volume of information, thereby keeping trial times within reason. The judge has significant discretion to determine what information is admissible as evidence and what is to be excluded.

There are two sources of evidence law: common law and statute law. Most evidence law is based on common law principles, but federal and provincial/territorial statutes may alter or add to common law evidence rules.

Administrative tribunals generally adhere to the same general principles of evidence law, but the rules of evidence are not applied as strictly as they are in courts.

In alternative dispute resolution systems, such as arbitration and mediation, and in the military justice system, the results for admitting and considering evidence are different from those in the criminal or civil adversarial system.

KEY TERMS

administrative tribunals, 26
admissible evidence, 21
court martial, 32
excluded evidence, 21
hearsay evidence, 21
judicial discretion, 21
natural justice, 28
principled approach, 21

NOTE

1   Only Alberta and Newfoundland and Labrador do not provide a provincial statutory hearsay exception for business records. See the following for the business records provisions: *Canada Evidence Act*, RSC 1980, c C-5, s 30 and RSBC 1996, c 154, s 23; CCSM, c E150, s 49; RSNB 1973, c E-11, ss 49 and 51; RSNS 1989, c 154, s 23; RSO 1990, c E.23, s 35; RSPEI 1974, c E-10, s 32; and RSS 1978, c S-16, s 32.

REFERENCES

Canadian Charter of Rights and Freedoms, Part I of the *Constitution Act, 1982*, being Schedule B to the *Canada Act 1982* (UK), 1982, c 11.

Lévesque, R v, 2000 SCC 47, [2000] 2 SCR 487.

Statutory Powers Procedures Act, RSO 1990, c S.22.

APPENDIX: EVIDENCE ACTS IN CANADA

Canada, *Canada Evidence Act*, RSC 1985, c C-5.

Alberta, *Alberta Evidence Act*, RSA 2000, c A-16.

British Columbia, *Evidence Act*, RSBC 1979, c 116.

Manitoba, *Manitoba Evidence Act*, RSM 1987, c E150.

New Brunswick, *Evidence Act*, RSNB 1973, c E-11.

Newfoundland and Labrador, *Evidence Act*, RSNL 1990, c E-16.

Northwest Territories, *Evidence Act*, RSNWT 1988, c E-8.

Nova Scotia, *Evidence Act*, RSNS 1989, c 154.

Nunavut, *Evidence Act*, RSNWT 1988, c E-8.

Ontario, *Evidence Act*, RSO 1990, c E.23.

Prince Edward Island, *Evidence Act*, RSPEI 1988, c E-11.

Saskatchewan, *Saskatchewan Evidence Act*, RSS 1978, c S-16.

Yukon, *Evidence Act*, RSYT 1986, c 57.

REVIEW QUESTIONS

1. What are the primary reasons for excluding evidence?

2. What do we mean when we say that the rules of evidence are flexible?

3. What role does the judge play in the admission and exclusion of evidence?

4. What is the primary source of evidence law? What is the secondary source?

5. In what circumstances will the courts overturn decisions on admission or exclusion of evidence made by administrative tribunals?

DISCUSSION QUESTIONS

1. Do you think the wide discretion afforded to judges in the application of evidence law is justified? Should the rules be more flexible? Less flexible?

2. Compare the treatment of evidence in administrative tribunals and in courts. Do you think there should be any difference in the rules of evidence between these settings? Why or why not?

Burden of Proof and Standard of Proof

3

LEARNING OUTCOMES

After completing this chapter, you should be able to:

■ Explain the issues of burden of proof.

■ Define the different kinds of standard of proof.

■ Understand *prima facie* cases and motions for dismissal for failure to meet a *prima facie* case.

■ Identify presumptions and the different kinds of judicial notice, and explain how they assist parties and courts in establishing facts that might otherwise be elusive and next to impossible to prove.

Introduction

This chapter explores how each party in a proceeding bears the burden to introduce sufficient evidence to prove its case. It explains the standard or level of proof the parties must meet, and compares the different standards of proof required in criminal and non-criminal matters.

Burden of Proof

burden of proof
a party's obligation to prove certain facts or matters in issue

If a burden is thought of as a weight on someone's shoulders, then **burden of proof** implies the weight of an obligation to prove certain facts or matters in issue. We say that the burden falls on the Crown to prove that an accused committed an offence. The accused has no obligation to prove anything but is presumed innocent until the Crown has met the onus or obligation of proving the accused's guilt. In a civil matter, the plaintiff has the burden of establishing the claim against the defendant. Like a defendant in a criminal matter, the defendant in a civil matter has no obligation to call evidence to refute the plaintiff's claim. If the plaintiff fails to establish her claim, the defendant is entitled to judgment in his favour.

For this reason, a judge in a criminal or civil matter will ask the defendant if he has evidence to call after the Crown or the plaintiff has finished presenting her evidence. If the Crown or plaintiff's evidence is not sufficient to prove the charge or claim against the defendant, there may be no need to respond to it. The trick is that the trier of fact, whether judge alone or jury, will not deliberate on the issue whether the "burden has been satisfied" until the defendant chooses whether to call evidence. If the defendant assesses the circumstances incorrectly and decides not to call evidence, he cannot change his mind when the judge finds him guilty or, in a civil matter, finds in favour of the plaintiff.

There is one complication to this relatively neat analysis. The burden of proof may shift from one party to the other at certain points in a trial, usually over the issue of admissibility of evidence. For example, if the accused wishes to argue that a particular piece of evidence was obtained through a breach of the Charter and should therefore be excluded, he has the burden of satisfying the judge that a Charter breach occurred. In fact, in most instances the party seeking to challenge the admissibility of evidence is obliged to prove that the evidence is not admissible. The burden of proof shifts to the party who seeks to exclude evidence because the primary objective of the rules of evidence is to ensure that all relevant and material evidence is put before the trier of fact. (One exception to this thinking pertains to statements to persons in authority or confessions. The Crown must prove that the confession was made voluntarily, and, as we shall see in Chapter 11 on self-incrimination, there are extensive criteria for proof of voluntariness.)

rebut
to present opposing evidence or arguments

The need to prove a fact or matter is generally a legal burden, but it can also be a tactical burden. Sometimes, a party faces a strategic choice whether to present further evidence. For example, where the Crown has presented a case against the accused that will likely result in a conviction if the accused does not try to **rebut** it, then the tactical burden has shifted to the accused, even though the accused is still not required to call evidence. No one can make the accused call evidence, but if he does not, he will almost certainly be convicted.

The same applies to civil matters. The defendant is not required to present any evidence, but if he thinks the plaintiff is likely to win on the basis of the evidence she has presented, the defendant will usually want to present his own evidence in support of his position. In making a tactical decision whether to call evidence or not, the defendant must always keep in mind that the other party can also gain some advantage from any witnesses called. The trier of fact is not restricted to considering only Crown evidence against the accused or, in a civil matter, only the plaintiff's evidence against the defendant. Indeed, the trier of fact must consider all the evidence in reaching its conclusion, so the decision to be made is whether the defendant's chances are likely to be improved by calling additional evidence. In short, a tactical burden is a matter of strategy, and counsel must try to read the trier of fact to determine whether it is necessary or, more properly, whether it is advisable to call evidence to counter the opponent's case.

Air of Reality Test

Not all evidentiary situations are created equal. In some circumstances, an accused faces a hurdle in presenting certain defences to the trier of fact. In the past, some pretty ludicrous defences were actually successful in front of juries. In an effort to curtail such potential abuses of justice, judges required that certain defences pass a test, now known as the **air of reality test**. Although the test applies to all defences, it is particularly germane in cases where an accused seeks to rely on the defences of provocation, necessity, drunkenness, mistaken belief in consent (in sexual assault matters), self-defence, or duress. The accused must first convince the trial judge that there is an air of reality to that defence. The question for the judge is whether the evidence before the court reasonably lends itself to such a defence. For example, where there has been a violent sexual assault that leaves the victim in hospital for two weeks, the suggestion by the defendant that the defence of mistaken belief in consent ought to be put to the jury would likely fail because there is no air of reality to that defence. The test is imposed between the hearing of the evidence and the instructions to the jury. If the judge decides that a defence does not pass the test, she will instruct the jury to disregard it. The goal is to ensure that jurors do not consider ridiculous defences that might confuse their deliberations and potentially lead to miscarriages of justice.

Interestingly, a judge is required to put to the jury any defence that would meet the air of reality test whether or not the accused specifically raised that defence. This issue can be raised on appeal for the first time and permit the accused to succeed in a bid for a new trial. In 2002, the Supreme Court of Canada reviewed the air of reality test in *R v Cinous* (2002 SCC 29, [2002] 2 SCR 3). In this case, the accused was a career criminal who thought two of his accomplices intended to kill him. He agreed to go with the accomplices to steal some computers. He was very nervous because he was driving the van the three of them were in and one of the accomplices was behind him. The two accomplices were also wearing gloves, one of them surgical gloves, which the accused associated with situations where a person expects there to be a lot of blood.

air of reality test
test of whether the defence to a charge is reasonable in light of the evidence

He pulled into a gas station and went in to buy something. Upon returning to the van, he opened the back door, pulled out his gun, and shot one of the men in the back of the head, killing him. The accused sought to have the judge instruct the jury on self-defence. In considering whether this defence should have been put to the jury, the Supreme Court stated (at paras 50-51):

> The principle that a defence should be put to a jury if and only if there is an evidential foundation for it has long been recognized by the common law. This venerable rule reflects the practical concern that allowing a defence to go to the jury in the absence of an evidential foundation would invite verdicts not supported by the evidence, serving only to confuse the jury and get in the way of a fair trial and true verdict. …
>
> The basic requirement of an evidential foundation for defences gives rise to two well-established principles. First, a trial judge must put to the jury all defences that arise on the facts, whether or not they have been specifically raised by an accused. Where there is an air of reality to a defence, it should go to the jury. Second, a trial judge has a positive duty to keep from the jury defences lacking an evidential foundation. A defence that lacks an air of reality should be kept from the jury. … This is so even when the defence lacking an air of reality represents the accused's only chance for an acquittal.

On the issue whether the air of reality test usurps the jury's role as the sole determiner of the facts, the Supreme Court stated:

> Indeed, the air of reality inquiry has been found not only to be consistent with the traditional division of labour as between judge and jury, but actually to *enhance* the jury's ability to carry out its task. Again, Cory J's statement in *Osolin* … is apposite:
>
>> The jury system has in general functioned exceptionally well. Its importance has been recognized in s. 11(f) of the *Charter. One of the reasons it has functioned so very well is that trial judges have been able to direct the minds of jurors* to the essential elements of the offence and *to those defences which are applicable.* That process should be maintained. The charge to the jury must be directed to the essential elements of the crime with which the accused is charged and defences to it. *Speculative defences that are unfounded should not be presented to the jury. To do so would be wrong, confusing, and unnecessarily lengthen jury trials.* [Emphasis added.]

Clearly, the determining factor is that the jury deserves to be protected from mischievous defences that serve to complicate and confuse its task and have no merit other than to mislead jurors into acquitting where the evidence does not support such a defence.

Standard of Proof

In both criminal and civil matters, the party who carries the burden of proving its case must meet a standard of proof. In criminal matters, that standard is proof beyond a reasonable doubt; in civil matters, the standard is proof on a balance of probabilities.

The Criminal Standard: Beyond a Reasonable Doubt

In a criminal matter, the Crown must prove its case against the accused **beyond a reasonable doubt**. Judges often say that triers of fact instinctively know what this term means, but when a person's freedom is at stake, judges and juries alike are not comfortable in leaving the definition that loose. In defining "reasonable doubt" for juries, judges have described it as being "not an imaginary or frivolous doubt," but one based on reason and common sense. However, because the use of this term in legal proceedings demands more than just "common sense," the Supreme Court of Canada has given very clear directions about how trial judges should explain the term, as well as very clear warnings of the dangers. In *R v Lifchus* ([1997] 3 SCR 320), the court stated (at para 36):

> It should be explained that:
>
> - the standard of proof beyond a reasonable doubt is inextricably intertwined with that principle fundamental to all criminal trials, the presumption of innocence;
> - the burden of proof rests on the prosecution throughout the trial and never shifts to the accused;
> - a reasonable doubt is not a doubt based upon sympathy or prejudice;
> - rather, it is based upon reason and common sense;
> - it is logically connected to the evidence or absence of evidence;
> - it does not involve proof to an absolute certainty; it is not proof beyond *any* doubt nor is it an imaginary or frivolous doubt; and
> - more is required than proof that the accused is probably guilty—a jury which concludes only that the accused is probably guilty must acquit.

On the issue of what the definition of reasonable doubt should *not* contain, the Supreme Court stated the following references should be avoided (at para 37):

> - describing the term "reasonable doubt" as an ordinary expression which has no special meaning in the criminal law context;
> - inviting jurors to apply to the task before them the same standard of proof that they apply to important, or even the most important, decisions in their own lives;
> - equating proof "beyond a reasonable doubt" to proof "to a moral certainty";
> - qualifying the word "doubt" with adjectives other than "reasonable," such as "serious," "substantial" or "haunting," which may mislead the jury; and
> - instructing jurors that they may convict if they are "sure" that the accused is guilty, before providing them with a proper definition as to the meaning of the words "beyond a reasonable doubt."

Finally, the Supreme Court attempted to set out a "model charge" to overcome the challenge facing all trial judges instructing juries in criminal trials (at para 39):

> The accused enters these proceedings presumed to be innocent. That presumption of innocence remains throughout the case until such time as the Crown has on the

beyond a reasonable doubt
very high standard of proof in criminal matters

evidence put before you satisfied you beyond a reasonable doubt that the accused is guilty.

What does the expression "beyond a reasonable doubt" mean?

The term "beyond a reasonable doubt" has been used for a very long time and is a part of our history and traditions of justice. It is so engrained in our criminal law that some think it needs no explanation, yet something must be said regarding its meaning.

A reasonable doubt is not an imaginary or frivolous doubt. It must not be based upon sympathy or prejudice. Rather, it is based on reason and common sense. It is logically derived from the evidence or absence of evidence.

Even if you believe the accused is probably guilty or likely guilty, that is not sufficient. In those circumstances you must give the benefit of the doubt to the accused and acquit because the Crown has failed to satisfy you of the guilt of the accused beyond a reasonable doubt.

On the other hand you must remember that it is virtually impossible to prove anything to an absolute certainty and the Crown is not required to do so. Such a standard of proof is impossibly high.

In short if, based upon the evidence before the court, you are sure that the accused committed the offence you should convict since this demonstrates that you are satisfied of his guilt beyond a reasonable doubt.

Perhaps an example will help. In a murder case, one of the elements of the offence that the Crown must prove beyond a reasonable doubt is that the alleged victim is in fact dead, not just missing or in hiding. Usually, this element is not at all difficult to prove because there is a dead body that can be identified and then sent to a pathologist, who can usually determine the cause of death—strangulation, drowning, blow by a blunt instrument, and so on. Where there is a body, there is no doubt at all that the victim is dead. But what happens if there is no body?

The absence of a body does not automatically mean that the Crown cannot prove beyond a reasonable doubt that the victim is deceased. It certainly presents a challenge for the prosecution but not an insurmountable one. For example, say that the victim is a young female college student who is extremely close to her family. She also has some close, long-time friends with whom she is in almost daily contact. One day, she disappears under mysterious circumstances and is never seen again. Her car is found with her blood inside. Her bank accounts and credit cards are never touched after her disappearance. She is gone for several years. After a long investigation, the police arrest her boyfriend and charge him with murder. The theory is that she was about to jilt him and so he murdered her.

At trial, the Crown must prove that the young woman is dead, that she was the victim of a murder, and that the accused killed her. While the Crown may have trouble proving beyond a reasonable doubt that the accused murdered her, it will likely be able to pass the first step and convince the trier of fact that she is deceased. It is not an absolute certainty. However, given all the circumstances, reason and common sense would indicate that she is dead. It is beyond reasonable doubt, not beyond any doubt, that the victim is deceased. (This example is based on the facts in *R v Baltovich* ((2004), 73 OR (3d) 481 (CA).) While Baltovich's conviction was overturned by the Ontario Court of Appeal and there is little doubt that he was wrongly convicted of murder, no legal question remains that the victim is deceased.)

The Civil Standard: Balance of Probabilities

The standard of proof in civil matters is not as high as it is in criminal proceedings. This is because the defendant is not in danger of losing his liberty and so the fundamental principle of presumption of innocence in criminal cases does not apply. The civil standard is proof on the **balance of probabilities**. Other terms for it include "preponderance of the evidence," "50 percent plus one," or simply "more likely than not." It is up to the judge or the trier of fact to weigh the evidence presented by the plaintiff and the defendant. Picture the scale held aloft by the statue of blind justice. If the plaintiff's evidence is heavier—more convincing—than the defendant's, the plaintiff wins; if it is not, the defendant wins. For example, if the plaintiff claims that the defendant caused injury to him through her negligence, the trier of fact must look at the evidence and determine whether it is more likely than not that the plaintiff has established the defendant's negligence. At the end of the trial, on the basis of all the evidence before it, the trier of fact must determine whether the existence of the defendant's negligence is more likely than the non-existence of her negligence. If, finally, the trier of fact finds that the arguments for and against the plaintiff's position are equal, then the plaintiff has "failed to discharge his burden" or has lost the case. Because the plaintiff has the obligation to prove his case, a tie goes to the defendant.

balance of probabilities
standard of proof in civil matters, determined on the basis of more likely than not

Standard of Proof in Administrative Tribunal Hearings

Administrative tribunals are civil processes and thus apply a civil standard of proof on the balance of probabilities in assessing the evidence before them. In some rare instances, that standard is raised, requiring proof on "clear and convincing evidence." This higher standard is typically used in circumstances where professional misconduct is alleged, which could result in the loss of a person's capacity to practise his or her chosen profession or where there are penalties that make the proceedings quasi-criminal.

The burden of proof usually lies with the party who initiates the proceeding in the tribunal. Typically, an individual applicant is seeking to overturn a decision of a government body, and therefore the applicant is required to establish her case in order to succeed. In some instances, the legislation governing a tribunal reverses the burden of proof. For example, when an applicant has been denied employment insurance benefits pursuant to sections 30 to 33 of the *Employment Insurance Act* (dismissal due to misconduct), the government body (the Canada Employment Insurance Commission) must establish that an employee was terminated due to actions that amounted to misconduct (see *NS v Canada Employment Insurance Commission*, 2014 SSTGDEI 142). Where a tribunal finds that the evidence is equally balanced, the benefit of the doubt goes to the applicant (*Employment Insurance Act*, s 49(2)).

Prima Facie Case

A *prima facie* **case** is one in which there is sufficient evidence on its face that no further proof is required for a party to succeed. In a criminal matter, if the Crown has established a *prima facie* case, it has established all the elements of the offence

prima facie **case**
case in which there is sufficient evidence on its face that no further proof is required for a party to succeed

beyond a reasonable doubt and will obtain a conviction unless the accused is able to call evidence to shake the reasonable doubt. Similarly, in a civil matter, if the plaintiff has established a *prima facie* case, she will succeed if the defendant does not call any evidence.

In some circumstances, a party must establish a *prima facie* case. For example, at the end of the Crown's case in a criminal matter, if the Crown has failed to establish a *prima facie* case, the accused may make a motion for a **directed verdict**. The Crown has failed to provide evidence on all material matters and, as a result, a jury could not find the accused guilty. If a person is accused of robbery and none of the witnesses identifies him, then he must be acquitted, identification being a matter in issue in the proceedings.

The Crown must also establish a *prima facie* case in a preliminary inquiry. It must show that there is some evidence on all material issues upon which a reasonably instructed jury could convict. For the purpose of assessing whether the Crown has made a *prima facie* case in a preliminary inquiry, the judge must assume that all the evidence presented is true, even where it was unconvincing to her. In the past, judges were not permitted to "weigh" the evidence in order to determine whether they would convict on the evidence, or even whether they would likely convict. Instead, they were restricted to assessing whether a jury could convict on the evidence. Recently, however, courts have undertaken the task known as "limited weighing." In this process, the preliminary inquiry judge assesses the evidence and considers whether a properly instructed jury could draw an inference of guilt. Only where the evidence appears so weak that a jury could not draw such an inference can the judge dismiss the charge. This same standard is applied in extradition hearings, where the court considers evidence presented by a foreign jurisdiction in order to determine whether the applicant has established that there is a criminal case to meet in the foreign court and that the accused should be sent there to answer the charges against him.

In a civil case, if the plaintiff does not establish a *prima facie* case, the defendant need not call any evidence but, instead, may make a motion to have the case against him dismissed. This is sometimes referred to as a motion for **non-suit**. The basis of the motion is that since the plaintiff has not proved all the elements of her case, there is no case for the defendant to meet. For example, in a torts case, if the plaintiff is unable to establish that the defendant owed her a duty of care—one of the elements of a claim for negligence—then the defendant could move for dismissal of the case against him.

Presumptions

A **presumption** is a thing that is taken to be true. In criminal and civil proceedings, presumptions are a way of assisting parties in proving facts that they must establish in order to succeed in their case, in circumstances where it would be unfair to make them prove the facts. By their very nature, presumptions are rebuttable. That is, the person against whom the presumption operates has an opportunity to call evidence to show that the presumption is not accurate and should be disregarded. There are presumptions that operate in both criminal and civil proceedings.

directed verdict
order from the judge to acquit the accused because the Crown has not made a *prima facie* case

non-suit
order from the judge dismissing the case because the plaintiff has failed to meet a *prima facie* case

presumption
a fact that is taken to be true without the requirement of formal proof

Presumptions in Criminal Cases

In criminal matters, the most fundamental presumption is the presumption of innocence. That is, the accused starts off with a clean slate and is presumed to be innocent. This presumption helps the accused person in her case because the obligation of proof is clearly laid at the Crown's feet. Another fundamental presumption is the presumption of mental competence. That is, any witness is presumed to be sane and if a party wishes to convince the judge that a person's evidence ought not to be accepted because she is suffering from a mental disability, then it is up to the person making that allegation to prove it. Thus, any person who calls a witness is aided in that she does not have to prove that the witness is sane before the evidence can be admitted.

Because proof beyond a reasonable doubt in criminal matters is a very high standard to meet, and owing to the fact that some things are hard to prove because the only person who really knows is the accused, presumptions are employed to permit the trier of fact to make certain conclusions unless the accused proves otherwise. This process helps the Crown overcome its burden of proof. Some examples may aid in clarifying this concept.

EXAMPLE 1

A driver collides with another vehicle. She gets out of her car, quickly surveys the damage, then hops back into her car and speeds off. A passerby witnesses this, follows the driver to her home, and calls the police on his cellphone. The driver is charged with "leaving the scene of an accident in order to avoid criminal or civil liability." At trial, the Crown establishes that it was in fact the accused who was driving this vehicle and that she was involved in this accident. The Crown seeks to rely on the following presumption in section 252(2) of the *Criminal Code*:

> In proceedings under subsection (1), evidence that an accused failed to stop his vehicle, ... offer assistance where any person has been injured or appears to require assistance and give his name and address is, in the absence of evidence to the contrary, proof of an intent to escape civil or criminal liability.

The Crown is still required to prove that the accused left the scene without leaving her name and offering assistance, but once that has been established, the Crown is entitled to rely on the presumption that the accused did this in order to avoid civil or criminal liability. Once the preliminary points have been established, the trier of fact must conclude that the accused left the scene to avoid civil or criminal liability unless there is "evidence to the contrary," likely from the accused. Because we can never know what is in a person's head, where there is one logical conclusion that arises from the proof of certain facts, the legislation provides for this presumption, which is really a logical inference.

A presumption has three important components:

1. The Crown must prove the basic fact.
2. The presumed fact follows on proof of the basic fact.
3. The accused can rebut the presumption by disproving or raising a doubt about the basic fact.

EXAMPLE 2

A young man, upon reaching the age of majority, spends an evening drinking with his friends. As he is driving home he is stopped by the police for not signalling a lane change. The police demand a breath sample and his reading an hour and a half later is 140 milligrams of alcohol per 100 millilitres of blood. Because he is over the 80-milligram limit, he is charged with impaired driving. At trial, the Crown proves that the accused was the driver and that he "blew" 140 on the Breathalyzer after a proper demand. The Crown then seeks to rely on the presumption that the reading on the machine equals his blood-alcohol level and that this was the level he had at the time of driving.

In this case, the trier of fact is required to conclude that the reading accurately reflects the blood-alcohol level at the time of driving. In fact, the reading may not be accurate. The Breathalyzer machine measures the amount of alcohol in a person's breath, and the science behind the machine says that it is possible to make a reasonably accurate extrapolation from that to conclude that if the machine measures X amount of alcohol in a person's breath then there will be, say, 140 milligrams per 100 millilitres of the person's blood. There are many variables from person to person, and the machine, in spite of careful standardizing and testing, can be wrong. For example, a number of years ago, after Breathalyzer machines had been in use for many years, it was discovered that police officers' radios (the ones strapped to their service belts) could cause the machines to give erroneous readings.

The protection afforded to the accused is that he can call "evidence to the contrary." In Breathalyzer cases, evidence to the contrary would likely involve the accused's testifying about his pattern of drinking and related matters, as well as an expert witness calculating from the pattern of drinking what the actual blood-alcohol level would be. Faced with this evidence contradicting the machine readings, if the court did not disbelieve the accused's testimony about his drinking pattern, the judge would have to acquit.

Problems with Reverse-Onus Presumptions in Criminal Cases

In a case where a presumption operates, as we have seen, the Crown is not required to prove the presumed fact beyond a reasonable doubt. The trier of fact may presume that the fact is true unless the defence can effectively challenge or rebut the presumption. In other words, if there is a presumption that the Crown may rely upon, the only way that the defence can challenge the presumption is to call evidence. Therefore, the usual burden on the Crown to prove all the material facts has been "reversed" so that the accused is required to disprove some of the facts. This is called a **reverse onus**. Reverse-onus provisions are necessary in some instances, but they can be dangerous because they may require the trier of fact to make conclusions that are not logical.

reverse onus
situation where the obligation to prove a fact is shifted from the Crown to the accused

In *R v Oakes* ([1986] 1 SCR 103), the Supreme Court of Canada reviewed the issue of whether reverse-onus provisions violate the Charter-protected right to be presumed innocent. The court made a number of important points in reviewing and clarifying where and when such reverse-onus provisions would meet the standard for acceptability. The legislation at issue in *Oakes* was section 8 of the *Narcotic Control Act*. It provided that when an accused person was determined to be in possession of a narcotic, the trier of fact must conclude that the accused possessed the narcotic for the purpose of trafficking, unless the trier of fact is satisfied by evidence to the contrary that it was "simple possession"—essentially, for personal use.

The Supreme Court concluded that the presumption contained in section 8 of the *Narcotic Control Act* was a presumption of basic fact (proof that the accused possessed a narcotic) that was mandatory but rebuttable. It found that such a presumption violated section 11 of the Charter:

> I am in no doubt whatsoever that [section 8 of the *Narcotic Control Act*] violates s. 11(d) of the *Charter* by requiring the accused to prove on a balance of probabilities that he was not in possession of the narcotic for the purpose of trafficking. Mr. Oakes is compelled by s. 8 to prove he is not guilty of the offence of trafficking. He is thus denied his right to be presumed innocent and subjected to the potential penalty of life imprisonment unless he can rebut the presumption.

The court went on to consider whether the violation could be "saved" by section 1 of the Charter as a limitation that was acceptable in a free and democratic society. We will review this test in Part III of the text, dealing with the Charter and adherence to a higher standard. The *Narcotic Control Act* has been repealed and replaced with the *Controlled Drugs and Substances Act*, in which there is no similar presumption.

Most legislated presumptions are mandatory; otherwise, there would not be much point in having such a presumption. An example of a permissive presumption is the presumption that a person intends the natural consequences of his actions. This presumption *permits* a trier of fact to conclude that if a person drives his car into a crowd, the person intends to cause injury to persons there, without any other evidence of his intention. However, the trier of fact is not *required* to come to that conclusion, even where there is no evidence led by the accused to counter that presumption.

Presumptions are designed to aid the Crown in proving its case against an accused, particularly where a component of the Crown's case is elusive, inside the accused's mind. Although it may be very difficult for the Crown to obtain a conviction in some circumstances, the *Oakes* case tells us that any attempt to simplify or streamline that process must still comply with the Charter. Whether the wording of a provision violates section 11(d) is a matter for the court's interpretation, but generally speaking, if the provision does not require the Crown to prove very much of anything before the burden shifts to the accused to prove his innocence, the provision will be seen as a Charter violation.

Presumptions in Civil Cases

There are a number of presumptions in the common law. For example, it is presumed that an adult is mentally competent. There is no need to prove that fact. In contrast, a party who wishes to challenge an adult's mental competency bears the onus of proving incompetence.

Tort law has a number of presumptions. One basic presumption is *res ipsa loquitur*, which is a Latin expression that means "the thing speaks for itself." In other words, something is so obvious that it needs no further explanation. In cases of negligence, for example, the plaintiff usually has the burden of proving all the elements of negligence, including that the defendant did not meet a proper standard of care in dealing with the plaintiff. The plaintiff would be required to call evidence of what the defendant did or did not do in taking care not to cause injury. However, in many instances, the plaintiff has absolutely no knowledge of what the defendant did that was careless and has no way of reasonably finding out. In these instances, applying the principle of *res ipsa loquitur* relieves the plaintiff of the burden of proving how a defendant who owes a duty of care was negligent where it is obvious that there must have been negligence for the injury to happen.

For example, if the plaintiff drinks a bottled beverage that had been sealed until she opened it and discovers a dead snail at the bottom of the bottle, she has no reasonable way of learning how the snail came to be there. It must have occurred at the manufacturing plant, because the bottle was sealed until the plaintiff opened it. But what exactly happened? Did the manufacturer have inadequate sterilization equipment? Was the storage facility improperly maintained? Perhaps an employee purposefully put the snail there to get back at the employer? All of these things are possibilities, and the law says the manufacturer would be responsible in all these instances. The principle of *res ipsa loquitur* operates in circumstances like these where the thing that caused the damage was under the sole control of the defendant, the injury could not have happened without negligence, and the facts of the incident are not known to the plaintiff. Of course, the defendant is entitled to call evidence to rebut the presumption and show that he was not negligent. (See *Donoghue (or McAlister) v Stevenson*, [1932] All ER 1, [1932] AC 562 (HL).)

Judicial Notice

To a layperson, it may seem that the legal process is largely about the creation of confusion through the overcomplication of matters. This may be because so many interests and considerations must be balanced in the delicate act of attempting to achieve justice. In some instances, evidence law is refreshingly logical in attempting to put reliable information before the trier of fact with the least amount of cost and frustration.

judicial notice
a judge's recognition of a fact without requiring a party to prove it

Judicial notice permits the judge to recognize or "take note of" the existence of a particular fact without requiring a party to formally prove it. If the judge is sitting alone, she will just state that she is taking judicial notice of a particular fact. If there is a jury, the judge will direct the jury that certain facts are to be taken as proven. The facts must be so commonly accepted in the community that no reasonable person could challenge them. These include some facts that can be easily ascertained by consulting sources that are acknowledged as accurate. Such facts are frequently referred to as **notorious facts**. (The term simply indicates the notoriety or recognition of the facts; it does not imply anything improper in them.)

notorious fact
a fact that is so generally known and accepted that it may not reasonably be disputed

In assessing whether a fact is a notorious fact, a court may ask:

1. Is this a fact that is part of society's common knowledge?

2. Is this a fact that is commonly known in this locality?

3. Is this a fact that is commonly known to a specific group within the community or locality?

If any of these questions can be answered "yes," the court may permit the fact to be proved by way of judicial notice.

One of the primary virtues of employing judicial notice as a means of proving a fact is that one or more of the litigants, as well as the court, are saved the time and expense of proving it. With the cost of legal proceedings today, this can be a considerable economic saving.

Examples of Judicial Notice

There is no exhaustive list of matters of which judicial notice may be taken, but some possibilities include the hour the sun sets in a particular location at a particular time of year, the impact of a recession on real estate prices, traffic patterns (rush hour), the impact of a loss of electrical power on perishable foods, activities that were widely publicized in the newspapers, the fact that Christmas day is a holiday, and that certain expressions commonly used by a prostitute and a potential client constitute an offering of sexual services. Further examples of judicial notice include determining the definition of a word by consulting a dictionary, or determining a geographic location by consulting an atlas. At least part of the rationale for provisions for judicial notice is that the justice system would look silly if "indisputable" facts were ignored by the courts. Consider the following examples.

EXAMPLE 1

In a criminal case involving a home invasion, the Crown asks the judge to take judicial notice of the approximate location of a cellphone at the time a particular telephone call was made based on the cellphone tower that received the signal, and to determine the directional movement of the phone in question over a particular time period by reference to the location of the different cellphone towers that received signals from that phone over a specific period of time. May the judge do so without requiring an expert opinion? The Ontario Court of Appeal said yes. (*R v Ranger*, 2010 ONCA 759.)

EXAMPLE 2

The accused were charged with wilfully promoting hatred against an identifiable group, namely the Roma, contrary to section 319 of the *Criminal Code*. They had appeared outside a motel housing Roma refugee claimants, carrying signs saying such things as "Honk if you hate gypsies," and yelling derogatory statements about gypsies. At the end of the Crown's case, the defence argued that the demonstrations were directed against "gypsies" and there was no evidence that "Roma" and gypsies are the same group. Could the trial judge take judicial notice that that the two terms referred to the same identifiable group? The Supreme Court of Canada said yes. (*R v Krymowski*, 2005 SCC 7, [2005] 1 SCR 101.)

EXAMPLE 3

The plaintiff was suing his former employer for wrongful dismissal. As part of the damages, he was claiming lost salary because he said he was not able to find another job for a number of months. Could the judge determine that the plaintiff had not taken sufficient steps to locate other employment by taking into consideration an ad in the paper seeking a person with his qualifications, during the specific period of his unemployment? The Newfoundland Court of Appeal said no. (*McHugh v City Motors (Nfld) Ltd*, 1989 CanLII 265 (NLCA).)

Administrative Tribunals

Administrative tribunals have considerable latitude in the exercise of judicial notice, or what is sometimes referred to as "administrative notice" (given that tribunal members are not actually judges). Most administrative tribunals are made up of persons who have considerable experience in the particular area of the tribunal's jurisdiction (for example, labour relations or environmental regulation). Tribunal members are often in possession of a multitude of facts that are commonly known in the area, and thus they may choose not to require the parties to go through the process of formally proving those facts.

Social Framework Facts

There is a very interesting area of judicial notice that has had a huge influence on recent developments in the law, particularly in the age of Charter challenges. This involves the court's taking judicial notice of "social framework facts." The idea is that the court should be able to review scholarly studies and research in relation to social conditions without having to call the author of the study as an expert witness (see *R v W (S)* (1991), 6 CR (4th) 373 (Ont CA)). The concept is that the court should be able to create a background of social context in which to determine the facts of a particular case. An example of this is the family law case *Moge v Moge* ([1992] 3 SCR 813). The issue in *Moge* was whether Ms. Moge was entitled to ongoing maintenance many years after the marriage had come to an end. She was working as she had throughout the marriage. The amount of maintenance at stake was only $50 per month, but the case went right up to the Supreme Court of Canada.

The Supreme Court permitted the presentation of evidence regarding the impact of divorce on the incomes of former spouses. This evidence relied heavily on research that showed that, after divorce, women and children almost invariably ended up in worse economic condition while the financial fortunes of men improved. This information formed a backdrop or foundation for the judgment which, in simple terms, held that the economic impact of divorce should be equally shared by former spouses.

In *R v Zundel* (1987 CanLII 121 (Ont CA)), the accused was charged with inciting hatred against an identifiable group, contrary to section 319 of the *Criminal Code*, in that he was publicly denying that the Holocaust occurred. The court was asked by the Crown to take judicial notice that the Holocaust did occur. If we are talking about something that the community in general (as opposed to a fringe community that chooses to deny the existence of the Holocaust) accepts as historically indisputable, then there should be no problem with the Crown's request. However, the Ontario Court of Appeal was concerned that allowing the Crown to establish an essential component of its case without formal proof would be prejudicial to the defence. The appellate court upheld the decision of the trial judge to exercise his discretion not to take judicial notice of the Holocaust.

The Court of Appeal said:

> However, if the trial judge had taken judicial notice of the existence of the Holocaust, he would have been required to so declare to the jury and to direct them to find that the Holocaust existed, which would have been gravely prejudicial to the defence in so far as it would influence the drawing of the inference concerning the appellant's knowledge of the falsity of the pamphlet. In our view, the judge exercised his discretion judicially in refusing to take judicial notice of the Holocaust.

An interesting case involving judicial notice took place in the Maritimes. In *R v S (RD)* ([1997] 3 SCR 484, 10 CR (5th) 1), a young person was charged with assaulting a police officer. The evidence was that the police were arresting another youth and that the accused interfered with this arrest. Both the trial judge and the accused were black and had roots in the local black community. The police officer was white. The accused and the police officer were the only witnesses called to give evidence, and they gave very different versions of the events. In response to a rhetorical question posed by the Crown, asked while she was delivering her reasons for acquitting the accused, the judge commented that police officers had been known to mislead the court and overreact, particularly in dealing with black youth, although she specifically said that her comments were not directed to the officer in this case. The judge was drawing on her life experience in reviewing the evidence and making her judgment. The Crown appealed the acquittal of the accused, claiming that it was based on a reasonable apprehension of judicial bias. The decision eventually came before the Supreme Court of Canada, where the majority of the court ruled that the judge was entitled to take notice of social conditions and that her comments did not amount to a reasonable apprehension of bias. Although the court expressed some concern about the wording used by the trial judge, her acquittal of the accused was upheld.

In the subsequent case of *R v Spence* (2005 SCC 71, [2005] 3 SCR 458), the Supreme Court again reviewed the scope of judicial notice. The accused was black and the victim of the robbery was South Asian. The defence wanted to question prospective jurors on whether the fact that the accused was black and the victim South Asian would prejudice their decision-making. The justification for this question was the defence theory that jurors of South Asian descent were more likely to sympathize with the victim, and thereby the right of the accused to a fair trial would be impaired. The trial judge did not permit the "interracial" question and limited the question only to potential bias in regard to the race of the accused. The accused was convicted and the matter wended its way to the Supreme Court of Canada. The court upheld the conviction on the basis that the question the defence wished to use was not based on any generally held knowledge that jurors of a particular race tend to sympathize with victims of the same race.

Writing for the court, Binnie J stated:

> The courts have acknowledged that racial prejudice against visible minorities is so notorious and indisputable that its existence will be admitted without any need of evidence. Judges have simply taken "judicial notice" of racial prejudice as a social fact not capable of reasonable dispute: *R v Williams*, [1998] 1 SCR 1128. It is not at all apparent, however, that as defence counsel put it in oral argument, "a potential juror, seeing a victim of his or her own race, there might be that sympathy, natural sympathy, or tendency to favour someone of your own race, [whether] minorities or majorities" (transcript, at p. 6). Such a proposition, it seems to me, takes us beyond the legitimate sphere of judicial notice. …

In other words, while judicial notice may be taken of the existence of racial prejudice, particularly as it may apply to the accused, when specific biases that aren't generally regarded as well-known facts are put before the court, there must be some evidence presented to support the fact. This type of evidence would normally be provided by expert witnesses.

CASE IN POINT

Judicial Notice Gone Awry

R v MacIsaac, 2015 ONCA 587

Mr. MacIsaac was charged with aggravated assault. He was playing in a non-contact recreational hockey league when, during the last few seconds of the game, he allegedly deliberately delivered a blindside hit on a player on the opposing team, causing him injury. The defence's position was that the contact was an unavoidable accident and therefore not criminal in nature.

The witnesses called by both the Crown and the defence, including the accused and the victim, all told slightly different versions of what they had seen on the ice. After hearing all the evidence, the trial judge decided to apply her personal knowledge of hockey to determine what actually happened. As a result of her analysis, Mr. MacIsaac was convicted. He appealed to the Ontario Court of Appeal.

The Court of Appeal determined that the trial judge had improperly speculated on the facts, using her personal knowledge of hockey, which turned out to be inaccurate and contrary to the evidence. For instance, she decided that one of the accused's witnesses had not actually been on the ice because it would have meant that there were three defencemen playing in the last minute of the game, which she described as "not logical" (at para 34).

The Court of Appeal said (at paras 35, 51):

> The trial judge appears to be taking judicial notice of hockey strategy and using that as a basis for rejecting the testimony. Her conclusion about who would be on the ice at the end of the game is entirely speculative and is also contrary to the evidence of Mr. Shorey that, in the final stages of games in the Ottawa senior men's league, teams play the most skilled players, regardless of their positions. …
>
> … hockey strategy is not a proper subject for judicial notice. From the sports pages to social media, it is abundantly clear that reasonable Canadians often disagree about what constitutes a rational hockey strategy in a given situation. Nor is there any source of indisputable accuracy by which to settle these disagreements. Neither branch of the test for judicial notice is fulfilled.

Mr. MacIsaac's conviction was overturned and a new trial ordered.

CHAPTER SUMMARY

The burden of proof in criminal and civil matters requires the Crown (in criminal cases) or the plaintiff (in civil cases) to prove certain facts or matters in issue. At certain points in a trial, however, the burden can shift to the accused or the defendant. In some special criminal cases, when certain defences are raised, the accused must also meet the air of reality test; that is, the accused must prove that the defence has the air of reality before it can be considered by the trier of fact. When the Crown or plaintiff has met the burden of proof, we say that a *prima facie* case has been made.

The standard of proof in criminal cases is proof beyond a reasonable doubt; in civil cases, it is proof on a balance of probabilities. Presumptions assist parties in proving facts that they must establish in order to succeed in their cases, but by their nature presumptions are rebuttable by opposing parties.

In certain circumstances, through the operation of judicial notice, a judge is able to "take note" of facts that would otherwise have to be proven.

KEY TERMS

air of reality test, 37
balance of probabilities, 41
beyond a reasonable doubt, 39
burden of proof, 36
directed verdict, 42
judicial notice, 46
non-suit, 42
notorious fact, 46
presumption, 42
prima facie case, 41
rebut, 36
reverse onus, 44

REFERENCES

Baltovich, R v (2004), 73 OR (3d) 481 (CA).

Canada Evidence Act, RSC 1985, c C-5.

Canadian Charter of Rights and Freedoms, Part I of the *Constitution Act, 1982*, being Schedule B to the *Canada Act 1982* (UK), 1982, c 11.

Cinous, R v, 2002 SCC 29, [2002] 2 SCR 3.

Controlled Drugs and Substances Act, SC 1996, c 19.

Criminal Code, RSC 1985, c C-46.

Donoghue (or McAlister) v Stevenson, [1932] All ER 1, [1932] AC 562 (HL).

Employment Insurance Act, SC 1996, c 23.

Lifchus, R v, [1997] 3 SCR 320.

MacIsaac, R v, 2015 ONCA 587.

Moge v Moge, [1992] 3 SCR 813.

NS v Canada Employment Insurance Commission, 2014 SSTGDEI 142.

Oakes, R v, [1986] 1 SCR 103.

S (RD), R v, [1997] 3 SCR 484, 10 CR (5th) 1.

Spence, R v, 2005 SCC 71, [2005] 3 SCR 458.

W (S), R v (1991), 6 CR (4th) 373 (Ont CA).

Zundel, R v, 1987 CanLII 121 (Ont CA).

REVIEW QUESTIONS

1. Which party usually bears the burden of proof in a civil case? In a criminal case?

2. What is the air of reality test, and what unique position does it play in some criminal defence issues?

3. Explain the difference between a civil standard of proof and a criminal one and why such a difference exists.

4. What is meant by the term *prima facie* case? Give some examples of its significance.

5. What role do presumptions play in both the burden and standard of proof?

6. What does it mean when we say that a presumption is rebuttable?

7. When may a judge take judicial notice of certain facts?

DISCUSSION QUESTIONS

1. Discuss the difficulties that a reverse-onus provision presents in relation to the Charter.

2. Review the reference to a model jury charge offered in *R v Lifchus*, [1997] 3 SCR 320 at para 39, below. Are there any problems with the wording that Justice Cory suggests?

(3) Suggested Charge
39. Instructions pertaining to the requisite standard of proof in a criminal trial of proof beyond a reasonable doubt might be given along these lines:

The accused enters these proceedings presumed to be innocent. That presumption of innocence remains throughout the case *until such time as the Crown has on the evidence put before you* satisfied you beyond a reasonable doubt that the accused is guilty. [Emphasis added.]

What does the expression "beyond a reasonable doubt" mean?

The term "beyond a reasonable doubt" has been used for a very long time and is a part of our history and traditions of justice. It is so engrained in our criminal law that some think it needs no explanation, yet something must be said regarding its meaning.

A reasonable doubt is not an imaginary or frivolous doubt. It must not be based upon sympathy or prejudice. Rather, it is based on reason and common sense. It is logically derived from the evidence or absence of evidence.

Even if you believe the accused is probably guilty or likely guilty, that is not sufficient. In those circumstances you must give the benefit of the doubt to the accused and acquit because the Crown has failed to satisfy you of the guilt of the accused beyond a reasonable doubt.

On the other hand you must remember that it is virtually impossible to prove anything to an absolute certainty and the Crown is not required to do so. Such a standard of proof is impossibly high.

In short if, based upon the evidence before the court, you are sure that the accused committed the offence you should convict since this demonstrates that you are satisfied of his guilt beyond a reasonable doubt.

Fundamental Principles

4

LEARNING OUTCOMES

After completing this chapter, you should be able to:

■ Explain the threshold tests for evidence.

■ Distinguish between relevance and materiality, and define conditional relevance.

■ Understand how evidence is weighed for its probative value and its prejudicial effect.

■ Distinguish between direct and circumstantial evidence, and explain why relevance is an issue with circumstantial evidence.

■ State the general principles of evidence regarding consciousness of guilt and prior judicial determinations.

Introduction

In this chapter, we will look at the first or fundamental test for deciding whether or not evidence can be admitted in a proceeding. This type of basic test is called a "threshold test" because it is the beginning of the process. A threshold is an entry point, through the door and into the room. In the legal sense, it is the test that leads to considering further questions that may need to be asked about the admissibility of a piece of evidence. But those questions cannot be asked until the first test has been passed.

The threshold test for the admission of any evidence requires that it be both relevant and material. While the concepts of relevance and materiality are related, they are not the same. We will examine both relevance and materiality, and learn what answers to the test are needed before we can move on to additional questions.

The Threshold Test: Relevance and Materiality

The determination of whether or not an alleged fact is admissible into evidence, and therefore something that the trier of fact may consider in deciding a case, is based on a series of questions about the fact. The very first of these questions is: Is the fact both relevant and material? Because it is the first question that must be answered, we say that it is the "threshold test" for the admissibility of all evidence. As discussed in Chapter 1, the role of the judge is like that of a gatekeeper who decides what evidence gets in through the gate. Evidence that does not meet the test of being relevant and material will not be admitted.

However, just because evidence must be relevant and material to be admitted does not mean that all relevant and material evidence will automatically be admitted. If the trier of law decides that a piece of evidence is relevant and material, she must then ask another series of questions about it, all of which must be answered in the affirmative before the evidence can be considered by the trier of fact. Those questions are the topics of subsequent chapters. But if the evidence is not relevant and material, it will automatically be excluded and no further questions need to be asked about it.

It is important to distinguish between the concepts of relevance and materiality. Many practitioners often fail to differentiate the two concepts when examining the facts, which can lead to confusion in their legal arguments. Proposed evidence can be both irrelevant and immaterial, relevant but immaterial, or irrelevant but material. Thus, potential for confusion abounds in this area.

Materiality Explained

We begin with the concept of materiality because it is easier to explain and understand than relevance. In any legal dispute, there is something that the parties are arguing about. In a case about a car accident, the parties are probably arguing about who caused the accident—who is at fault. That is the major dispute before the court. There are likely numerous smaller or subordinate disputes as well, such as how fast the defendant was driving before the collision, whether the plaintiff ran a red light, or whether the defendant was intoxicated. In a criminal case, the major issue in dispute between the Crown and the accused is the guilt of the accused. There are also likely to be many smaller disputes in the case. A fact that relates to any matter in dispute between the parties is a **material fact**.

material fact
a fact that relates to any matter in dispute between parties

EXAMPLE 1

Joe is charged with stealing Frank's car. Joe wishes to introduce evidence that Frank works as a waiter and does not declare all his tips, and therefore is cheating on his income tax. According to Joe's convoluted thinking, Frank bought his car using money that should have gone into the tax system; therefore, the car belongs to all Canadians. Because Joe is a Canadian, he has a right to take the car whenever he wishes.

Assuming that the judge does not agree with Joe's logic, the information about Frank's cheating on his taxes will not be admitted because it is immaterial to the proceedings before the court. It does not relate to any matter in issue before the court in Joe's criminal charge. If Frank finds himself in Tax Court at a later date, the information about not declaring his tips would be entirely material—in fact, it could be the main matter in issue between him and the Canada Revenue Agency.

EXAMPLE 2

Terry is suing Jan as a result of a car accident. There is a dispute about who was at fault. In her cross-examination of Jan, Terry's lawyer demands to know whether or not Jan is retired. Jan's lawyer objects to the question as immaterial.

The judge upholds the objection. The information about Jan's retirement cannot assist the trier of fact in determining fault, so the judge must not allow it as evidence.

Relevance Explained

A fact is relevant if it logically helps to prove a material fact in the proceeding. It does not have to prove the entire matter in dispute, only a small point that will help logically bolster the proof of something that is material. Relevance is best thought of as a logical support for an argument. That is, for the question, "Is this fact relevant?" we can substitute the question, "Does this fact logically lead to something that is important to prove in the case?" For example, if one wished to prove that a thief was a certain height, would it be logical to establish that he was wearing white running shoes? Not likely. The fact that the accused was wearing white running shoes does not have a logical connection to what one is trying to prove—his height. The colour of the running shoes would therefore not be a **relevant fact**.

relevant fact
a fact that logically supports a proposition

Relevance requires a determination of whether, as a matter of human experience and logic, the existence of Fact A makes the existence of Fact B more probable than it would be without Fact A. If it does, then Fact A is relevant. As long as Fact B is a material fact in issue, or relevant to a material fact in issue, then Fact A is *prima facie* admissible. For example, take a case in which the Crown is trying to prove that Eddy is the killer, and there is evidence that the killer was seen running down the alley wearing a black toque. DNA evidence showing that Eddy's hair was recovered from a black toque in a garbage can in that same alley would make the proposition that Eddy was the killer more likely. The DNA evidence is therefore relevant to the Crown's case.

EXAMPLE

In a personal injury case, the plaintiff is trying to prove that the defendant was negligent because he was driving too fast for the road conditions. The plaintiff says that there was frost on the roads and the defendant should have been travelling more slowly, more cautiously. The accident took place in Calgary, Alberta. As part of her case, the plaintiff seeks to introduce into evidence meteorological reports showing that at the time of the accident it was –5 °C in Edmonton. Should the judge permit the admission of meteorological evidence that relates to Edmonton into a trial dealing with an accident in Calgary? If the defendant objected to the evidence, would the objection be that the evidence is irrelevant or immaterial?

Let's consider the issue of materiality first because it is usually easier to sort out. Does evidence about the likelihood of frost on roads relate to a matter in issue between the parties? Yes, because the issue is whether the defendant was driving too fast for the road conditions. So, in general terms, the plaintiff is on the right track. The problem is that putting information about road conditions in Edmonton before the trier of fact won't assist it in coming to conclusions about the material issues. There is no logical connection between the weather conditions in Edmonton and the road conditions in Calgary—the two cities are over 250 kilometres apart. It is illogical to conclude that the road conditions in Edmonton at any particular time were the same as those in Calgary. The plaintiff may want to introduce the evidence about Edmonton because her brother-in-law works for the Edmonton weather channel, so it is cheaper for her to find out this information. Or, even though she knows that the weather was different in Edmonton, she may want to mislead the court into inferring that it was the same. Or, she may want to introduce the evidence for any number of other reasons.

In determining the admissibility of this evidence, the trier of law asks, is it logical to conclude that information about the road conditions in Edmonton makes the trier of fact better able to draw conclusions about the road conditions in Calgary? The answer is no, there is no logical connection between the two. More importantly, admission of the evidence is dangerous because the trier of fact may conclude from the fact that the judge let the evidence in that it has some importance or value and may therefore give it weight, even though it deserves no weight. The result could be an unjust decision. In our system of justice, the trial judge must keep out information that will diminish or impair the ability of the trier of fact to render a just and reasonable verdict.

Conditional Relevance

In a court case, it is often difficult to present evidence in the chronological order in which events occur. One witness is called and tells his or her version of events. Another witness, or even several other witnesses, must be called to fill in the rest of the story. It is not until all the witnesses have testified that the complete story emerges.

Because evidence is often presented in this way, there are times when the relevance of evidence is not immediately apparent.

Recall the murder case involving Eddy and the black toque. The Crown is trying to prove that Eddy murdered the victim. The first witness called says that she saw a man, identified as Eddy, running down the street, near the alley, at about the same time as the murder. This evidence puts Eddy in the general vicinity of the murder, but the witness did not see him wearing a toque or any other type of hat. In fact, she says she is absolutely certain that Eddy was bare-headed.

The next witness called is the police officer who found the black toque in the garbage can in the alley. This black toque seems to have nothing to do with Eddy, because the first witness said he was not wearing a hat when she saw him. The fact that the officer found a black toque does not logically connect, at this point, to the proposition that Eddy is the murderer. It appears to be irrelevant. However, the Crown's third witness, a forensic scientist, will testify that she examined the hat and tested the hair inside it, and found Eddy's DNA in the hair.

When the police officer describes finding the hat, Eddy's lawyer may want to object to the admission of this information into evidence on the ground that it is irrelevant. In defending the admission, the Crown would argue that the finding of the hat will be linked to a relevant point but that several witnesses will be needed to do it. The Crown will ask that the evidence be admitted on condition that it is properly and logically tied to a relevant fact by the end of the presentation of the Crown's case. The judge would then admit the evidence on the ground of its **conditional relevance**. That is, the evidence is admitted on the condition that its relevance will be established as the case goes along and more evidence is presented. If the Crown is unable to establish relevance by the end of its case, the judge will direct the jury to ignore that evidence.

conditional relevance
term describing evidence that may not initially appear relevant but is admitted on condition that its relevance will be established

Weight of Evidence Versus Admissibility

As we have discussed, the threshold test for the admissibility of evidence is whether it is both relevant and material. Sometimes, as we will discuss later on when examining the rules of evidence in more detail, not all evidence that is relevant and material will be admitted for consideration by the decision-maker because of circumstances that raise questions about its reliability. For example, hearsay evidence—a witness repeating in court what someone else has told him—is not usually admissible, even if it is relevant, because the reliability of the statement cannot be tested in the normal manner (through cross-examination). So, relevance and admissibility are not the same thing, but we will take a closer look at this issue in later chapters.

It is also important to note that each piece of admissible evidence does not have the same importance. A piece of evidence that is admitted is put into a pool with all the other admissible evidence. It is up to the decision-maker to decide which pieces of evidence have the most importance in terms of determining what is at issue in the court case. We say that the most important evidence has the most **probative value**. The probative value of evidence is its value to the decision-maker in proving what is at issue in the proceeding. This process of considering each piece of evidence independently and deciding on its probative value is referred to as weighing the evidence.

probative value
the degree to which a potential piece of evidence helps prove a proposition; the value or strength of a fact in proving what the party seeks to establish

For example, in a case where two experts are called, such as one by the Crown and one by the defence in a criminal case, and the expert evidence is contradictory, the decision-maker would tend to give more weight to the evidence of one witness over the other if that witness was the professor who taught the other witness in the specific area of expertise and the former student kept referring to the textbook written on the subject by the former professor.

EXAMPLE

The accused, Jimmy, is charged with murder. A witness, who knows Jimmy slightly from the neighbourhood and who was standing 10 metres away from the scene of the crime, gives evidence that he saw Jimmy stab the victim in the chest with a butcher knife. Another witness, Jimmy's girlfriend, tells the court in her testimony that Jimmy was with her at the time of the murder and they were watching television at her house on the other side of town. The decision-maker may tend to give the eyewitness evidence more weight than that of the girlfriend.

There may be reason to give the evidence of the girlfriend less weight, because she may have a motivation to lie to protect Jimmy. However, if it was a dark evening and pouring rain on the night of the stabbing, the decision-maker may give less weight to the evidence of the eyewitness based on his ability to be able to clearly see the person who committed the murder. The lack of a clear view may diminish the probative value of the eyewitness's evidence particularly because he knew Jimmy only slightly, but if he was a long-time friend of Jimmy's, his evidence may have more weight because he would be better able to identify Jimmy even from a distance on a dark night.

The probative value or importance attached to a piece of evidence is largely a matter of common sense. No arbitrary rules or formula can determine how much importance each piece of evidence should be given. The weight given to a piece of evidence depends on numerous factors that are specific to each case. Before the decision-maker can make a decision, each piece of evidence must be given weight, and each component must be considered in relation to all the other admissible evidence.

Some factors affecting the weight given to evidence include

- the circumstances surrounding the event about which the witness is testifying;
- the witness's ability to properly observe the events;
- any bias the witness may have toward or against one of the parties;
- the consistency the evidence has with other reliable and credible evidence;
- any benefit that the witness may gain by testifying;
- any special qualifications and knowledge of the subject on which the witness is testifying;
- the demeanour of a witness while giving evidence; and
- any history the witness may have of dishonesty or lying.

This list of factors is by no means exhaustive, and factors will differ from case to case.

Weighing Probative Value Against Prejudice

It is the role of the trier of fact to weigh the reliability and credibility of evidence. However, the trier of law also weighs the evidence to ensure that its probative value exceeds its prejudice. As we have learned, the probative value is the degree to which a proposed piece of evidence helps prove something at issue in the case. The proposition that a party wishes to prove may be a small part of the case, such as the date the plaintiff signed a contract, or it may be the whole case, such as who murdered the victim.

A factor that bears particularly on the issue of admissibility—and therefore is dealt with by the trier of law—is the strength of the inferences that can be drawn from the proposed evidence. For example, DNA testing of blood on the accused's clothing that shows it matches the victim's blood has very strong inferential value. The evidence establishes the strong likelihood that the accused was close to or in contact with the victim when the victim was bleeding. On the other hand, testing of fibres in the accused's car that shows they match the make of carpet in the victim's home—carpet that was installed in thousands of homes—has less probative value. This evidence does not offer much help at all in proving the Crown's proposition that the accused murdered the victim. The only proper inference to be drawn from such fibre evidence is that the accused or someone else using his car was in one of the thousands of homes that have this carpet.

EXAMPLE

The accused is stopped by police near the scene of a violent murder. The victim was slashed with a knife and blood was spattered all over the room. The clothes of the accused appear to have dark "blood-like" stains. Testing shows that the stains are in fact blood. However, the blood does not match the victim's or the accused's, but five other people's. Should this evidence be admitted?

If the victim's blood had been on the accused, that evidence would clearly be very probative, because it would place him at or near where the victim suffered an injury. Instead, he has five other people's blood on him, which may be suspicious but is not helpful to the trier of fact, beyond wild speculation. It is that wild speculation that the judge must guard against. The probative value of the evidence is very slight. In weighing the probative value of this evidence, the trier of law must also consider the **prejudice** of the evidence, or the likelihood that a jury hearing this information will give the evidence more weight than it deserves. Clearly, in this instance, the probative value of the evidence is exceeded by the prejudice.

prejudice
the potential for a trier of fact to give evidence more weight than it deserves

---

In considerations of the probative value of a proposed piece of evidence, the line between factors that are under the judge's authority (the strength of the inferences that may be drawn from the evidence) and those that are under the jury's authority (the credibility and reliability of the evidence) can become blurred. Where the judge thinks the jury may give the evidence much more weight than it deserves, even if it is otherwise valuable to them, the judge can protect them from this prejudice by excluding the evidence. This commonly occurs with crime scene photos. While such photos are clearly relevant and material to the proceedings, they often cause a very emotional reaction and can lead jurors to distort or abandon the logical processes they are required to carry out. Consider how logical you are when you get into a heated argument. When angry, jealous, frustrated, or hurt, most people say and do things that they would not do in a calm or rational frame of mind. The prejudice inherent in the gory photos is that the jurors may become incapable of objectivity and rational assessment, and reach a decision against the accused regardless of the lack of evidence against him. Thus, a judge needs to consider credibility to a degree, because evidence that is biased or otherwise wholly untrustworthy, if given weight by the trier of fact, can result in a very wrong decision.

Prejudice, then, must be measured and weighed against the probative value of evidence. Historically, prejudice referred only to the potential for the trier of fact to give the evidence more weight than it deserves, and it was usually considered only in criminal matters and only in relation to the accused. More recently, however, the concept of prejudice has been broadened to include other considerations. The concept of fairness to the parties is now applied to persons other than the accused—the complainant in a sexual assault trial, for example. In weighing the prejudicial value of proposed evidence, judges also consider whether the evidence will absorb an undue amount of court time, whether it was presented by one party with little or no warning to the other, whether it will distract the trier of fact from the issues, and whether it will simply demean the judicial process by insulting or otherwise emotionally abusing witnesses.

Probative Value Versus Prejudice

The following chart shows the factors that a judge considers in weighing the probative value of the evidence against its prejudice.

Probative Value	Prejudice
Strength of the evidence in proving what the party proposes	Potential to be given undeserved weight by the jury
Benefits of credibility and reliability: • credibility only where it is not so suspect as to be misleading • reliability only where it is not so suspect as to be misleading	Costs of presenting the evidence, including: • excessive use of court time • fairness to the parties • potential to confuse the issues

It should also be noted that evidence is not automatically excluded just because it is prejudicial. Sometimes, despite throwing a very negative light on the accused, a piece of evidence has sufficient probative value that it ought to be before the trier of fact. Consider an accused who is charged with breaching a condition of his parole by being at an elementary school. The fact that the restriction was placed on the accused as a result of a conviction for the sexual assault of a child would certainly be prejudicial in the sense that it would show the accused in a bad light, but it would likely be admissible so that the trier of fact could understand the basis for the original order.

Relevance and Circumstantial Evidence

Evidence can be categorized as either direct or circumstantial evidence. **Direct evidence** is given when a witness offers testimony about a material fact, and that material fact is something that he actually experienced—saw, heard, touched, and so on. Recall that a material fact is one that relates to any matter in dispute between the parties. If the trier of fact believes the witness when he says he saw what he says he did, that is the end of the fact-finding on that issue. The credibility of the witness is the deciding point. The trier of fact can believe or disbelieve the witness, but she need not make any logical inference about the direct evidence.

For example, if the Crown is trying to prove that Sam stabbed Joe but Sam is denying his guilt, whether Sam stabbed Joe is a material issue in the case because it is a matter in dispute between the parties. If there is a witness who says she saw Sam stab Joe, her testimony is direct evidence of a material fact. The trier of fact has to determine only whether the witness is credible. If she is, then the trier of fact will decide that Sam stabbed Joe.

Circumstantial evidence is not as straightforward. It is indirect evidence from which the trier of fact can logically infer the existence of a material fact. In other words, there is a chain of facts that can be followed to a logical conclusion about an issue in dispute between the parties even though there is no direct evidence. The trier of fact must make a logical jump or inference to reach the determination of the material fact.

For example, say the witness in the scenario above, instead of seeing Sam stab Joe, saw a man with one leg stab Joe. Sam has one leg. There is also evidence that Sam had a long-term grudge against the victim. There is no direct evidence that Sam stabbed Joe. No one can actually identify him as the person who did the stabbing. However, the trier of fact may logically follow the indirect evidence and make a logical inference that Sam stabbed Joe. Circumstantial evidence involves a two-step process. The trier of fact must first decide that the witness is credible and should be believed when she says she saw a one-legged man stab Joe. Second, even if she accepts the witness's testimony, the trier of fact must make an inference that the stabber was Sam and not some other one-legged man.

Relevance is a central issue in circumstantial evidence but not in direct evidence. Direct evidence is always relevant once it has passed the test of materiality. Circumstantial evidence must first pass the materiality test, but it then must also be tested for its relevance to the matter at hand.

Sometimes TV shows or movies suggest that circumstantial evidence is not as good as direct evidence. That is not necessarily the case. Circumstantial evidence can often be very helpful to a case, while direct evidence can be a major problem. For example, it is well established that eyewitness testimony, which is direct evidence, is one of the most unreliable forms of evidence available. People tend to see things and events from their own perspectives and through their own filters—it is quite common that two people witnessing the very same incident will "see" it differently. Many factors come into play, such as the witnesses' own conscious or unconscious biases, their ability to observe detail, or their physical location in relation to the occurrence.

direct evidence
evidence given by a witness about a material fact that the witness experienced

circumstantial evidence
indirect evidence from which the trier of fact can logically infer the existence of a material fact

Some Relevance Rules of Thumb

Over time, general principles about types of evidence and the issue of relevance have been established, such as an accused's post-offence conduct, and prior judicial determinations related to a matter.

Post-Offence Conduct

Evidence regarding an accused's behaviour after the alleged offence is circumstantial, and the Supreme Court of Canada in *R v White* ([1997] 2 SCR 72, 125 CCC (3d) 385) defined the type of behaviour at issue as follows:

> Evidence of after-the-fact conduct is commonly admitted to show that an accused person has acted in a manner which, based on human experience and logic, is consistent with the conduct of a guilty person and inconsistent with the conduct of an innocent person.

At one time, this type of evidence was referred to as "consciousness of guilt" in reference to the conduct of the accused, but in the *White* case, the Supreme Court of Canada, while not rejecting the nature of the evidence itself, said that this term should not be used. The problem with the label, said the court, is that it can mislead juries because it implies guilt before all the evidence is analyzed. Despite the court's advice, the term "consciousness of guilt" is still sometimes used to refer to post-offence conduct.

In criminal cases, the behaviour of the accused may be admitted as evidence that he was behaving in a "guilty manner"—for example, running away from the scene of the crime, lying about his whereabouts on the night in question, or altering his appearance immediately after the offence was committed. The trier of fact is asked to draw the inference from the circumstantial evidence of the accused's post-offence conduct that he behaved as a guilty person would in trying to escape the scene or cover up the evidence.

Post-offence conduct may be admitted into evidence on the basis that it is relevant. Of course, there may be logical reasons for the accused's behaviour that have nothing to do with guilt. The judge must therefore be extremely vigilant in advising the jury as to the proper use of post-offence conduct evidence, because it could be misused otherwise. It is to be treated by the trier of fact as only one piece of evidence among all the other evidence, and guilt should not be inferred from the post-offence conduct alone.

CASE IN POINT

Post-Offence Conduct

R v Angelis, 2013 ONCA 70

Demetrios Angelis was charged with second-degree murder in the death of his wife, Lien, to whom he had been married for 16 years. He did not deny killing her but denied that he had intended to kill her and instead had acted in self-defence when she attacked him.

Angelis's marriage was disintegrating, largely due to the fact that Mr. Angelis had recently discovered that his wife had been having an affair with another man for 13 years. Although there had been no history of violence during the marriage, after the affair came to light, the relationship became more acrimonious.

On the day of his wife's death, Mr. Angelis was getting ready to take his children to church when he and his wife began to argue. The argument escalated into a brief but very violent struggle in which his wife, who was a small woman, ended up on the floor with the much heavier accused on top of her. At that point, she suddenly stopped breathing. A subsequent autopsy could not clearly point to the cause of death, but the pathologist said asphyxiation was possible. This could have been caused by smothering or strangulation or by the accused sitting on the victim, which could have interfered with her breathing.

Mr. Angelis did not attempt to help his wife when she stopped breathing. Although he was a registered nurse, he did not attempt CPR to try to revive her, nor did he call 911. He said he was in shock.

He then, among other things, wrapped her body in a rug and dragged her into the bedroom. Leaving the body there, he dressed, gathered his children, and took them to church, where he took part in the services. It was only after returning home that he called 911, some three to four hours after his wife's death. During the 911 call, he was calm and composed.

At trial, the accused did not deny that he had caused his wife's death, but he argued that it was caused unintentionally. If the jury found that he had not intended to cause the death, he could not have been convicted of murder but could have been convicted of manslaughter, a lesser offence that does not require the intent to kill. The trial judge instructed the jury that they could take into account Mr. Angelis's post-offence conduct in determining whether he intended to kill his wife.

Mr. Angelis was convicted of second-degree murder. He appealed the conviction on the charge of murder to the Court of Appeal for Ontario. The judge's instruction to the jury with respect to his post-offence conduct was central to the appeal.

The Court of Appeal determined that this instruction was a legal error. While the post-offence conduct could certainly be considered by the jury in deciding whether the accused did something wrong, it could not be used to determine whether he had an intent to kill in this case. Mr. Angelis's post-offence conduct was equally consistent with a finding of manslaughter as it was with a finding of murder.

The court set aside the conviction and ordered a new trial.

In civil cases, the equivalent to post-offence conduct is the concept that is often referred to as "subsequent repairs": the defendant has done something following the harm to the plaintiff to rectify the situation that the plaintiff claims resulted in her injury. For example, if the defendant has repaired the broken tiles in the floor that the plaintiff said she had tripped over, this would be evidence of subsequent repairs and would play the same role that post-offence conduct does in criminal cases. In other words, the evidence is usually admissible, and the trier of fact is asked to infer that the defendant's action to rectify the situation of which the plaintiff is complaining is one piece of evidence of liability on the defendant's part.

However, an offer to settle in a civil case is not admissible into evidence. If the defendant has offered the plaintiff an amount of money to settle the case, this is a fact that the trier of fact will not hear. Although one might infer liability on the basis of such an offer, the courts have ruled that offers to settle should be encouraged because of their benefits to the justice system by cutting down on trial time and the attendant costs of litigation.

Prior Judicial Determinations

A single incident can result in both criminal and civil legal proceedings. For example, if a drunk driver hits a pedestrian, the driver will be charged with the criminal offence of impaired driving and it is quite likely that the pedestrian will sue, in civil proceedings, for his injury. If the driver is convicted of impaired driving in the criminal proceeding, the courts have ruled that that conviction is admissible into the civil proceeding as *prima facie* proof of the act. The defendant in such a civil proceeding thus bears the onus of rebutting or disproving the act. If a person is found criminally responsible for a certain action, it is highly unlikely that a civil court will find otherwise.

However, it is entirely possible for a defendant to be acquitted in the criminal case and still be found liable in the civil case. This can happen because of the different standards of proof required in each type of proceeding. In a criminal case, the Crown may not be able to prove beyond a reasonable doubt the guilt of the accused, but a plaintiff in a civil proceeding, relying on the same facts, may be able to establish the defendant's civil liability on the balance of probabilities. In any event, the criminal case is always tried before any civil proceedings in order to avoid undue prejudice toward the defendant, whose right to remain silent would be prejudiced in defending the civil action.

CHAPTER SUMMARY

The threshold test for the admission of any evidence requires that the evidence be both relevant and material. It is the very first question one must ask about potentially admissible evidence. To be relevant, evidence must have a logical connection to what one is trying to prove. To be material, evidence must relate to any matter that is in dispute between the parties. While the concepts of relevance and materiality are related, they are not the same. Because proposed evidence can be both irrelevant and immaterial, or relevant but immaterial, or irrelevant but material, there is considerable potential for confusion.

Evidence may also be conditionally relevant and admitted on the proviso that what appears to be an irrelevant fact will be rendered relevant by the admission of additional evidence.

Once a fact has been found to be relevant and material, the judge may still exercise discretion to exclude it from evidence if its prejudicial effect outweighs its probative value.

Evidence can be either direct or circumstantial. Direct evidence involves a witness's first-hand, personal knowledge of a material fact. Relevance is not an issue with direct evidence. By comparison, circumstantial evidence is less straightforward. The trier of fact must make an inference, based on the circumstantial evidence, that a material fact exists. Because an inference must be made, relevance is a central issue with circumstantial evidence.

Finally, there are a couple of "rules of thumb" about relevance. First, in both criminal and civil cases, evidence that the accused or defendant attempted to cover up his actions or involvement in the alleged offence or incident is referred to as post-offence conduct. It is usually viewed as relevant and, therefore, admissible as one piece of evidence to be considered by the trier of fact in relation to the guilt or lack of guilt of the accused. Second, a prior judicial determination based on the same set of facts is usually admitted into evidence as being relevant. However, it is admitted only as one piece of evidence; it does not necessarily determine the decision in the later judicial proceeding.

KEY TERMS

circumstantial evidence, 61
conditional relevance, 57
direct evidence, 61
material fact, 55
prejudice, 59
probative value, 57
relevant fact, 55

REFERENCES

Morris, R v, [1983] 2 SCR 190, 7 CCC (3d) 97.

White, R v, [1998] 2 SCR 72, 125 CCC (3d) 385.

REVIEW QUESTIONS

1. Why is the requirement that evidence, to be admissible, must be both relevant and material called a threshold test?

2. What is a material fact?

3. How is a fact determined to be relevant?

4. What is conditional relevance, and why may some evidence be admitted on the basis that it will later be shown to be relevant?

5. When we say that a piece of evidence is more probative than prejudicial, what do we mean?

6. What is meant by the term "direct evidence"? Give an example.

7. What is meant by the term "circumstantial evidence"? Give an example.

8. Why is relevance a central issue with circumstantial evidence but not with direct evidence?

9. What is post-offence conduct? Give an example.

DISCUSSION QUESTIONS

The following questions deal with relevance and materiality.

1. The accused has been charged with first-degree murder in the killing of an eight-year-old girl who lived next door to him. The Crown wishes to lead evidence from the investigating officer that the attention of the police was drawn to the accused because he looked and acted "weird" when the police first canvassed the neighbourhood to see whether any neighbours had seen anything suspicious. The accused refused to participate in the search for the missing child and did not seem particularly upset after her body was discovered. Why might the evidence of the police officer be admissible or inadmissible?

2. The accused has been charged with the murder of his daughter. The child's dismembered body was found in various places around the city. The first body part found was discovered by a woman walking her dog on the beach. The woman saw a couple acting suspiciously, and they left a bag on the rocks. When she went to take a look after they were gone, she found the child's head in the bag. It was obviously a horrible and grisly discovery.

   The accused has admitted to killing his daughter but says it was an accident. He says he dismembered the body after the accidental death because he was an illegal immigrant and was afraid he would be deported. He also admits to going to the beach with his wife and leaving the bag with the head inside. The Crown has refused to accept a plea bargain for either manslaughter or second-degree murder and is trying the accused on first-degree murder.

   At the trial, the Crown calls the woman who discovered the child's head in a plastic bag on the beach. First, counsel asks her what her marital status is. Then he asks about the breed of her dog. He then asks her to describe the events of the morning when she saw the suspicious couple and what they looked like. He also asks about the nature of her discovery.

   Are there specific objections the defence can make to any or all of these questions? If so, what are they?

3. The accused and several others were charged with conspiracy to import and traffic in heroin from Hong Kong. The Crown's case is based on surveillance and wiretap evidence. When the accused was arrested, a newspaper article entitled "The Heroin Trade Moves to Pakistan," written two years prior to the offence, was found in the accused's apartment. Crown counsel argues that the presence of the newspaper article in the accused's apartment raised the inference that the accused had taken preparatory steps to import heroin or had contemplated it, even though the article referred to the heroin trade in Pakistan and not Hong Kong. Defence counsel objects on the basis that the evidence is not relevant. Do you think he is right?

4. The accused is charged with importing a narcotic. He had asked his mother if she would store some furniture for his friends who were then travelling in South America. The mother agreed. When she was notified by the airline that the furniture had arrived, she advised them to deliver it to her. Before the furniture was delivered, the RCMP examined it and found marijuana concealed in a cupboard with a false bottom. The RCMP allowed the furniture to be cleared through customs and delivered it to the mother's house, and then placed the house under constant surveillance. Four days passed and no one collected the furniture. The RCMP then seized the furniture containing the marijuana. Later in the day, they conducted a search of the accused's apartment.

At trial, the examination-in-chief of one of the RCMP officers proceeded in part as follows:

> **Constable King:** So I entered the apartment and found no one at home.
>
> **Crown Counsel:** Did you find anything relevant to this case?
>
> **Constable King:** Well, I found a small metric scale, some pipes, some magazine articles talking about sources of marijuana, and a pot that contained a green substance.
>
> **Defence Counsel:** Your Honour, I object. I fail to see the relevance of all this.
>
> **Crown Counsel:** Your Honour, the paraphernalia illustrates that the accused is a marijuana user, the scale shows he's a trafficker, and all together this shows a motive to import and, from there, knowledge of the marijuana in the furniture.
>
> **Defence Counsel:** The probative value, if any, is weak and the prejudice to my client is enormous. I ask you to exercise your discretion and exclude.

Do you agree with the Crown or the defence in relation to the admissibility of this evidence?

PART II

Exclusion of Evidence That May Be Relevant and Material

Hearsay

5

LEARNING OUTCOMES

After completing this chapter, you should be able to:

■ Define hearsay.

■ State the fundamental rule about the admissibility of hearsay.

■ Understand when an out-of-court statement may be admitted to show state of mind.

■ Distinguish between the two types of implied statements and their admissibility.

Introduction

hearsay
statement, originally
made out of court, that
is repeated in court for
the truth of its contents

Hearsay is a statement, originally made out of court, that is repeated in court for the truth of its contents when the maker of the statement is not available for cross-examination in the proceeding (*R v Khelawon*, 2006 SCC 57 at para 35, [2006] 2 SCR 787). The fundamental rule about hearsay is: *Hearsay is not admissible evidence unless it meets a specific exception that permits it to be admitted.*

Hearsay is one of those concepts that are simple and yet elusive. The idea behind restricting the admissibility of hearsay is that a witness should not repeat in court a statement made outside court if the purpose of presenting the statement is to have the trier of fact accept it as true. Hearsay is at best second-hand evidence because the person who made the statement is not making it in court and the reliability of the statement cannot be tested through cross-examination. Typically, someone else is repeating what they heard or what they think they heard.

Think of the game of Broken Telephone, where one person in the circle starts by whispering a sentence in the ear of the person next to her. That person then "repeats" the sentence by whispering in the ear of the person next to him. After going through perhaps 20 people in the circle, the statement "Many people are called but few serve" may turn into "Come to McDonald's where billions are served." This may be a fun exercise around the campfire but it is a very dangerous one in a court of law. The reliability of second- or third-hand evidence cannot be tested and examined in court in the same way that first-hand evidence can be tested and examined.

The trier of fact was not there when the events that are the focus of the proceeding occurred. In order to come to conclusions of fact, the fact-finder must take the evidence that is presented and weigh it so as to determine what actually occurred. A number of safeguards or tests have been established to ensure that reliable evidence is obtained from witnesses. Chief among these are the following:

1. The person who made the statement is testifying under oath and subject to sanctions or penalties for perjury.
2. The trier of fact can observe the person making the statement and assess her reliability and truthfulness.
3. The opposing party has an opportunity to cross-examine the witness and attack her testimony to test its truthfulness.

In essence, hearsay is generally not admissible because its reliability cannot be tested and examined in the same manner as other evidence. The statement is not made under oath, the trier of fact does not have the opportunity to assess the demeanour of the statement-maker in court, and most importantly, there can be no cross-examination of the person making the statement. When a witness merely repeats what he or she heard, and is not the actual person who made the statement, all that can be tested is whether or not the witness is giving reliable evidence about hearing the statement. For example, if Joe is giving evidence that Sami told him that Sami's brother had murdered the victim, there is no way for the trier of fact to test whether Sami made the statement that Joe thought he heard, or to understand the basis on which Sami made the statement. To avoid this problem, Sami himself should be called to give evidence. Sami would then be placed under oath and cross-examined.

The Test for Hearsay

In assessing whether proposed evidence is hearsay, we must go right back to the basics and see whether the statement falls under the definition:

1. Is the proposed evidence a statement originally made outside the courtroom?
2. Is it being submitted in court to show that what was said is true?
3. Is the maker of the statement not available to be cross-examined in the proceeding?

If the answer to questions 1 and 2 is yes and the answer to question 3 is no, the proposed evidence is hearsay and is not admissible unless it falls within one of the exceptions to the rule. It should also be noted that hearsay statements do not have to be made orally; they can be made in writing or even implied.

While the test appears to be simple, in reality it is not as easy to apply as it might seem at first glance.

Out-of-Court Statements That Are Not Hearsay

Generally, an out-of-court statement may not be admissible when it is offered for the truth of its contents. However, it may be admissible for other purposes that have nothing to do with whether the contents of the statement are true. If the statement is not offered for its truth, *it is not hearsay* and may therefore be admitted simply on the threshold basis for the admission of all evidence—its relevancy. One must ask whether there is a relevant purpose for having the statement admitted, aside from for the truth of its contents. If there is such a purpose, the statement may be admissible.

Consider a criminal case in which a police officer, acting on information given to him by an anonymous informant who cannot now be found, searches a suspected drug dealer in a pub and finds her holding a considerable quantity of heroin. The officer had no reason other than the statement of the informant for suspecting that the accused was trafficking in narcotics. At the trial of the accused, the Crown wants the officer to give evidence as to what he was told by the informant in order to show that he had reasonable and probable grounds for conducting a search. The statement of the informant is admissible not for the truth of its contents—that the accused is a heroin trafficker—but rather to show the basis for the arresting officer's actions in searching the accused.

Consider a civil case in which the defendant is being sued by another driver who is claiming the defendant was negligent in backing out of a driveway because he did not look behind him. The defendant states that his passenger got out of the car to direct him because his line of vision was blocked and that the passenger said, "Nothing is coming. It's okay to back up." The statement is admissible not for the truth of whether or not it was actually safe to exit the driveway but for whether or not the defendant had a reasonable basis to believe that it was safe and therefore that he met a reasonable standard of care.

In both of these examples, the statement is used to show what the person who heard the statement was thinking, not whether what he heard was true. When arguing to admit these kinds of statements, counsel are seeking to show the state of mind of the person.

The leading case on the admission of statements to show state of mind is the Privy Council decision in *Subramaniam v Public Prosecutor* ([1956] 1 WLR 965 (PC)).[1] The accused was charged with possession of ammunition during a period in Malaysia marked by many terrorist actions. As a defence to the charge, Subramaniam raised the issue of duress. He told the authorities that he had been taken prisoner by terrorists who told him they would kill him unless he assisted them. The trial judge ruled that the statement was hearsay and could not be admitted. As a result, Subramaniam had no way to prove his state of mind—namely, that he felt compelled to help the terrorists—and therefore could not make out the defence of duress. He was convicted and sentenced to death. On appeal, it was held that the statement was admissible. The appeal court ruled that the accused was not seeking to have the statement admitted to prove the fact that the terrorists were going to kill him, but rather to prove what he believed to be the case.

The court held (at 970):

> Evidence of a statement made to a witness by a person who is not himself called as a witness may or may not be hearsay. It is hearsay and inadmissible when the object of the evidence is to establish the truth of what is contained in the statement. It is not hearsay and is admissible when it is proposed to establish by the evidence, not the truth of the statement, but the fact that it was made.

In summary, it does not matter whether someone was carrying drugs, whether it was safe to back out of the driveway, or whether terrorists really would have killed Subramaniam. The statement is not being admitted to prove that it was true. It is being admitted to show what the person who heard the statement thought after hearing it. In other words, the statement is being admitted to show its effect on the person who heard it and his state of mind.

Implied Statements

implied statement
action, behaviour, or course of conduct that conveys information to observers

An **implied statement** can qualify as hearsay. An implied statement is made when a person performs an action or engages in conduct that conveys information to the observers. There are two types of implied statements and they tend to be treated differently by the courts.

The first type of implied statement involves an action by which a person intends to communicate information non-verbally. For example, nodding the head up and down to answer "yes" and pointing a finger at someone when asked who has the stolen goods are actions intended to convey a message. The person performing such actions intends to convey certain information through his action. When a witness is asked to testify about this kind of non-verbal communication made by another person, the issue of hearsay arises. For example, the witness wants to say, "I accused Tom of stealing the petty cash and he nodded his head up and down, agreeing with me," or, "When Mack heard that I was going to testify against him he stared me straight in the eye and slid his thumb across his throat," or, "The flag person waved her arm in a circle, beckoning us forward." These are all examples of communication without the use of spoken or written language but in a manner that deliberately attempts to communicate a meaning nevertheless. These kinds of implied statements are hearsay and are treated the same as any other hearsay statement—that is, they are not admissible unless they meet one of the exceptions to the hearsay rule (*R v MacKinnon*, 2002 BCCA 249, 165 CCC (3d) 73).

There is a second kind of conduct that conveys information, even though the actor does not directly intend to do so. Sometimes, a person's action or behaviour implies that she believes certain facts even though the purpose of her action is not to communicate a message. For example, a rich, elderly man has a nightcap every evening before heading off to bed. One night, he falls asleep before he has a chance even to sip his drink. It is later discovered that the drink was spiked with enough rat poison to kill a human being. The day after the drink was poisoned, the niece, who stands to inherit the intended victim's fortune, was observed letting out a cry of shock upon seeing her uncle come down the stairs in the morning. One could argue that the niece's shock implied knowledge of the poison in the uncle's drink because she was taken aback by the ordinary morning activity of his coming down to breakfast. Is this type of implied assertion hearsay?

Although there is some judicial inconsistency in and academic debate over the admissibility of this kind of implied statement, generally, Canadian courts tend to treat this type of conduct as admissible. If the action is not *intended* to convey information, then it cannot be a statement. If it cannot be a statement, it follows that it cannot be hearsay either. Therefore, if the action is relevant and not more prejudicial than probative, a description of it will be allowed into evidence.

Analysis

Let us work through a few examples to clarify the concept of hearsay.

EXAMPLE 1

Tim is charged with impaired driving. Sally testifies that she was at a party where Tim was and someone said to her, "I hope Tim isn't planning on driving, he's as drunk as a skunk." Tim was stopped by the police an hour later but the Breathalyzer machine malfunctioned and they could not get any blood-alcohol readings for him. Can Sally's comment be admitted to prove that Tim was drunk?

In this example, Sally would be testifying about what someone else told her. The evidence would be presented for its truth (that Tim was intoxicated), so it fits the classic hearsay definition and, in the absence of some exception, would be excluded.

EXAMPLE 2

Douglas Radler collapsed on the street. An ambulance attended. As he was being loaded into the ambulance, Radler was heard to say to the paramedics, "I've got a heart condition but I'm allergic to nitro." On the way to the hospital the paramedics gave him nitroglycerin. He had a massive allergic reaction and died as a result. Radler's family is now suing the ambulance service for wrongful death. At trial, Radler's family—in order to prove that he was alive and coherent when he was placed in the ambulance—wishes to present evidence from a witness at the scene that Radler said those words. The defence objects, saying that this evidence is hearsay and inadmissible. Is it?

In this example, the witness would testify about what he heard the deceased say to the ambulance attendants. Because the witness would be repeating in court something heard elsewhere, this evidence is hearsay on its face. Is the potential evidence being offered for its truth? That is, is it being presented to show that the ambulance attendant was warned about Radler's allergy? According to the plaintiff, the evidence is being offered simply to establish that the deceased was alive and coherent when he was loaded into the ambulance. If this is the reason the evidence is being presented, then it should be admitted. The problem is that the evidence contains additional information that may be prejudicial to the defence. It would be better if the witness were simply to testify that the deceased was alive and talking in a coherent manner when he was loaded into the ambulance, without getting into the details. The testimony would provide valuable evidence without having a prejudicial impact.

EXAMPLE 3

Frank and Bob are charged with robbing a bank. Two weeks after the robbery, the police, acting on a tip, intercept a letter sent to Frank in Montreal that has $500 cash in it. The serial numbers of the bills confirm that they are all from the bank robbery. The handwritten note says, "Frank, Here's your share of the loot. Anytime you want to partner up again for some quick money, let me know. Bob." The police conduct a search of Bob's apartment and locate a pad of the same type of paper. The top page has impressions on it, indicating that someone wrote a note on a piece of paper on top of the pad and tore it off. A police expert examines the note and the pad and concludes that the note was written when this paper was on the pad found in Bob's apartment. The Crown wishes to introduce this evidence to establish a connection between Bob and the stolen money found inside the letter to Frank. Bob's counsel objects to the admission of such hearsay evidence. Should it be admissible?

In this example, as in example 2, the issue revolves around why the evidence is being presented. The statement about sharing the loot is clearly prejudicial to the defence's case, but the note does link the stolen money to Bob. The statement could be dealt with by having the police expert testify that the note accompanying the money was written while the note paper was on top of the pad found in Bob's apartment. The content of the note is irrelevant to this analysis. It could have said, "Having a great time in Vancouver, wish you were here." So the evidence would not be hearsay if it were presented for the purpose of establishing the connection between the money and Bob. However, it would be hearsay if it were used for the purpose of demonstrating the truth of the contents of the note—namely that Bob and Frank robbed the bank together. If the content of the note is irrelevant, the evidence should be given without quoting the statement; the expert should simply explain the connection between the note and the pad found in Bob's apartment.

EXAMPLE 4

In a family law case, a witness begins to testify that he was standing with his friend when the defendant walked by. The friend commented, "That's the guy I saw smacking his kid around in the parking lot yesterday." The defendant's counsel objects to this as hearsay. Plaintiff's counsel points out that the witness heard it with his own ears, so it is not hearsay at all. Who is right?

This example illustrates a common problem with hearsay. Just because someone heard a statement "with their own ears" does not mean that the statement is not hearsay. Once again, the issue of admissibility turns on the reason for admitting the comment. If the comment is being admitted to show that the friend spoke, then it is not hearsay. However, it is difficult to imagine why the statement should be admitted for that purpose, because the fact that the friend spoke does not itself seem relevant. Rather, it is what the friend said that is important. That is, the witness's evidence is being presented to show the truth that "the guy" did strike his child. Plaintiff's counsel should have called the friend to give direct evidence of what he saw in the parking lot the previous day.

CHAPTER SUMMARY

Hearsay is a statement, originally made out of court, that is repeated in court for the truth of its contents and for which the maker of the statement cannot be cross-examined. Hearsay is not admissible unless it fits within one of the exceptions to the rule, because its reliability is at issue. It is a statement that cannot be tested for reliability because it was not made under oath nor is it possible to cross-examine the maker of the statement in court.

Some statements at first glance may appear to be hearsay but in fact are not. Out-of-court statements that are presented to establish the state of mind of the accused are not hearsay and therefore are admissible if they meet the threshold test for all evidence—namely, that they are relevant and material. The hearsay rule does not apply to them because they are not hearsay.

Implied statements, of which there are two types, may or may not be hearsay. The first type, such as the nod of a head to indicate agreement or assent, is intended to convey information and is therefore treated as a statement. Because it is a statement, it is governed by the hearsay rule and is admissible only if it satisfies one of the exceptions to the rule.

The second type of implied statement also involves actions and behaviour that convey a message. However, this type of action or behaviour is not intended by the actor to communicate information in the same manner as the first type of implied statement. In many instances, the action or behaviour sends a message despite the intention of the actor. This second type of implied statement is usually admissible in Canadian courts. The thinking is that, because the actor did not intend to convey information, it is not a statement in the true sense and therefore is not governed by the hearsay rule. The second type of implied statement is admissible if it is relevant and more probative than prejudicial.

KEY TERMS

hearsay, 72
implied statement, 74

NOTE

1   The Privy Council in the United Kingdom served as the final court of appeal for decisions made in many Commonwealth courts. It was the final arbiter of Canadian law until 1949, when the right to appeal to the Privy Council was eliminated from Canadian law and the Supreme Court of Canada became the final court of appeal for Canada.

REFERENCES

Khelawon, R v, 2006 SCC 57, [2006] 2 SCR 787.

MacKinnon, R v, 2002 BCCA 249, 165 CCC (3d) 73.

Subramaniam v Public Prosecutor, [1956] 1 WLR 965 (PC).

REVIEW QUESTIONS

1. Define hearsay. What are the four specific facets of this definition?

2. What is the general rule in relation to hearsay?

3. What three safeguards to reliability are missing with hearsay evidence?

4. Give two examples of out-of-court statements that are not hearsay.

5. Explain the difference between the two types of implied statements. Why is the admissibility of one type governed by the hearsay rule and the other not?

DISCUSSION QUESTIONS

1. Two young boys were playing Cowboys and Indians when one was struck in the eye with an arrow. The statement of claim alleges that the adult defendants were negligent in permitting their son to have a bow and arrows. The plaintiff seeks to introduce evidence that the defendants paid medical bills incurred as a result of the plaintiff's injury. Identify any potential hearsay issue and discuss whether or not the payment of the medical bills is admissible evidence.

2. The plaintiff is suing the defendant for damages for personal injury incurred as a result of the defendant's motor vehicle running her down as she was walking across an intersection. After the incident, a number of spectators gathered and the plaintiff overheard one of them saying, "There's no question that fellow ran the yellow light. I saw him do it." The plaintiff is also prepared to testify that although she was dazed at the time, she distinctly heard a voice, which she could not identify, say, "But I never even saw her until the last moment." The plaintiff also seeks to call a witness who will testify that, shortly before the accident, the defendant's vehicle passed him in an erratic manner and his wife remarked, "Here's a driver looking for an accident." Discuss whether any of these statements are hearsay.

3. The accused is charged with credit card fraud. He wants to testify that his friend, who has since died, told him, "This is my card and you may use it if you wish." Is this statement admissible? If so, on what basis?

4. Joe has been accused of public mischief. The allegation is that, as a joke, he shouted, "Bomb! Run for your life!" on a crowded subway platform. A huge panic ensued as people rushed to escape. The arresting officer wants to testify that when he asked the subway passengers to identify who shouted that there was a bomb, several people pointed at Joe. Discuss whether or not the officer will be able to give this evidence.

Traditional Exceptions to the Hearsay Rule

6

LEARNING OUTCOMES

After completing this chapter, you should be able to:

■ Identify the traditional exceptions to the hearsay rule.

■ Explain the circumstances in which the traditional exceptions to the hearsay rule do and do not allow the admission of evidence.

■ Explain the reasoning behind the traditional exceptions to the hearsay rule.

Introduction

As we saw in Chapter 5, the common law general rule that hearsay is not admissible into evidence was developed to address issues of truth and reliability. If a witness did not testify in person and thus could not be evaluated for truthfulness by the trier of fact, could not be cross-examined, and was not subject to sanctions, her statement was viewed as less trustworthy.

However, over time, the courts developed a variety of exceptions to the hearsay rule that became part of the common law. In some exceptional situations, hearsay statements are reliable and it does not make sense to exclude them. The current state of the law is that if a hearsay statement fits into one of the common law exceptions, it can be admitted into evidence.

This chapter examines these traditional common law exceptions.

Admissions of a Party

admission of a party
anything said by a party by way of word or conduct that the other party wishes to introduce against that party

The general rule regarding the **admission of a party** is that anything said by a party by way of word or conduct may be admitted into evidence and used against him. The rule is applicable to both civil and criminal cases. Although the rule is very broad, there are some limitations on it.

Formal Versus Informal Admissions

The admission process can be either formal or informal. In the formal process, a party to the proceeding admits that certain facts are true, thereby relieving the opposing side from proving those facts at trial. Once a formal admission is made, the party is bound by this admission and usually may not withdraw it. The purpose of formal admissions is to avoid spending valuable trial time proving facts that are not in dispute. For example, in a civil case, the defendant may admit to liability but wish to contest the amount of damages. The defendant is not challenging the factual circumstances of the incident giving rise to the lawsuit, so there is no reason to require the plaintiff to prove them. Formal admission of liability focuses trial time on evidence regarding the amount of damage caused or the degree of injury suffered by the plaintiff. Both parties benefit from this approach because they are not paying lawyers to prepare and argue points that are not in dispute. The rules of civil procedure provide the form, content, and time requirements for formal admissions. In a criminal case, the accused may admit to killing the victim but wish to dispute whether the killing was manslaughter as opposed to murder. Such admissions save valuable trial time and enable the fact-finder to focus on the issues in dispute.

In a civil case, the rules of procedure for the superior courts of all the provinces provide for a process of formal admissions. These rules of court require the party seeking specific admissions to give notice to the opposing party, who then has an opportunity to respond. Failure to respond results in a deemed admission of fact. In addition, there may be serious cost consequences for refusal to admit a fact that is subsequently proved to be true at a hearing. Consider a case involving a motor vehicle accident. The notice to the opposing party may include a number of necessary but uncontroversial matters such as dates and times, ownership of vehicles, even who was at fault for the accident. The admission of fault is less common than the admission of other facts, but the real issue between the parties may not be who caused the accident but the extent of the damage caused by it. It is rational to acknowledge the uncontroversial matters and move on to the real issues, thus saving money and court time in the process. A formal admission can come from pleadings, admissions of fact in writing, or simply from the mouth of counsel, thus dispensing with the need for the other party to prove the facts that have been conceded.

According to section 655 of the *Criminal Code*, admissions can be formally used in the criminal process, although they are less commonly used than in non-criminal cases. Since the Crown bears the onus of proof of establishing the elements of the offence beyond a reasonable doubt, defence counsel in criminal matters are more guarded about a formal admission that would lower the burden of proof on the prosecution. However, formal admissions do have a role to play in criminal court in some cases. The tendency today is to make use of admissions at trial authorized by section 655 where appropriate.

For example, consider a case in which the accused has been charged with murder. He does not dispute that he killed the victim but is claiming that the offence was actually manslaughter, which requires a different level of intent than murder and carries a lesser sentence. The defence may make a formal admission for trial purposes that the accused caused the death of the victim and argue the *mens rea* issue, seeking conviction on the lesser offence.

Formal admissions, as described above, do not create hearsay difficulties, but admissions can also be informal. It is this type of informal admission that is an exception to the hearsay rule. Generally, a statement made by a party outside of court can be admitted against him by an opposing party for the truth of its contents. For example, in a negligence case against the defendant, the plaintiff wants to call a witness to give evidence that she heard the defendant say to his passenger right after the collision, "I guess I shouldn't have come out of the parking lot so fast." The reason for seeking to put the defendant's statement in evidence is for the truth of its content that he was negligent for going too fast.

Statements made by a party outside of court may also be used in criminal cases but generally only against the accused who made the statement. They may not be used against a co-accused except in very specific circumstances. For instance, if an accused makes a statement to his girlfriend that he shot the victim, that evidence could be used in court against him for the truth of its contents. But if he said, "John and I shot him," that statement could be used only against the person making the statement and not against John in his trial for the same murder (see the discussion under the heading "Conspiracies and Admissions by Co-Defendants" on page 87).

It is important to note that in criminal cases, admissions of an accused are an exception to the hearsay rule only if the statement is made to a person who is not in authority (see *R v Oickle*, 2000 SCC 38, [2000] 2 SCR 3). If the statement is made to a person in authority, such as a police officer, the statement may fall into the category of being a confession. Confessions follow very different rules than do admissions of a party. The topic of confessions is dealt with in detail in Chapter 11, which addresses issues of self-incrimination in criminal cases.

In both criminal and non-criminal cases, the statement need not be intended as an admission. It can be any statement a party made that may be used against him. The criteria examined below are used to consider whether a statement of a party will be an admission.

Different Forms of Admission

Admissions may take a number of different forms. They may be written or spoken, or even communicated by action, conduct, or gesture. As we have seen, they do not need to be made with knowledge that they might hurt the speaker in future litigation. But there are unexpected ways that a litigant can be harmed by admissions. The expression "loose lips sink ships" comes to mind because it is often through inadvertent disclosures that a case is mortally wounded.

Vicarious Admissions

vicarious admission
admission made
by an authorized
speaker for a party

A **vicarious admission** is a statement made by an authorized speaker for an individual, business, group, organization, or other recognized entity that may be used against the party in subsequent litigation. When a party authorizes a person to speak on their behalf, the party can be held accountable for what that person says. It is important to note that the content of what the agent, employee, or representative says does not have to be authorized; it is enough that the person is authorized to speak for the party. Carefully worded communiqués that have been approved by a company's legal team seldom provide information that is useful for a plaintiff and damaging to the defendant company. Rather, damaging or incriminating statements usually come from the offhand comments of spokespersons or representatives who have not thought through all the ramifications of their statements.

For example, a few years ago, one of the major automobile manufacturers was producing a minivan with defects. At certain speeds on the highway, the back door of the van would open when it hit a bump. Not only that, the back seat, which was designed to be removable, would actually pop out of the vehicle. Minivans are often used by families for transporting a lot of passengers, including children, so these were very serious defects. What if, after a mishap, a news crew rushes to the factory to interview the vice-president in charge of safety, but when they get there the only person around is the night watchman? With a looming deadline, the news crew interviews the night watchman, who is happy to share his opinions. He says, among other things, "I keep telling them they have to put safety latches on those vehicles but they say it's too expensive and that they'd rather just settle the lawsuits." Can the night watchman's statement be used as an admission against the car manufacturer? As tempting as it is to say yes, the answer is no, the statement cannot be used, because the night watchman is not authorized to speak about safety matters. If the vice-president had been available and he said the same thing, adding, "Those cameras aren't rolling yet, are they?," his statement would be admissible—and damning evidence, indeed.

Finally, it is important to note that vicarious admissions need not be intentionally revealed to the outside world. In fact, admissions are often secret communications within a company. For example, in the Enron scandal of 2001, emails that were meant to be kept from regulators, because they exhorted traders to "sanitize" their files, ended up as devastating evidence of impropriety.

In summary, the criteria for determining whether vicarious admissions are admissible are as follows:

1. There must be proof that the speaker was an agent or employee of the party at the time the statement was made.

2. The speaker must have been authorized to speak on the topic in issue.

3. The statement must have been made to a third party.

Admissions by Action

A person can also make an admission without uttering any words. Meaning or intention can be communicated by an act or gesture rather than by spoken or written language. **Admission by action** goes beyond the communication that happens non-verbally when a person answers a question by nodding or shaking her head "yes" or "no," or when making other gestures that communicate meaning, although these types of gestures would be admissions. Admissions by action that can be used against a person include the destruction of evidence, lying about material matters, giving a false alibi, changing one's name or appearance, asserting a lie, resisting arrest, or failing to appear for a hearing. The point is that these types of actions may imply a sense of guilt in the accused. These admissions, generally referred to as post-offence actions, can be countered by the party against whom the admission has been made, but the party may be strategically pressed into the defensive position of explaining it away.

For example, in a criminal case, the Crown wishes to introduce evidence of flight, or running away, as an accused's acknowledgment of a guilty mind. The underlying question is whether an innocent party would run from the police. Your response to that question would have a lot to do with your life experience with the police and whether you have an expectation of a fair hearing if you chose to await the arrival of the authorities or turn yourself in. In other words, there may be many reasons why someone would flee the scene of a crime—concern for her personal safety, fear that she will be railroaded into a conviction, or many other factors that have nothing to do with guilt. But the trier of fact may draw a negative inference from the accused's running away from the scene of the crime or other post-offence behaviour. This does not mean that the actions are, on their own, definitive of guilt. They are circumstantial evidence that may be considered along with other relevant evidence. At one time, the term for these post-offence actions that can result in the drawing of negative inferences was "consciousness of guilt." More recently, courts have frowned on the use of this term, as it may convey a stronger implication of guilt than is appropriate and may cause confusion to jury members (see *R v White*, [1998] 2 SCR 72).

In civil matters, a current hot topic is whether subsequent remedial actions of a defendant can be used to prove negligence. Suppose, while leaving a grocery store, you slip and fall on the stairs and hurt your back. You complain to the store manager, who looks at your shoes and says that you shouldn't wear heels like that in freezing weather. The next week you pass the same store and notice a new railing on the

admission by action
meaning or intention conveyed by an act or gesture

stairs and a sign that says, "Caution, stairs may be slippery." Can you use this information to prove that the stairway was hazardous when you fell? There are policy considerations that come into play in answering this question. On the one hand, we want to encourage people and businesses to remedy safety hazards as soon as they become known. On the other hand, people and businesses might be reluctant to take such measures if they knew that these remedial steps could be used against them and contribute to damage awards that they would have to pay.

One solution to this dilemma is to make such measures "off-limits" to litigation. This is the approach that has been taken in the United States, where the federal *Rules of Evidence* state that evidence of subsequent remedial measures is not admissible to prove negligence, culpable conduct, a defect in a product or design, or a need for a warning. Individual litigants may feel hard done by because remedial measures appear relevant and probative to their issue, but the greater good would be served by not admitting this evidence. Moreover, if the evidence were admissible, the remedial measures may never be taken, so potential evidence would never materialize. In that sense, nothing is lost. This same issue arises where a defendant makes a voluntary payment, say, for medical treatment or to compensate the plaintiff for some material loss. Is this an admission of liability? Should it be?

In Canada, we have taken the approach that defendants should not avoid taking remedial measures and thus incur potential greater liability. The thinking was that if such measures were admissible, owners of land where hazards existed would not repair them, thus exposing the public to ongoing risk. The statement by Bramwell B. in *Hart v Lancashire and Yorkshire Ry Co* ((1869), 21 LT 261at 263 (Eng Ex Ct)), an old English legal decision from the 19th century, is often quoted by Canadian courts for this principle:

> People do not furnish evidence against themselves simply by adopting a new plan in order to prevent the recurrence of an accident. I think that a proposition to the contrary would be barbarous. It would be, as I have often had occasion to tell juries, to hold that, because the world gets wise as it gets older, therefore it was foolish before.

However, this rule has been altered over time so that evidence of remedial measures taken may be admissible not as an admission of liability but to support facts that are relevant to the issue of negligence. Essentially, it is circumstantial evidence dealing with the issue of liability.

Admissions by Silence

Although admissions are most commonly made in words, in some circumstances silence may also be an admission. If a person remains silent in the face of an accusation, the failure to make a denial may be admitted into evidence as an implied admission. However, silence will be an implied admission only if the silence manifestly implies an admission (see *R v Christie*, [1914] AC 545 (HL), *R v Conlon* (1990), 1 OR (3d) 188 (CA), and *R v Pammer*, [1979] MJ No 149, 1 Man R (2d) 18 (CA)). Not all statements made in the presence of a party who remains silent amount to an admission, but only those in which denial would be reasonably expected. However, because it is the right of an accused to remain silent, failure to make a denial to a police officer does not constitute an admission. Moreover, silence in the face of questioning by the police cannot be admitted as post-offence conduct from which a negative inference of guilt may be drawn by the trier of fact (see *R v Turcotte*).

Whether or not silence in the face of allegations of wrongdoing is an admission would be determined by way of a voir dire. The judge must determine whether there is sufficient evidence to show that the silence amounted to an adoption of the allegation by the party. This is a difficult proposition to establish and, as a result, silence will only rarely be found to be an admission.

Criteria for Admissions

1. Admissions include any statement or act by an opposing party that the other side wishes to use in evidence against the party who made the statement.

2. The statement need not be knowingly made against interest.

3. A statement made to a person in authority, such as a police officer, in a criminal case is a confession, and different rules apply (see Chapter 11, Self-Incrimination).

4. Admissions include any statement by an agent or employee authorized to speak on behalf of the other party.

5. Admissions may be made, in some circumstances, by conduct.

Conspiracies and Admissions by Co-Defendants

As a general rule, an admission may be used in evidence only against the party who made it. Therefore, an admission against one co-defendant is usually not admissible against anyone but the person who made the statement. For example, if Joe admits that he and Amit robbed the bank, the statement is admissible only against Joe. It cannot be admitted into evidence against Amit. The case against Amit must be made out in some other way.

The exception to this rule occurs when the parties are involved in a common design. For example, in a civil case, when a partnership is suing or being sued, a statement by one partner may be used against all the partners. In a criminal context, **conspiracy** is a common design. When parties are involved in a conspiracy, they are working together to plan a criminal act. Any statements made by any of them in the furtherance of the conspiracy may be used against all the conspirators, not just the one who made the statement. This principle is based on hundreds of years of common law; the Supreme Court of Canada applied it in *R v Mapara* (2005 SCC 23, [2005] 1 SCR 358). It is important to note that statements that are not part of or in furtherance of the conspiracy are not admissible against anyone but the maker of the statement because the statement does not form part of the conspiracy. Thus, the guilty plea or the confession of one conspirator is not admissible against the other alleged conspirators because the statement is not part of the conspiracy, but is made after the fact.

conspiracy
a common design or plan by two or more persons to commit a criminal act or omission

Proof in a conspiracy trial goes through three stages. In the first stage, the Crown establishes that a conspiracy actually existed. In the second stage, the Crown establishes who members of that conspiracy are. In the third stage, the fact-finder in relation to those proven members of the conspiracy then moves on to consider whether those conspirators are guilty beyond a reasonable doubt. It sometimes happens that the Crown can establish that a conspiracy existed but lacks sufficient evidence to establish that certain of the accused persons were part of the conspiracy. In that case, those persons are acquitted of the conspiracy charge and free to go unless they are facing other charges. However, if the Crown establishes that a conspiracy did exist and that certain persons were part of that conspiracy, then any evidence that is admissible against one member of the conspiracy is evidence against all members of the conspiracy. So evidence that would usually be inadmissible against one defendant—for example, because it is a tape-recorded telephone conversation between two other defendants—becomes admissible against the first defendant even though it is hearsay in relation to him. The reason for this unique approach is simple: because of the intense secrecy surrounding conspiracy offences, the Crown would be handicapped in ever obtaining a conviction without a relaxation in the evidentiary approach. This relaxation of the hearsay rule is referred to as the **co-conspirator exception**.

During trial, hearsay statements by alleged co-conspirators are **conditionally admissible**, meaning that they may be admitted and form the body of evidence that the jury considers when determining whether a conspiracy exists. The conditional evidence cannot be used in determining whether the accused is a member of the conspiracy.

It should be noted that not all statements made by a co-conspirator are admissible, but only those statements made when the conspiracy was active and that can be classified as being "in furtherance" of that conspiracy. It should also be noted that the first stage above involved consideration of "all the evidence," which includes evidence that in the second stage ought not to be considered against individual persons. Hearsay, then, is available to the jury to determine whether a conspiracy existed, but not to determine whether the accused is a member of the conspiracy. However, once the accused is determined to be a member of the conspiracy, hearsay is again admissible to consider whether the accused is guilty beyond a reasonable doubt. It is like a hearsay sandwich—admissible in the first stage and the last but not in the middle.

Some authors argue that the first stage does not involve hearsay at all because the truth of the statements is not the issue, just that they were said—that there were conversations that appear to be in furtherance of a common design or the commission of an offence. This seems to put too narrow an interpretation of the "truth of its contents" aspect of hearsay. For example, suppose the police wiretap a conversation like this:

Dan: I've got $50,000 to invest in a cocaine smuggling operation but I need some trustworthy people who know how to get through Customs.

Biff: My cousin Eddie works for Customs, and I know he'd turn a blind eye if we paid him $3,000 each time.

Dan: Sounds like a plan.

The argument is that this is not hearsay because it does not matter whether Dan has really got $50,000, or for that matter whether Biff's cousin Eddie works for

co-conspirator exception
rule allowing evidence against one member of a conspiracy as evidence against all other members

conditionally admissible
term describing evidence that is admitted for a specific purpose but that is not at that stage admissible on the larger issue

Customs. They could all be lying about this information but still be conspiring to commit a criminal offence. The difficulty with this approach is that the contents of the statements are in fact the offence. If Dan really has no money or Biff has no cousin in Customs, how can their statements be anything more than exaggeration or bragging? It is not a criminal offence to lie or exaggerate. The contents of the statements are essential to the offence and must be true to the extent that they are not "fantastical"; otherwise, there is no offence. In conspiracy cases, the contents of the statements are relevant; therefore, a hearsay exception is necessary in order to consider conversations involving some members of the alleged conspiracy, in order to determine whether a conspiracy exists.

As complex as this all may seem, the Canadian approach is to have the trier of fact, the jury, make the determinations regarding the existence of a conspiracy and membership in the conspiracy, in addition to whether the Crown's case has been proved beyond a reasonable doubt at the end of the day. The mental exercise would be difficult for the legally trained, but it is a very tall order indeed for a jury of laypersons.

In a civil context, the co-conspirator rule is modified to take into account the different standards of proof. In *Insurance Corp of British Columbia v Sun* (2003 BCSC 1059), Groberman J restated the rule as follows:

- The trier of fact must be satisfied on the *balance of probabilities* that a conspiracy alleged by the plaintiff existed.

- Then, the trier of fact must review all the evidence that is directly admissible against the defendant to see whether it establishes a *reasonable likelihood* that the defendant is a member of the conspiracy.

- If the trier of fact reaches this conclusion, it must then decide whether the plaintiff has established membership on the balance of probabilities. In doing this, the trier of fact can apply the hearsay exception to acts and statements of co-conspirators, making them evidence against the plaintiff.

This analysis must be conducted separately for each defendant and for each conspiracy alleged.

Conspiracy and Admissions

1. The fact-finder must consider all the evidence to decide whether the Crown has proved beyond a reasonable doubt that the conspiracy existed.

2. If the conspiracy is found to have existed, the fact-finder must consider only the evidence that is directly admissible against each accused to determine whether, on the balance of probabilities, that accused is a member of the conspiracy. (The co-conspirator exception does not come into play yet.)

3. If the accused is determined to be a member of the conspiracy, then the co-conspirator exception applies and any acts and statements of co-conspirators may be used to determine whether the Crown has proved beyond a reasonable doubt that the conspiracy exists and the accused is a member of that conspiracy. (This is the co-conspirator exception.)

Declarations Against Interest

declaration against interest
a statement made by a party that is against the party's legal interest

Declarations against interest, or statements made by parties against their own interests, are admissible into evidence if they fit within the criteria for the admissions exception to the hearsay rule that we have just considered. When a person who is not a party to a proceeding makes a statement against his or her own interest, it may be admissible if it falls within the declaration against interest exception. Admissions and statements against interest are similar in that they involve a person making a statement that acknowledges facts that could have negative repercussions, but the declaration against interest exception is essentially used against non-parties.

There are two categories of "against interest" that have traditionally led to the admissibility of third-party hearsay. One involves statements against pecuniary or proprietary interest. The second relates to statements against penal interest.

Declarations Against Pecuniary or Proprietary Interest

pecuniary or proprietary interest
concerned with financial or ownership matters

The term **pecuniary or proprietary interest** is another way of saying financial or monetary interest. Where a person makes statements that can cost him money, the statements are considered sufficiently reliable that they should be admitted into evidence. This does not mean that the trier of fact should accept the statements as true without weighing them; it just means that the trier of fact will get to see or hear these statements. The elements of the test for admissibility of statements against pecuniary interest are outlined below, followed by some examples that may or may not satisfy the test.

Declarations Against Pecuniary or Proprietary Interest

The common law test for admissibility of declarations against pecuniary or proprietary interest was applied by the Supreme Court of Canada in *Demeter v R* ([1978] 1 SCR 538).

1. The person making the statement must be unavailable to testify.
2. The statement must be against the person's interest.
3. The person making the statement must have had personal knowledge of the facts (that is, no "double hearsay").
4. The economic prejudice to the person making the statement must have been immediate.
5. The person making the statement must have known about the prejudice.

EXAMPLE 1

Jennifer is a passenger in Dharma's car when it is cut off by another car and ends up in a ditch. Jennifer is heard to state, "What was that other driver thinking? It's not your fault there are idiots like that on the road." When Jennifer sues Dharma alleging negligent driving, Dharma's counsel seeks to introduce that statement as a statement against pecuniary interest because if Dharma didn't cause the accident, Jennifer can't recover from him for her injuries.

EXAMPLE 2

Allan cashed a cheque from Kay and wrote on the back, "Accepted as full payment for purchase of 1985 Dodge." However, before ownership of the vehicle is transferred, Allan dies and the executor refuses to transfer Allan's 1985 Dodge to Kay's name. When Kay seeks an order requiring the executor to transfer the car to her, she wishes to rely on the notation on the cheque as a statement by the deceased against his pecuniary interest.

EXAMPLE 3

There was an issue of proof in a case about when Johnny Randall was born. According to his rich uncle's will, he had to be born by April 1, 1970 in order to inherit a share of the estate. He had been born at home and delivered by a midwife who has since died. Both his parents are also deceased. To top it off, the province made an administrative error in recording the child's birth, so there is no official record and the lawyer representing Johnny wants to admit a written statement from the midwife's bookkeeper dated March 31, 1970 and signed by the midwife that says, "Received from Mrs. Randall, $400 for the delivery of her son Johnny." Although it is clearly hearsay, the written statement was admissible because it was against the financial interests of the midwife to have given the statement to her bookkeeper for entry into her financial records unless it was likely true. If she said she was paid, she couldn't then claim she was not.

Will the facts in these scenarios satisfy the test for admissibility of statements against pecuniary interest? Let us look at the logic at play here.

1. The person making the statement must be unavailable to testify. The person may be dead, too ill to testify, insane, outside the jurisdiction of the court, or missing. In some instances, evidence against pecuniary or proprietary interest has been permitted when the person making the statement has simply refused to testify.

2. The statement must be against the person's interest. All the scenarios given in the examples appear to fit these criteria. Jennifer, by acknowledging that Dharma was not negligent, may compromise her ability to recover damages from Dharma for personal injuries she suffered. This applies whether or not Jennifer has made a claim; the simple fact that she prejudiced her right to claim is enough. The same reasoning essentially applies to Allan's acknowledgment of payment for the car. By acknowledging full payment, he has given up his right to collect again—it was against his monetary interest that he acknowledged the payment. Finally, the midwife's bookkeeper's acknowledgment of payment for the delivery of the Randalls' child is against the midwife's interest, but without getting into whether the bookkeeper may have an economic interest in this transaction, we encounter another problem in the following.

3. The person making the statement must be speaking from personal knowledge. There is nothing to indicate that the midwife's bookkeeper was

present at the birth, so she would have been relying on what she was told to conclude that the baby was born on March 31, 2000. The bookkeeper's statement would not be admissible under this exception.

4. The economic prejudice to the person making the statement must have been immediate. In such a case, there are too many contingencies that remove the certainty that makes the statement inherently reliable.

5. The person making the statement must have known about the prejudice. Unless the person knows that the statement will cost him money or a chance to recover money otherwise owed to him, then it lacks the force or reliability that would overcome the hearsay rule.

It should be noted that a statement against pecuniary or proprietary interest need not be a public statement. It could be written in a diary, which the person keeps under lock and key. A private statement against interest that comes to light counts as a statement against pecuniary interest.

Declarations Against Penal Interest

penal interest
matter that could
result in the person's
being incarcerated

The term **penal interest** implies that the individual could be charged with a criminal offence as a result of the information supplied in the statement. The declaration against penal interest exception to the hearsay rule arises where a person, who is not a party to a proceeding, acknowledges that he or she committed a criminal offence, sometimes even one for which another person is on trial. There are strict rules for the use of such evidence, which may reflect the fact that these declarations are usually made by persons of unsavoury or criminal background. The position taken by the Supreme Court of Canada in *Lucier v R* ([1982] 1 SCR 28) makes this exception exceedingly narrow and of little practical use.

One early case dealt with by the Supreme Court of Canada provides an excellent example of how this provision will or will not come into play. In *R v O'Brien* ([1978] 1 SCR 591), the accused was charged with possession for the purpose of trafficking (PPT) jointly with a man named Jensen. O'Brien stood trial and was convicted, while his co-accused Jensen fled Canada. Jensen later returned and indicated to his lawyer that he was solely responsible for the drugs and that O'Brien was innocent of the charge. Jensen agreed to testify to that effect in order to provide new evidence for O'Brien's appeal; however, he died before the hearing. The Court of Appeal, though, allowed the statement to be entered and directed an acquittal against O'Brien on the PPT charges. Overturning the Court of Appeal decision, Dickson J for the Supreme Court stated:

> The guarantee of trustworthiness of a statement made out of court flows from the fact that the statement is to the "deceased's immediate prejudice." To be admissible there must be realization by the declarant that the statement may well be used against him. That is the very thing Jensen wished to avoid. He had no intention of furnishing evidence against himself. His obvious desire was not to create damaging evidence, detrimental to his penal interest. Yet, that is the very basis upon which admissibility of extra-judicial declarations of penal interest rests. In my opinion, the statements of Jensen to Mr. Simons failed to meet the requirements for admissibility.

One positive aspect for the accused is that the Crown cannot make use of a declaration against penal interest by a deceased person to implicate the living accused, because it remains inadmissible hearsay.

Declarations Against Penal Interest

In *Demeter v R*, the Supreme Court of Canada set out the following test for the admissibility of declarations against penal interest:

1. The person making the statement must be dead, insane, out of the jurisdiction, or too ill to testify. Refusal to testify is not sufficient.

2. The person making the statement must believe that he or she is vulnerable to criminal prosecution as a result of making the statement.

3. The vulnerability to criminal prosecution cannot be remote (that is, a vague possibility).

4. The court should consider whether there is any other evidence supporting the statement against penal interest and whether there is a connection between the person making the statement and the accused person.

5. The court will look at the totality of the circumstances surrounding the making of the statement to determine its admissibility. Some statements may be somewhat inculpatory (tending to incriminate) and somewhat exculpatory (tending to exonerate) and would not meet the test.

Some examples of penal interest will illustrate.

EXAMPLE 1

George tells his lawyer, "You know that pig farmer guy; well, he's going to take the fall for me. I guess I was pretty smart after all to dump those bodies on his farm." Can George's statement be admitted as a declaration against penal interest?

EXAMPLE 2

Tonya admitted to her friend Joey that she robbed the Lower Mainland Savings Credit Union all by herself. Frank is charged with the offence and Tonya promised to come and testify on his behalf, but she became ill with giardiasis (beaver fever) and is in hospital in Oregon. Though lucid, she may not recover in time to testify. Can her statement to Joey be admitted as a declaration against penal interest?

In the first example, George has made his statement with full assurance that it is confidential and will never come to the attention of the authorities. It was not made with a belief that criminal prosecution may result and therefore would not be admissible under this exception. In the second example, Tonya is unable to come to Canada but that does not mean that her evidence cannot be obtained. She could be examined in Oregon under oath with both parties present, or her evidence could be presented through live video conferencing. Unless these options are ruled out, the evidence would not be admissible.

Dying Declarations

dying declaration
statement made by a
person who is certain he
or she is about to die

A **dying declaration** is the statement of a dying person. For example, Sameer is bleeding to death from a bullet hole in his chest and gasps out with his last breath, "Robert shot me!" His statement is a dying declaration. The dying declaration exception to the hearsay rule applies only in criminal cases. It has no applicability in civil matters.

Dying Declarations

1. The maker of the statement must be deceased.

2. At the time of making the statement, the person making it must have known that he or she was going to die almost immediately.

3. The statement must be one that would have been admissible if the person who made it had lived.

4. The statement is about who or what caused the maker of the statement to die.

5. The criminal case in which either the Crown or the defence is seeking to admit the statement is one in which the charge relates to the death of the statement-maker (see, for example, *R v Aziga*, 2006 CanLII 38236 (Ont SC)).

CASE IN POINT

Deceased Wife's Statements to Cousin, Doctor Not Admissible Against Husband

R v Czibulka (2004), 189 CCC (3d) 199 (Ont CA)

In this case, the Ontario Court of Appeal considered the admissibility of a deceased woman's statements about her husband. It ruled that Maria Czibulka's complaints of abusive treatment by her husband Louis ought not to have been admitted against him at his murder trial.

Louis and Maria, both alcoholics, had a physically abusive relationship. The scene facing the police when they responded to Louis's 911 call suggesting his wife had overdosed on drugs looked very suspicious. She was lying face down on the living room floor, clad in only a bra and underpants. Her body was covered in bruises and the autopsy confirmed that she had 25 fractured ribs, a fractured skull, a ruptured diaphragm, and internal bleeding. Clumps of her hair had been pulled out and were found in the apartment, and DNA tests confirmed the presence of Louis's skin under her fingernails.

All of that evidence was properly admissible against Louis, but the trial judge went too far in admitting statements she made to her cousin in California and to her doctor. The judge made the mistake of relying on the truthfulness of the contents of the statements to determine their reliability. He also made the classic mistake of concluding that the absence of evidence was evidence of absence.

In overturning the trial court decision, the Ontario Court of Appeal stated (at paras 35 and 44): "The absence of evidence of motive to fabricate is not the same as evidence of the absence of motive to fabricate. … In other words, a finding that there is simply no evidence one way or the other that the declarant had a motive to fabricate cannot be converted into a finding in favour of the proponent that the declarant had no motive to fabricate."

Essentially, if the authorities fail to discover a motive to fabricate, that does not mean that the court is entitled to conclude that none existed. The trial judge stated that there was no motive for the deceased to fabricate in her discussions with her doctor. In fact, however, there was substantial motive to fabricate, because she was contemplating litigation against her husband and stated to the doctor that she was visiting him to get the evidence "on the record." In relation to her request for shelter with her cousin in California, the deceased could have exaggerated the abuse she was receiving from her husband in order to "obtain sympathy from her cousin so he might change his mind."

The Court of Appeal ordered a new trial for Louis but without the statements from the deceased.

We can see from the criteria for the dying declarations exception that the statement must be made when the speaker has lost all hope of living and thus (it is thought) has no reason for worldly gain in lying. The deceased person's comments cannot include hearsay statements and must be directed at the cause of her untimely death. Julius Caesar's dying comment, "Et tu, Brute?," would not work if he had said, "Flavius told me that Brutus was in on the stabbing."

Res Gestae or Spontaneous Statements

Res gestae is a Latin term used to refer to what in English have come to be called **spontaneous statements**. These are statements that are made in an excited state or that express an existing physical, mental, or emotional state. There are many variations on such statements, and we will look at the most common of these. The idea underlying the exception for such statements is that when an event takes place and a person comments on the event, without having an opportunity to fabricate a story, then the concern about concoction or lying is minimized.

For example, during renovations on your house, a carpenter is in the other room. You hear methodical hammering and then, all of a sudden, you hear what you assume is the hammer dropping and the carpenter shouting, "Ow! my thumb!" If you were to repeat this in court, the statement would be hearsay if you were being called to prove that the carpenter hurt his thumb on the job. However, the spontaneous scream of pain may very well be admissible under this exception to the hearsay rule. The immediacy of the comment and the unlikelihood that a person would drop his hammer and quickly concoct a story about hitting his thumb tend to make this statement reliable.

On the other hand, if the carpenter tells you three days later, "You know, when I was working on your house, I hit my thumb with the hammer," that statement would also be hearsay and not admissible to prove the fact that he hit his thumb. The statement in this instance would not be spontaneous, and there would have been time for the carpenter to make up a story about an injury.

Spontaneous statements can include "excited utterances" and statements of present impressions of physical or mental condition.

Excited Utterances

An **excited utterance** is a comment made almost immediately following a startling event. The comment does not have to be immediate, but it must be close enough in time to it that the trier of law can determine that the mind of the speaker was still

res gestae or spontaneous statement statement made in an excited state or expressing an existing physical, mental, or emotional state

excited utterance statement made while the speaker's mind is still dominated by a startling event

dominated by the event. The sort of events that qualify as startling are serious accidents, bodily threats, observing a death—anything that would cause the person making the comment to suspend his or her ability to invent a story. The person's mind must be dominated by the events in question when the words are spoken.

One of the problems with this exception is that the meaning of "immediate" in relation to the event being described has been interpreted in different ways. In one case, the statement of a person who had just been in a fight and was calling out, "She stabbed me," was not considered immediate enough because the act of stabbing was not ongoing (see *R v Leland*, [1951] OR 12 (CA)). In another, a stabbing took place, considerable time elapsed, and a statement was made to ambulance attendants, yet the statement was still considered sufficiently immediate for the court to allow the exception (see *R v Andrews*, [1987] 1 AC 281, below). While it is true that a judge must consider how startling an event was, one stabbing is probably pretty much as startling as another.

The *R v Andrews* case is a well-known example of the principles applicable with *res gestae* or spontaneous statements. A couple of robbers, armed with a bread knife and a paring knife and disguised under a sheet, entered Alexander Morrow's apartment and stabbed and robbed him. The sheet came off during the attack and Morrow was able to identify them. After his attackers left, he went upstairs for aid and the police arrived shortly thereafter. Morrow died in hospital a few months later. At trial, the Crown sought to admit his statements to the police identifying his attackers.

The House of Lords identified a number of factors that must be considered in looking at the admissibility of such evidence:

- Can the possibility of concoction or distortion be disregarded?
- Was the event so startling or dramatic as to dominate the thoughts of the victim, giving no real opportunity for reasoned reflection?
- The statement must be so closely associated with the event that it can fairly be stated that the mind of the person making the statement was still dominated by the event.
- Is there anything in the circumstances to imply any special reason for concoction, such as malice or a history of dispute?
- Are there any special circumstances that increase the potential for error, such as excessive alcohol consumption?

Statements of Present Impressions or Physical or Mental Condition

In general, a statement made by a person about his or her present impressions or physical or mental condition is admissible. However, the statement must relate to an impression or condition that the maker of the statement is experiencing at the time the statement is made. Recalling or remembering the condition will not suffice.

A **present impression** is essentially what it sounds like—a statement such as "I'm cold," "The room is spinning on me," or "The wheel on that truck in front of us looks like it's about to come off." In effect, the person is making a narrative statement in

present impression
statement regarding a person's perception of their immediate physical surroundings or actions

real time, describing events as they unfold. For example, following the volcanic eruption of Mount St. Helens in 1980, a person caught in the fallout zone audio-recorded his experience. He was walking along seeking a clear patch where he would be safe but expected that he was going to die. As he walked, he commented on the ash burning his eyes and throat, the difficulty he was having in breathing, and everything he could or could not see. His narrative was a simultaneous translation of his experience and precisely what the present impression exception deals with. To meet the exception, a present impression statement does not have to be made in a life-threatening situation, but the comments do have to be almost instantaneous, with no opportunity for concoction.

Statements regarding present physical or mental condition are particular types of present impression statements. In statements regarding present physical condition, the speaker is reporting physical sensations that he or she is experiencing as they happen. Examples of such statements are, "Do you have any Tylenol 3 for this throbbing headache?" "I'm feeling numb on my left side," and "I think my knee just gave out."

Statements regarding a present mental condition include statements of emotion, intention, or planning that a person is experiencing at a particular point in time. Consider someone found dead of a drug overdose who made the statement awhile earlier, "I've got nothing to live for." The statement would not be admissible for the truth of its contents—that she had no reason to live—but would be admissible for the inference that she was depressed and perhaps suicidal.

Business Records

The Common Law Rule

There are many "mechanical" recordings that are made by individuals in the course of performing their duties of employment. These **business records** can range from the notes made by a nurse about a hospital patient's temperature on his daily chart, to the serial number of a CD player manufactured in Japan, to the cash register receipt given at a store, to the sign-in records of the probation office showing whether the accused kept his appointment as required by his probation order, to a multitude of other recordings that are made in any number of different circumstances.

business record
record made in the ordinary course of business by an individual performing the duties of employment who has no motive to fabricate

The case of *Ares v Venner* ((1970), 12 CRNS 349 (SCC)) opened up the admissibility of such business records, in both written and oral form, in recognition that there are many reliable sources of recorded information that can be accessed for litigation purposes, and that calling the person who actually made the recording is not only of little use but a waste of time and the litigants' money. In the absence of the business records rule, the following line of questioning would be necessary:

> Now, Mrs. Masuda, I understand that you work at Toshiba Electronics in Osaka, Japan. You were working on the assembly line on June 23, 2013 recording the serial numbers of CD players being manufactured for the North American market. I am showing you a Toshiba CD player here. Can you tell me whether you remember this particular number?

Any number of other similarly futile questions could be asked, because the person who recorded the information could provide specifics only by reference to the very records that the party is seeking to admit. Why not, then, simply admit the records for whatever help they may be to the trier of fact, without having the person employed to record them testify?

As with any other hearsay exception, there should be assurance that the business records will be reliable by reference to the care taken in making and recording the observations.

Common Law Test for the Admissibility of Business Records

To ensure reliability of business records, the judge should consider the following criteria in determining admissibility (see, for example, *R v Monkhouse*, 1987 ABCA 227):

1. the records were made in the ordinary course of the business;
2. they were made by a person whose duty was to keep such records;
3. the person who made the records did so from personal knowledge;
4. the records were made contemporaneously (at the time of the event); and
5. the person making the records had no motive to misrepresent them.

The Statutory Rule

Most provincial evidence statutes,[1] as well as the *Canada Evidence Act*, contain specific provisions to permit the admission of business records that are in written or recorded form, whereas the common law rule set forth in *Ares v Venner* applies to both oral and written statements. It is important to note, however, that the statutory provisions do not replace the common law rule; rather, they work as an adjunct to it.

Unfortunately, the statutory provisions relating to business records are not uniform. Although all the evidence statutes require that written records be made in the usual or ordinary course of business, the statutes differ in their definition of the term "business." For example, the federal *Canada Evidence Act* includes government in the definition but the Ontario statute does not. As a result, there is Ontario case law that says that police officers' notes may not be admitted under the statutory provision (*Woods v Elias* (1987), 21 OR (2d) 840, 1978 CanLII 1256 (Co Ct)). However, in cases in which federal evidence law applied, the decision would likely be quite different because of the inclusion of government in the definition in that legislation. What this means is that as long as what the officer's notes say would be admissible if he were present to give oral evidence, then they would be admitted. For instance, if he took measurements at the scene of a hit-and-run accident and wrote them down, or made specific observations himself that there was blue paint on the side of the damaged car and recorded that observation in his notes, those would be admissible because he himself witnessed the facts. He would have had personal knowledge of content in the business record.

It is important not to confuse this issue with trying to admit an officer's notes that contain what other people told him, such as a witness to the accident telling the officer that she saw a blue car speeding away from the scene. That statement would not be admissible in court under the business record exception because the officer would only be repeating in his notes what someone else told him. He would have no personal knowledge of what he had recorded. If he were present in court to give evidence orally, he would not be able to repeat what the witness told him. The witness herself would have to be called to tell the court what she saw.

Approximately half of the statutes, besides requiring that records be made in the usual and ordinary course of business, also require that there be an actual duty to make the record. In other words, the person making the written record must be duty-bound to record the "act, transaction, occurrence or event" (see, for example, section 35(2) of the Ontario *Evidence Act*).

Another difference among the statutes is that some require that notice be given to the opposing party prior to a request to the court to admit the documents. Both the *Canada Evidence Act* and the Ontario *Evidence Act* provide that the opposite party must be given seven days' notice, while the British Columbia statute does not specifically require that any notice be given.

Technology and the ways in which electronic records are created and stored have resulted in changes or additions to some of the existing evidence acts to allow the admission of electronic business records. Given the nature of digital media and how computers operate, some or perhaps all of these electronic documents may not meet current statutory definitions of a "record." To ensure that such records are admissible, the federal government, as well as the provincial governments of a number of provinces, including Ontario, Saskatchewan, Manitoba, and Yukon, have enacted uniform electronic evidence provisions. These require authentication of a record to answer the specific questions: What is this document? Where did it come from? Who or what created it? The authentication must be provided by a witness who can give oral evidence to answer these questions.

In addition, the party that wishes to have electronic evidence admitted must satisfy the court that the record is the best evidence available. This requirement is necessary because traditional evidence rules have typically required the production of the original document. In computer terms, though, the notion of an "original document" can be problematic. Usually, an electronic record is not the original document. It is most often a printout of information previously stored on a computer, which may only ever exist in document format at the point it is printed out to become evidence in a trial.

Prior Testimony

The Canadian legal system often moves slowly. In a criminal case, the time between the laying of a charge and the completion of a trial can easily stretch into many years. Civil cases in a superior court may take even longer to work their way to trial. During that time, witnesses in a criminal matter may be called to testify at a preliminary hearing where the accused is represented by counsel and has an opportunity to cross-examine them. In a civil matter, there are likely to be examinations for discovery at which counsel have an opportunity to cross-examine an opposing party under oath.

In addition, the same incident may give rise to both a criminal charge and a civil suit for damages. If Bob gets angry and purposely drives his car into George, causing George serious injury, Bob is likely to be charged with a criminal offence. He may also be sued by George for the damages George suffered—loss of income, medical costs, pain and suffering, and so on. In situations where one incident gives rise to both criminal and civil liability, the criminal trial precedes the civil case.

It sometimes happens that a witness testifies at the preliminary hearing or the examination for discovery but then is unable to present testimony again at trial. The witness may be too ill to testify, or has left the country or disappeared, or has become mentally incapacitated, or has died. If a party wishes to have the absent person's sworn testimony admitted at trial for the truth of its contents, there is a hearsay issue. The prior testimony exception to the hearsay rule was developed to deal with this situation.

The Common Law Rule

According to *Walkerton (Town) v Erdman Estate* ((1894), 23 SCR 352, 1894 CanLII 9), oral evidence taken at another proceeding may be admitted at trial for the truth of its contents if

1. the witness is unavailable for the trial,
2. the material issues and the parties are substantially the same in both proceedings, and
3. the opposite party had the opportunity to cross-examine in the earlier proceeding.

These criteria provide protection against the prejudicial impact of having evidence presented where the other party has no opportunity to test the reliability of the evidence through cross-examination. It is the opportunity to cross-examine that is important, not whether the party actually used the opportunity.

CASE IN POINT

Testimony from First Murder Trial

R v Ellard, 2009 SCC 27, [2009] 2 SCR 19

Kelly Ellard was tried for the murder of Reena Virk in Saanich, British Columbia. The case received extensive, Canada-wide media coverage because of the circumstances. Both the victim and the accused were teenagers. Reena had been bullied and picked on by a group of her peers at school. She was lured to an isolated spot and swarmed and beaten by a group of teens, including Ellard. The victim managed to get away but was followed by Ellard and her boyfriend, who badly beat her again and left her to drown under a bridge. The boyfriend, in a separate trial, was convicted of second-degree murder. Over the course of more than a decade, Kelly Ellard had three trials and various appeals until her conviction was finally confirmed by the Supreme Court of Canada in 2009.

A Crown witness in Kelly Ellard's second trial for the murder of Reena Virk became ill before his cross-examination could be completed, so the evidence he gave at her first trial was admitted at the second. Justice Selwyn Romilly ruled that the evidence given by Lorne Lloyd-Walters at Ellard's first trial could be heard by the jury. It was the second time in the trial that the jury heard evidence from a witness who was unable to testify. Earlier, the jury heard an audiotape of testimony from a witness in the first trial who later died.

Section 715 of the *Criminal Code* allows testimony from an earlier trial to be used in a subsequent trial, in part to deal with the slow pace of litigation. Without such a provision, the prior testimony of witnesses who die or become incapacitated while a trial decision wends its way through the appeal process would be inadmissible, and without such evidence, a new trial would often be impossible and the administration of justice would fall into disrepute.

Prior Testimony Under the Civil Rules of Court

The procedural rules of most provincial superior courts provide for the admission of testimony from prior proceedings. These rules differ from province to province, but most of them strictly limit the type of evidence that may be admitted. For example, the Ontario *Rules of Civil Procedure* allow only for the admission of prior testimony taken during examinations for discovery, not evidence in any other proceeding:

> 31.11(6) Where a person examined for discovery,
> (a) has died;
> (b) is unable to testify because of infirmity or illness;
> (c) for any other sufficient reason cannot be compelled to attend at the trial;
> or
> (d) refuses to take an oath or make an affirmation or to answer any proper question,
> any party may, with leave of the trial judge, read into evidence all or part of the evidence given on the examination for discovery as the evidence of the person examined, to the extent that it would be admissible if the person were testifying in court.

This means that, in Ontario, if there had been a prior proceeding such as a criminal trial, any evidence from that proceeding could not be admitted under the rule. Instead, the party wanting to admit the earlier testimony would have to rely on either the common law rule or section 5 of the Ontario *Evidence Act*, which provides for the admission of recorded transcripts from prior proceedings.[2]

The British Columbia *Supreme Court Civil Rules*, however, provide a much broader rule of admission:

> 12-5(54) If a witness is dead, or is unable to attend and testify because of age, infirmity, sickness or imprisonment or is out of the jurisdiction or his or her attendance cannot be secured by subpoena, the court may permit a transcript of any evidence of that witness taken in any proceeding, hearing or inquiry at which the evidence was taken under oath, whether or not involving the same parties to be put in as evidence, but reasonable notice shall be given of the intention to give that evidence.

In civil proceedings in the British Columbia Supreme Court, recourse to the common law or the provincial evidence act would not be necessary because the rule permits the transcript of sworn evidence of "any proceeding, hearing or inquiry" to be admitted into evidence.

Prior Testimony Under the Criminal Code

There are provisions in the *Criminal Code* for the admissibility of prior testimony. As with the common law rule and provincial procedural rules, the intention appears to be to provide safeguards of necessity and reliability to ensure that the prejudice to the accused is minimized:

> 715(1) Where, at the trial of an accused, a person whose evidence was given at a previous trial on the same charge, or whose evidence was taken in the investigation of the charge against the accused or on the preliminary inquiry into the charge, refuses to be sworn or to give evidence, or if facts are proved on oath from which it can be inferred reasonably that the person
>> (a) is dead,
>> (b) has since become and is insane,
>> (c) is so ill that he is unable to travel or testify, or
>> (d) is absent from Canada,
>
> and where it is proved that his evidence was taken in the presence of the accused, it may be read as evidence in the proceedings without further proof, unless the accused proves that the accused did not have full opportunity to cross-examine the witness.

In this exception, the necessity criteria are clearly defined as being dead, insane, too ill to testify, or absent from Canada. The judge has the discretion to determine whether the latter three make the accused unable to testify. (The first criterion is something even a judge is powerless to correct.) Note that the evidence must be taken in the presence of the accused and that there must have been *full* opportunity to cross-examine. An accused who absconds before or during his trial is deemed to have been present, so that requirement in the above definition is met, even in the absence of the accused. Thus, a strategy of "taking off" until key witnesses are no longer available will not work.

Prior Statements Made by Witnesses

Until relatively recently, at common law, a prior statement made by a witness who was not a party to the proceeding has long been admissible to challenge the credibility of a witness, not for the truth of its contents. This is the classic "Are you lying now or were you lying then?" scenario. For example, Sally tells the police that she saw Matt steal money from a classmate's book bag, and then at Matt's theft trial she says she didn't see anyone steal the money. Under the common law rule, the prior statement—that Sally saw Matt steal the money—may be admitted only to show that Sally is not a very believable witness because she cannot get her story straight. This principle does not involve an exception to the hearsay rule because the prior statement is not being admitted for the truth of its contents.

More recently, the Supreme Court of Canada, in a line of cases, has examined the issue of whether prior statements may be admitted into evidence for the truth of their contents, not merely to challenge the credibility of a witness. In a number of instances, the cases involved videos of prior statements taken by the police during their investigation of an offence. The person videotaped is either unavailable to appear in court or is present in court and is now recanting, or changing his original story.

The issue was ultimately determined in the case of *R v Khelawon* (2006 SCC 57, [2006] 2 SCR 787). The court ruled that prior out-of-court statements, whether videotaped or not, and whether or not the witness was present in court to give evidence, are hearsay and cannot be admitted for the truth of their contents unless they fit within an exception to the hearsay rule. Over this same period of time, however, the court was also developing a line of cases that ultimately led to the creation of a new approach to examining hearsay in general, often referred to as the *principled approach* or the *principled exception*. We discuss both the *Khelawon* case and the principled exception in depth in Chapter 7, The Principled Exception to the Hearsay Rule.

For the purpose of this discussion, *Khelawon* established that if a prior statement can meet the two-pronged test of reliability and necessity, it may be admitted for truth. The central issue is one of reliability. If some solid, extrinsic reliability of the prior statement can be established, the statement may meet the criteria for admission under the principled exception to the exclusionary rule. Establishing the reliability of such statements is not an easy task. The major test for reliability is cross-examination at the point that the statement is being made, and that test is difficult to meet in out-of-court situations.

This does not mean that prior statements cannot continue to be admitted for purposes other than truth, such as to test witness credibility or to help a witness refresh her memory.

Identifications

In the matter of identifications, the law of evidence takes into account the practicalities of the litigation process and the frailties of human memory. An initial identification often takes place shortly after a crime. The witness may be shown a photo lineup or an in-person lineup, or may even pick out the suspect in a crowd or informal group. Then there will be a passage of time, usually many months or even years, before the witness sees the person again. At this point, the person is typically sitting beside his counsel in a courtroom and is well dressed and well groomed, and to one degree or another looks different from the way he did at the time of the offence. (Male accuseds often have either more or less facial hair; any accused may have a different hairstyle or may have gained or lost weight.) Not surprisingly, witnesses sometimes have difficulty identifying the accused in court.

The usual practice for presenting information regarding the prior identification of the person is as follows. The police officer who took the witness's original testimony testifies about the identification process—say, a photo lineup. The lineup array is presented as an exhibit, and the officer testifies about the selection made by the witness from the choices offered. The officer's instructions to the witness are crucial in determining the reliability of the identification. The witness should not have been influenced by the officer or the process and must not have concluded that she had to make a selection, or even that the offender was necessarily in the array. In other words, it is not acceptable for the witness to have picked the *closest* person to the perpetrator rather than the actual offender. Lineup identifications have resulted in many wrongful convictions and, while invaluable for the police, they are not very strong evidence in themselves.

Where the witness can positively identify the accused in court, particularly where the accused has gone through a radical transformation in appearance, the out-of-court identification can be considered by the trier of fact in determining whether identification has been proven beyond a reasonable doubt. This is the case where the witness can testify that she accurately identified the person previously as the offender. Although this evidence is hearsay, its reliability comes from the fact that the identification was made close to the events in question and the witness is available for cross-examination about the accuracy of that identification.

For defence counsel, the essential concern with these identifications is that one can never tell whether the witness is identifying the accused on the basis of her memory of the original incident or of her clearer and more recent memory of picking the accused out of a lineup. The opportunity for observation in a lineup is usually much better than during the actual, often chaotic occurrence of the incident. Because the lineup process takes place outside the view of the court, usually in circumstances where the police have selected someone they believe is the offender, there exists potential for subtle influence of the witness. Subsequently, in the period leading up to the trial and at the trial itself, a witness who does not want to acknowledge a mistaken identification or uncertainty may "dig in" and insist on the truth of her memory.

The rule on the admissibility of prior identifications has evolved out of necessity, given the sometimes very lengthy times between the commission of an offence and the trial. The justice system would be very poorly thought of if a criminal could elude justice after having been positively identified very close to the time of the offence but could not be identified years later, possibly because of his altered appearance.

The In-Court Identification Game

Defence counsel tend to be cynical about in-court identification of the accused by witnesses. It sometimes seems that a witness looks down at the defence table, passes over the man in the expensive suit, and picks the person beside him as the perpetrator. In an effort to combat this kneejerk identification, some counsel will have the accused sit in the body of the courtroom rather than beside them when identification testimony is being presented. It's hard to say how often this is a successful strategy for the defence. One problem may be that no one else in the courtroom is a likely candidate. The spectators may be elderly or they may not be from the same identifiable racial or cultural group. Defence counsel can overcome this problem by having their client bring a group of friends along with him and giving the witness a real test in identification.

There is an anecdote about a lawyer that had a client who was charged with stealing a car. When the lawyer showed up the morning of the trial, he approached the client and began talking about the case. The person to whom the lawyer was speaking interrupted and said, "I think you want to talk to my cousin." As it turned out, the client had brought his cousin with him and he wanted to see whether the police could pick him out of the body of the courtroom, with his relative there. The family resemblance between the client and his cousin was astounding: they could almost have been twins. The judge, too, was amazed at the family resemblance, but nevertheless he permitted the experiment.

The client, his cousin, and a few other unlikely suspects were in the body of the courtroom when the first officer testified. When the defence counsel got to the issue of identification, the officer unhesitatingly picked out the client. Thinking "Lucky guess," the lawyer continued cross-examination by asking the officer how he could be certain of the identification. The officer replied, "You'll notice, counsellor, that your client has a bit of a curve to his nose and his earlobes are longer than those of his friend. That's how I know he's the one I dealt with." The lawyer was startled, but on closer inspection he found that the officer was right. Not all witnesses are as good at identification as that officer, but he certainly was one whom it would be wise not to challenge in that way again.

Past Recollection Recorded

Sometimes a witness to an incident will, at the time or shortly after, write notes or otherwise record her perceptions of the incident as it occurred. However, given the length of time between the incident and the trial, the witness may not remember the specific details that she wrote down or recorded. The classic example is a situation where the witness writes down the licence plate number of a car speeding away from the crime scene. When called upon to testify months or years later, the witness can no longer remember the exact number and wants to refer to the note that she wrote at the time she witnessed the event in order to refresh her memory.

The note itself is hearsay. It is a written, out-of-court statement that counsel is trying to admit in court for the truth of its contents. In *R v Meddoui* ([1991] 3 SCR 320), the Supreme Court of Canada upheld criteria summarized by the Alberta Court of Appeal ((1990), 61 CCC (3d) 345 at 352 per Kerans JA), quoting *Wigmore on Evidence*, as the test for permitting a witness to refer to a written note or other recording:

1. The past recollection must have been recorded in some reliable way.
2. At the time, it must have been sufficiently fresh and vivid to be probably accurate.
3. The witness must be able now to assert that the record accurately represented his knowledge and recollection at the time. The usual phrase requires the witness to affirm that he "knew it to be true at the time."
4. The original record itself must be used, if it is procurable.

In other words, the information the witness wishes to refer to must have been made very close in time to the incident, in some reliable fashion, and the witness must be able to verify that she believed the information to be true when she recorded it.

This test has been explicitly adopted in numerous provincial court decisions and in the Supreme Court's decision in *R v Fliss* (2002 SCC 16, [2002] 1 SCR 535).

Oral Histories of Aboriginal Peoples

The law evolves over time, one hopes in ways that make it fairer and more accessible to the people to whom it applies. Evidence law is perhaps even more responsive to societal change because it is not subject to overtly political considerations but is intended to balance the rights of parties against the interests of society as a whole in seeing that justice is done. In recent times, the Supreme Court has recognized the admissibility of the oral histories of Aboriginal peoples.

Delgamuukw v British Columbia ([1997] 3 SCR 1010) was an Aboriginal title claim advanced by the Gitksan and Wet'suwet'en people to a vast area of land in British Columbia. In order to advance this claim, the Gitksan sought to show that they had title to this land prior to 1846 and that they had never relinquished this title.

The Supreme Court of Canada laid out the manner of proof of Aboriginal right in *R v Van der Peet* ([1996] 2 SCR 507 at paras 54-59). In summary, an Aboriginal claimant must prove that a modern practice, tradition, or custom has a reasonable degree of continuity with the practices, traditions, or customs that existed prior to contact. The practice, custom, or tradition must have been "integral to the distinctive culture" of the Aboriginal society, in the sense that it distinguished or characterized their traditional culture and lay at the core of the people's identity. It must be a "defining feature" of the Aboriginal society, such that the culture would be "fundamentally altered" without it. And it must be a feature of "central significance" to the people's culture, one that "truly made the society what it was."

The following components summarize the proof needed:

- there must be a modern practice, tradition, or custom (for example, salmon fishing for trade);
- there must be continuity from pre-contact times to the present;
- the practice, tradition, or custom must have been integral to the people's culture; and
- the people must have had a distinctive society.

Proof of Aboriginal *title* is more focused on occupation of the land than proof of Aboriginal right. It focuses on the time at which the Crown asserted sovereignty over the land, which in British Columbia was 1846. In *Delgamuukw*, the claim of the Gitksan and Wet'suwet'en people was a collective one and supported by collective oral history. The Supreme Court stated that in order to claim Aboriginal title, the following must be proved:

1. the land was occupied prior to sovereignty;
2. continuity exists between present and pre-sovereignty occupation; and
3. at the time sovereignty was asserted by the Crown, occupation of the land was exclusive.

Proof of occupation can be established by showing either actual occupation or that a system of law exists that asserts control over the land.

Oral history was validated by the Supreme Court of Canada in *Delgamuukw* and it was emphasized that no distinction could be made between oral history and documentary history. That is not to say that anything someone says is accepted unquestioningly, but rather that oral history should be assessed for reliability just like documentary evidence and given the weight it deserves:

> Notwithstanding the challenges created by the use of oral histories as proof of historical facts, the laws of evidence must be adapted in order that this type of evidence can be accommodated and placed on an equal footing with the types of historical evidence that courts are familiar with, which largely consists of historical documents. This is a long-standing practice in the interpretation of treaties between the Crown and aboriginal peoples.... . To quote Dickson CJ, given that most aboriginal societies "did not keep written records," the failure to do so would "impose an impossible burden of proof" on aboriginal peoples, and "render nugatory" any rights that they have ... . This process must be undertaken on a case-by-case basis. (para 87)

Oral histories, called *adaawk* and *kungax* by the Gitksan and Wet'suwet'en peoples, were admitted at their land claims trial. These histories are recitations of important events for these people, including migrations, origins, traditions, laws, and the territory falling under the jurisdiction of the various houses of the Gitksan and Wet'suwet'en chiefs. This evidence was offered as proof of historical use and occupation of a specific territory. While the trial judge admitted this evidence, he ultimately gave it no weight, saying that the oral histories were not "literally true," that they included material that was mythological, and that they offered a "romantic view" of the claimants' history.

The Supreme Court of Canada found that the trial judge erred in not giving weight to the oral histories and said that if the oral histories of Aboriginal peoples were not treated the same as documentary histories, they would "never be given any independent weight and are only useful as confirmatory evidence in aboriginal rights litigation" and thus would "be consistently and systematically undervalued by the Canadian legal system," making it virtually impossible for First Nations to litigate Aboriginal title claims. The court directed a new trial stipulating that this evidence be given weight on the issue of Aboriginal title.

CHAPTER SUMMARY

Despite the general rule that hearsay is not admissible into evidence because it cannot be tested in the normal way for reliability, the common law has developed a number of exceptions to the rule. In some exceptional situations, hearsay statements can be viewed as reliable and it does not make sense to exclude them. As a result, if a hearsay statement fits into one of the common law exceptions, it may be admitted into evidence.

KEY TERMS

admission by action, 85
admission of a party, 82
business record, 97
co-conspirator exception, 88
conditionally admissible, 88
conspiracy, 87
declaration against interest, 90
dying declaration, 94
excited utterance, 95
pecuniary or proprietary interest, 90
penal interest, 92
present impression, 96
res gestae or spontaneous statement, 95
vicarious admission, 84

NOTES

1   Only the evidence acts of Alberta and Newfoundland and Labrador do not provide a provincial statutory hearsay exception for business records. See the following for the business records provisions: federal—*Canada Evidence Act*, s 30; and provincial—British Columbia *Evidence Act*, s 23; *Manitoba Evidence Act*, s 49; New Brunswick *Evidence Act*, ss 49 and 51; Nova Scotia *Evidence Act*, s 23; Ontario *Evidence Act*, s 35; Prince Edward Island *Evidence Act*, s 32; and Saskatchewan *Evidence Act*, s 50.

2   See also *Manitoba Evidence Act*, s 27; *Alberta Evidence Act*, s 27; Nova Scotia *Evidence Act*, s 19; New Brunswick *Evidence Act*, ss 33 and 35; and Saskatchewan *Evidence Act*, s 50.

REFERENCES

Alberta Evidence Act, RSA 2000, c A-18.

Andrews, R v, [1987] 1 AC 281.

Ares v Venner (1970), 12 CRNS 349 (SCC).

Aziga, R v, 2006 CanLII 38236 (Ont SC).

British Columbia, *Evidence Act*, RSBC 1996, c 124.

British Columbia, *Supreme Court Civil Rules*, BC reg 168/2009, rule 31.

Canada Evidence Act, RSC 1985, c C-5.

Christie, R v, [1914] AC 545 (HL).

Conlon, R v (1990), 1 OR (3d) 188 (CA).

Criminal Code, RSC 1985, c C-46.

Customs Act, 1985, c 1 (2d Supp).

Czibulka, R v (2004), 189 CCC (3d) 199 (Ont CA).

Delgamuukw v British Columbia, [1997] 3 SCR 1010.

Demeter v R, [1978] 1 SCR 538.

Ellard, R v, 2009 SCC 27, [2009] 2 SCR 19.

Fliss, R v, 2002 SCC 16, [2002] 1 SCR 535.

Hart v Lancashire and Yorkshire Ry Co (1869), 21 LT 261 (Eng Ex Ct).

Higham v Ridgway (1808), 103 ER 717 (KB).

Insurance Corp of British Columbia v Sun, 2003 BCSC 1059.

Khelawon, R v, 2006 SCC 57, [2006] 2 SCR 787.

Leland, R v, [1951] OR 12 (CA).

Lucier v R, [1982] 1 SCR 28.

Manitoba Evidence Act, CCSM c E150.

Mapara, R v, 2005 SCC 23, [2005] 1 SCR 358.

Meddoui, R v (1990), 61 CCC (3d) 345 (Alta CA), aff'd [1991] 3 SCR 320.

Monkhouse, R v, 1987 ABCA 227.

New Brunswick, *Evidence Act*, RSNB 1973, c E-11.

Newfoundland and Labrador, *Evidence Act*, RSNL 1990, c E-16.

Nova Scotia, *Evidence Act*, RSNS 1989, c 154.

O'Brien, R v, [1978] 1 SCR 591.

Oickle, R v, 2000 SCC 38, [2000] 2 SCR 3.

Ontario, *Evidence Act*, RSO 1990, c E.23.

Ontario, *Rules of Civil Procedure*, RRO 1990, reg 194.

DM Paciocco & L Stuesser, *The Law of Evidence*, rev 5th ed (Toronto: Irwin Law, 2010).

Pammer, R v, [1979] MJ No 149, 1 Man R (2d) 18 (CA).

Prince Edward Island, *Evidence Act*, RSPEI 1988, c E-11.

Saskatchewan Evidence Act, SS 2006, c E-11.2.

Turcotte, R v, 2005 SCC 50, [2005] 2 SCR 519.

Van der Peet, R v, [1996] 2 SCR 507.

Walkerton (Town) v Erdman Estate (1894), 23 SCR 352, 1894 CanLII 9.

White, R v, [1998] 2 SCR 72.

Woods v Elias (1978), 21 OR (2d) 840, 1978 CanLII 1256 (Co Ct).

REVIEW QUESTIONS

1. What is an admission, and when can it be used?

2. In what circumstances does a person make an admission on behalf of a party?

3. Can an employee make an admission on behalf of an employer? If so, when?

4. Is it possible to make an admission without speaking?

5. What is the difference between an admission and a declaration against interest?

6. Give an example of a dying declaration that would be admissible, and an example of one that would not.

7. List the different types of spontaneous statements and state the circumstances in which each becomes admissible.

8. Why is there a business records exception, and when does it apply?

9. What is the common law rule creating an exception for prior testimony? How does it differ from the civil and criminal statutory exceptions?

10. In what circumstances can a prior inconsistent statement be admitted for the truth of its contents?

11. Why is there an exception for prior identification?

12. In what circumstance may a witness rely on a previously recorded statement?

13. Explain the basis for the development of the oral histories of First Nations exception.

DISCUSSION QUESTIONS

1. In a case involving a violation of the *Customs Act*, the Crown, in order to establish the country of origin, seeks to introduce the perfume seized from the accused, the bottles of which have labels reading, "Made in Paris." The Crown seeks to call Constable Smith, who will testify that the accused told him the perfume came from France and that, when asked how he knew, the accused replied, "Look at the label, dummy!"

   Identify the hearsay statements and discuss whether or not they will be admitted into evidence.

2. The accused is charged with murder. The Crown's main witness, Jones, will testify that the accused's brother advised him some weeks prior to the trial that he should be careful because the accused had "already killed once to save his hide." Jones is also prepared to say that the accused, the night before the trial, phoned him and said, "If you don't want what Smith got, stay off the stand tomorrow." The Crown is prepared to lead evidence that Smith was murdered some two years ago.

   Discuss whether or not each of these statements will be admissible.

3. A witness observes a hit-and-run accident and writes down the licence plate number of the fleeing vehicle. The witness later describes the vehicle to the investigating officer, who makes a note of it. Sometime before the trial the witness lost her note, and now at trial she cannot remember the licence plate number. Discuss whether or not the investigating officer can supply the missing number while giving evidence.

4. The accused, Butch, is charged with the murder of his estranged wife, Jill. The killing occurred in the early morning hours at the deceased's front doorway and was the result of several blows to the head with a small hatchet. Jack, the 14-year-old son of the couple, was roused from his sleep by someone knocking loudly at the front door. He testifies that he heard his mother go downstairs and then heard her screaming: "Butch, what are you doing? No! No! Please don't hurt me, Butch." Will the Crown be successful in having Jack's testimony admitted?

7

The Principled Exception to the Hearsay Rule

LEARNING OUTCOMES

After completing this chapter you should be able to:

- Analyze the traditional exceptions to the hearsay rule in terms of their necessity.

- Analyze the traditional exceptions to the hearsay rule in terms of their reliability.

- Explain the principled exception to the hearsay rule in terms of necessity and reliability.

- Understand the application of the principled exception to the hearsay rule.

Introduction

One of the major developments in Canadian evidence law in the last quarter-century was the Supreme Court of Canada's development of a new hearsay exception called the principled exception. As with many developments in law, the court looked to learned experts in legal matters, in this instance, Professor John Henry Wigmore. This chapter explains the development of the principled exception by the court, based on Wigmore's legal academic writings and analysis.

Wigmore's Criteria

John Henry Wigmore was one of the foremost experts on Anglo-American evidence law. In the early half of the 20th century, Wigmore wrote a multivolume text on evidence law that is still used by scholars and practising lawyers today. Besides dealing with the practical applications of evidence in the courtroom, he also analyzed the historical and academic principles of the common law of evidence. We will come across Professor Wigmore several times in our study of evidence law.

While some people might find the traditional, judge-made exceptions to the hearsay rule to be an unrelated hodgepodge of common law rules, Wigmore saw a common thread running through all of them, linking them together in a rational manner. Because the rule against the use of hearsay focuses on the difficulties of reliability and trustworthiness, Wigmore asked himself if there was some underlying reason the courts found the exceptions more reliable and trustworthy than hearsay that was not admissible.

The common themes that Wigmore saw as underpinning all the traditional exceptions to the hearsay rule were that the out-of-court statement is

1. *necessary* in the sense that the only way the evidence could be admitted would be through hearsay, and
2. relatively *reliable* in the circumstances in which the statement was made.

The *necessity* of the statement being admitted through hearsay usually arises because the person who made the statement is not available to give testimony in court by the time the case has reached trial. The witness may have died, or left the country and cannot be found, or suffered some deterioration in mental or physical health that makes appearing as a witness next to impossible. Another possibility is that the maker of the statement has now recanted or changed the statement. In some cases, there may be another evidence rule that prevents the person who made the statement from being summonsed or subpoenaed to give evidence. For example, in a criminal case, a spouse may claim privilege that protects spousal communication (see Chapter 10, Privilege).

With regard to *reliability*, the statement must have been made in circumstances where the court has determined that there is some trustworthiness to the statement, even though it was not made under oath and the maker of the statement cannot be cross-examined.

Let us take a second look at the traditional exceptions that we examined in Chapter 6. How might they meet the tests of necessity and reliability?

Admissions of a Party

This exception to the hearsay rules makes just about everything said by a party to the proceeding admissible against him or her in court.

Necessity

The opposite party must show that the only manner in which the statement can be admitted is by way of hearsay. If the maker of the statement is a party in the case, it is unlikely that he would not be available, but it is the availability of the evidence that is important. For example, in the time between the events that led to the court proceeding and the court proceeding itself, the party may have forgotten earlier statements or changed his story, or, in the case of a criminal charge, the accused may not be testifying at all and so cannot be cross-examined on his out-of-court statements.

Reliability

The type of admissions that an opposing party would want to enter into evidence would be statements that would help his or her case. These admissions would be ones that hurt the case of the party who made them. It seems to be human nature that people tend to lie to help themselves or to make themselves look better. They rarely lie to make themselves look worse. Although false confessions do occur, an accused thief is much more likely to claim that he did not steal the diamond ring than to falsely admit that he did. A defendant who is being sued for damages in tort is much more likely to deny negligence than to falsely admit it. Therefore, when a party makes an admission that would hurt his or her case, generally it is more likely to be reliable than not.

Declarations Against Interest

The two general principles relating to declarations against pecuniary or proprietary interest and declarations against penal interest are as follows:

1. The person making the statement must be unavailable.
2. The statement must be against the statement-maker's interest.

Necessity

One of the criteria for the admission of a non-party statement against interest is that the person who made the statement is unavailable to give evidence at the proceeding. In that circumstance, it is clear that the statement can be admitted only through hearsay.

Reliability

As with admissions of a party, a person is unlikely to make a statement that harms his or her interest unless it is true.

Dying Declarations

The test for the admissibility of dying declarations is as follows:

1. The maker of the statement must be deceased.
2. At the time of making the statement, the person making it must have known that he or she was going to die almost immediately.
3. The statement must be one that would have been admissible if the person who made it had lived.
4. The statement is about who or what caused the maker of the statement to die.
5. The criminal case in which either the Crown or the defence is seeking to admit the statement is one in which the charge relates to the death of the statement-maker.

Necessity

The person who made the statement must be dead.

Reliability

The notion of the reliability of a dying declaration probably arose at a time when society was more religious. From the viewpoint of a number of religions, a dying person is likely to tell the truth because she fears the deathbed consequences of going to meet her God. That is fine if we can rely on the statement-maker's belief, but there is no assurance of reliability if the dying person believes that she can lie with impunity. Unlike swearing an oath, which must also be binding on a person's conscience for there to be any assurance of truthfulness, there is no worldly consequence for a dying person who lies.

It might also be argued that a dying person will feel the need to leave this world with a clean slate, regardless of whether she believes that there are consequences in the "great beyond." That is a nice thought, but it is little more than a fairy tale—kind of a happy-endings belief. What if a person facing his own mortality is more inclined to get off one last practical joke, delighting in the thought of all the chaos that he will leave behind? We cannot know what goes through the mind of a person on the brink of death, but we have constructed a traditional exception to the hearsay rule that is based on the belief that a dying person's statement is more likely to be true than not. This exception applies only to criminal proceedings.

The statement must be made when the speaker has no hope of living and thus (it is thought) no reason for worldly gain in lying. The deceased person's comments cannot pass on hearsay statements from others and must be directed at the cause of her untimely death. Julius Caesar's dying comment, "Et tu, Brute?" would not work if he had said, "Flavius told me that Brutus was in on the stabbing."

Res Gestae or Spontaneous Statements

In general, the *res gestae* or spontaneous statement exception allows the admission of a statement made in an excited state or a statement expressing an existing physical, mental, or emotional state if the statement is made contemporaneously with, or very close in time to, the event.

Necessity

The party wishing to admit a spontaneous statement into evidence must establish that the statement could be admitted only by way of hearsay. This might be the case if the original maker of the statement is dead or otherwise unavailable to give evidence, or for some other reason, such as he could not remember the statement or had changed his story.

Reliability

The principle underlying this exception is that the statement was made so close in time to the occurrence that the there was no opportunity for the maker of the statement to reflect on it and invent a story. Therefore, he is assumed to have spontaneously stated the truth as he saw it. Of course, the statement may be untrue because of a mistaken perception, but the point is that the maker did not have time to fabricate it.

Business Records

This exception permits the admission of business records if

1. they were made in the ordinary course of the business,
2. they were made by a person whose duty was to keep such records,
3. the person who made the records did so from personal knowledge,
4. the records were made contemporaneously (at the time of the events), and
5. the person making the records had no motive to misrepresent them.

Necessity

It may be necessary to admit a business record through hearsay for several reasons. For example, in the case of hospital records or books of account, if a party was required to call every single nurse or bookkeeper who made entries into the record, trials could last a very long time. In these instances, it is necessary to admit the evidence to ensure that the justice system can deal with cases in a timely fashion.

Sometimes, it is nearly impossible to determine who actually made the business record. For example, the serial number stamped onto a CD player is a business record. As the player comes down the assembly line, an employee stamps the number onto the item. Three years later, in an attempt to show that the player was stolen, it would be next to impossible to determine which worker stamped the specific player. Instead, a representative of the manufacturer could identify the marking as a business record used by that company and could even specify the date that the player was made by reference to records kept by the manufacturer.

Reliability

The above criteria are designed to ensure reliability. The records were made as part of the usual business of the organization. An organization has an interest in maintaining accurate records. For example, in a hospital, the health and even the lives of the patients depend upon accurate recording. In a profit-making business, accurate records often determine the financial viability of the enterprise. We have additional assurance in the fact that the continued employment of the person who made the record, to some degree, depends on her accuracy in recording. When records are made within a reasonable time after the events, there is some assurance of reliability because intervening factors such as memory loss or third-party influence can be eliminated.

The final factor—that of having "no motive to misrepresent"—is intended to eliminate the prospect that the recording was made by someone who has an interest in the outcome of a dispute and who might doctor or modify the record to support one side.

Prior Testimony

Testimony given by a witness in a prior proceeding is generally admissible in another proceeding.

Necessity

The first requirement for the application of this exception, whether under the common law, statute law, or the procedural rules of provincial civil courts, is that the witness be unavailable.

Reliability

As we know, two of the major difficulties with hearsay evidence are that it is not taken under oath or affirmation and it cannot be cross-examined. These problems do not exist with prior testimony because it was sworn evidence and there was an opportunity to cross-examine in the earlier proceeding.

Prior Inconsistent Statements Made by Someone Other Than the Accused

In the cases of *R v B (KG)* ([1993] 1 SCR 740) and *R v U (FJ)* ([1995] 3 SCR 764), the Supreme Court of Canada dealt with circumstances involving recanting witnesses

—that is, witnesses who told one story at the time of the investigation and who then, at trial, tell another story that helps the accused. The court extended the use that could be made of prior inconsistent statements, which previously could be used only to challenge the credibility of the witness and not for the truth of their contents. It ruled that in very limited circumstances, prior inconsistent statements made by witnesses other than the accused may be admitted for the truth of their contents if, on a case-by-case basis, the trial judge determines that the prior statements meet the tests of necessity and reliability.

Necessity

In trials involving recanting witnesses, much if not all of the Crown's case may depend on the original, out-of-court statements, which cannot be admitted in any other way than through hearsay because the witnesses are now saying something entirely different from what they said initially. If this evidence were to be automatically excluded under the hearsay rule, it would invite witness intimidation by the accused, or by the accused's family and friends.

Reliability

As noted by the court in *R v B (KG)*, the availability at trial of a witness, even a recanting one, goes some distance toward curing the defect of the accused's not having had the opportunity to cross-examine the witness at the time the statement was made. The witnesses can be cross-examined in the proceeding on the change in their story, and the trier of fact has an opportunity to assess which of the statements, the original one or the one given in court, is the more reliable in relation to all the circumstances.

Identifications

When a witness has identified the accused from a lineup or a photo array shortly after the incident, the officer conducting the identification process may give testimony that the witness did verbally identify the accused.

Necessity

The rule on the admissibility of prior identifications has evolved out of necessity, given the sometimes very lengthy times between the commission of an offence and the trial. The justice system would be very poorly thought of if a criminal could elude justice after having been positively identified soon after the time of the offence but could not be identified years later, possibly because of his altered appearance.

Reliability

The witness can testify that she accurately identified the person previously as the offender. The reliability comes from the fact that the identification was made close in time to the events in question and the witness is available for cross-examination about the accuracy of that identification.

There are also strict requirements as to how the identification process is to be conducted. The witness cannot be coached or led to the identification in any manner.

Past Recollection Recorded

This exception requires the following conditions:

1. The past recollection must have been recorded in some reliable way.
2. At the time, it must have been sufficiently fresh and vivid to be probably accurate.
3. The witness must be able now to assert that the record accurately represented his knowledge and recollection at the time. The usual phrase requires the witness to affirm that he "knew it to be true at the time."
4. The original record itself must be used, if it is procurable.

Necessity

The witness cannot remember the details of the record he made of the incident. The witness is not able to give the evidence unless he can refer to the record he made of the incident or event.

Reliability

The requirement that the record be made contemporaneously with, or close to, the incident provides some assurance that it was very fresh in the recorder's memory and therefore is more reliable than information recorded sometime after the fact. This condition is bolstered by the requirement that the record be made in some reliable manner and that the original record be used, if at all possible.

Oral Histories of Aboriginal Peoples

The oral histories of Aboriginal peoples have been admitted in land claim cases.

Necessity

Most Aboriginal history is based on oral accounts rather than on written accounts. If the courts refused to give oral histories independent legal weight, it would be virtually impossible for First Nations to litigate Aboriginal title claims.

Reliability

In *Delgamuukw v British Columbia* ([1997] 3 SCR 1010), the Supreme Court of Canada determined that oral histories should be treated in the same manner as written histories in proof of Aboriginal land title issues. Oral histories are as reliable or unreliable as written histories. Oral history evidence is to be assessed just like any other fact. It can be tested for reliability in the same way as other evidence—through corroboration, consistency, potential for bias, and so on.

The Development of the Principled Exception

From their inception, the traditional hearsay exceptions were very rigidly applied by the courts. If the statement did not fit properly into the legal criteria required by the exception, it was not admissible into evidence. This approach began to change in the early 1990s when the Supreme Court of Canada heard the case of *R v Khan* ([1990] 2 SCR 531).

In *Khan*, a mother took her three-and-a-half-year-old daughter to see the family doctor. She left the child with the doctor for about half an hour. After leaving the doctor's office, she had a conversation with her daughter. During the chat, it became clear to the mother that Dr. Khan had sexually assaulted the little girl. The child herself clearly did not understand the nature of the assault and had not mentioned it until the mother struck up an innocent conversation. The child was taken to the police, who found physical evidence in the form of semen on the child's clothing. At the time, however, DNA tests were not well established as reliable evidence, and in any event, there was then no legal requirement for Dr. Khan to provide a DNA sample. At trial, the judge determined that the child was incapable of giving evidence because of her inability to understand the court process or the nature of the legal requirement to be truthful. Unless the mother was permitted to testify about what the child said to her, there would be no way of convicting Dr. Khan for this offence.

The difficulty was that none of the traditional exceptions to the hearsay rule applied in *Khan*. The Crown attempted to argue that the statement was a spontaneous one, but the statement could not be fit into the *res gestae* exception without doing serious damage to the intention or reason behind the exception. Therefore, the mother's evidence could not be admitted unless the Supreme Court analyzed the basic underpinnings of the exceptions to the hearsay rule and developed a new approach. This is exactly what it did.

In its analysis, the court went back to basics and looked at the reasons for the hearsay rule. Relying on Wigmore's earlier study of the issue, the court concluded that the basic principles supporting the existing exceptions to the rule were, indeed, necessity and reliability. It determined that, in addition to the traditional exceptions, there ought to be an exception that was founded on the principles underlying the development of the hearsay rule. The court called this additional exception the **principled exception**. This new approach stated that where necessity and reliability could be established, hearsay may be admitted, provided that the probative value of the evidence outweighed the prejudice.

principled exception
exception to the hearsay rule based on the principles of necessity and reliability

It must be necessary to rely on hearsay to admit the evidence. If the person who originally made the statement is available to give evidence, he or she must be called to testify in person. In looking at reliability, a court must find replacements for the above-noted credibility and reliability assurances. These replacement guarantees are often referred to as *circumstantial guarantees of reliability*. These can be seen by asking, "What is it about the circumstances of the statement being made that provide a guarantee of reliability?" If there are no circumstantial guarantees of reliability, then the long-standing hearsay dangers cannot be avoided and the evidence should not be admissible.

In the *Khan* case, the child's statements could be admitted only through her mother because the child was too young to testify. On the issue of necessity, the court weighed heavily the concern about the sexual abuse of young children and the fact that these incidents happen in private and often with very small children. Where a child does not satisfy the criteria for giving sworn or unsworn evidence, then his or her evidence, repeated to others, would be lost. In such circumstances, it would not be possible to obtain a conviction against offenders, regardless of the reliability attached to the statements. It was therefore necessary to admit the statements by way of hearsay. The court also stated that in some instances expert testimony about the unacceptably traumatic impact on a child of testifying might suffice to meet the necessity criteria.

With regard to the circumstantial guarantees of reliability, the court found that they could be established by the following conditions:

1. the child's statement was surprising and uncoached;
2. the child used age- and experience-appropriate language to describe an experience she did not fully understand;
3. there was semen on the child's clothing; and
4. her statement, particularly her concern over not getting the candy, had a disarming ring of truth.

The statement was determined by the Supreme Court to be sufficiently reliable to justify its admission.

Since the decision in *Khan*, the principled approach has become the governing exception to the hearsay rule. Evidence that would previously have been excluded automatically by the rigid application of the traditional hearsay exceptions is now admissible if it meets the tests of necessity and reliability.

Applying the Exceptions

In the years immediately following *Khan*, it was not entirely clear whether this new principled approach replaced all the existing hearsay exceptions or whether these traditional rules still had application in Canadian courts. Was the principled exception to be used only when the evidence did not fit within any of the existing exceptions? If that was to be the rule, there would likely be cases where a statement might fit within one or more of the traditional hearsay exceptions and still not meet the tests of being necessary and reliable.

For example, a spontaneous statement, made in the immediate aftermath of an event, might not be reliable for any number of reasons. Perhaps the maker of the statement was so in shock that any perception he had of the incident was clouded by the physical and emotional trauma he had suffered. Nevertheless, if the traditional *res gestae* exception was applied, the statement would automatically be admissible.

In other words, although the traditional exceptions were developed with the underpinnings of necessity and reliability, there were instances where they might not meet the tests of necessity and reliability. However, if the traditional exceptions were completely eliminated from the law of evidence and only the principled approach applied, the examination of the admissibility of a hearsay statement would be greatly expanded, leading to lengthy trials and unpredictability in the process.

The issue of the traditional exceptions and the principled approach was further canvassed by the Supreme Court of Canada in *R v Starr* (2000 SCC 40, [2000] 2 SCR 144). The difficulty with the *Starr* case is that the court was divided and the test for reliability was somewhat convoluted. In the later case of *R v Khelawon* (2006 SCC 57, [2006] 2 SCR 787), the court clarified the reliability discussion in *Starr* and asserted that it should no longer be used.

However, in the majority decision, Iacobucci J made it very clear that even the traditional exceptions that apply are to be scrutinized to determine whether the evidence meets the criteria of necessity and reliability. In the subsequent cases of *R v Mapara* (2005 SCC 23, [2005] 1 SCR 358) and *R v Khelawon*, the court reaffirmed the continued applicability of the traditional exceptions and summarized the governing framework for the analysis of the hearsay exceptions.

In its simplest form, the test that a court will apply in determining whether hearsay will be admissible is as follows:

1. Does the hearsay fall within one of the traditional exceptions?

2. Does it meet the tests of necessity and reliability as set out in the principled approach? If it does not, it will not be admitted even if it meets the criteria of that traditional exception.

3. If so, it will be admissible as long as it is not more prejudicial than probative.

4. Evidence that does not meet one of the traditional exceptions may be admitted as long as it meets the tests of necessity and reliability established by the principled approach.

CASE IN POINT

Videotaped Statements by Deceased Complainants

R v Khelawon, 2006 SCC 57, [2006] 2 SCR 787

In 1999, Ramnarine Khelawon, the manager of a retirement home, was charged with aggravated assault in relation to alleged attacks on five of the home's elderly residents. The assaults first came to light when a cook at the home found one of the residents, Mr. Skupien, badly injured in his room with his belongings packed in green garbage bags. Skupien told the cook that Khelawon had beaten him and threatened to kill him if he didn't leave the home. The cook took him to her home and then to a doctor. The doctor found that the victim had three fractured ribs and bruises, and later testified at trial that these injuries were consistent with an assault but also with a fall.

The police then became involved. Upon an investigation at the home, they found four other residents who also alleged that they had been assaulted by Khelawon. Videotapes were made by the police of the statements made by the complainants, including Skupien. His videotaped statement was not made under oath, but he did say that he understood the importance of telling the truth and that he could be criminally charged if he did not.

It was also established from medical records that Skupien had been treated for several psychiatric problems including paranoia and depression, although a psychiatrist did give expert opinion evidence at trial that Skupien had capacity and understood the need to tell the truth. At trial, the defence argued that the cook, whose employment at the home had been terminated, held a grudge against Khelawon that had caused her to negatively influence Skupien against the accused.

By the time of the trial, none of the complainants were available to testify. Four of them, including Skupien, had died, and the fifth was found to be lacking capacity because of mental deterioration.

The major issue in this case was the admissibility of hearsay statements of the complainants in the videotapes under the principled exception because there was no applicable traditional exception.

The trial judge admitted some of the tapes, including that of Skupien, and Khelawon was convicted of several charges. At the Ontario Court of Appeal, the court excluded the tapes and entered an acquittal on all charges. The Crown appealed the acquittal to the Supreme Court of Canada, and on the appeal was granted leave to have the court deal only with Skupien's taped statements.

The Supreme Court conducted an extensive overview of the case law related to hearsay, the traditional exceptions, and the principled approach, as well as the approach's application as developed through *Khan* and the subsequent decisions of the Supreme Court.

The Definition

Hearsay is an (1) out-of-court statement (2) presented for the truth of its contents but (3) for which there is no contemporaneous cross-examination available.

How to Apply the Rule

1. If the statement meets the definition of hearsay, it is presumptively inadmissible unless it fits within an exception to the rule. The traditional exceptions to the hearsay rule remain presumptively in place.

2. The traditional exceptions are to be tested for necessity and reliability, as required by the principled approach.

3. In "rare cases," a traditional exception may not meet the test of necessity and reliability, depending on the facts of the case.

4. If a statement does not fit within a traditional exception to the rule, it may still be admitted under

the principled exception if it meets the test for necessity and reliability.[1]

Application of the Rule to This Case

1. The videotaped statement of Mr. Skupien is hearsay because the Crown wants to admit it for the truth of its contents—that Mr. Khelawon assaulted him—and because Skupien cannot be cross-examined in court.

2. The statement does not fit within any traditional exception, so it should be analyzed under the principled exception of necessity and reliability.

3. The statement is clearly necessary because Skupien is deceased and obviously not available for cross-examination.

4. When examining the statement for reliability, the court found that it did not meet the test for the following reasons:

   a. The reliability of the statement could not be tested in the normal manner through cross-examination.

   b. On the facts of this case, there was no adequate substitute for cross-examination that would establish sufficient reliability of the statement because

      i. there was at least some indication from the medical examination, at the time of making the statements, including mental health issues;

      ii. the cook was a disgruntled employee who may have influenced Skupien to make the allegations of assault; and

      iii. expert evidence established that, aside from assault, there were other possible explanations for Skupien's injuries, such as a fall.

The Decision

The police videotapes were ruled inadmissible hearsay owing to their failure to meet the reliability test of the principled exception. Khelawon was acquitted of the outstanding charges against him.

CHAPTER SUMMARY

The traditional common law exceptions to the hearsay rule can be looked at in terms of their necessity and reliability. Wigmore's analysis of these criteria in the traditional exceptions provided the basis for the principled exception as established by the Supreme Court of Canada in the case of *R v Khan*. The application of the principled exception was clarified in the *Starr* decision.

The principled exception does not replace the traditional exceptions. Rather, it is used to ensure that the traditional exception being applied in a particular case is in fact necessary and reliable. Only if the facts of the case do not permit the application of the traditional exceptions does the court look to the principled exception to determine the admissibility of a hearsay statement.

KEY TERM

principled exception, 119

NOTE

1   In its analysis of the application of the rule, the court summarized the governing framework as set out in the prior case, *R v Mapara*, at para 15.

REFERENCES

B (KG), R v, [1993] 1 SCR 740.

Delgamuukw v British Columbia, [1997] 3 SCR 1010.

Khan, R v, [1990] 2 SCR 531.

Khelawon, R v, 2006 SCC 57, [2006] 2 SCR 787.

Mapara, R v, 2005 SCC 23, [2005] 1 SCR 358.

Starr, R v, 2000 SCC 40, [2000] 2 SCR 144.

U (FJ), R v, [1995] 3 SCR 764.

REVIEW QUESTIONS

1. Identify the two cornerstones of the principled exception to the hearsay rule.

2. Explain how necessity and reliability are applicable to each of the traditional exceptions to the hearsay rule.

3. How is the principled exception to be applied?

DISCUSSION QUESTIONS

1. Go back to the Discussion Questions at the end of Chapter 6. Discuss how the principles of necessity and reliability apply to each of the hearsay statements in questions 1 to 4.

2. Parminder was rushed to the hospital by her sister with a severe case of suspected tetanus. She could not speak, but her sister told the nurse that Parminder was allergic to penicillin. Parminder was given penicillin and is now in a coma from which she may never recover. Tragically, in an unrelated incident, her sister was later killed in a car accident.

   The parents of the girls are now suing the hospital for the damage suffered by Parminder. They want to call another patient who was in the emergency waiting room the day Parminder was admitted to hospital. He will testify that he heard Parminder's sister tell the nurse that Parminder was allergic to penicillin.

   Discuss whether or not you think this evidence will be admitted.

3. Max was charged with impaired driving after he was stopped as a result of a 911 call. The person who called 911 was another driver who had been following Max on the highway and was extremely concerned: Max was driving erratically, was weaving over the lines on the highway, and had already almost hit three other cars. The Crown wants to admit the tape of the 911 call as evidence of just how badly Max was driving.

    If you were the judge, would you allow this evidence? On what basis would you admit the evidence or exclude it?

Character Evidence

8

LEARNING OUTCOMES

After completing this chapter, you should be able to:

- Understand the value and danger of character evidence.

- Recognize when character evidence is admissible and when it is not.

- Describe how a person's criminal record can be used in a trial.

- Understand the value and danger of similar fact evidence.

- Recognize the difference between character evidence and expert evidence of propensity or disposition.

- Understand the role of third-party character evidence.

- Discuss the differences between criminal and civil trials in relation to character evidence.

Introduction

Character evidence is evidence of the type of person someone is—honest, dishonest, calm, ill-tempered, generous, selfish, and so forth—as demonstrated by the person's past conduct. It draws inferences from past conduct—did Sam kill on this occasion because he has killed in the past? In other words, character evidence is a type of circumstantial evidence that involves drawing conclusions based on behaviour from past conduct.

Overview of Character Evidence

When considering the reliability of the information put before it by a witness, the trier of fact may be assisted if it has reliable information about the witness's character, because there is some truth to the proposition that bad people do bad things and good people do good things. This is the main reason that early English juries were chosen from people who were familiar with the parties to the dispute.

In our present legal system, the courts view character evidence with suspicion, not because it has no value, but because it may be given far greater value than it deserves. Although character evidence may have **probative value**, the courts are reluctant to admit this type of evidence because of its **potential prejudice**. The courts have recognized a strong human inclination to speculate and to jump to conclusions based on available information, and with this in mind have imposed strict limits on the admissibility of character evidence. Where the available information casts the accused in a bad light because of his unrelated behaviour, a great risk exists that the trier of fact will leap to the conclusion that the accused is guilty even though the reliable evidence is not sufficient to support such a conclusion.

Character evidence is presented to try to establish that a person who holds certain characteristics either did or did not act a certain way on a specific occasion—in other words, that the person "acted in character." The proposition is not without merit, because people are creatures of habit and tend to repeat the same types of actions—they tend to act in character. However, people act "out of character" as well. People do things that we never would have thought they were capable of. Therefore, one has to be very careful when asked to extrapolate consistent behaviour from past behaviour. Such extrapolations can lead to incorrect conclusions, as shown in the example below:

> Elly is charged with stealing a smartphone.
> Elly has a criminal record for shoplifting.
> Elly must have stolen the smartphone.

Similarly, extrapolations from presumed behaviour can lead to incorrect conclusions, as shown in the example below:

> Dennis is charged with stealing a smartphone.
> Dennis is a priest.
> Priests are honest.
> Dennis could not have stolen the smartphone.

As stated above, people tend to give greater value to character evidence than it deserves and draw incorrect conclusions on its basis. They also show a tendency to want to convict an accused of the crime in question for his past crimes. This issue is described more fully in the sections below.

Considerations in Measuring Probative Value

1. Proximity in time between the offence and similar acts
2. Similarity between the charged conduct and similar acts
3. Number of similar acts
4. The circumstances surrounding the similar acts
5. Distinctive features that unify the incidents
6. Existence of any intervening acts
7. Any other factors that support or rebut the underlying unity of the acts

R v Handy, 2002 SCC 56 at para 82, [2002] 2 SCR 908.

Against Whom May Character Evidence Be Presented?

Although we think of the accused as the person against whom character evidence is presented, character evidence may be presented against a complainant as well.

The distinction that has just been raised between leading evidence of bad character against a person accused of a crime or against the complainant is an important one. How the common law rules that govern the admissibility of character evidence are applied largely depends on the context within which the evidence is being offered. The important considerations that a judge takes into account in deciding to admit or refuse evidence are whether the evidence is being tendered in a civil or criminal trial, who the evidence would be used against, and whether the evidence is of good or bad character, because these considerations will determine the degree of injustice that will flow from the misuse of evidence. For example, in a criminal trial, the liberty of an accused is at stake and the courts have always treated this as a more important consideration than the loss of money that is usually at stake in a civil trial. Finally, character evidence can be led against third-party witnesses. This topic is discussed below under the heading "Testimony and Credibility of Third Parties."

Character Evidence of a Person Charged with a Criminal Offence

Generally, in a criminal trial, prosecutors are not permitted to introduce information about an accused's bad character in order to assist the trier of fact in concluding that the accused was also bad on this particular occasion. An accused who has broken into houses in the past to rob them may be more likely than a person on the street to be the person who robbed a little old lady at the automated teller. However, there are a lot of people who fit into the category of persons who rob houses and quite a lot who have even robbed little old ladies, so establishing that the accused robs houses does not help much in proving that he robbed the woman at the automated teller. It does show that he belongs to that group of people capable of stealing, but this group is so large that it would be dangerous to give significant weight to this fact. The danger is that the trier of fact, when presented with this evidence, will give it much more weight than it deserves. In the opinion of the courts, on a scale of 1 to 100, where 1 is the tiniest bit of proof, barely registerable, and 100 is absolute certainty, this sort of information deserves about a 2 or a 3.

In assessing the value of such information, the court needs to ask: In what way is the house robber more likely to have robbed the old lady than the person who cheats on his income taxes, buys a flat-screen television for $50 out of the back of somebody's car, or neglects to report a bank error that is $150 in his favour? All these people are arguably stealing and are, at the very least, guilty of moral lapses that show they are capable of taking from someone else for their own advantage. A politician who has voted himself a generous salary increase may be called many things, but this does not mean that he is more likely to have robbed the little old lady than any other person on the street.

The house robber may in fact be less likely to have robbed the little old lady because she may remind him of his own grandmother whom he dearly loves, or he may choose to rob only empty houses because he is terrified of confrontation with people, no matter how old or frail. So, while there may be some value to the information that the accused has a record for robbing houses, the value it provides is far outweighed by the danger it poses in a criminal case, where it may be assigned more weight than it deserves by the trier of fact. Thus, the judge performs a gatekeeping function by screening out this information because it is dangerous.

CASE IN POINT

Bad Character and an Accused

R v Soikie, 2004 CanLII 1849 (Ont SC)

This case dealt with the issue of the admissibility of bad character evidence against an accused. Mr. Soikie was charged with murder. He claimed to have killed the deceased in self-defence and as a result of provocation. He did not suggest in his testimony that he was a man of good character, but his counsel attacked the character of the deceased by leading evidence of prior violent acts perpetrated by the deceased. In response, the Crown was permitted to lead evidence of the peaceful disposition of the deceased. The issue was whether the Crown would be permitted to attack the accused's character by showing him to have a violent disposition. The trial judge declined to permit such an attack, stating that admitting the Crown's evidence would result in both moral and reasoning prejudice and tend to distract the trier of fact because the evidence was inflammatory. The judge ruled that evidence of the accused's character did not advance the issue whether the deceased was the aggressor, and its probative value did not exceed the prejudice that would result from its admission.

Criminal Record and the Accused

Because an accused has a right to be presumed innocent, a criminal record may not be admitted into evidence by the Crown. An exception to this is when the accused chooses to testify.[1] In this case, it is felt that the record goes to the issue of general credibility of the accused. In other words, the criminal record is not to be used to show that the accused is more likely to have committed the offence for which he is charged, but to show that his sworn testimony is less worthy of belief in light of his past dishonest behaviour. As the gatekeeper, the judge still has the discretion to disallow the criminal record, though in practice, the record is almost always admitted. In performing her gatekeeper function, the judge will weigh the prejudicial effect of the record against its probative value. One factor that plays heavily in this assessment is the age of the record—an old record followed by a legally blameless life may very well be excluded.

Whether the accused's criminal record is admitted is particularly important where the Crown's case is circumstantial and the record is one that casts the accused in a particularly bad moral light, as with someone charged with sexual offences who has one or more convictions for similar offences.

An accused who does testify is taken to have put his credibility in issue, and by taking the stand to tell his story, the accused places himself in a position where his criminal record may be introduced into evidence. This can strongly discourage an accused from testifying. For example, in a sexual assault case, once the jurors learn that the accused was convicted of rape eight years ago, it will be difficult for them to listen dispassionately to the evidence in relation to the sexual assault charge, ignore the criminal record, and impartially weigh the evidence of guilt presented by the Crown.

The jury's inability to overlook a similar conviction undoubtedly contributed to the conviction of Norman Fox in Vancouver on June 21, 1976. He was convicted of sexual assault largely based on his previous conviction for rape. He spent eight years and six months in jail for a crime that someone else committed. This was one of the earliest well-publicized wrongful conviction cases. Interestingly, the commissioner who reviewed the case, to determine whether compensation should be paid to Fox for his wrongful conviction, pressured him into agreeing to share the compensation award with the woman he was legitimately convicted of raping many years before. His prior offence still tarnished him to the degree that the commissioner, rather than simply compensating him for the wrong done to him by the system, made clear that he felt giving money to a rapist was distasteful.

Other Dangers of Character Evidence

There are other dangers in presenting bad character evidence to the jury. The jurors may use it to justify a conviction for the wrong reasons. There is a significant danger that the accused will be convicted as additional punishment for past wrongdoings, or that he will be punished because he is not likeable, or that the jury will convict him simply to bring closure to the matter. The jury, out of laziness, may be unwilling to conduct a thorough and exhaustive analysis of the evidence, particularly when the accused is viewed as an undesirable element in society. Their thinking may be, "It's not like we're convicting Snow White here—look at his record."

How to Make the Best of a Bad Situation

Often, an accused is not called to testify because he has a criminal record. The defence knows that the accused will be cross-examined by the prosecution on his record. What if the accused feels compelled to testify and tell his side of the story? Is there anything that can be done to cast the accused in a better light?

The impact that the record has on the trier of fact can be diminished by dealing with the record in direct examination. By raising the record first, the accused will appear more forthright and candid. The accused is effectively saying, "Yes, I did those things, and I'm not trying to hide anything." However, the accused will appear far less forthright and believable if the matter of the record is first raised by the prosecution in cross-examination. Better yet for the accused is having pleaded guilty for the previous convictions. In that case, the accused might truthfully testify, "I pleaded guilty to every one of those offences because I did them, but I won't plead guilty to this one because I didn't do it."

Good Character Evidence

People charged with criminal offences often claim to their legal representatives that they can get two dozen character witnesses to testify on their behalf. In reality, presenting good character evidence does not happen very often. This is partly because the criminal courts are filled with people accused of crimes who do not stand to gain much from a character contest with the Crown. But the main reason is that, at the heart of it, good character evidence is not very meaningful because even people of good character do bad things. Who among us has not been guilty of some transgression? It may be impossible to find a person who has led a life filled with only positive acts and has not committed a wrongful act at some point in her life. Entire novels have been built on morally upright persons succumbing to temptation.

In spite of the fact that such evidence has limited merit in the eyes of the court, some accused persons do present evidence to try to show that they are not the kind of people to commit the type of offence they have been charged with. Generally, evidence of good character is restricted to the accused's reputation in the community rather than specific past good deeds.[2]

Most often, when an accused chooses to lead evidence of his good character, he calls friends and neighbours to testify about his reputation in the community. Such testimony can be helpful, although a cardinal rule is to be sure that the people chosen to testify know the substance of the charge facing the accused. It undermines the accused's case if the Crown in cross-examination asks, "Did you know that four women have testified that the accused exposed himself to them while performing a solitary sexual act?" and the witness reacts with surprise and revulsion. The jurors are likely to entirely discount the friend's or neighbour's good character evidence, or worse, think badly of the accused for not being forthright with his chosen witness. They conclude, "If he can't be honest with his friends, then he surely must be lying to us."

An accused person can also testify about his own good character, but such testimony is self-serving and likely to be greeted with cynicism. Jurors are likely to think, "What else would you expect him to say?" Another approach is to present expert evidence on the topic of good character, but a good character expert sounds a little silly to most jurors, who feel they don't need an expert to tell them what constitutes good character. Instead, what experts usually testify about is very specific behaviour and the accused's predisposition toward it. For example, a person charged with sexually assaulting a child who can demonstrate through an expert that he does not have the psychological profile of a pedophile would stand a better chance with a jury than another person who cannot advance this sort of evidence.

However, once the accused calls good character evidence, he is taken to have put his character in issue and the Crown is then entitled to attack his character by cross-examining the accused's witnesses, calling its own witnesses who can challenge this version of the accused's character, and calling its own experts. In other words, once the accused has opened the door by calling evidence of good character, the Crown is free to lead evidence of bad character. The accused will almost certainly have his criminal record put to him and may have to answer to other evidence showing that he committed similar crimes in the past. An accused can even put his character in issue inadvertently, as happened in *R v McFadden* ((1981), 65 CCC (2d) 9 (BCCA)). In this case, the accused, who was married, was charged with the indecent assault and murder of another woman. In defending the charge, he stated, "I have the most beautiful wife in the world." He was taken to have implied that he would never become sexually involved with another woman. This would permit the Crown to explore any infidelities or even marital problems that the accused might have.

In another matter, *R v Tierney* ((1982), 70 CCC (2d) 4821(Ont CA)), the accused stated that he was not the sort to commit sexual assault of a woman. A psychiatrist for the Crown then testified that the accused possessed an abnormal disposition to react violently if rejected by a woman, providing devastating evidence against him. Of particular danger to an accused is the fact that because reputation evidence is by its nature hearsay, then rebuttal to reputation evidence can also be hearsay. Witnesses for the accused can therefore be asked what rumours they have heard about the accused. These rumours can be plentiful and vicious, and they can damage the accused's character. As these examples show, the decision to call good character evidence is one that should be considered cautiously.

Character Evidence and Expert Evidence of Propensity or Disposition

Often, when judges talk about character evidence and evidence of propensity or disposition, they mean the same thing. However, while the concepts may appear to be similar, they are fundamentally different. As stated earlier in this chapter, character evidence is evidence of the type of person someone is as demonstrated by the person's past conduct. When people use the term "propensity" or "disposition" in this context, they are really talking about character evidence, which, as we have seen, is generally not admissible to establish that the accused committed the acts complained of. **Propensity or disposition evidence** can be better understood as proof of a person's *psychiatric* tendencies, as provided by an expert. Because this type of evidence is given by an expert, it is taken as psychiatric fact. For example, character evidence

propensity or disposition evidence
evidence of an accused person's psychiatric tendency to act a certain way

may show, on the basis of a person's past violent acts, that the person is violent, while propensity evidence may show, on the basis of a psychiatric assessment, that the person has violent tendencies. Sometimes this distinction may be blurred, but it is important to keep in mind that while anyone can testify as to character, only a properly qualified expert can offer evidence of a person's propensity or disposition to act in a certain manner. (See also the discussion of expert opinion in Chapter 9.)

Propensity and disposition evidence creates extreme prejudice for the accused and for this reason will not be admitted merely to demonstrate the propensity of an accused to act a certain way. This may sound illogical, but it makes perfect sense if we look at the rationale behind the rule against admitting evidence of bad character. It is dangerous to conclude that someone committed an act because he acted the same way in the past. Similarly, in the case of propensity and disposition evidence, it is equally (and perhaps even more) dangerous to conclude that an individual acted in a certain manner simply because of a psychological predisposition.

The common law position is that propensity or disposition evidence may be admitted only if it is analogous to a physiological fact. Therefore, it would not be permissible to lead evidence that the accused had abnormal violent tendencies to support an inference that he killed the victim. However, it may be permissible to lead such evidence to demonstrate that the accused or the perpetrator of the crime "has distinctive behavioural characteristics such that a comparison of one with the other will be of material assistance in determining innocence or guilt" (see *R v Mohan*, [1994] 2 SCR 9 at para 37). For example, if a crime showed clear signs of psychopathological origin, it may be permissible for the Crown to demonstrate that the accused shares these specific psychopathological tendencies with the perpetrator. Thus, a perpetrator who tortures his victim with electric shocks as a precursor to a sexual assault would likely demonstrate a very specific psychological profile. Evidence that the accused does or does not share the same profile may very well be admissible. In any event, evidence of propensity or disposition of the accused would be admitted only if the probative value of the evidence is so high that it displaces the extreme prejudice that the accused would suffer from the admission of the evidence.

Similar Fact Evidence

similar fact evidence
evidence that shows that an accused committed similar offences in the past, which may be admitted provided that it is relevant in establishing an important matter other than the accused's predisposition to commit that type of offence

Similar fact evidence is evidence that shows that the accused committed similar offences in the past. Although a general prohibition exists against the use of bad character evidence, there are some instances where the evidence is so valuable, so convincing, that to deny it to the fact-finder simply because it shows the accused in a bad light would be unjustifiable. It is very tempting for a prosecutor to see great value in similar fact evidence, because it will help the jury come to the conclusion that the prosecutor feels is just. However, the fact remains that a person charged with a crime is not on trial for past transgressions. It is essential to avoid drawing the prohibited inference that the accused is guilty of the offence simply because he has committed similar acts in the past.

If it can be clearly shown that the accused has demonstrated in his behaviour a pattern or design, then it is logical to admit similar fact evidence to imply that it is likely that the same person who committed similar acts in the past committed the outstanding offence. Although there may be some appeal in this proposition, the law is quite settled that while similar fact evidence may indeed be admissible for certain purposes, it is not permissible for the Crown to lead the evidence for the prohibited inference that owing to a predisposition, the accused is more likely to have committed this particular offence.

The classic example is the case of *Makin v AG for New South Wales* (see Case in Point), a case against a married couple who were suspected of murdering 12 infants, in which the prosecution sought to introduce evidence of infant burials in the backyards of two of the couple's previous residences.

CASE IN POINT

Birth of the Principle of Similar Fact Evidence

Makin v AG for New South Wales, [1894] AC 57

The Makins presented as a lovely couple with four daughters of their own ranging in age from 11 to 17. They advertised in the *Sydney Morning Herald* that they would adopt or take in children for a fee. This was an appealing prospect to many young unwed mothers who could not adequately provide for their babies but wanted to ensure that they got a better life. The Makins took in many such babies; however, few survived their guardianship. On October 11, 1892, a worker was digging in the backyard of a house in Macdonaldtown, a suburb of Sydney, trying to clear a blockage in a drain. His gruesome discovery was that the blockage was caused by two bundles of baby clothing containing the decaying remains of two infants. The police dug up the backyard and located another five sets of infant remains. Tenancy records soon revealed that John and Sarah Makin were the former tenants of the cottage. The police also determined that the Makins had a former address in Redfern, where more bodies of babies were discovered. The Makins were eventually tracked to another home in nearby Chippendale, and yet more baby bodies

were found in the backyard of that property. In all, the grisly total grew to 12.

In the sensational trial of the Makins, evidence was presented through Amber Murray and numerous other mothers who had entrusted their children to the Makins for a weekly fee of 10 shillings. In the end, the Makins' own daughter Clarice testified against them, linking clothing found on the buried corpses to her parents and confirming that Amber Murray's infant child Horace did not survive to make the move to Macdonaldtown from Redfern. This evidence was significant because it helped establish the monetary motive for the killings—John Makin had continued to collect the 10 shillings from Amber Murray well beyond Horace's death. Though the Makins testified on their own behalf, their credibility was destroyed when the prosecution caught them in lies and inconsistencies. Both were convicted and given the only sentence available, death. John was hanged, but Sarah had her sentence commuted to life imprisonment. She was released after 19 years, in 1911.

Given the primitive state of forensic evidence at the time, a conviction against the Makins was by no means a certainty. After all, infant deaths were common, and it was not unheard of for children who died in childbirth or shortly after to be buried in backyards. The contribution that *Makin* made to the law of evidence was to establish the principle at the root of similar fact evidence. The court developed the principle in the following passage:

It is undoubtedly not competent for the prosecution to adduce evidence tending to shew that the accused has been guilty of criminal acts other than those covered by this indictment, for the purpose of leading to the conclusion that the accused is a person likely from his criminal conduct or character to have committed the offence for which he is being tried. On the other hand, the mere fact that the evidence adduced tends to shew the commission of other crimes does not render it inadmissible if it be relevant to an issue before the jury, and it may be so relevant if it bears upon the question whether the acts alleged to constitute the crime charged in the indictment were designed or accidental, or [if the evidence is used] to rebut a defence which would otherwise be open to the accused.

Evidence that some infant corpses were found in the backyard of a home that the Makins occupied was not admitted to prove that they committed the act for which they were standing trial. Rather, the evidence was used to rebut an argument that the deaths were accidental. In other words, coincidence could be ruled out because there were a dozen similar deaths. The strength of the evidence lay in the sheer unlikelihood that the Makins innocently happened to rent houses with backyards filled with baby corpses.

Development of the Similar Fact Evidence Rule

The leading case on similar fact evidence in Canada, and the one that developed the test for the admissibility of similar fact evidence, is *R v Handy*. In this case, the accused was charged with sexual assault causing bodily harm. He claimed that the complainant consented to the manner of sexual interaction, but she stated that while she had initially consented, she had withdrawn her consent when the sexual interaction became violent. She stated that Handy would not take no for an answer. At trial, the Crown sought to introduce evidence from the accused's former wife stating that he had sexually assaulted her seven times and enjoyed inflicting pain on her when they had sex. The accused alleged that the complainant and his former wife had colluded in their stories. He was convicted by the jury.

On appeal, in finding that the similar fact evidence had been wrongly admitted, the Supreme Court set out the test for admissibility (*R v Handy* at para 55):

> Similar fact evidence is thus presumptively inadmissible. The onus is on the prosecution to satisfy the trial judge on the balance of probabilities that in the context of the particular case the probative value of the evidence in relation to a particular issue outweighs its potential prejudice and thereby justifies its reception.

Using this test, a trial judge starts from the proposition that similar fact evidence should not be admitted. In assessing whether an exception should be made for evidence that the Crown seeks to admit, the judge requires the Crown to first show that the evidence is relevant to some other issue beyond the disposition or character of the accused. The obvious difficulty is to identify the "other issue" to which the accused's past acts are relevant. The general disposition of the accused does not qualify as "some other issue." Examples of "other issues" may include identification, guilty knowledge, intent, improbability of coincidence or accident, or rebutting a defence advanced by the accused. However, these "other issues" are not categories of admissibility. They are elements in the admissibility analysis. The issues must derive from the facts alleged against the accused or from any defence raised or reasonably antici-pated. They must be a live issue in the trial to which the evidence relates. If an issue is no longer in dispute—for example, where the accused admits a fact—then the evi-dence is no longer relevant to a material issue and is excluded.

The Crown must then establish that the inevitable prejudice that accompanies such evidence is outweighed by the value of the evidence—its contribution to proving the Crown's case. Any evidence that merely shows prior convictions can be seen only as general propensity evidence and cannot have greater probative value than the preju-dice it introduces. The Crown's task is even more difficult when the accused has num-erous convictions, because the greater the number of convictions, the more likely the jury will see them as conclusive of guilt in the outstanding offence and abandon the arduous task of weeding through the maze of evidence admitted against the accused.

Finally, the judge must assess the similarity of the evidence of prior bad acts to the case before the court by applying a number of criteria. The distinctiveness of the events is one such criterion. For example, the fact that two sexual assaults were com-mitted does not meet the criterion of distinctiveness, but the occurrence of two sex-ual assaults during which the assailant was wearing a *Phantom of the Opera* mask and singing opera is strikingly distinctive. Another consideration is the number of sim-ilar incidents. The probative value increases with the increase in the number of inci-dents. The number of details that match will enhance the probative value of the evidence, provided, however, that there is a link to the accused. A judge may also look at any surrounding circumstances and the absence of intervening events in as-sessing the probative value of the evidence.

Another important criterion is proximity in time. Generally, the greater the per-iod of time between the present offence and past similar offences, the more caution must be exercised in determining the admissibility of the similar fact evidence. In *R v Atlin* (2003 YKCA 5), an appeal from a conviction for sexual assault from the Yu-kon that was heard shortly after the Supreme Court of Canada's decision in *Handy*, the appeal court considered what impact the passage of time should have in the weight given to the similarity of facts. There was evidence that the accused had com-mitted similar acts between 1972 and 1975, and the matter in issue took place around 1987. The court stated (at para 18):

> One matter that seems to me troubling in the instant case is the temporal aspect. By that I mean that the incident involving M.J. occurred at a time when the appellant was quite a young person and the incidents involving S.J. occurred when he was an adult. It is entirely possible that as an individual matures there can be a change in their attitude, way of life and such. While it is not always going to be a conclusive fact where there are other very cogent badges or indicia of similarity, it seems to me that in general the greater the temporal space between the alleged similar acts and the acts that are alleged in the counts before the Court in the indictment, the more care or caution that will have to be exercised by the [judge] in analyzing the ques-tion of how that circumstance will impact on admissibility. It is fair to say that this will often be a very salient factor in the analysis concerning admissibility.

The Test for Admissibility of Similar Fact Evidence

1. The judge starts from the proposition that evidence of bad character should not be admitted.
2. The Crown must establish that bad character evidence is relevant to some other issue beyond the disposition or character of the accused.
3. The Crown must show on a balance of probabilities that the probative value of the evidence outweighs the prejudicial effect.

How Similar Is Similar?

If a court is prepared to look at an accused's past acts to detect a pattern or design, then the admissibility of such evidence must in part be determined by the degree of similarity between the past acts and the circumstances of the present case. Simply put, similar fact evidence put forth by the Crown must be evaluated to determine how similar the acts are to one another. In such instances, the court will look for unique characteristics of the acts—a fingerprint, so to speak. There have been cases, however, where the court has made dubious conclusions in this regard. One such case is *R v Arp* ([1998] 3 SCR 339), where the judge allowed evidence to be admitted regarding two incidents that had occurred over three years apart. During these incidents, intoxicated young women were taken to remote locations near Prince George, British Columbia and killed, and their bodies were left at the site. Their clothing, some of which had been cut by a sharp tool, had been removed and was scattered about. Unfortunately, there is not much that is unique in these incidents. The kidnapping and murder of young women, their sexual assault, and the abandonment of their naked bodies are by no means "fingerprints." The only somewhat uncommon incident is the cutting of the clothing, which is not a rare occurrence in crimes of this kind. In Arp's situation and others like it, the accused is faced with the additional hurdle of overcoming the prejudice generated by being linked in the mind of the trier of fact to another horrific crime. The prejudice is compounded if there are many similar crimes that the accused is linked to.

There is no hard and fast rule when it comes to the question of how similar the similar facts must be before they can be introduced as evidence against an accused. Obviously, the greater the similarity to the facts of the present case, the more likely it is that the similar facts will be admitted. But is partial similarity sufficient? If an accused has demonstrated a bad temper in the past by yelling and screaming at the slightest provocation but not resorting to violence, then can that evidence be introduced if the present allegations are that the accused lost his temper and killed in a blind rage? Most of us would probably have great difficulty accepting a link between those similar facts and an accused charged with murder. Although both situations clearly relate to a bad temper, the accused never demonstrated any physically violent acts in the past. If anything, his past actions demonstrate that the accused possesses the ability to refrain from violence even when in an angry and agitated state.

Thus, the lawyer should focus on the degree of similarity when arguing in court for or against the admissibility of similar fact evidence. Often, it is possible to make a persuasive argument either for or against the admissibility of the same set of similar facts. Many courts have adopted the phrase "striking similarity" when determining whether a set of similar facts are sufficiently similar to the case at hand, especially when the issue is identity. It is conceded that the "striking similarity" test falls short of establishing a definitive and objective standard of comparison. However, the same can be said for the concept of reasonable doubt.

Assessing the Degree of Prejudice in Similar Fact Evidence

In *Handy*, the Supreme Court of Canada described two types of prejudice that can result from the admission of similar fact evidence and instructed the courts to weigh such prejudice against probative value. The first, **moral prejudice**, results when the evidence of bad character shows the accused in a bad light, as a morally bad person, and leads the fact-finder to infer guilt. If the fact-finder reasons that the accused must be guilty because she is the kind of person who commits immoral acts, then there is moral prejudice to the accused.

The second type of prejudice is **reasoning prejudice**. This form of prejudice results when evidence that is presented interferes with the trier of fact's reasoning process by acting as a kind of red herring that distracts the trier of fact from the task of objectively evaluating the legitimate evidence. The trier of fact can become confused or distracted and decide the issue on the basis of evidence that is not legitimately before it. Judges may be tempted to admit the evidence because the more similar the evidence is, the stronger the probative value. However, this also means that there is a greater chance that the trier of fact could mistakenly mix together the two matters, weighing information from the similar fact matter as if it were evidence in the present matter. In such instances, the trier of fact has blended the two offences and not limited the similar fact offence to consideration of the issue that it was admitted to establish.

One of the difficulties of assessing probative value and prejudice is that the two concepts do not operate in the same plane. The probative value of evidence goes to the proof of an issue, while the prejudicial effect goes to the fairness of the trial. One concept is not necessarily related directly or adversely to the other. As probative value increases, prejudicial effect does not necessarily recede. However, probative value and prejudicial effect do pull in opposite directions when assessing the admissibility of similar fact evidence (*R v Handy* at paras 148, 149).

Although the Crown must establish that the similar fact evidence is admissible for some other purpose than to show bad character, the evidence is not inadmissible simply because it does show bad character, particularly when the evidence has high probative value. Thus, we see another important aspect of similar fact evidence. While such evidence is presumed inadmissible because of its potential for prejudice, if it has high probative value it will be admissible, in spite of the prejudice that it has. The cause of justice would not be served if a truly bad person were permitted to wear a blanket of protection that kept out highly relevant evidence, simply because it made him look bad. As with most aspects of evidence law, a balancing of the accused's rights and the need for society to protect itself is at play.

moral prejudice
prejudice that results from the admission of evidence of bad character showing the accused to be a morally bad person and leading the trier of fact to conclude that he is guilty

reasoning prejudice
applies to evidence that, if admitted, may confuse the trier of fact or distract it from the issue it must decide

Balancing Probative Value and Prejudicial Effect

R v Johnson, 2010 ONCA 646

Kristin Johnson was found guilty of second-degree murder in the 2005 death of 17-year-old Katrina Kiyoshk. Johnson appealed his conviction to the Ontario Court of Appeal on several grounds, including the improper admission by the trial judge of two pieces of similar fact evidence. The trial judge had permitted the Crown to introduce similar fact evidence in the form of two previous incidents involving the appellant.

The events on the night of the victim's death were disputed, but all parties agreed that Johnson and a friend of his, Nathaniel Shipman, had been "cruising" around Walpole Island while drinking, and before the victim's death, both Johnson and Shipman had sex with her. The two previous incidents similarly involved cruising around Walpole Island and violence by Johnson toward women. One previous incident involved the victim, and the other involved intoxication.

There were several grounds of appeal raised by the appellant, including that the trial judge improperly permitted these two incidents to be introduced as similar fact evidence. The Court of Appeal agreed that the trial judge improperly admitted the similar fact evidence and ordered a new trial. What is particularly interesting is how the court balanced the probative value of the evidence against its prejudicial effect.

The court found that the first incident had very little probative value as identification evidence because it did not exhibit a significant degree of similarity with the events surrounding the death of the victim. Without this degree of similarity, all that was left was evidence that the appellant was a bad, violent person, and therefore more likely to have committed the offence. The only similarities between the two incidents were that both involved cruising around Walpole Island with one man and one woman, and that the accused exhibited animus towards the female passenger while intoxicated. There was no sexual component to the incident and, although it was reasonably proximate in time to the alleged offence, the incident was an isolated occurrence that did not establish a pattern of behaviour. The court noted (at paras 116, 118) that

> There were no distinctive features unifying the incidents. The Crown failed to show that the appellant's conduct on this occasion was distinctive. To the contrary, there was evidence that drinking and cruising was a behaviour that was practised in the area. The incident thus simply did not exhibit sufficient similarities

> to render it particularly probative with respect to identity. … At best this evidence might establish that the accused was violent when intoxicated.

The court found that the probative value of the second incident was not particularly high for different reasons, noting that it could arguably show that the appellant disliked the victim, even to the point of violence, but it did not show some dispute between victim and accused that provided a motive for the crime. The court stated that "the animating context of the appellant's actions in the White Truck incident was entirely unconnected to the animus that was supposed to have motivated the alleged offence" (para 121). The evidence did have some probative value on the issues of identity and credibility, because the appellant did act violently toward the victim herself. However, again, there was a lack of distinctive features when comparing the incident with the circumstances surrounding the death of the victim.

A trial judge will decide whether to admit similar fact evidence after measuring and weighing the probative value and the prejudicial effect of the proposed evidence. A trial judge has no discretion to admit proposed similar fact evidence that is more prejudicial than probative. However, a trial judge's decision is afforded deference given the difficulty in the balancing of probative and prejudicial effects. One problem in this case was that the trial judge's reasons contained no analysis of the potential for the moral or reasoning prejudice identified as required by *Handy*. As a result, the court conducted its own analysis of the prejudicial effect of the evidence and concluded that there was a real risk of both forms of prejudice in this case.

In assessing the risk of moral prejudice, the court noted that both similar facts involved evidence of bad character and reprehensible conduct. The first incident "showed the appellant to be a person who seeks to inflict serious injury without any provocation or cause." The second incident "was worse: it demonstrated an actual attack that had gone entirely unpunished. Presented with this evidence, a fair-minded juror might well conclude that the appellant was simply a bad person" (para 129).

As a result, the court concluded that the "similar fact incidents gave rise to a strong risk of an unfocused and distracted approach to the case. This, combined with the real risk of moral prejudice and the marginal probative value of the evidence, ought to have resulted in a ruling that the evidence was inadmissible" (para 132).

The court concluded with the following helpful summary of the law in this area (at para 140):

> The rule against bad character evidence is a long standing one, justified by well accepted policy considerations. It is one of the central exclusionary rules in the law of evidence designed to ensure that an accused's right to a fair trial is maintained. Similar fact is an exception to this exclusionary rule and the case for making such an exception was simply not made out on this record.

Prior Acquittals and Similar Fact Evidence

What of the situation where an accused committed a prior similar act but was acquitted? Should evidence of the prior act be admissible as similar fact evidence? The position in Canada is that an acquittal places the similar fact evidence off-limits in future prosecutions (see *R v Grdic*, [1985] 1 SCR 810). Even a stay of proceedings, which means that the Crown chooses not to proceed with the charges (usually because a conviction is unlikely), has been determined to have the same result as an acquittal in relation to similar fact evidence. Some theorists argue that the probative value of the evidence is independent of whether a conviction or acquittal arose. In other words, the similar nature of the evidence can support an inference that the same person committed both offences and assist the trier of fact in its determination regardless of whether the accused was acquitted. The argument is that the trial judge in the present matter should be entitled to look behind the acquittal when a completely unrelated issue resulted in the acquittal, such as a breach of the accused's right to counsel, because there is no diminishment of the probative value of the facts from the prior trial.

Others have had considerable difficulty with this reasoning. They contend that to categorize acquittals differently or to create a hierarchy of acquittals is a slippery slope and would be a serious setback to the presumption of innocence. If an accused is truly entitled to be presumed innocent, then an acquittal makes the first allegation a nullity, as if it never existed. Fortunately for accused persons, similar fact evidence from a prior acquittal or stay of proceedings remains off-limits at this time.

Character Evidence and Co-Accused Persons

In an interesting twist, in cases where the Crown is not entitled to present bad character evidence, a co-accused may be entitled to present evidence that the other person charged is of bad character, provided that the judge does not conclude that the prejudicial effect is greater than the probative value. By doing so, the co-accused attempts to show that the other person charged is more likely to have committed the crime, essentially saying, "The other guy did it—after all, look at his record." The impact of taking this course of action, however, is that the co-accused person puts his own character in issue and is open for attack by the other person or the Crown.

Often, these character battles work to the advantage of the Crown, with both accused pointing fingers at each other and each damaging the character of the other. Sometimes, though, the case can turn out badly for the Crown if the jurors find both accused to be lacking in credibility and conclude, "These guys are both bad news but we can't tell which one of them did it." An acquittal of both accused, where the jury is certain that one of them committed the offence, is necessary in such cases but certain to leave a bad feeling among the public.

Character Evidence and Prior Convictions in Civil Matters

Character evidence is rarely led in civil cases and is usually not admissible. Most of the common law rules that relate to character evidence and virtually all of the statutory modifications to the common law have arisen in the context of criminal cases. However, evidence of a party's character is admissible if the character of the party is at issue. For example, in many jurisdictions, an alleged case of defamation can be decided against the plaintiff if the statements made by the defendant are shown to be true; defamation occurs only if the statements the defendant has made about the plaintiff are false. It would therefore be appropriate for the defendant to lead evidence that such statements are true. Apart from those situations where the character of a party is at issue, evidence that a party is of bad character is generally inadmissible in civil cases. Similarly, rarely will a party be entitled to present evidence of her good character.

There is, however, a special rule that has been developed to deal with circumstances where a person has acted in such a way that he attracts both criminal and civil liability. If the person is convicted of a criminal offence—say, assaulting the complainant—the complainant can then sue the perpetrator in civil court, using the conviction as *prima facie* proof that the defendant committed the assault. What this means is that, absent proof to the contrary, the trier of fact must conclude that the assault has been proven in the civil matter. In this instance, the "prior" bad act alleged is in fact the same act but proven to a criminal standard, so in the subsequent civil case, the trier of fact may start from the proposition that the defendant has already been convicted of the alleged assault beyond a reasonable doubt.

Testimony and Credibility of Third Parties

Witnesses who are not parties in a trial are presented as truth-tellers and will be accepted as such unless the opponent challenges the witness's credibility or general character. The person calling a witness is not entitled to bolster that witness's credibility with evidence of the witness's good character or honesty. It should be noted that it is common to provide a brief introduction of the witness to the trier of fact so that the witness's evidence may be put into context, but it is not permissible to attempt to enhance the witness's credibility through this avenue. The dialogue below illustrates a permissible introduction of a witness:

> **Counsel:** Calling Frances Moorley to the stand. … Now, Ms. Moorley, I understand that you are an accountant and have been for the past 10 years.
>
> **FM:** Yes, I work at General Motors in the Finance Department.

Counsel: And you are a mother of two teenaged children and have resided in Littletown for the past eight years.

FM: That's correct, we moved here from Bigtown just over eight and a half years ago.

Counsel: Now, you observed a matter on June 21 that brings you to court today; could you tell us about that?

This exchange gives the trier of fact a sense of the witness without going overboard and attempting to enhance her credibility. If counsel were to take it a step further and ask about the witness's church attendance, volunteer work, and medal for bravery, that would constitute an attempt to present the witness as being more believable than a typical witness and would not be acceptable.

Clothes Make the Witness

In an anecdotal account of one jury trial, the accused was charged with insurance fraud by claiming to have a passenger in his car when he was involved in an accident. It was a very rainy October night and the other vehicle came through an intersection, striking the accused's car as he was turning left. The drivers pulled their vehicles to the side of the road and exchanged information in the rain at the back of the other driver's vehicle. At trial, the accused stated that his passenger remained in the vehicle because it was raining.

It was not until a year later, after medical benefits had been paid to the alleged passenger, that a new insurance adjuster noted that the other driver stated there was only a driver (and no passenger) in the vehicle he collided with. Thus, the adjuster concluded that this had been an attempt to obtain "no fault" benefits by fraud. The issue at trial was whether the other driver could have been mistaken in concluding that there was no passenger in the accused's vehicle. The problem was that the other driver was an off-duty police officer; therefore, the police and Crown believed him. Although it was clear that the other driver could be mistaken, particularly given that it was raining and dark outside, no amount of arguing by the defence would dissuade the Crown from proceeding with the charges.

On the first day of the trial, the Crown called its first witness, the police officer, who showed up for court in uniform, even though he was off duty at the time. So why was he wearing his uniform? If he had been a painter, would he have turned up in paint coveralls, or if he had been a doctor, would he have turned up in scrubs? Obviously not. This was a thinly disguised attempt to bolster his credibility. The defence objected, but the judge, particularly because the officer was there and ready to testify, permitted him to give his testimony in uniform. As it turned out, the officer had to be recalled later in the trial, and this time the judge directed that he not wear his uniform. Interestingly enough, his evidence was much less impressive the second time around. The accused was ultimately acquitted.

In a criminal trial, witnesses who are not parties to the case are not entitled to the same protection against bad character evidence as an accused. The particular protection against bad character evidence afforded an accused stems from the fact that his liberty is at stake. Witnesses who are not parties to the case do not have their liberty at stake, and their credibility can be attacked as long as the questions asked of them are relevant to the testimony they give. Normally, any evidence that attacks the credibility of a witness that is not relevant to a material issue is not admissible. This is often referred to as the **collateral facts rule** (see *R v Prebtani*, 2008 ONCA 735 at para 130). Because a witness always puts her credibility at issue when she testifies, an exception is made where the witness is caught lying: in such instances, the general credibility of the witness can be attacked (see *R v Biddle*, [1995] 1 SCR 761 at para 20). The following example illustrates such a situation.

collateral facts rule
rule that limits the calling of additional evidence on immaterial issues between the parties

> ### EXAMPLE
>
> **Attacking the Credibility of a Lying Witness**
>
> In the novel *A Time to Kill*, by John Grisham, defence counsel calls a psychiatrist to testify that the accused was insane when he killed the two men who raped his daughter. The prosecution attacks the character of the psychiatrist, asking whether he has any criminal convictions. The defence lawyer makes the mistake of not objecting to this question about the psychiatrist's past criminal history, which is irrelevant to his testimony. The psychiatrist states that he has no criminal convictions, but it comes out that he has a 30-year-old conviction for statutory rape. Because the psychiatrist has lied, evidence of his past criminal history is admitted because it becomes relevant to the issue of his general credibility.

As with the case of a person charged with a criminal offence, section 12 of the *Canada Evidence Act* also permits any witness to be examined on his or her criminal record.

The testimony of third parties has been used in murder and assault trials to show that the victim had a disposition toward violence, thus supporting the accused's plea of self-defence. This sort of evidence has been admitted even where the accused was unaware of the deceased's violent tendencies because it supports the proposition that the accused had little choice but to defend himself when faced with a violent attack. However, when an accused calls a third-party witness to testify about the deceased person's predisposition for violence, he risks putting his own character in issue, and as a consequence the Crown would be in a position to attack the character of the accused in much the same manner as it could attack any other witness.

Third-Party Character Evidence in Sexual Assault Cases

rape shield provisions
provisions in the *Criminal Code* that forbid the admission of evidence of a complainant's sexual history to support an inference that she is more likely to have given consent or is less worthy of belief

The specific subset of third-party character evidence that relates to complainants in trials for sexual offences has been the subject of legislative and judicial intervention. The **rape shield provisions** in sections 276 and 277 of the *Criminal Code* state that the prior sexual conduct of the complainant is presumptively inadmissible. Section 276(1) states:

[E]vidence that the complainant has engaged in sexual activity, whether with the accused or with any other person, is not admissible to support an inference that, by reason of the sexual nature of that activity, the complainant

    (a) is more likely to have consented to the sexual activity that forms the subject-matter of the charge; or

    (b) is less worthy of belief.

Section 277 states:

In proceedings in respect of an offence under section 151, 152, 153, 153.1, 155 or 159, subsection 160(2) or (3) or section 170, 171, 172, 173, 271, 272 or 273, evidence of sexual reputation, whether general or specific, is not admissible for the purpose of challenging or supporting the credibility of the complainant.

Although the argument that sexually experienced persons will have sex with anyone or cannot be believed is absurd, it has proven to be very persuasive to juries. Time and again, juries have acquitted persons accused of sexual offences after the credibility of the victim was undermined in this manner. This was done through questioning: how often she had sex, whether she had sex with more than one partner, whether she had sex more than once an evening—even questions about fantasized sex were sometimes allowed.

This era of victim abuse was finally put to an end with the Supreme Court's decision in *R v Seaboyer; R v Gayme* ([1991] 2 SCR 577). In that case, the court found that the provisions of section 277 did not infringe the provisions of the *Canadian Charter of Rights and Freedoms* because the section excludes evidence that can serve no legitimate purpose. However, the court found section 276 unconstitutional because it was too broad in excluding evidence. The court distinguished between the *use* and *misuse* of evidence of sexual activity and set out rules to regulate the questioning of a complainant about her prior sexual history. The decision places the onus on the accused to convince a judge that such questions are relevant to a legitimate issue for the defence. It explicitly prohibits questioning that is directed toward the twin myths that sexually experienced complainants are either less worthy of belief or more likely to have consented because of their sexual history. By way of example, Seaboyer sought to question the complainant about prior sexual activity that might explain bruising that she claimed resulted from the alleged sexual assault, and Gayme, an 18-year-old student, sought to question the 15-year-old complainant about her sexual history in relation to other students at the same school where the alleged assault took place. He claimed that she was the sexual aggressor. In both cases, the accused were denied the right to question the complainants on their prior sexual history.

CHAPTER SUMMARY

Character evidence is evidence of the type of person someone is, as demonstrated by the person's past conduct. Although character evidence has probative value, it also carries the potential to create prejudice in the eyes of the trier of fact and is admitted by the court only under strict circumstances. It is generally not admissible as circumstantial evidence of guilt in criminal cases. Evidence of propensity is distinct from character evidence in that it is evidence of a person's psychiatric tendencies as attested to by an expert.

Similar fact evidence can have great probative value, but it has a very high potential to create moral prejudice and reasoning prejudice and will be admitted only if it passes the test set out by the Supreme Court of Canada.

Character evidence is rarely permitted in civil cases. The character evidence rule does not normally operate to protect third parties to a criminal case such as the complainant. Third-party character evidence has been limited in sexual assault cases by the rape shield provisions in the *Criminal Code* and by the Supreme Court of Canada.

KEY TERMS

character evidence, 126
collateral facts rule, 142
moral prejudice, 137
potential prejudice, 126
probative value, 126
propensity or disposition evidence, 131
rape shield provisions, 142
reasoning prejudice, 137
similar fact evidence, 132

NOTES

1   Section 12 of the *Canada Evidence Act* sets out the procedure for cross-examining a witness about a prior conviction.

2   The leading case is an old English case, *R v Rowton*. The Ontario Court of Appeal commented more recently on this concept in *R v Clarke* at para 28.

REFERENCES

Arp, R v, [1998] 3 SCR 339.

Atlin, R v, 2003 YKCA 5.

Biddle, R v, [1995] 1 SCR 761.

Canada Evidence Act, RSC 1985, c C-5, as amended.

Clarke, R v, 1998 CanLII 14604 (Ont CA).

Criminal Code, RSC 1985, c C-46, as amended.

Grdic, R v, [1985] 1 SCR 810.

Handy, R v, 2002 SCC 56, [2002] 2 SCR 908.

Johnson, R v, 2010 ONCA 646.

Makin v AG for New South Wales, [1894] AC 57 (PC).

McFadden, R v (1981), 65 CCC (2d) 9 (BCCA).

Mohan, R v, [1994] 2 SCR 9.

Prebtani, R v, 2008 ONCA 735.

Rowton, R v (1865), 169 ER 1497.

Seaboyer, R v; R v Gayme, [1991] 2 SCR 577.

Soikie, R v, 2004 CanLII 1849 (Ont SC).

Tierney, R v (1982), 70 CCC (2d) 481 (Ont CA).

REVIEW QUESTIONS

1. What are the dangers of admitting character evidence?

2. What is the value of character evidence?

3. What is similar fact evidence, and what criteria apply to its admissibility?

4. What are the rape shield provisions, and how might an accused get evidence of a complainant's sexual history admitted?

DISCUSSION QUESTIONS

In the following scenarios, (a) determine whether the evidence is admissible and if not, why not, and (b) if the evidence is admissible, determine for what purpose it is being admitted.

1. Glen Bainbridge is charged with murder in the death of his wife. The prosecution wishes to lead evidence that Glen had beaten his wife on two previous occasions.

2. Allen Abdi is charged with sexually assaulting a young boy who visited him at his home. The prosecution wants to lead evidence that the accused molested five other boys, two of whom obtained multi-million-dollar settlements to buy their silence. The alleged past activities include hugging, kissing, and fondling the other boys. These incidents go back in time between 12 and 15 years, and only one of the boys will testify in person. The other evidence will be provided by third parties.

3. Peter Savard is charged with the murder of a 17-year-old cheerleader, whose killer carved the number "666" into her flesh. The prosecution wants to lead evidence that Peter has just been paroled after serving 20 years for killing a 17-year-old cheerleader and carving the number "666" into her body.

4. Ronald Pritchard is charged with common assault. The defence wishes to lead evidence that Ronald had been beaten by the complainant in the past and evidence about the complainant's past violent acts.

5. Scott Nardella is charged with sexual assault. The defence wishes to lead evidence that Scott had a past sexual relationship with the complainant and evidence about the complainant's other past sexual relationships.

6. Trevor McDonald has been charged with smuggling diamonds into Canada. His defence is that he "forgot" to declare the goods and lacked criminal intent. His lawyer wishes to lead evidence that Trevor is a deeply religious and honest person.

7. Nadia Ali was a passenger in a motor vehicle that was driven by her boyfriend, Steven Ancheta. Steven drove under a transport truck and Nadia was decapitated. Nadia's parents sued Steven and the truck driver, Joe Dietrich. During his discovery, Joe stated that he is not presently working because he lost his licence after being convicted of drunk driving while taking his mother to bingo.

8. Reginald Stein, a police officer, has been charged with second-degree murder in the death of Ellen Selkirk. The defence is based on "justifiable force." Reginald wishes to lead evidence that he was awarded a citation for Top Cop after saving three children from a burning car. He also wishes to lead evidence that Ellen is known to have a terrible temper. The Crown wishes to lead evidence that Reginald was once suspended for hitting a motorist and charged (but acquitted) of assault.

Opinion Evidence

9

LEARNING OUTCOMES

After completing this chapter, you should be able to:

■ Demonstrate an understanding of when the opinion evidence of a lay witness can be admitted and when it cannot.

■ Demonstrate an understanding of when the opinion of an expert witness can be admitted and when it cannot.

■ Describe the process of qualifying an expert witness.

■ Describe how various statutes have modified the rules respecting the admissibility of expert evidence.

■ Explain the limitations on expert evidence.

Introduction

The primary purpose of evidence law is to ensure that reliable information is put before the trier of fact. With this purpose in mind, the courts developed the rule that witnesses are not to express opinions, but merely state facts that are within their knowledge, observation, and experience. In the classic 1950s TV series *Dragnet*, Detective Sergeant Joe Friday frequently urged excited witnesses, "Just the facts, ma'am."

In the courtroom, the witness and the finder of fact have clearly differentiated roles: The witness supplies the facts, and the trier of fact evaluates them and determines what to make of them. This differentiation of roles is particularly important, given that in most instances the witness has only a piece of the puzzle, whereas the trier of fact is given information from many sources and can see how the pieces fit together. The trier of fact is thus better positioned to draw conclusions from the evidence put before it. But as with most rules that arise in evidence law, this one has significant exceptions. Where the trier of fact is in need of help from a witness that can come only in the form of an opinion, the witness may, in certain situations, be permitted to express an opinion. Mostly, this will happen when the witness is determined by the judge to be an expert in a particular area, but laypersons are also permitted to express their opinions in certain circumstances.

The Rule Against Opinion Evidence

The rule against opinion evidence can be stated in simple terms:

> Opinion evidence is not admissible unless it is either the opinion of a layperson that is helpful for a clear understanding of his or her testimony or the opinion of an expert.

Of course, if the rule against opinion evidence were as straightforward as it appears to be in the above passage, there would be no need to continue reading this chapter. However, the details and the application of the rule can be confusing. First, we must ask what we mean when we talk about an opinion.

What Is an Opinion?

The best way to understand what is meant by "opinion evidence" is first to look at what it is *not*. It is not evidence of fact. Rather, **opinion evidence** is evidence that is based on conclusions or inferences that are drawn from facts or observations. If a witness states that she observed a dead body being placed into the trunk of a vehicle, she is stating her opinion as to the state of the body. She may have drawn this conclusion from the fact that the person was not moving or that his clothes were bloodstained, but it is unlikely that the witness was able to observe as a fact that the person being put into the trunk was deceased. The witness will be permitted to state her personal observations, but not her inferences or conclusions based on those observations. The conclusions of the witness are only her opinion, not matters of fact. It is

opinion evidence
evidence given by a witness that is based on conclusions or inferences drawn from facts or observations; generally, the witness is not permitted to state the conclusions or inferences themselves, only the observations

up to the trier of fact to look at all of the evidence and then to draw the appropriate conclusions. However, this does not mean that a witness would never be able to testify that a person was deceased, even if it involved the drawing of an inference from personally observed fact. This situation is discussed below under the heading "Layperson's Opinion."

An excellent illustration of prohibited opinion evidence is the legendary story, said to be true, of a witness testifying at an assault trial. During direct examination, the witness testified that the accused bit the victim's ear off in the fray. In cross-examination, defence counsel challenged the witness, "Now, you didn't actually see the accused bite the complainant's ear off, did you?" "No," replied the witness. "Then how can you say for sure that it was the accused who bit the complainant's ear off?" "Because I saw the accused spit out the ear," was the reply. The observed fact was the spitting out of the ear. The opinion was that the accused had bitten off the victim's ear. The point is that the witness has direct knowledge of what he saw, the spitting out of the ear, and drew the inference that the accused bit off the ear.

Layperson's Opinion

What if, in the first example above, the witness had instead observed a decapitated body being placed in the trunk of car? Is there any real danger in permitting the witness to offer a **layperson's opinion** as to whether the victim was alive or deceased at the time? Is the trier of fact in any better position than the witness to conclude that the victim was indeed dead when placed in the trunk? Clearly, the witness is in as good a position as the trier of fact—if not better—to conclude that the victim was deceased where the signs of death are obvious and overwhelming.

There are certain instances where allowing opinion evidence to be admitted can help the trier of fact and where there is little potential for harm. For example, lay witnesses are permitted to offer an opinion that a layperson could ordinarily be expected to arrive at. Lay witnesses are thus permitted to offer an opinion on such matters as a person's age, height, race, or other physical characteristics. It is understood that the trier of fact will regard these opinions as approximations or best estimates rather than exact statements or gospel truths.

Similarly, where the subject matter of the opinion is within the knowledge and expertise of the average person, an opinion will usually be permitted. Thus, lay witnesses are permitted to answer such questions as "What speed was the car travelling at?," "What time of day was it?," "What colour was her dress?," "How old was the victim?," and "How far away was the shooter?" A lay witness has been permitted to express an opinion on whether an accused was intoxicated on a particular occasion; the emotional state of a person; the condition of things (worn, shabby, used, or new); and the identification of persons, things, and handwriting. The trier of fact knows, or is reminded by the judge, that the witness is only giving her best estimate and that different witnesses have different abilities to judge or approximate and different experiences on which they base their opinions. However, if the information provided by the witness requires specialized knowledge that is beyond that of the average person, the witness must be qualified as having the expertise to make those conclusions.

layperson's opinion
opinion given by an ordinary witness on a matter of ordinary experience; permitted where the opinion does not unnecessarily encroach on the trier of fact's role

The courts apply the following general criteria to determine whether the opinion evidence of a lay witness can be accepted:

1. The opinion is one that a layperson could ordinarily be expected to arrive at.
2. The lay witness has sufficient experience to draw these conclusions.
3. The lay witness is better situated than the trier of fact to form the conclusions.

In addition, a lay witness may be permitted to present his evidence in opinion form where it is difficult for him to express the information without stating an opinion. For example, "He was drunk" is clearly an opinion, but it is more easily expressed than "His eyes were bloodshot, he was weaving back and forth, he stank of alcohol, and he had urinated in his pants." The latter presentation of facts (although those facts still contain some opinions) is far more helpful to the trier of fact, but many witnesses, particularly those who are testifying for the first time, would have difficulty expressing the precise basis upon which they came to the conclusion that the person was drunk. The statement "He was drunk" has some value but should be given less weight than the other, more factual description of what was observed. Where a witness includes opinions in her testimony, this is sometimes referred to as a **compendious mode of expressing facts**, and permitting the witness some latitude in testifying is a way of making the legal process approachable to the average person (see *Graat v The Queen*, [1982] 2 SCR 819).

compendious mode of expressing facts
testimony in which the witness mixes opinion into his narrative in order to express himself; permitted by the court where it is difficult for the witness to express the information without stating an opinion

Expert Opinion

The Expert Opinion Rule

An **expert opinion** is just what it sounds like: it is one where a person with specific expertise in an area that is in issue before the court testifies in order to assist the trier of fact in coming to conclusions of fact in that area. The trier of fact will almost never be an expert in blood-spatter analysis, accident reconstruction, stress loads in bridge construction, DNA analysis, Breathalyzer readings, or any number of scientific or knowledge-based fields. Because litigation often involves understanding and interpreting complex and narrow fields of study, experts can be extremely helpful to the trier of fact. The rule permitting expert evidence can be summarized as follows:

expert opinion
testimony given by a properly qualified person with specific expertise in an area that is in issue before the court; permitted in order to assist the trier of fact in coming to conclusions of fact in that area

> A properly qualified expert will be permitted to provide his or her opinion if that specialized knowledge will permit the trier of fact to better understand the facts or evidence before it.

Experts are helpful in sorting out some of the issues facing the trier of fact in litigation and in criminal trials. Often they are essential. However, some safeguards exist to ensure that the trier of fact is not unduly influenced by the opinions of expert witnesses and that the persons testifying are indeed experts in their fields. In *R v Mohan* ([1994] 2 SCR 9), the Supreme Court of Canada developed four criteria to help determine whether a witness may be qualified as an expert and thus give opinion evidence:

1. *Relevance:* There are two aspects of this determination. The first is simple, logical relevance. Does the information that counsel seeks to introduce via the expert logically promote the proposition that has been advanced? Second, even if the information is relevant, do the benefits of this sort of evidence outweigh the risks?

2. *Necessity:* Is the expert needed to assist the trier of fact in coming to conclusions on the issues before the court?

3. *Qualifications:* Is this particular expert qualified in the field he would provide evidence in? It is noteworthy that some experts are presented and qualified to give evidence in one area but in the course of their testimony stray into areas that are beyond their expertise.

4. *The absence of any exclusionary rule:* There cannot be a rule prohibiting the evidence. In other words, counsel cannot use the expert to get information before the trier of fact that is otherwise inadmissible, such as privileged information or evidence obtained in violation of a person's Charter rights.

The Mohan Factors

Relevance

In assessing whether the relevance requirement has been met, a judge starts by asking whether the information helps make the point it is being presented to prove. If it does not, then it is not admitted as evidence. If it does, then the judge goes on to weigh the information to determine whether it ought to be admitted. This process is similar to a cost–benefit analysis. The judge asks what cost or potential for distortion or damage the information represents, and what benefit exists for the trier of fact in hearing the proposed evidence. In short, does the probative value outweigh the prejudice?

In considering the probative value of the evidence, the court will generally consider three criteria:

1. *The connection between the expert opinion and facts proven in evidence:* The closer the connection, the more weight the opinion deserves.

2. *The strength of the expert evidence:* How important is the evidence in proving the proposition it is presented to support?

3. *The importance of the evidence:* Is the issue being proved central to the proceedings? The more significant or important the issue is, the more likely the court will find there to be a benefit in allowing the evidence.

In relation to the last point, counsel or the legal representative that hopes to have expert evidence admitted needs to avoid the "so what" factor. It is not very helpful if the trier of law says, "If I admit the e vidence or not, so what? How will that have any impact on the outcome of the proceedings?" The point is that importance is not an all-or-nothing proposition. It is something that is normally defined in terms of degrees, not absolutes.

The prejudicial effect of evidence relates to the unwanted negative effect of the evidence on the trial itself—for example, if the evidence would unduly delay or lengthen the trial. Evidence is also prejudicial if its effect is out of proportion to its reliability (see *R v BM*, 1998 CanLII 13326 (Ont CA)). In this respect, the trier of law must also weigh the risk that admitting too much evidence will overwhelm the trier of fact, or that the proposed evidence will confuse the trier of fact.

Necessity

A judge cannot simply look at the expert evidence and determine that it would be helpful to the trier of fact. Setting the bar that low invites the admission of all kinds of evidence that the trier of fact might like, because it would make its job easier, but also invites reliance or dependence on evidence that provides easy answers but not necessarily the right ones. Necessity means what it implies: Unless the trier of fact cannot reasonably come to the right conclusion without the expert evidence, the evidence should not be permitted. There must be the potential for a wrong determination or an inability to understand or "access" the information before expert evidence can be admitted. From this perspective, a wrong determination in a criminal case implies the potential for a wrongful conviction, and thus the courts have been broad in their interpretation of necessity when considering the evidence of criminal defence experts. This approach ensures that the accused has the opportunity for "full answer and defence."

Qualifications

In order for expert evidence to be admitted, the expert must be qualified in the field she provides evidence in. Thus, counsel that seeks to have an expert testify about the effect of glue-sniffing on the accused's state of mind when he assaulted his teacher would likely be successful in convincing the judge that expert evidence regarding the toxicology of glue is both necessary and relevant. If the witness is a toxicologist with advanced degrees, publications on the subject, and 20 years of experience, the judge will very likely qualify the expert to testify. If counsel attempts to have one of the client's glue-sniffing friends give evidence about the impact of glue on the brain, the judge is likely to refuse the testimony, notwithstanding that the witness would have a basis for testifying that is far more intimate than the conventionally schooled expert.

The Absence of Any Exclusionary Rule

The issue here is that a party should not be able to present evidence through an expert that it could not present directly. So, where an accused speaks to a psychiatrist, who is later called to testify, the psychiatrist should not be able to relate an excuse or a justification given by the accused for his actions ("He attacked me with a shovel, so I stabbed him"), thus permitting that information to get before the trier of fact without the accused's facing cross-examination. Or, where a Crown expert makes reference to a confession from the accused that was beaten out of him and thus is not admissible, the expert's comment should not be admitted. In both cases, the expert evidence would not be admissible to the extent that it violates an exclusionary rule.

CASE IN POINT

Revisiting the Mohan Test

R v Abbey, 2009 ONCA 624

The Ontario Court of Appeal revisited the *Mohan* test in the 2009 decision of *R v Abbey*. That case involved a bloody turf war between two rival Toronto gangs, the Galloway Boys and the Malvern Crew. It was conceded at trial that one or more of the Malvern Crew had shot and killed Simeon Peter, believing him to be a member of the Galloway Boys. About four or five months after the shooting, the accused had a small teardrop tattoo inscribed on his face. As part of its case, the Crown sought to introduce evidence from Dr. Totten, a sociologist, as an expert in the culture of urban street gangs in Canada. In particular, the Crown proposed to have Dr. Totten provide his opinion as to the meaning of a teardrop tattoo within urban street gang culture in Canada and also his opinion of the meaning of the accused's teardrop tattoo.

It was Dr. Totten's opinion that a teardrop tattoo signified one of three possible events: First, that a gang member or close friend had died; second, that the person had served a custodial sentence; or third, that the person had killed a rival gang member. The Crown then wanted Dr. Totten to answer a hypothetical question that would eliminate the first two meanings in this case and essentially opine that the accused had inscribed a tattoo because he had killed a rival gang member. The trial judge rejected this evidence on the basis that it was not reliable for a number of reasons.

In allowing the Crown's appeal, the court applied the *Mohan* criteria but drew a distinction in the analysis of logical and legal relevance and set out a two-step process for admitting expert evidence. The first stage involves the consideration of certain preconditions of admissibility; evidence that does not meet these preconditions is excluded. The preconditions of admissibility include the *Mohan* criteria, but the court will consider only whether the evidence is logically relevant at this stage. The cost–benefit analysis of the evidence, or legal relevance, is performed at the second step. An analysis of the necessity of the proposed evidence is conducted as part of the larger cost–benefit analysis. The trial judge, in exercising the gatekeeper function, must determine whether the evidence is "sufficiently beneficial to the trial process to warrant its admission despite the potential harm to the trial process that may flow from the admission of the expert evidence" (see *R v Abbey* at para 76).

While the two-stage analysis set out in *Abbey* has not appeared to gain traction with trial courts in Ontario or with other provincial courts of appeal, there is an interesting feature of this case that may prove to be durable in its application. The court clarified that the trial judge, in performing the gatekeeper function, need not treat expert evidence as an "all or nothing" proposition. Remember, evidence generally may be admissible for one purpose but inadmissible for another. The same is true for expert evidence. In *Abbey*, the expert was not permitted to testify regarding the reason the accused obtained the tattoo, but was permitted to offer an opinion on the significance of a teardrop tattoo within gang culture.

The Process of Qualifying an Expert

Before a witness will be permitted to provide expert evidence, the judge will need to determine whether the evidence that is being adduced is admissible, and whether the witness is properly qualified to provide the evidence. If there is no jury and there is no dispute regarding the admissibility of expert evidence in the circumstances, the process of qualifying the expert is usually brief. Counsel will typically lead the witness through her resumé and may ask a few questions pertaining to her qualifications. Opposing counsel will be given the opportunity to ask questions, and the judge may question the witness as well. Counsel will then request that the judge qualify the witness as an expert.

If there is a jury, or if the necessity for expert evidence or the witness's qualifications are in dispute, the process of qualifying the witness as an expert may be more rigorous. The party attempting to put forth the evidence will have to demonstrate that the evidence meets the four criteria set out in *R v Mohan*.

Limits on the Number of Expert Witnesses

One of the problems with expert testimony is that, on any topic, a plaintiff or the Crown can find a dozen experts to support its contention, while the defendant or the accused can find an equal number whose evidence leads to the opposite conclusion. As a point of fact, many jurisdictions limit the number of experts who can testify on a point so that the exercise does not become simply a numbers game, leading the trier of fact to conclude that the side that presents the most experts must be right.

The *Canada Evidence Act* limits the number of experts that can be called by any party without leave of the court to five; the limit under the Ontario *Evidence Act* is three. However, exceptions can be granted to permit more experts to be called than are provided for in the *Canada Evidence Act* and in provincial statutes. Leave may be granted even after a party has called expert witnesses.

Hired Gun Syndrome

A related issue is the "hired gun" syndrome. It is remarkable (and not entirely coincidental) how often the same expert will testify in many different trials but only for the defence, or only for the Crown. For example, certain toxicologists are well-known defence witnesses and have never testified for the Crown. Similarly, there are doctors who consistently will provide evidence for defendants, while others are known as "plaintiffs' doctors."

Experts are usually paid by the party who has retained their services. This is not to suggest that expert evidence can be bought, but that some experts may be predisposed to viewing matters in a way that is helpful to the plaintiff or to the defendant. In instances where the court determines that an expert is biased or has adopted an adversarial stance toward the other party, that evidence can be excluded or given diminished weight.

CASE IN POINT

The Biased Expert

R v Natsis, 2014 ONCJ 532

Dr. Christy Natsis was charged with a number of *Criminal Code* offences, including offences related to impaired driving, arising out of a motor vehicle accident that occurred on March 31, 2011. The SUV driven by Dr. Natsis collided head on with a pickup truck driven by Bryan Casey, who died from the injuries he suffered in the collision.

At Dr. Natsis's trial, the Crown sought to introduce the evidence of three police officers as experts in accident reconstruction. The defence objected to the admissibility of this evidence on the basis that all three officers were biased and partial to the prosecution. The defence set out a total of 69 specific reasons in relation to the three officers in support of its position.

After an extensive review of the case law, the trial judge concluded (at para 160):

> Clearly, it is open to a trial judge in an appropriate case to exclude expert evidence that is biased or partial, as opposed to admitting it subject to weight. O'Connor, A.C.J.O. in *Carmen* … suggests that this discretion be reserved for cases where "the evidence is so tainted by bias or partiality as to render it of minimum or no assistance."

In assessing the defence's claims of bias, the trial judge considered especially a number of emails sent by Constable Kelly, one of the proposed expert witnesses, noting that (at para 168)

> [a] fair reading of these emails supports the conclusion that Kelly—almost from the outset of his involvement in this matter—crossed the line from technical traffic collision investigator to general investigation of the offence. He immediately asserted himself as advisor and counsel to the officer in charge. He sought to be included in—and even to initiate—meetings with Besner and all others with a *"vested interest"* in the case. [Emphasis added]

After carefully considering the arguments of the parties, the trial judge excluded a significant portion of Kelly's evidence, while the evidence of the two other officers was admitted subject to weight.

Provincial and Territorial Rules Regarding Expert Evidence

Most experts are busy practising in their fields and may find it difficult to fit a trial into their schedules. For example, a doctor may have a waiting room filled with patients or may be scheduled to perform surgery on the same day that she is expected to testify in court. To address this, many provincial/territorial evidence acts have special provisions that are designed to streamline the presentation of expert evidence and accommodate experts.

Under section 52(2) of the Ontario *Evidence Act*, a party may, with leave of the trial judge, use the report of an expert at trial instead of calling the expert as a witness. In Manitoba, a medical report is admissible without leave of the court by virtue of section 50(1) of the *Manitoba Evidence Act*. Prince Edward Island and Saskatchewan also have provisions in their legislation permitting the use of medical reports. In section 10 of British Columbia's *Evidence Act*, any expert report is admissible as evidence. Both the Yukon and the Northwest Territories have adopted provisions similar to those of British Columbia.[1] Additionally, most provincial superior courts have rules that allow for the use of expert reports. All of these statutes generally permit a party to compel the attendance of a medical practitioner or other expert if necessary or to test his or her evidence by cross-examination, but many provide cost sanctions for calling the expert unnecessarily (for example, section 52(5) of the Ontario *Evidence Act*). Any party that wishes to rely on any of these statutes should review the applicable provisions carefully, because there are special procedural and notice requirements.

Limitations on Expert Evidence

We have seen that a judge, as a gatekeeper, is charged with determining whether or not to admit the evidence of an expert witness. Even when an expert's testimony is admitted by the court, it is still subject to several limits that determine the weight it is given by a judge or a jury.

1. Foundation of the Expert's Opinion

In order for an expert's opinion to have any value, it must be based on proven facts. An opinion based on facts not proven is of very little value and will be given little, if any, weight by the trier of fact. Where the trier of fact is a jury, the judge will instruct it to give the opinion little or no weight. For example, if an expert states that the deceased died from stab wounds without first examining the deceased or her medical records, that opinion is of scant help to the trier of fact because it is little more than speculation or conjecture. It is therefore crucial that both sides understand the factual underpinnings of any expert's opinion. Expert evidence can be attacked by skillful cross-examination that uncovers the absence of a factual basis for the expert's opinion. Similarly, it is equally important for a party calling an expert to build a proper foundation upon which the expert can base an opinion or risk having the evidence be given little weight.

The foundation of an expert's testimony is usually established by posing a hypothetical question for the expert to answer. The hypothetical question is typically formulated by asking the expert to assume certain facts upon which to base an opinion. Later, if the facts are not proven at all or the trier of fact rejects the assumed facts, the opinion is treated with far less deference.

The hypothetical question will often be worked out ahead of time with the expert's help and will carefully track the evidence that has come out in court. So, for example, where an expert is called in an impaired driving trial, the purpose is usually to challenge the accuracy of the Breathalyzer readings. The hypothetical question would establish a pattern of drinking and ask the expert what the blood-alcohol level would be in light of those facts. In this example, the hypothetical question might be phrased as follows:

> Hypothetically, if a person weighing 100 kilograms were to begin drinking at 8:30 p.m. and consume 200 millilitres of 40 percent alcohol at an even rate between 8:30 p.m. and 11:00 p.m., and that person was detained by the police as the driver of a vehicle at 11:25 p.m., what would this person's blood-alcohol level be at the time of driving?

It is relatively easy for the trier of fact to determine how much of the information contained in the hypothetical question is based on evidence presented to the court. The trier of fact will weigh the evidentiary foundation of the opinion before ultimately deciding the degree, if any, to which the opinion is accepted.

2. Hearsay

Sometimes, the foundation of an expert's evidence is based on hearsay evidence. Experts may testify in innumerable areas of specialized or scientific endeavour. In preparing a report to be used in litigation, an expert will often obtain information from sources that are not presented in evidence by either side in the litigation. The expert has thus relied on information that is not before the trier of fact. This can be problematic for the trier of fact, who is usually faced with two different expert opinions on the same topic and must evaluate which opinion deserves more weight. If the opinions are based solely on the evidence that is before the trier of fact, then the trier of fact simply weighs the evidence presented by the two experts and determines which opinion is more persuasive.

Where an expert has conducted an interview with a person who does not testify in court or where, for example, a psychologist has spoken with an accused who does not testify, then the expert's opinion must be influenced to a degree by this inadmissible hearsay evidence. To safeguard the trier of fact from being unduly and indirectly influenced by inadmissible hearsay evidence, the courts have developed a rule that the expert's evidence is to be discounted according to the degree to which the inadmissible hearsay evidence has influenced the expert's opinion. In order for the expert's opinion to be given any weight, there must be some admissible evidence that goes to the foundation of the expert's opinion. The more the expert relies on hearsay evidence, the less weight the evidence can be given. Where the expert opinion is based mainly on inadmissible hearsay evidence, the trial judge may in fact instruct the trier of fact to give it no weight at all (see *R v Lavallee*, [1990] 1 SCR 852).

3. *Ultimate Issue Opinions*

Historically, no expert witness, or any other witness, could express an **ultimate issue opinion**—that is, an opinion on the ultimate issue that is before the trier of fact. Here are some examples:

> "He can't be criminally responsible, because he was obviously suffering from a mental disorder at the time of the offence."
> "They must have known that dumping those chemicals would kill the fish."
> "The plaintiff caused the accident and now he's trying to rip off the system."
> "The building collapsed because the contractor used shoddy materials."

The reason the courts did not permit this type of evidence is that the trier of fact is charged with the responsibility of drawing conclusions based on the facts. If the trier of fact is exposed to opinions on the ultimate issue between the parties, it may be swayed by those opinions and not decide the issues on the basis of the admissible evidence. This can occur when the expert witness is persuasive, when the trier of fact is lazy, or when the matter is so confusing to the trier of fact that a clearly stated opinion on these issues is welcomed. In other words, by having witnesses express their own opinions on the ultimate issues, they are usurping the role of the trier of fact.

The Supreme Court of Canada has made clear that the common law rule prohibiting expert evidence on the ultimate issue no longer applies in Canada (see *R v Burns*, [1994] 1 SCR 656 at para 25). Experts may now express opinions on the ultimate issue where such evidence will be of assistance to the trier of fact. It is still not, however, appropriate for the witness to say, "He's as guilty as hell." That is clearly for the trier of fact to determine. But the expert witness may say, "In my opinion, Mr. Abbey was suffering from a mental disorder at the time that he killed his wife." This is an opinion that will assist the trier of fact in determining the accused's criminal responsibility for the offence with which he is charged.

If the expert's evidence begins to drift into areas normally reserved for the trier of fact, it should be assessed with special scrutiny, and less weight will likely be placed on it. The witness may be permitted to continue his testimony, but the judge will try to steer him away from stating any opinions on the issues or questions reserved for the trier of fact, and any that slip through are likely to be given very little, if any, weight.

ultimate issue opinion opinion on the ultimate issue that is before the trier of fact; generally, witnesses are not permitted to give an ultimate issue opinion because the trier of fact could be swayed by it

Expert Evidence on the Ultimate Issue

Hartley v Cunningham et al, 2013 ONSC 2929

This case, a 2013 decision of the Ontario Superior Court of Justice, concerned a dispute between two neighbours about the location of a tree. The issue was whether the applicant required the consent of her neighbours to remove the tree. The applicant sought a declaration that the tree was situated on her property and that she owned the tree, arguing that the trunk of the tree was entirely on her property where it emerged from the ground.

The respondents countered that the tree straddled the property line between their property and the applicant's. The respondents based their argument on the opinion of several experts, whose evidence was that consideration must also be given to the root ball and canopy of a tree to determine where it was situated:

> Mr. Radecki, one of the respondents' experts, provided evidence in this matter. He explained that the applicant's position that tree trunk position should be measured at ground soil level is arbitrary and although some municipalities use that measurement location for their purposes and while he is aware of competing definitions of boundary trees, he rejects them as inconsistent with the conventional wisdom. He stated, and I accept his reasoning, that: a great deal of caution must be exercised when measuring trees at ground level. This is because establishing the base of the tree is often difficult and controversial. The base of the tree contains the root flare which may be broader than the trunk itself and the trunk of the tree at ground level is

ambiguous and not necessarily a useful measure of where the tree trunk transfers into the root system (the true base of the tree).

While Moore J found the opinions of the experts helpful to better understand the anatomy and development of a growing tree, he did not rely on their opinions to the extent that they might appear to address the ultimate issue of the interpretation of the meaning of the relevant legislation. To address that issue, the court examined the history of the legislation and the common-sense and dictionary meanings of "trunk":

> In my view, the meaning of the words in section 10(2) is clear. It includes within the ambit of the meaning of a tree trunk growing on a boundary line the entire trunk from its point of growth away from its roots up to its top where it branches out to limbs and foliage. In any event, it is not only the arbitrary point at which the trunk emerges from the soil that governs.
>
> I accept the respondents' evidence and submissions that to interpret the legislation otherwise may lead to anomalous results where a property owner chooses to add soil or other materials to the base of the tree to artificially raise the soil up and away from the roots, perhaps to a portion of the trunk, not on the boundary line.

Moore J ultimately found that the tree was a boundary tree and could not be removed by the applicant without the consent of the respondents.

4. Rule Against Oath Helping

The rule against oath helping holds that evidence adduced solely for the purpose of proving that a witness is truthful is inadmissible.

When one witness enhances the evidence of another by approving of him or commenting favourably on his credibility, the witness has engaged in the prohibited practice of oath helping. The following is an example: "My good friend, Dr. Freud, who testified earlier, is the most prominent and respected psychoanalyst in the field." The rule against oath helping holds that evidence adduced solely for the purpose of proving that a witness is truthful is inadmissible. In the view of the courts, a witness should have her testimony evaluated on its own without the need for another witness bolstering that testimony. Statements such as these hinder the trier of fact and raise a number of concerns. Would the trier of fact then be weighing the expert witness's credibility, or would the trier of fact be swayed by the oath helper's opinion that the expert witness is the salt of the earth? Would the trial be distracted if a battle of the supporting witnesses were to ensue? Would the trier of fact defer to the opinion of the expert who is the most highly spoken of by the other witnesses, thus determining the dispute on the basis of the expert's popularity rather than the facts relating to the dispute that were before the trier of fact?

There is, however, an exception to the rule against oath helping. In certain situations, it is permissible to lead evidence from expert witnesses that is general in nature where the evidence provides information to the trier of fact that will assist it in evaluating the general credibility of certain types of witnesses. For example, where there are allegations of sexual abuse against family members, and a child complainant testifies to the abuse before the trial begins, it is quite common for the child complainant to retract her allegations between the time of her testimony and the trial. She may do so for a number of reasons: Family members may pressure her to withdraw the allegation for fear that the family breadwinner will be jailed; she may have been removed from her home and misses her siblings and parents; the family may have been thrown into chaos with the revelations of abuse and she may decide that things were better off for everyone before the disclosure; or family members may deny that the abuse occurred and she may become confused and uncertain about what, if anything, did happen. The trier of fact will ultimately have to evaluate the validity of the initial allegation and will have to decide what to do with the fact of the retraction. This is where expert evidence comes in.

An expert can testify that such retractions are quite common in situations of familial sexual abuse, although the expert must not specifically comment on whether any particular witness is telling the truth in her testimony. Thus, the trier of fact will be able to put the retraction in context—it may be a valid retraction or it may be a manifestation of the factors mentioned above. At least the trier of fact will not feel compelled to treat the retraction as conclusive on the issue of whether or not the abuse took place. It becomes one factor to consider among all the other admissible evidence.

CASE IN POINT

Oath Helping

R v Bernardo (2000), 48 OR (3d) 135 (CA)

Notorious serial killer Paul Bernardo appealed his first-degree murder convictions in the deaths of Leslie Mahaffy and Kristen French in part on the basis that the evidence of two experts called by the Crown amounted to oath helping. At trial, Bernardo maintained that it was his wife, Karla Homolka, who alone was the murderer and that he was guilty only of manslaughter. As part of the Crown's case, two experts gave evidence to explain battered woman syndrome and the associated post-traumatic stress disorder to assist the jury in assessing Homolka's evidence and to help them decide who killed the two victims. The trial judge did not, however,

permit the experts to offer an opinion on whether Homolka suffered from this syndrome. The Ontario Court of Appeal, in dismissing Bernardo's appeal, found that the evidence did not amount to oath helping (at para 17):

> The battered woman syndrome is a recognized psychiatric condition and expert evidence explaining this syndrome has been admitted by many courts since the decision of the Supreme Court of Canada in *R v Lavallee* … . The expert evidence in this case would have helped the jury to determine whether there was an explanation for what might be regarded by the

average person as conduct by Homolka that was inconsistent with that of a truthful witness. The syndrome explained how some people react to certain experiences. The jury would have had the benefit of this explanation, among a host of other relevant considerations, in assessing Homolka's credibility.

The court recognized that the evidence may very well have the effect of bolstering Homolka's credibility if the jury accepted the validity of this syndrome and that Homolka suffered from it, but that alone did not make the evidence inadmissible. The evidence was relevant not because it amounted to an opinion on whether Homolka was telling the truth, but because it might explain her behaviour.

5. Novel Science

New and emerging scientific endeavours may become relevant in a dispute. Because the judge is charged with the task of determining what information will be admitted on the basis of whether it will help or hinder the trier of fact, she will have to determine whether to accept expert evidence in new and somewhat untested sciences. In her role as gatekeeper, the judge must give special scrutiny to the proposed evidence so that the trier of fact is not subjected to unreliable evidence cloaked in the mystique of science. Expert evidence is routinely admitted in proven scientific areas. Fingerprint experts testify about whether a print lifted from a crime scene matches the accused's and inform the jury regarding the uniqueness of a person's fingerprints. Even with this well-established science, there is some dispute about how many matching characteristics are required before the expert can confirm a match. Where fingerprint experts testify on both sides of an issue, the trier of fact will have to determine which expert to give more weight to.

DNA Evidence

DNA evidence was first admitted into evidence in England in the late 1980s and has since exploded in use and popularity all over the world. It has been responsible for the location and conviction of numerous violent offenders and, equally important, for the exoneration of many wrongfully convicted persons.

Although DNA evidence has found a significant place in police work and is routinely accepted as expert evidence in courts of law, some controversy continues about how definitive the results are. Some proponents put the probability of wrongful identification in the range of one in several billion, while critics point out that within certain more isolated communities where marriages between close relatives are common, the certainty plummets to one in 100,000. To put this statistic into perspective, if the real certainty of a mismatch is one in 100,000, this means that in a country the size of Canada there are potentially more than 300 other people who would also be matches. This and other factors, such as improper handling and collection, contamination, and shoddy lab work, will influence the ability of scientists to make definitive statements about the certainty of a match. Clearly, DNA evidence has been shown to be helpful to triers of fact, but the courts are mindful of its limitations when DNA evidence is presented in the course of expert testimony.

The Supreme Court of Canada dealt with the issue of the admissibility of novel science in *R v J-LJ* (2000 SCC 51, [2000] 2 SCR 600). This was a case where the accused sought to lead expert evidence to address his contention that the sexual offences he was charged with were performed by a particular type of sexual deviant and that he did not demonstrate those deviant sexual characteristics. The psychologist he wished to have testify was a pioneer in Canada of a device known as the penile plethysmograph. This device measures changes in the flow of blood to or circumference of the penis in response to the subject's being presented with visual stimuli—for example, pictures of a child in a sexual context. If the subject reacts to such stimuli, then the theory is that his true sexual interests are revealed notwithstanding his protestations to the contrary.

In commenting favourably about the factors that would be helpful in evaluating the soundness of novel science, the Supreme Court referred to the US case of *Daubert v Merrell Dow Pharmaceuticals, Inc* (509 US 579 (1993)). In *Daubert*, the US Supreme Court identified four factors to consider in evaluating a novel theory or technique (at paras 593-94):

(1) whether the theory or technique can be and has been tested:

> Scientific methodology today is based on generating hypotheses and testing them to see if they can be falsified; indeed, this methodology is what distinguishes science from other fields of human inquiry.

(2) whether the theory or technique has been subjected to peer review and publication:

> [S]ubmission to the scrutiny of the scientific community is a component of "good science," in part because it increases the likelihood that substantive flaws in methodology will be detected.

(3) the known or potential rate of error or the existence of standards; and,

(4) whether the theory or technique used has been generally accepted:

> A "reliability assessment does not require, although it does permit, explicit identification of a relevant scientific community and an express determination of a particular degree of acceptance within that community." …
>
> Widespread acceptance can be an important factor in ruling particular evidence admissible, and "a known technique which has been able to attract only minimal support within the community," … may properly be viewed with skepticism.

In commenting on this last factor, the Supreme Court of Canada concluded (*R v J-LJ* at para 34):

> Thus, in the United States, as here, "general acceptance" is only one of several factors to be considered. A penile plethysmograph may not yet be generally accepted as a forensic tool, but it may become so. A case-by-case evaluation of novel science is necessary in light of the changing nature of our scientific knowledge: it was once accepted by the highest authorities of the western world that the earth was flat.

In assessing whether the special scrutiny test outlined by Sopinka J in *Mohan* was met, the Supreme Court analyzed the matter as follows (*R v J-LJ* at para 35):

> The penile plethysmograph, as noted by Fish JA, is *generally recognized by the scientific community* and is used by psychiatric facilities such as the Institut Philippe Pinel de Montréal to monitor the result of treatment for sexual pathologies. The plethysmograph enables the medical staff to assess the progress of therapy of known and admitted sexual deviants. This is inapplicable to the respondent. He denies he is part of such a group. He is not undergoing therapy. *Dr. Beltrami is a pioneer in Canada in trying to use this therapeutic tool as a forensic tool where the problems are firstly to determine whether the offence could only be committed by a perpetrator who possesses distinctive and identifiable psychological traits, secondly to determine whether a "standard profile" of those traits has been developed, and thirdly to match the accused against the profile.* Dr. Beltrami's evidence is therefore subject to "special scrutiny." While the techniques he employed are not novel, he is using them for a novel purpose. *A level of reliability that is quite useful in therapy because it yields some information about a course of treatment is not necessarily sufficiently reliable to be used in a court of law to identify or exclude the accused as a potential perpetrator of an offence.* In fact, penile plethysmography has received a mixed reception in Quebec courts. … Efforts to use penile plethysmography in the United States as proof of disposition have largely been rejected … . [Emphasis added.]

Another factor that was very important in this particular case was that, by Dr. Beltrami's admission, the penile plethysmograph detected a sexual deviant only 47.5 percent of the time. In other words, in a population of sexual deviants, the plethysmograph worked in detecting the deviant less than half of the time. This level of reliability did not impress the Supreme Court. This case provides an excellent example of how courts will go about the process of assessing novel science using the special scrutiny test.

CASE IN POINT

Post-Hypnosis Evidence

R v Trochym, 2007 SCC 6, [2007] 1 SCR 239

The Supreme Court of Canada affirmed this approach to novel science in *R v Trochym*, where the issue was the admissibility of post-hypnosis evidence. Stephen Trochym was charged with second-degree murder in the death of his girlfriend. Forensic evidence established that the victim had been killed early on Wednesday, October 14, 1992 but that her body had been repositioned some 8 to 12 hours later to make it look like the murder had been sexually motivated. The theory of the Crown's case was that the killer had returned to the scene sometime later the same day to cover his trail. A neighbour spoke to the police a few days after the murder and told them that she had seen the accused leaving the victim's apartment on Thursday, October 15, 1992. This evidence did not place the accused at the scene when the body of the victim had been repositioned.

The police asked the neighbour to undergo hypnosis to improve her memory. The neighbour agreed and during the session remembered seeing Trochym leave the apartment at 3:00 p.m. on the day of her daughter's piano lesson, which was the Wednesday in question. The neighbour subsequently adopted these memories in her testimony. This evidence placed Trochym at the scene during the time the body had been repositioned, and he was subsequently convicted of second-degree murder. The accused appealed his conviction to the Supreme Court of Canada.

In evaluating the effects of hypnosis on memory, Deschamps J for the majority wrote (at para 40):

There is a general consensus that most individuals are more suggestible under hypnosis, that any increase in accurate memories during hypnosis is accompanied by an increase in *inaccurate* memories, that hypnosis may compromise the subject's ability to distinguish memory from imagination, and that subjects frequently report being more certain of the content of post-hypnosis memories, regardless of their accuracy. In sum, while it is not generally accepted that hypnosis *always*

produces unreliable memories, neither is it clear when hypnosis results in *pseudo-memories* or how a witness, scientist or trier of fact might distinguish between fabricated and accurate memories.

The majority of the court viewed this evidence as novel science and was not satisfied that the post-hypnosis evidence met the four criteria identified in *R v J-LJ*. In the result, Trochym's appeal was allowed and a new trial was ordered.

Criteria for the Admission of Novel Science

In order to be admissible, the novel science must meet the following criteria:

1. *It must be essential.* The trier of fact cannot come to a satisfactory conclusion without this aid.

2. *It must withstand special scrutiny.* The reliability of the science must be established because the scientific community has not generally accepted it yet.

3. *It must satisfy even stricter necessity and reliability requirements* where it approaches the ultimate issue in the matter.

6. Junk Science

This chapter has emphasized that there are risks associated with placing too much reliance on science and the evidence of experts. Still, even with all of the safeguards that the courts have adopted to protect the integrity of the trial process, wrongful convictions happen all too frequently. There are several reasons that people are convicted of crimes they have not committed. Historically, wrongful convictions were chiefly attributable to eyewitness misidentification, bad legal representation, false confessions, the use of unreliable informants, and government misconduct. Over the past few decades, however, a troublesome new cause has emerged—convictions that are based primarily on faulty science. The sheer volume of wrongful convictions and judicial findings in the United States from the use of questionable scientific methodology has resulted in this dubious evidence being commonly referred to as "junk science."

Junk science is not new, nor is it entirely worthless. Modern chemistry traces its roots to the alchemists who spent centuries searching for the "elixir of life" and a way to turn base metals into gold. However, it is one thing to venture on an unknown scientific voyage and quite a different matter to base a conviction in a murder case on bad science. Unfortunately, the latter has happened too frequently.

DNA evidence has been used to help convict the guilty and exonerate the innocent since the late 1980s. In the United States, about half of the original convictions in DNA exoneration cases involved unvalidated or improper forensic science[2] such as hair microscopy, bite mark comparisons, firearm tool mark analysis, shoeprint comparisons, and improperly conducted serology, commonly known as blood typing. These techniques are now known to be unreliable and inaccurate.

It is therefore understandable that the Supreme Court of Canada rejected the post-hypnosis evidence of a witness that placed the accused at the scene of the murder on the date in issue. What may be surprising to some is that the trial judge initially admitted this evidence and that the Ontario Court of Appeal affirmed the conviction. Even the Supreme Court was split, with three justices ultimately dissenting from the outcome in *Trochym*. The point made is that while it may be easy to be critical of flawed science, especially after the fact, it is much more difficult for a judge to perform the gatekeeper function when assessing whether the evidence is "sufficiently beneficial to the trial process to warrant its admission despite the potential harm to the trial process that may flow from the admission of the expert evidence" (see *R v Abbey* at para 76).

POLYGRAPH EVIDENCE: TRUTH OR FICTION?

Polygraphs of one sort or another have been in use since 1924. Police forces across the world use polygraphs as an investigative tool to assist them in narrowing their list of suspects and in extracting confessions. In most violent offences, the perpetrator is someone close to the victim. Thus, if six close friends and family take the polygraph test and five pass according to the technician, the police will focus their efforts on the remaining person. Canadian courts, however, have treated polygraph evidence with suspicion. They have not been prepared to take the leap of faith that the police forces have and have not accepted polygraph evidence in courts of law.

The courts have perceived a great danger in the admission of evidence from a device that is commonly referred to as a "lie detector." If the trier of fact hears that an accused failed the lie detector test, then the trier of fact may conclude that the accused is lying and convict the individual on this basis. The danger is that the trier of fact will take this information as absolute and abandon its task of weighing all the evidence for and against the accused. What the polygraph does is measure a number of physiological responses in the subject. The responses are correlated to the questions being asked and graphed to determine whether there is a relation between false responses and the graph. Ideally, a certain pattern on the graph that is the same pattern that resulted from responses when the subject is known to have lied would appear when other questions are being asked. This pattern, then, points to further lies. Typically, the polygraph plots at least three physiological responses: blood pressure, pulse, and respiration.

Polygraphs may also test muscular movement and the electrical conductivity of the skin, which is reduced if the subject perspires. Critics of the polygraph point out that emotional stress generated by the test itself can cause heightened blood pressure, pulse rate, and respiration, as well as changes in the electrical conductivity of the skin. They also point out that a pathological liar would not react to the questions in the manner that a "normal" person would, thus eliminating the validity of the test for this group.

Polygraph evidence has not found general approval or acceptance by the scientific community, and an argument for the admissibility of such evidence must be determined having regard to the principles of novel science. It may very well be that polygraph testing will evolve and become much more reliable at some future time. Even if it does, it is unclear whether the courts would ever be prepared to admit polygraph evidence to help the trier of fact make findings of fact or credibility.

7. *Expert Evidence Amok*

Sometimes we become too comfortable with our science. The courts have also found comfort with specific sciences. For example, DNA evidence is now routinely admitted. But DNA evidence did not exist 50 years ago and was once itself a novel science. Most people will agree that the emergence of DNA evidence has proven to be invaluable in the administration of justice. But that is not always true of science, even science that has gained near-universal acceptance.

Dr. Charles Smith was once considered a leader in the field of child forensic pathology. For 24 years—from 1982 to 2003—he was head pediatric forensic pathologist at Toronto's Hospital for Sick Children. Dr. Smith performed over 1,000 child autopsies and, in the case of suspicious or sudden deaths, often had to determine whether the infant died from a fall or as a result of being shaken violently, commonly referred to as "shaken baby syndrome." As a result of Dr. Smith's findings, dozens of parents were charged with causing the deaths of their children. The cases against these parents were built almost entirely around Dr. Smith's findings, and his evidence was regularly accepted by the courts. We now know that he was wrong far too often.

Concerns about Dr. Smith's competence first arose in 1991 in a case where a 12-year-old babysitter was charged in the death of a 16-month-old infant. The trial judge was highly critical of Dr. Smith's methodology and conclusions. Over the next decade, there were other warning signs about Dr. Smith's competence and professionalism, but his reputation as a leading expert in the field continued to grow. Eventually, the warning signs could no longer be ignored, and in 2005, an Ontario coroner's inquiry reviewed 45 of Dr. Smith's autopsies that had resulted in a finding that the cause of death was either homicide or criminally suspicious. The review found that Dr. Smith had erred in 20 of these cases, 12 of which resulted in convictions. This discovery prompted the Ontario government to order a full public inquiry into Dr. Smith's practice. The Honourable Stephen T. Goudge was appointed commissioner of the Inquiry into Pediatric Forensic Pathology in Ontario.

On October 1, 2008, the commissioner released a comprehensive four-volume report that made sweeping recommendations, including several concerning the role that courts play in admitting and relying on expert evidence. The commissioner cautioned that judges bear a heavy burden as the ultimate gatekeepers in protecting our judicial system from unreliable expert evidence that, in the case of Dr. Smith, contributed to miscarriages of justice. The report sets out a number of specific recommendations to assist judges in performing this task.[3] The following recommendation (at 487) addresses how judges should assess expert evidence before admitting it at trial:

> A concern about the reliability of evidence is a fundamental component of the law of evidence. Threshold reliability plays an important role in determining whether proposed expert evidence is admissible under the *Mohan* test. Reliability can be an important consideration in determining whether the proposed expert evidence is relevant and necessary: whether it is excluded under any exclusionary rule, including the rule that requires evidence to be excluded if its prejudicial effect exceeds its probative value and whether the expert is properly qualified. Trial judges should be vigilant in exercising their gatekeeping role with respect to the admissibility of such evidence. In particular, they should ensure that expert scientific evidence that does not satisfy standards of threshold reliability be excluded, whether or not the science is classified as novel.

CHAPTER SUMMARY

The courts are reluctant to permit witnesses to express opinions or come to conclusions based on evidence that is presented in court because this function is reserved for the trier of fact. A lay witness is qualified to testify as to what he actually saw or heard, but is usually in a worse position than the trier of fact to draw conclusions on the facts. Experts are given more leeway, but before expert evidence is admitted, the four criteria of relevance, necessity, qualifications, and the absence of any exclusionary rules must be met. The rationale for permitting expert evidence is that such evidence allows the trier of fact to make better sense of technical matters or those requiring specialized knowledge. However, in light of the inherent dangers of placing too much reliance on the evidence of experts, the courts have placed limitations not only on the admissibility of such evidence, but also on the weight it is given by the trier of fact.

KEY TERMS

compendious mode of expressing facts, 150
expert opinion, 150
layperson's opinion, 149
opinion evidence, 148
ultimate issue opinion, 157

NOTES

1   At the time of writing, Alberta, Nova Scotia, New Brunswick, and Newfoundland and Labrador did not have any provisions in their evidence acts permitting the use of medical or expert reports.

2   See Innocence Project, "Unvalidated or Improper Forensic Science," online: <http://www.innocenceproject.org/causes-wrongful-conviction/unvalidated-or-improper-forensic-science>.

3   The executive summary and the complete report are available online at: <http://www.attorneygeneral.jus.gov.on.ca/inquiries/goudge/report>.

REFERENCES

Abbey, R v, 2009 ONCA 624.

BM, R v, 1998 CanLII 13326 (Ont CA).

Bernardo, R v (2000), 48 OR (3d) 135 (CA).

British Columbia, *Evidence Act*, RSBC 1979, c 116.

Burns, R v, [1994] 1 SCR 656.

Canada, *Canada Evidence Act*, RSC 1985, c C-5.

Canadian Charter of Rights and Freedoms, Part I of the *Constitution Act, 1982*, being Schedule B to the *Canada Act 1982* (UK), 1982, c 11.

Criminal Code, RSC 1985, c C-46.

Daubert v Merrell Dow Pharmaceuticals, Inc, 509 US 579 (1993).

Goudge, Stephen T, *Inquiry into Pediatric Forensic Pathology in Ontario*, online: <http://www.attorneygeneral.jus.gov.on.ca/inquiries/goudge/report>.

Graat v The Queen, [1982] 2 SCR 819.

Hartley v Cunningham et al, 2013 ONSC 2929.

Innocence Project, "Unvalidated or Improper Forensic Science," online: <http://www.innocenceproject.org/causes-wrongful-conviction/unvalidated-or-improper-forensic-science>.

J-LJ, R v, 2000 SCC 51, [2000] 2 SCR 600.

Lavallee, R v, [1990] 1 SCR 852.

Manitoba Evidence Act, RSM 1987, c E150.

Mohan, R v, [1994] 2 SCR 9.

Natsis, R v, 2014 ONCJ 532.

Ontario, *Evidence Act*, RSO 1990, c E.23.

Trochym, R v, 2007 SCC 6, [2007] 1 SCR 239.

REVIEW QUESTIONS

1. Give some examples of novel science and explain how its admissibility would be tested.

2. Explain the reason for the rule against the admissibility of opinion evidence.

3. List the criteria in the *Mohan* test for the admissibility of expert evidence.

4. What is meant by the term "hired gun syndrome"?

DISCUSSION QUESTIONS

Review the following scenarios. For each, discuss whether the testimony is admissible. Why or why not? If the testimony is not admissible, is there any way for the statement to be rephrased so that it would be admissible?

1. Ricardo Thanderys testified, "I knew that the guy did it because he was the only one in the bunch who was shaking."

2. George Jankowski testified, "The car was speeding, maybe 120 kilometres an hour, before it struck the deceased."

3. Baligha Ahmed testified, "I knew the guy was dead because I saw the train hit him."

4. Dr. Hans Everthen, a pathologist, testified, "The victim died of natural causes as a result of a heart attack, not from the blow to his head."

5. Dr. Mary Distu, a toxicologist, testified, "The victim was impaired by the consumption of alcohol and probably attacked the accused first."

6. Rob Dapur, an expert in alienology, testified, "The accused could not have been present when the deceased died because the accused had clear and obvious signs on her body that she had been abducted by aliens at that time."

7. Susan Holgado, a handwriting expert, testified, "The deceased did not write the words 'Kent did it.' The words were written by someone else."

8. Albert Mackay, a highly respected psychiatrist, testified, "The accused could not be guilty of murder because he was clearly and obviously suffering from a mental disorder at the time."

10

Privilege

LEARNING OUTCOMES

After completing this chapter, you should be able to:

- Define privilege.

- Explain the circumstances in which privileged communications are not admissible.

- Demonstrate an understanding that all forms of privilege are subject to a public safety exception.

- Explain the differences between solicitor–client privilege and litigation privilege.

- Discuss the distinction between privilege by class and privilege by case, and identify relationships that may attract privilege on a case-by-case basis.

- Understand and apply Wigmore's four criteria for assessing privilege.

Introduction

We have already seen that not all evidence that is relevant and material is admitted in court. If it were, evidence law would be simple. The courts choose to operate in this manner not to complicate the litigation process unnecessarily, but for the good reason that if the process operated with no exceptions, there would be unfortunate unintended consequences. The legal system must be fair, and wherever fairness comes into play, there is usually a balancing of interests. In some instances, certain communications—for example, letters or conversations—will be kept from the trier of fact. This information is often reliable and probative; it may even contain confessions of guilt or information that would resolve a civil dispute with a high degree of certainty. The reason for excluding such information is based on the balancing of interests—not only those of the parties, but those of society as well.

There are some situations in which another value is seen as more important than the principle of maximizing reliable information placed before the trier of fact. In these cases, the value of preserving the privacy of certain communications is seen as more important than the value of placing reliable and probative information before a judge or a jury.

Privilege Defined

privilege
status accorded communicated information that makes the information unavailable to the trier of fact

The concept of **privilege** is that certain information is off-limits to the litigation process. No matter how relevant and material, the information cannot be available to the trier of fact. Indeed, some privileged information is so valuable that it would determine the outcome of the litigation and easily allow the trier of fact to determine that the right disposition of the litigation had been achieved.

For this reason, judges are hesitant to endorse claims of privilege except in situations where there are clear historical grounds for the claim and where the competing interests are substantial. Privilege can attach to verbal or written communications, and once a judge has determined that the communication is privileged, it cannot be introduced into evidence, no matter how valuable or determinative it may be. In this respect, the judge acts as gatekeeper by shielding the trier of fact from information that it should not hear or see.

privilege by class
privilege based on the relationship between the communicator of information and the recipient

Privilege is generally placed into two categories: privilege by class and privilege by case. **Privilege by class** is based solely on the type of relationship between the communicator and the recipient of the communication. It arises upon the establishment of any class of relationship that has been accorded this privilege. In other words, to invoke the privilege, a party need show the court only that the communication was made within a prescribed class of relationships. After privilege by class is established, all communications within that class are protected, subject only to situations where public safety is endangered. On the other hand, **privilege by case** is determined on a case-by-case basis. It is not primarily dependent on the type of relationship between the person making the communication and the person to whom the communication was made. However, this is not to say that the nature of the relationship is not important. It clearly is, but whether privilege extends to any communication is determined by the court on a case-by-case basis and not by class membership.

privilege by case
privilege extended to communication on a case-by-case basis

It is important to understand that although privilege is an exception to the rule that relevant and material evidence is generally admissible, there are many situations where courts refuse to exclude evidence that appears to attract a claim of privilege. This is done either by applying the privilege exceptions narrowly and thus saying that privilege does not apply to the unique circumstances before the court, or by carving out exceptions to the exception itself.

Public Safety Exception

All forms of privilege are subject to the **public safety exception**. Basically, this means that privilege is overridden when there is a threat to public safety. Although the issue usually arises within the context of the doctor–patient relationship, it can exist elsewhere. For example, if a client confides to his lawyer that he plans to murder his wife, the public safety exception is invoked and the intended victim must be warned. The Canadian case that set the standard is *Smith v Jones* ([1999] 1 SCR 455). In this case, the Supreme Court of Canada laid out clear criteria for the exception to privilege. The duty to warn intended victims exists where

1. the risk is to a clearly identifiable person or group;
2. the risk of harm includes severe bodily injury, death, or serious psychological harm; and
3. the risk is imminent.

("Imminent" means that the nature of the relationship creates a sense of urgency; this requirement does not necessarily impose a time limit on the risk.)

All three elements must be present. Because the standard is high, this exception to privilege is applied infrequently and only to the extent necessary to warn the intended victim or victims of the danger. Furthermore, the exception cannot be used to disclose past acts, only intentions to commit future acts.

public safety exception
an exception to privilege when the otherwise protected communication poses a threat to public safety

Privilege by Class

Because privileged communications are generally not admissible as evidence, and it is the aim of the courts to put as much relevant and material information before the trier of fact as possible, courts and judges take a very narrow or restrictive approach when privilege is claimed by class. If the relationship does not clearly and obviously fall within a prescribed class, the claim will fail. (Keep in mind, however, that if privilege cannot be established by class, it may still be made out in an individual case, as discussed below under the heading "Privilege by Case.") The following are some classes of privilege that have developed over time.

1. Solicitor–Client Privilege

Solicitor–client privilege is one of the oldest and most entrenched forms of privilege. It protects communications between a lawyer and her client. The reason this form of privilege is so universally respected is that it is accepted that a client could

solicitor–client privilege
privilege that protects communications between lawyer and client made for the purpose of obtaining legal advice

not obtain proper legal advice if he were afraid of telling his lawyer the whole truth about the matter. Once the client does reveal the whole truth, the lawyer is in a position to give proper advice. Not only does this serve the best interests of the client, it often translates into great savings of court time and efficiency in the process if an early resolution of the matter is achieved.

There is a distinction between solicitor–client privilege and a lawyer's or legal representative's duty to keep the affairs of a client confidential. Solicitor–client privilege is an evidentiary rule that has evolved over the years into a rule of substantive law, while **confidentiality** is a professional obligation imposed by a regulatory body.

confidentiality
the ethical duty of a law professional not to disclose information related to the representation of a client

One notable feature of solicitor–client privilege is that the privilege belongs to the client and survives his death. Thus, the lawyer is not released from her obligations to keep her client's secrets even after the client dies. This rule exists because the client's interest in privacy can extend beyond his death, as when an action against an individual is pursued through an estate trustee. It is not up to former counsel to determine what would have been or should be waived in terms of their communications with former clients.

Solicitor–client privilege is one major exception to the rule that relevant and material evidence is always admissible. But, as with many areas of evidence law, there are exceptions to the exception. There are a number of situations where communications between a lawyer and someone else are not privileged, or where the law has carved out an exception to the rule that communications between lawyer and client are excluded as evidence, such as the public safety exception. In those instances, the communications can be disclosed to the court.

Not everything that a client says to a lawyer will attract privilege. Even where it is established that the communication was made or received by a client, this fact is not sufficient to establish privilege over disclosure of the communication. To attract privilege, the communication must be confidential and relate to the seeking, forming, or giving of legal advice. So, it is only where a client is communicating with a lawyer in order to get legal advice that the conversation or written communication is protected.

In addition, a client who wishes to claim privilege is responsible for protecting the information. If the client has a loud conversation with his lawyer in a restaurant or at a party, and details of the matter are overheard, the client has let the information out into the public and privilege cannot be restored. The analogy of closing the barn door after the horse has fled applies here. In the view of the courts, the privilege holder has essentially waived his right to rely on privilege by either intentionally or inadvertently publicizing the information. Thus, the concept of privilege is applied to the source of the information—a lawyer's contact with a client—but not the information itself, if it is not properly guarded. Although carelessness may effectively waive privilege, documents that have made their way into other hands by mistake, theft, or trickery will likely maintain their privileged character in Canada. This would apply, for example, in a situation where a privileged email was sent in error to opposing counsel (see *Celanese Canada Inc v Murray Demolition Corp*, 2006 SCC 36, [2006] 2 SCR 189).

Privilege does not attach simply because someone is a lawyer. A lawyer working as the president of a company does not have privilege attach to communications made or received in her capacity as president. (Of course, communications she has as president of the company with the company's lawyers to obtain advice on a legal matter are protected.)

In-House Counsel

Pritchard v Ontario (Human Rights Commission), 2004 SCC 31, [2004] 1 SCR 809

A decision of the Supreme Court of Canada confirms that in-house counsel who provide opinions for administrative tribunals will have those communications protected by solicitor–client privilege. In *Pritchard v Ontario (Human Rights Commission)*, Ms. Pritchard was appealing a decision of the Human Rights Commission not to deal with her complaint that her former employer, Sears Canada, had discriminated against her. Ms. Pritchard wanted to have disclosure of a legal opinion provided to the commission by in-house counsel on the issue whether her claim ought to be dismissed as a bad-faith application because she had signed a release against Sears Canada dealing with these same complaints.

The court treated the situation the same as with corporate in-house counsel or in-house counsel for a government department dealing with litigation against it. In the appeal, the court found that the Human Rights Commission was a party to the proceedings before the court and thus in no different position from any other litigant. It therefore ruled that the "communication between the Human Rights Commission and its in-house counsel is protected by solicitor–client privilege."

Often in legal matters, a strict application of legal principles by a judge would result in an absurdity. Fortunately, common sense usually prevails. Such is the case where communications between a solicitor and a client are criminal in themselves. These conversations are not protected. An example would be the case where a lawyer is involved in a criminal conspiracy, as has happened on occasion where lawyers have been involved in drug-conspiracy or money-laundering schemes. Lawyers are also not ethically permitted to advise clients on how to commit crimes so that clients can get away with criminal acts. For example, advice to a client on how to circumvent money-laundering laws would not be protected by privilege.

Solicitor–Client Privilege

Communications between a solicitor and client that

1. are of a confidential nature,
2. relate to the seeking, forming, or giving of legal advice, and
3. are not criminal in themselves and do not facilitate criminal activity

are privileged, *except*

    a. where they are necessary to establish the innocence of an accused person *or*

    b. where public safety is at risk.

There is a distinction to be made, however, between past and future crimes. A client can expect his solicitor to keep his communications confidential even where he admits to horrendous past crimes. Unless and until the client indicates he will go out and harm another person or group of persons *in the future*, his communication cannot be disclosed by the lawyer. However, any acknowledgment of past offences remains privileged. As well, telling a lawyer about future non-violent crimes will not trigger the public safety exception, and the communication will continue to attract protection from disclosure. Where, however, the lawyer has received information that public safety is at risk, the duty to warn intended victims set out in *Smith v Jones* applies. The lawyer must then take whatever steps she can to protect the person or group exposed to the threat. Usually this means calling the police. However, the lawyer may reveal only as much confidential information as is necessary to protect the threatened party.

Exception to Solicitor–Client Privilege Where the Innocence of an Accused Is at Stake

An accused may seek to have third-party communications between a solicitor and her client admitted in order to help establish his innocence. This exception to solicitor–client privilege is referred to as **innocence at stake** and is consistent with the accused's right to make full answer and defence, as afforded by section 7 of the *Canadian Charter of Rights and Freedoms*. The exception also reflects the view of the court that an accused cannot be seen to defend himself properly where a lawyer, an officer of the court, withholds information that could clear him.

However, the innocence at stake exception to solicitor–client privilege is applied narrowly by the courts because of the deference given to protecting these communications. It is clear from *R v McClure* (2001 SCC 14, [2001] 1 SCR 445) that before the courts will even consider the exception, an initial threshold must be met whereby "the accused must establish that the information he is seeking in the solicitor-client file is not available from any other source and he is otherwise unable to raise a reasonable doubt as to his guilt in any other way" (at para 48).

What this means is that the courts will not consider an innocence at stake exception if the accused is able to raise a reasonable doubt without violating solicitor–client privilege. In other words, the innocence at stake exception is not open if other evidence is available to the accused that would raise a reasonable doubt. This is in keeping with the purpose of the exception, which is to prevent wrongful convictions, not to permit the accused to mount a more complete defence.

Some commentators have argued that the initial threshold set out in *McClure* is too stringent. In order to pass the threshold, the accused must demonstrate an inability to raise a reasonable doubt otherwise. This is essentially an acknowledgment that the accused has a weak defence. How can an accused later put forth a credible defence if the *McClure* test is not met?

If the accused is able to meet this initial threshold, there follows a two-part test, as set out in *McClure*. The accused must first clear a less stringent hurdle—establish that communications exist that could raise a reasonable doubt. If this test is met, the judge must then look at the solicitor–client communications in order to decide whether they are likely to raise a reasonable doubt. All of the above must be shown by the accused on a balance of probabilities.

If the accused is successful, the judge orders that only those communications that are necessary to establish the accused's innocence be admitted into evidence. (Note: If those communications in fact establish that another person committed the crime that the accused is charged with, the communications will not be made available to the Crown in a subsequent trial against that other person. They continue to be

innocence at stake exception

an exception to solicitor–client privilege when the otherwise protected communication is necessary to establish a person's innocence

protected in relation to that person by solicitor–client privilege, and that person is not taken to have waived that privilege.)

One thing to remember is that throughout this whole process, the accused is "shooting in the dark"—he will likely have some reason to suspect that this information will assist him, but he will not know for sure. If he did have positive proof, then the privilege would likely have already been waived by the other party. Let's say Winston is asked to hold a briefcase for a friend. It turns out that the briefcase was stolen in a particularly violent robbery, and the police find the briefcase when conducting a lawful drug search of Winston's apartment. Winston ends up being charged for the robbery, but before he can convince his friend to testify that he was the one who committed the robbery, the friend dies. This friend has a criminal lawyer with whom he has been dealing. Winston surmises that the friend would have told his criminal lawyer about his involvement in the robbery, so Winston wants the lawyer to tell the court about the friend's involvement. We know that the friend cannot waive the solicitor–client privilege—he is dead—so Winston would have to rely on the innocence at stake provisions and convince the judge that the lawyer has evidence that would assist his case and that he would otherwise likely be convicted. Note, though, that Winston is focusing his energy on trying to convince a judge that he will likely be convicted without this evidence when there is no guarantee that the evidence will be admitted.

Innocence at Stake Test

1. Threshold
   a. The accused must establish that there is no other source for the exonerating information.
   b. The accused must establish that he would otherwise be unable to raise a reasonable doubt.
2. Two-Part Test
   a. The accused must establish that communications exist that *could* raise a reasonable doubt regarding his guilt.
   b. If the accused establishes that such communications exist, then the judge will examine them to determine whether they are *likely* to raise a reasonable doubt.

2. Litigation Privilege

Similar to solicitor–client privilege, **litigation privilege** is a concept that has developed to facilitate a smoothly functioning legal system. This class of privilege applies to communications between a client's lawyer and third parties, provided that the litigation was commenced or anticipated at the time of the communications and that the dominant purpose of the communications was to obtain information for the litigation. In the case of an unrepresented litigant, the privilege covers communications between the litigant and the third party (see *Blank v Canada (Minister of Justice)*, 2006 SCC 39, [2006] 2 SCR 319). This group is usually composed of persons

litigation privilege
privilege that protects communications between a client's lawyer or law firm and third parties

who provide expert opinions on some aspect of the litigation, which the lawyer then uses to formulate legal advice to the client. The reports containing the expert opinions may be released to the other side, in which case privilege no longer attaches, but if they are kept secret, they are protected from disclosure. The reason for this rule is that, with the increasingly complex litigation today, no lawyer is in a position to properly advise all clients at all times without the assistance of third parties. If clients were afraid to obtain this information for fear that opposing counsel would use the information against them, that would undermine the parties' ability to pursue legal remedies and, almost as importantly, would limit the lawyer's or law firm's ability to achieve a settlement without the need for a trial.

Although litigation privilege does remove some relevant information from review by the trier of fact, it is information that might not exist at all without the rule, and it is greatly beneficial to all parties to have such a provision in place. There are a few distinctions between litigation privilege and solicitor–client privilege that are worth noting. Litigation privilege can be claimed only if the information was requested because of or in contemplation of litigation. This is not the case with solicitor–client communications. These must be in relation to obtaining legal advice, but litigation need not be involved. As well, litigation privilege is not restricted to communications between a lawyer and client. Third-party communications gathered for the purpose of litigation are more broadly protected than third-party solicitor–client communications where the third party is an agent of the lawyer, such as a translator or a psychiatrist.

Litigation Privilege

1. Applies to communications between a lawyer or law firm and third parties.
2. Litigation must have been commenced or anticipated at the time of communication.
3. The dominant purpose of the communication is to assist in the litigation.

Another interesting difference between litigation privilege and solicitor–client privilege is that solicitor–client privilege lasts forever. Litigation privilege dies with the litigation because, after the litigation has ended, there is no longer an interest to protect. Unlike solicitor–client privilege, litigation privilege "is neither absolute in scope nor permanent in duration" (see *Blank v Canada (Minister of Justice)* at para 37). Finally, litigation privilege may be more easily overridden than solicitor–client privilege on the basis of fairness or process arguments. The rationale of litigation privilege is to facilitate the litigation process rather than to protect the solicitor–client relationship. The Ontario Court of Appeal in *General Accident Assurance Company v Chrusz* (1999 CanLII 7320 (Ont CA)) stated that "litigation privilege is being defined by the rules as they are amended from time to time." The rules provide for disclosure of privileged documents to ensure a fair trial.

Comparison of Solicitor–Client Privilege and Litigation Privilege

A comparison of solicitor–client privilege and litigation privilege is provided in the chart below.

Solicitor–Client Privilege	Litigation Privilege
Protects confidential communications between lawyer and client.	Communications need not be made in confidence, just in the process of litigation.
Applies to communications made in order to obtain legal advice.	Applies only to communications made in the context of litigation and is not applicable to post-litigation communications.
Does not expire with the end of the relationship or the death of the client or lawyer.	Exists only during the subsistence of the litigation.
Great deference is given to solicitor–client communications, so solicitor–client privilege is not easily overridden.	More easily overridden on the basis of fairness or process arguments.
Third-party communications are protected where the third party is an agent of the lawyer such as a translator, or a psychiatrist examining the client for the lawyer.	Third-party communications are much more broadly protected where information is being gathered for the purpose of assisting the lawyer with anticipated or ongoing litigation.

A good example of how the question of admissibility arises is an accident involving a railroad authority. The authority always investigates accidents and produces an occurrence report. If the authority is sued, the report may assist its counsel in litigation. If it is simply a safety report, then it is discoverable, but if its dominant purpose was in contemplation of litigation, then it is not discoverable. However, because these reports are routinely produced for every accident, the courts have been wary of excluding them when litigation privilege is asserted. The reasoning is that these authorities cannot be expected to be sued for every accident, regardless of severity or fault, and therefore the reports do not meet the requirement of having been requested in contemplation of litigation.

3. Settlement Negotiations

Settlement negotiations enjoy a form of privilege that serves an important purpose in litigation. This class of privilege protects both sides from having sensitive information about settlement discussions revealed to the court. Settlement privilege by its nature implies that the information has been revealed to the other side, usually in the form of settlement discussions, a letter, or an offer to settle. This information is not provided to the judge, specifically so that each side can explore settlement without fearing that it is raising or lowering its bottom line in court with each concession that it makes. Thus, these negotiations are **without prejudice**—that is, none of the discussions, offers, or compromises may be used in subsequent court proceedings.

without prejudice protection claimed for information provided by a party that prevents the information from being used in court

The purpose of settlement privilege is to facilitate settlement. Parties would not make offers or compromise their positions if these acts could be used against them to prove liability or guilt. The privilege wraps a cloak of inadmissibility around the efforts that the parties make to resolve their differences. What is said in settlement discussions will be more open and therefore more fruitful when the parties know that the discussions are completely "off the record." While in most cases it is in the best interests of the parties to settle their dispute without incurring further legal costs, there is also an overriding public interest in favour of settlement. The wheels of justice would soon grind to a stop if every case went to trial. The courts have long recognized the value of this form of privilege and protect genuine efforts to settle from being used against a litigant.

Settlement Privilege

The test for determining whether settlement privilege exists has three steps:

1. There must be actual or contemplated litigation.
2. The communication must be intended to be confidential.
3. The purpose of the communication must be an attempt to effect settlement of some or all of the issues in the dispute.

CASE IN POINT

Settlement Privilege in Canada

Sable Offshore Energy Inc v Ameron International Corp, 2013 SCC 37, [2013] 2 SCR 623

The leading case on settlement privilege in Canada is the 2013 Supreme Court of Canada decision in *Sable Offshore Energy Inc v Ameron International Corp*. In that case, the plaintiff sued several defendants and settled with some, but not all of them. This permitted the settling defendants to withdraw from the litigation.[1] The issue was whether the non-settling defendants would be entitled to disclosure of the amounts of the settlement. In unanimously rejecting the arguments of the non-settling defendants, the court made the following five key points:

1. **Substance triumphs over form.** Courts will look at the substance of the communication instead of how it is categorized by the parties. Often settlement communications are prefaced by the words "without prejudice." These words by themselves do not operate to magically transform ordinary correspondence into a *bona fide* attempt to resolve some or all of the issues in dispute. The court will look at the content of the communication to determine whether the communication is privileged.

Conversely, a communication may be privileged when those words do not appear. The test is whether the communications were made in confidence with the intention to resolve any matters in dispute (para 14).

2. **Settlement privilege exists in both civil and criminal matters.** The privilege protects communications intended to resolve civil, criminal, and quasi-criminal prosecutions (para 16).

3. **Settlement privilege is not dependant upon a successful resolution.** Communications that do not end with a settlement continue to be protected (para 17).

4. **Settlement privilege covers both the communication and the agreement.** This decision clarified some confusion in earlier cases (para 18).

5. **There is an exception to this form of privilege** if a party establishes, on a balance of probabilities, that there is a competing public interest that outweighs the public interest in encouraging settlement (para 19).

One distinction that is important, but is sometimes overlooked, is that although settlement discussions are protected, the common law does not protect admissions of liability unless it is made clear that all settlement discussions are privileged. For example, the statement "I'm sorry, don't worry, I'll pay to have your car repaired" may very well be admissible as an admission of liability. It is therefore advisable for parties to make clear that any settlement discussions are to be privileged, and it is still a good idea to preface any offers with the words "without prejudice," notwithstanding the Supreme Court's decision in *Sable Offshore Energy Inc.*

In Ontario, rule 49 of the *Rules of Civil Procedure* specifically protects formal offers to settle from disclosure to the trial judge for the purpose of establishing liability. However, the rule allows disclosure after judgment when dealing with the issue of costs. Other provinces have similar rules. The idea is that while a judge cannot hear any offers when dealing with the question of liability and damages, she can look at offers made by a party when addressing the issue of costs. A litigant who made a reasonable offer is normally rewarded by an award of costs. Of course, this means that the party who was stubborn in continuing the litigation may be punished by an award of costs against itself.

All Canadian provinces now have a form of mandatory mediation to help resolve private lawsuits. The information that is shared in these sessions is normally made privileged by the statute or rule that created the mediation in the first place. However, it is now settled that a form of confidentiality is inherent in mediation because the parties are attempting to settle their dispute. This means that discussions and conversations in mediation are protected by the common law settlement privilege (see *Union Carbide Canada Inc v Bombardier Inc*, 2014 SCC 35 at para 39, [2014] 1 SCR 800). Still, most mediators will err on the side of safety and have their clients sign a confidentiality agreement prior to the mediation session.

4. Apology Legislation

Because an apology is normally admissible as an acknowledgment of liability against the person making it, people may be afraid to offer an apology following an accident or an unfortunate event. In fact, most liability insurance policies prohibit insured persons from admitting liability or compromising the defence of an action, thus effectively preventing an apology. For this reason, physicians who had caused a patient death or injury, whether negligently or not, could not apologize or express their regret to patients or their families even though many felt that an expression of regret, such as "I am sorry that this happened," would be welcomed. Doctors, nurses, and other health care providers supported legislation that would permit an acknowledgment of regret without fear of legal repercussions. The position of these health care workers found support in legal circles, and some provinces responded by enacting "apology legislation." Most Canadian provinces (with the exception of Quebec and Newfoundland and Labrador) have now adopted some form of apology legislation.

An apology is generally defined in the various statutes as an expression of sympathy or regret and as a statement that a person is sorry, or as any other actions or words indicating contrition or commiseration, whether or not the words or actions admit or imply fault or liability. Generally, the statutes make an apology inadmissible as an acknowledgment of liability or fault in a civil or administrative proceeding (but not in criminal or quasi-criminal proceedings). Of course, any apology made during the course of giving evidence in any proceeding would be admissible to establish liability against the apologizing witness in that proceeding.

In Ontario, section 2(1) of the *Apology Act, 2009* provides as follows:

> 2(1) An apology made by or on behalf of a person in connection with any matter,
>> (a) does not, in law, constitute an express or implied admission of fault or liability by the person in connection with that matter;
>> (b) does not, despite any wording to the contrary in any contract of insurance or indemnity and despite any other Act or law, void, impair or otherwise affect any insurance or indemnity coverage for any person in connection with that matter; and
>> (c) shall not be taken into account in any determination of fault or liability in connection with that matter.

The Power of an Apology

In 2008, some meat products from Maple Leaf Foods of Toronto were found to contain the listeria bacteria. Fifty-seven people contracted listeriosis after consuming contaminated meat. Twenty-two fatalities were attributed to the breakout. Maple Leaf CEO Michael McCain did something very unusual—he publicly admitted fault for the outbreak and unequivocally apologized in every available media outlet. As part of his apology, Mr. McCain stated:

> Going through the crisis there are two advisers I've paid no attention to. The first are the lawyers, and the second are the accountants. It's not about money or legal liability; this is about our being accountable for providing consumers with safe food. This is a terrible tragedy. To those people who have become ill, and to the families who have lost loved ones, I want to express my deepest and most sincere sympathies. Words cannot begin to express our sadness for your pain.

Many observers credit Mr. McCain's heartfelt apology as the reason the company was able to survive the listeriosis crisis.

Tony Wilson, "The Best Legal Advice Is Often an Apology," *The Globe and Mail* (1 February 2011), online: <http://www.theglobeandmail.com>.

5. Crown Privilege or Public Interest Immunity

Public interest immunity is founded in common law. This immunity prevents relevant evidence from being disclosed or being found admissible when considerations of public policy are found to be more important than the full disclosure of facts. The immunity enjoyed by governments used to be unassailable; it was a blanket class immunity that flowed simply from an assertion by the responsible minister that the documents were privileged "in the public interest." This is no longer the case.

Today, the interests of the justice system are balanced with the public interest. On the one hand, the administration of justice depends on the availability of reliable information, whatever the source, even if that source is the government. On the other hand, protecting sensitive governmental information may be in the public interest. Let's say that the provincial government decides to request tenders on a catering contract for a conference. A losing bidder sues the government, claiming racial profiling and discrimination as the basis for not getting the contract. The plaintiff's counsel seeks government documents dealing with the conference. The government discloses some, but declines to disclose all of the documents, claiming public interest in keeping security measures secret. Depending on the specific documents being sought, public interest may well trump the plaintiff's right to know.

In order to determine whether privilege has been properly claimed, the common law permits a court to examine the documents in issue. The documents will be disclosed if the court concludes that the public interest in the administration of justice outweighs the claimed public interest.

One area where absolute privilege applies without any balancing by the court is with federal Cabinet documents. Section 39 of the *Canada Evidence Act* provides that the disclosure of Cabinet documents can be refused without examination or hearing of this information by any court, person, or body. The policy argument in favour of this approach is that if bureaucrats and others who advise the Cabinet had constantly to look over their shoulders and hedge their language, then the government would not be getting clear and honest advice in order to make decisions. The courts, however, have rejected this form of "blanket" class privilege in the case of provincial cabinets where there is no similar legislative protection. These documents are treated like other claims of public interest immunity, and the competing interests will be weighed by the trial judge to determine whether the documents should be disclosed (see *Carey v Ontario*, [1986] 2 SCR 637).

6. National Security Matters

In the wake of the September 11, 2001 terrorist attacks on the United States, additional security measures have been put in place in Canada that appear to permit various government agencies and departments to operate under a veil of secrecy by claiming that there are national security interests to protect.[2] Where an issue of disclosure of **sensitive information** or **potentially injurious information** arises, the parties are obliged to inform the Attorney General of Canada. The judge is required to seal the information or otherwise give direction that will prevent disclosure. A hearing is then held in the Federal Court of Appeal to determine the validity of the national security claim.

The novel aspect of this procedure is that the hearing is held *in camera*, without notice to any parties, and without the right by any party to make representations unless the judge so determines. No one is permitted to disclose the existence of the application. Even if the judge determines that the government has not made its case for protection of the information, the Attorney General can override that decision by simply filing a certificate. The certificate is good for 15 years. The danger with this kind of power is that the government, for political reasons, can restrict information that might injure it. Although the Federal Court of Appeal has the power to override the certificate, the criteria to override are extremely difficult to meet. The national security claim will stand as long as the government can show some relevance of the certified information to the area for which the government claims protection.[3]

sensitive information
information relating to international relations, national defence, or national security that is in the possession of the Government of Canada, whether originating from inside or outside Canada, and is of a type that the Government of Canada takes measures to safeguard

potentially injurious information
information of a type that, if it were disclosed to the public, could injure international relations, national defence, or national security

in camera **hearing**
a private hearing, often in a judge's chambers, that is closed to the public

7. Informer Privilege

Another class of privilege in the public interest is privilege that protects against disclosure of a police informer's identity. Informants are a "necessary evil" within the justice system. Police investigations often hinge on information that is provided by criminals who obtain some benefit from cooperating with the police. If this source of information were to dry up, many serious crimes would remain unsolved. In exchange, the informants, often petty drug dealers, thieves, and other miscreants, are able to ply their trade under an umbrella of immunity. They may be caught committing less serious offences, but they have confidence that if they have some information to exchange or if they have been valuable to the police in the past, their case will not proceed to trial. Occasionally, money is exchanged for information, but the greatest inducement to informing is that the police will forgive the charges for informants' low-level criminal activity.

The reason for providing protection from disclosure of an informant's identity is twofold. First, without this protection, the informant would be useless to the police in future investigations. He would be marked in the criminal community and would no longer have access to helpful information for the police. The reason informants are so valuable and necessary is that they have access to places and information that the police do not. Second, if the informant's identity were disclosed, he might be murdered for having assisted the police. Disclosure of an informant's identity at a preliminary inquiry increases the likelihood that the informant will not live to see the trial. Without this protection, few people would be willing to work with the police, even where they receive some consideration in the form of forgiven charges in exchange for their help.

The Supreme Court of Canada has consistently held that informer privilege renders a matter beyond the discretion of the trial judge. Once the trial judge is satisfied on a balance of probabilities that informer privilege exists, there is a "complete and total bar on any disclosure of the informer's identity" (see *Named Person v Vancouver Sun*, 2007 SCC 43 at para 30, [2007] 3 SCR 253). Unlike other forms of public interest privilege, there is no balancing of interests at all. The protection of the identity of an informant is absolute and non-discretionary. The only time the rule can be abridged or modified at all is to establish innocence in a criminal trial under the innocence at stake exception. Disclosure of an informant's identity would be permitted only if it were the only way to establish the innocence of a person charged with a criminal offence. Disclosure is not justified on any other basis, including the right of a person charged with a criminal offence to make full answer and defence or the right of an accused to receive disclosure from the Crown (*Named Person v Vancouver Sun* at paras 27-28).

The duty to protect an informant's identity extends to both the trial judge and Crown counsel. Sometimes the defence may have serious questions about whether the person claiming the privilege is in fact a police informer. In those cases, and in situations to determine whether the innocence at stake exception applies, an *in camera* hearing is normally held to determine whether the identity of the putative informant can be made public. The participation of defence counsel in the *in camera* hearing is limited to making submissions to the court regarding who might legitimately constitute a confidential informant and suggesting questions that the judge may put to any witnesses at the *in camera* proceeding (see *R v Basi*, 2009 SCC 52 at para 56, [2009] 3 SCR 389).

8. Spousal Privilege

Generally, husbands and wives, as well as married same-sex spouses, cannot be compelled to disclose to the court any communications between them made during their marriage. This class of protection is known as **spousal privilege**. The principle of spousal **incompetence** and **non-compellability** is an old one, likely born of the concept of the unity of husband and wife. According to this concept, spouses are not separate persons in the eyes of the law, and spousal incompetence and non-compellability are simply an extension of the right not to be compelled to testify against oneself. Additional policy considerations have evolved over time, including the support or respect that society has for the family unit and the importance of safeguarding the relationship and preserving the marriage. However, in 1853, the British Parliament passed the *Evidence Amendment Act*, which made married spouses competent and compellable in civil proceedings. Before this, spouses were not able to testify either for or against their wife or husband. But it was not long before marital communications attracted privilege in criminal proceedings. Today, spousal privilege is codified in the *Canada Evidence Act* as well as in various provincial acts.[4] Recent amendments to the *Canada Evidence Act* now make spouses competent and compellable as witnesses in criminal proceedings against the other spouse, but generally continue to make communications that arise during the marriage privileged. Section 4(3) of the *Canada Evidence Act* states:

> No husband is compellable to disclose any communication made to him by his wife during their marriage, and no wife is compellable to disclose any communication made to her by her husband during their marriage.

Note that in order to claim privilege, the parties must be legally married. It has been determined that privilege does not apply to irreconcilably separated married persons (see *R v Salituro*, [1991] 3 SCR 654). Historically, it has not applied to common law spouses. So, in essence, persons married for two weeks had greater protection from being compelled to testify than common law couples who had been together for 40 years. Currently, the law is in a state of flux, with some Canadian courts using the provisions of the Charter to extend this form of privilege to unmarried spouses, while others have not (see *R v Nguyen*, 2015 ONCA 278 and *R v Legge*, 2014 ABCA 213). (The Charter, and how it is used by the courts, is fully discussed later in this text in Part III, Evidence and the Charter.) Interestingly, section 4(3) of the *Canada Evidence Act* previously gave no protection to same-sex couples because they could not legally marry.

Another important component of section 4(3) is that spousal privilege attaches only to communications. Thus, a spouse can be compelled to testify about anything dealing with her mate, except interactions that qualify as communications. Therefore, a husband or wife may be compelled to testify about things that he or she has observed. For example, a wife whose husband hands her bloody clothes with the

spousal privilege
privilege based on the spousal relationship that prevents one spouse from testifying against the other

incompetent witness
an incompetent witness is one who is *legally unable* to give evidence in a proceeding

non-compellable witness
a non-compellable witness is one who *cannot be legally required* to give evidence in a proceeding

instructions, "See if you can get that nasty stain out of my favourite shirt; that Alfred bled like a stuck pig," could not be compelled to repeat his words, but could be compelled to disclose her observations about the bloody laundry.

An interesting distinction between spousal privilege and other forms of privilege is that although the spouse who receives the communication cannot be compelled to disclose it, if she volunteers the information, the court welcomes it. This rule appears to be a compromise that attempts to maximize the amount of information available to the court. In effect, the court is saying, "We won't make you talk about it, but if you want to, we're happy to hear it."

Spousal Privilege in Brief

1. The persons in the relationship must be married or be spouses.
2. Privilege applies only to communications during the marriage and does not survive the ending of the marriage.
3. Privilege applies only to communications, not observations.
4. The spouse who receives the communication cannot be compelled to disclose it, although he or she may volunteer it.

There are some nuances to the spousal privilege rule that increase the amount of information available to the trier of fact. The communications must have originated during the marriage, and the privilege survives only as long as the marriage lasts. So, if the marriage ends through divorce or separation or the death of a spouse, privilege no longer applies. The idea here is that there is no longer a relationship to safeguard, so there is no longer a need to restrict the available information in order to protect the marriage. Similarly, communications between two spouses before they marry are not privileged. In addition, spouses who are careless and reveal their secrets to third parties are not protected, although communications that are intercepted by wiretap pursuant to a wiretap authorization are protected (see *Lloyd et al v The Queen*, [1981] 2 SCR 645).

There are further limitations placed on the extent to which communications between spouses are privileged. Under the common law, the privilege does not apply when a spouse is charged with an offence involving the person, life, or health of the other spouse (see *R v McGinty* (1986), 52 CR (3d) 161 (YKCA)). So if a husband says something to his spouse while committing an offence against her, the communication would not be privileged and would be admissible in a case concerning the offence. Similarly, any threat against a spouse or a child of the spouse would not be privileged (see *R v Schell*, 2004 ABCA 143).

Bill C-32, or as it was known by its short title, the *Canadian Victims Bill of Rights*,[5] received royal assent on April 23, 2015. This bill amended the *Canada Evidence Act* by making spouses competent and compellable witnesses in proceedings against the other spouse. Prior to this, there was some confusion in the case law between the concepts of spousal incompetence and spousal non-compellability. However, the Bill did not repeal or amend section 4(3), which continues to protect any *communications* that arise during the marriage. It is clear now that a spouse can be called as a witness against the other spouse, but the spouse may continue to invoke spousal privilege where it exists.

9. Judicial Privilege

Judges and members of administrative tribunals cannot be compelled to testify or disclose any information regarding their deliberations or reasoning in coming to a decision. This class of protection is known as **judges' privilege**. This makes perfect sense given the independence of the judiciary. Judges must be free to make what are often difficult decisions without fear that their conduct in coming to a decision will be placed under a microscope.

Similarly, deliberations by jurors are also protected by law (see section 649 of the *Criminal Code*). It is only when there is a concern regarding juror misconduct, or the veracity of juror deliberations, that jurors are required to disclose what went on during their discussions. The extent of any such disclosure is confined to dealing with those concerns only.

Additionally, communications made within or incidental to a judicial proceeding are shielded from any defamation claims (see *1522491 Ontario Inc v Stewart et al*, 2010 ONSC 727). The reason for the rule is that participants in litigation would not be able to perform their functions properly if they always had to look over their shoulders in fear of being sued for what they said. This protection extends to everyone involved in the litigation, including judges, adjudicators, legal representatives, and witnesses.

judges' privilege
privilege that protects judges and administrative tribunal members against disclosing information behind their decisions

Privilege by Case

There are other classes of relationships that appear to be of sufficient importance to attract privilege. However, the courts have been reluctant to extend privilege to other classes. In *A (LL) v B (A)* ([1995] 4 SCR 536), the Supreme Court of Canada expressed its view that "class privilege presents many impediments to the proper administration of justice and … has not been favoured in Canada" (at para 65).

There are many relationships for which a layperson, or even a person in such a relationship, may form the erroneous opinion that any communications within the relationship are privileged—for example, many people assume that communications made to a priest or a therapist are confidential. Communications that arise within these relationships may indeed give rise to a claim of privilege, but whether privilege attaches or not depends on the case, not simply the existence of the relationship. It is crucial to maintain a clear distinction between privilege by class and privilege by case. In the former, privilege arises automatically; in the latter, privilege is determined on a case-by-case basis.

The American jurist John Henry Wigmore developed four criteria for assessing claims of privilege in areas where the claim has traditionally not been accepted by the courts on the basis of privilege by class. These criteria have been adopted by Canadian courts and are commonly referred to as the **Wigmore test**. The criteria are as follows:

Wigmore test
four criteria for assessing case-by-case claims of privilege

(1) The communications must originate in a confidence that they will not be disclosed.

(2) This element of confidentiality must be essential to the full and satisfactory maintenance of the relationship between the parties.

(3) The relation must be one which in the opinion of the community ought to be sedulously [persistently and diligently] fostered.

(4) The injury that would inure to the relation by the disclosure of the communications must be greater than the benefit thereby gained for the correct disposal of litigation.

Wigmore's Four Criteria

1. The communications must originate in a confidence that they will not be disclosed.

In assessing whether privilege should attach to communications between individuals in a circumstance where there is no legislated or historically recognized privilege, the first criterion identified by Wigmore was whether the communication originated in confidence. In other words, if the parties at the time did not think that the communications were confidential, then there is no confidential relationship to protect and a litigant cannot claim privilege as an afterthought.

What kind of communications originate in confidence? In fact, there are a great number of relationships that are confidential in nature. Take, for example, the relationship between an accountant and his client. Not only will the client sometimes disclose information to the accountant that she does not want the tax authorities to know about; she likely also would not want such information shared with her neighbours or co-workers. Therefore, communications with an accountant almost certainly originate in confidence. Similarly, communications with a banker, doctor, or escort service are confidential in nature. Even communications with a hairdresser, personal trainer, or car mechanic may be confidential. In these and other such relationships, individuals want to know that their privacy is respected. All these communications will likely originate in confidence that the professional will not disclose the private information.

2. This element of confidentiality must be essential to the full and satisfactory maintenance of the relationship between the parties.

The second of Wigmore's criteria deals with the importance of confidentiality to the maintenance of the relationship. The court considers whether it is necessary to protect the communication in order to preserve the relationship. Take the classic situation of the confessional. Great deference is given to communications between a person who is unburdening her conscience and the religious figure that she confides in. This relationship would be ruined in no time at all if this confidential information was made public. Similarly, the Greenpeace activist who drives a high-performance car that has some of its anti-pollution devices circumvented would require discretion. Disclosure of such information might be embarrassing to the activist and would undoubtedly damage his relationship with his mechanic. However, if the court were to grant privilege, relevant and material evidence would be lost to the trier of fact in both situations.

3. The relation must be one that in the opinion of the community ought to be sedulously fostered.

This aspect of Wigmore's criteria deals with the value that the community places on the relationship. For example, a bookie and his client would satisfy the first two criteria because their communications would originate in confidence and confidentiality is essential to the relationship. However, the community does not value this relationship above the correct disposal of litigation. The same is true of the relationship between a hit man and his mob boss or a drug addict and her dealer.

There are many relationships where confidential communications are essential to the relationship but do not attract any protection from disclosure. Relationships that may attract protection include therapeutic relationships, such as that between a psychotherapist and a client who has suffered abuse. The court must weigh the benefit to the victim of being able to trust that her innermost thoughts will be protected from exposure, particularly to the abuser. Clearly, the court must consider the value that the community puts on this relationship and the importance of having information available for the correct disposition of the dispute.

4. The injury that would inure to the relation by the disclosure of the communications must be greater than the benefit thereby gained for the correct disposal of litigation.

This is the overall balancing criterion. With this, the court must assess whether the damage to the relationship that would result from the release of the information is greater than the benefit that would be gained by having this information available to correctly dispose of the litigation. For example, in *R v RJS* ((1985), 45 CR (3d) 161 (Ont CA)), a father was charged with sexual assault of his stepchild. He agreed to participate in therapy sessions to help the child, and in those sessions accusations of sexual assault were levelled at him. He did not respond to the allegations, through a denial or otherwise. The Crown sought to introduce the allegations and lack of a denial as evidence against the accused, and the accused sought to have the communications designated as privileged. In looking at the therapeutic nature of the communications, the court determined that Wigmore's first three criteria were met. However, the court found that the importance to the correct disposal of the litigation outweighed the potential for injury to the relationship between the father and the therapist.

In the example above, it seems obvious that allowing evidence that will aid in convicting a child abuser outweighs any damage to the relationship between the father and the therapist. However, it is important to consider carefully what is gained and what is lost. It can be extremely important for an abused person to have an opportunity to confront the abuser in a safe and professionally supervised setting. This may be key to the abused person's recovery. If the communications in the therapy sessions are disclosed, the accused person knows that his continued involvement in this forum could be used against him in court and he would not continue to involve himself in this process. Thus, by making such a ruling, the court captures information on one occasion but scares away all future positive involvement of accused persons in the recovery of their victims. This could translate into a net loss when weighed by the court. The focus therefore is not only on the specific individual relationship in issue, but also on broader policy considerations.

Paralegal–Client Privilege

Under the *Law Society Act* of Ontario, licensed paralegals are authorized to provide specified legal services to the public. The question of whether solicitor–client privilege extends to non-lawyers performing lawyer-like functions was canvassed by Master Ronald Dash in *Chancey v Dharmadi* (2007 CanLII 28332 (Ont SC)). It should be noted that *Chancey* was decided before paralegals were formally recognized as a profession in Ontario.

CASE IN POINT

Paralegal–Client Privilege

Chancey v Dharmadi, 2007 CanLII 28332 (Ont SC)

In this case, the plaintiff sued the defendant for damages arising from a motor vehicle accident for which the defendant was charged with careless driving under Ontario's *Highway Traffic Act*. The defendant retained a "paralegal" to represent her in the *Highway Traffic Act* matter. During her discovery in the civil suit, the defendant was asked to produce the paralegal's file to the plaintiff. The defendant refused, claiming that the communications were privileged. At the time, paralegals were not formally recognized as a profession, although there were numerous agents representing people charged with *Highway Traffic Act* matters and other provincial offences. The issue before the court was whether the contents of the file were privileged. In assessing whether solicitor–client privilege extended to paralegals and their clients, Master Dash stated:

> Prima facie it appears that the rationale for granting class privilege to communications between a solicitor and his client made in the course of giving legal advice applies equally to communications between a paralegal and his client in the course of giving legal advice.

However, Master Dash found that solicitor–client privilege did not apply in the circumstance of this case:

In my view, there is no principled reason why a class privilege should not be extended to paralegal-client communications; however, it must be restricted to communications with an identifiable group, namely paralegals licensed by the Law Society [of Upper Canada]. Since the paralegal with whom the defendant communicated was not a licensed paralegal, no class privilege can be said to apply. No declaration should be made at this time, on the facts of this case, with respect to the existence of a class privilege over paralegal-client communications. Such determination should be made at a time when it is supported by an appropriate factual matrix. In other words, determination of the existence of a class privilege over paralegal-client communications should be determined in a proceeding in which privilege is claimed over communications between a paralegal licensed by the Law Society and his client.

This ruling did not finally determine the issue before the court, and Master Dash then applied the Wigmore test to the facts of the case and decided that the communication satisfied all four Wigmore criteria. As a result, the paralegal's file was not produced in the civil suit and was kept confidential.

This case suggests that solicitor–client privilege may now extend to paralegals and their clients, although it is not determinative of the issue. At any rate, it is difficult to see how most *bona fide* paralegal–client communications would not be protected on a case-by-case basis using the Wigmore criteria.

Relationships Not Protected by Class

Most patients mistakenly assume that what they have told their doctor is private and protected from disclosure. Similarly, both priest and penitent often share the view that confessions cannot be disclosed. However, courts have traditionally been reluctant to expand the classes to which privilege attaches because this evidence is usually highly probative and very reliable. Often, it is the best evidence available to the trier of fact. Communications from such relationships may be privileged, but only on a case-by-case basis and if they meet the Wigmore test. Because many relationships enjoy widespread popularity, the courts have struggled with preserving the integrity of some of these relationships while also attempting to ensure that relevant and probative evidence is not excluded without sufficient justification.

1. Relationship Between Doctor and Patient

As discussed above, no class privilege exists for communications between a doctor and her patient. Claims of privilege in these situations are determined on a case-by-case basis having regard to the Wigmore criteria. However, doctors, psychiatrists, and psychologists all have strict codes that forbid them from revealing confidential information provided to them by their patients. As far back as the time of Hippocrates and the Hippocratic Oath, doctors were exhorted to keep secret those confidences entrusted to them:

> Whatsoever things I see or hear concerning the life of men, in my attendance on the sick … I will keep silence thereon, counting such things as sacred secrets.

Yet this duty to respect the secrets of the patient is not absolute. It has become increasingly clear that society is prepared to intercede in the relationship between doctor and patient where there is a risk to an identifiable person or group. However, the dilemma facing the physician remains. By breaching client confidentiality where a risk to an identifiable person is revealed, the physician exposes herself to sanctions for professional misconduct if her governing body second-guesses her decision. In addition—and this is one of the more compelling arguments put forth by medical professionals—the more often doctor–patient confidentiality is breached, the less likely it will be that sick people seek help.

The position of the courts with regard to doctor–patient confidentiality is set out in *Smith v Jones*, discussed earlier in this chapter under the heading "Public Safety Exception." After *Smith*, there can be no doubt that in law the duty to protect outweighs patient confidentiality.

As a result of *Smith*, a psychiatrist must take effective steps to warn an intended victim or the authorities but should reveal only as much information as is necessary to protect the potential victim. In the psychiatrist's assessment, probably the most difficult task is to determine the degree of risk. Psychiatrists have applied a standard of "more likely than not." For example, if a patient who is involved in a billing dispute with the telephone company confides to a psychiatrist that he would like to "blow away some of the telephone repairmen," the psychiatrist will assess whether it is more likely than not that the patient will kill or seriously harm the repairmen. The Canadian Psychiatric Association has expressed concern that it is not possible to treat serious psychiatric disorders if the patient is not free to discuss his problems with his therapist. However, the duty to warn remains, which could have devastating financial repercussions through civil suits against the psychiatrist if her assessment of the patient turns out to be wrong.

Physicians also find themselves in circumstances where their duty of confidentiality to their patients conflicts with their duty to the public at large. Such is the case where a person with a sexually transmitted disease is not prepared to treat it or avoid unprotected sexual contact. The same criteria that apply to psychiatrists would apply to other physicians in those circumstances.

2. Relationship Between Religious Leader and Adherent

Many Canadians feel very strongly about what Catholics would call the "sanctity of the confessional" or protection from disclosure of communications between an individual and a religious leader or adviser. Yet the law does not treat such communications as privileged in the way that solicitor–client communications are privileged. The law in Canada remains as it was decided in the case of *R v Gruenke* ([1991] 3 SCR 263). Although the case was not unanimously decided, Lamer CJ, writing for the majority, stated (at 288):

> [A] prima facie privilege for religious communications would constitute an exception to the general principle that all relevant evidence is admissible. Unless it can be said that the policy reasons to support a class privilege for religious communications are as compelling as the policy reasons which underlay the class privilege for solicitor-client communications, there is no basis for departing from the fundamental "first principle" that all relevant evidence is admissible until proven otherwise.

The argument of the majority that distinguishes solicitor–client communications as more deserving of the application of privilege than religious communications is that this relationship is essential to the functioning of the legal system. It is, of course, a matter of perspective. Judges, first being lawyers, naturally are inclined to see communications between lawyers and clients as having greater importance than any other communications. But a priest, rabbi, or imam who was charged with determining which type of communications should receive the highest protection would likely say that religious communications trump all others.

Nevertheless, religious communications must meet the Wigmore test on a case-by-case basis. Although some have argued that the disclosure of religious communications infringes an individual's right to protection of freedom of religion as guaranteed by the Charter, the courts have ruled (as in *R v Gruenke*, above) that disclosure can be justified and is dependent on the particular circumstances that come before the court. The courts have also ruled that the approach must be a "non-denominational" one. The religious leader or adviser need not be ordained, and the communications need not be in the context of a formal confession. Thus, in considering the circumstances of the communication, the courts give great deference to the multicultural nature of Canadian society.

3. Relationship Between Complainant and Another Party in Criminal Matters

A matter of considerable controversy in recent years has been whether privilege should attach to private communications of complainants where an accused person seeks to have them disclosed as part of his defence. *R v O'Connor* ([1995] 4 SCR 411) brought this simmering issue to a head. Bishop O'Connor was charged with a number of counts of sexual assault that dated back about 30 years. The defence sought production of psychiatric records dealing with the treatment received by the complainants over the intervening period since the alleged assaults. There are two arguments to be made for the defence in this respect. First, the records may shed light on the incidents and support defences available to the accused, such as the defence of consent. Second, where the complainant has been injured and the accused has been found guilty, the records may assist the defence in qualifying the degree of injury caused by the accused, and thus bring a lighter sentence.

In *O'Connor*, the trial judge was satisfied that the records sought by Bishop O'Connor were relevant and ordered them disclosed by the Crown, who had them in her possession. This ruling was appealed through to the Supreme Court of Canada, where the Crown urged the court to consider three criteria for keeping the records private:

1. Societal interest in encouraging the reporting of sexual offences
2. Societal interest in encouraging complainants to seek treatment
3. Impact of the decision on the integrity of the trial process

In rejecting the criteria, the Supreme Court provided specific guidelines for when such records would be discoverable by the defence, setting out a two-stage process, which is discussed below.

First Stage

- The accused must establish that the information he seeks is "likely to be relevant" to his defence.
- There is no balancing of interests, just relevancy as a test.
- If this test is met, the information is produced for the judge to review; if the test is not met, the information is not disclosed.

Second Stage

- If the test in the first stage is met, the trial judge reviews the records and determines whether and to what extent the records will be produced.
- The judge must balance the interests of the accused in obtaining a fair trial against the societal and privacy interests of the complainant.
- The reviewing court must consider
  a. the necessity of the records for the accused to defend himself,
  b. the probative value of the records,
  c. the complainant's privacy expectation,
  d. whether production of the record is based on a discriminatory belief or bias, and
  e. the impact on the dignity or right to privacy of the complainant.

In the end, the Supreme Court rejected the appeal and the records were disclosed. The decision caused a considerable backlash as victims' support groups rallied against a determination that would increase the possibility that complainants would see their most personal thoughts and confidences made public and thus available to their abusers. In reaction to the *O'Connor* case, Parliament enacted sections 278.1 to 278.91 of the *Criminal Code* in 1997. These sections set out a multi-staged procedure for an accused to seek production of records where there is a privacy interest of another person. The process may include a written application, a subpoena served on the person who holds the record, an *in camera* hearing, a judge's review of the actual records, and a decision by a judge as to whether any, part, or all of the record should be disclosed.

An accused can potentially be stopped even prior to the judge's reviewing the records, should the judge feel that the exercise is akin to a fishing expedition. Under the legislated provisions, the two-stage process is maintained. In fact, the first stage is essentially the same: The accused must convince the trial judge that the information is likely to be relevant. What the legislation does, however, is specifically indicate 11 assertions that are out of bounds to an argument of relevance. The inability of the trial judge to consider these assertions when assessing reliability essentially gives effect to the three criteria noted above that the Supreme Court of Canada rejected in *O'Connor*. In other words, what the Supreme Court of Canada said was not applicable to the determination of relevancy, Parliament determined to be relevant.

4. Other Confidential Relationships

There are many other relationships that could potentially be covered by Wigmore's four criteria and granted privilege. Consider again the relationship between an accountant and his client. If one is skirting the line between tax avoidance and tax evasion, the information communicated to an accountant is definitely intended to be confidential. One tax lawyer has advertised that he may be able to reach an agreement with the Canada Revenue Agency, on an anonymous basis, to pay tax on undeclared income. This advertisement goes on to mention that both tax consultants and accountants can be forced to disclose information about their clients while a lawyer cannot be required to do so. Is this advertisement accurate, or does it mislead the public? The advertisement suggests that communications between accountants and their clients are not privileged. This may not be entirely accurate, because privilege is determined on a case-by-case basis in these instances. It is difficult to envision how a court would justify not upholding the claim for privilege by an accountant who is providing essentially the same service as a lawyer.

In other relationships, such as that between a reporter and her source, the courts have not recognized class privilege. Some reporters have been jailed for contempt of court for refusing to divulge the source of their information during court proceedings. For example, in 2005, *New York Times* reporter Judith Miller was jailed because she refused to identify her confidential source in the case where someone in the Bush administration had leaked the identity of CIA operative Valerie Plame. Although Ms. Miller was not the one to publish the identity of the CIA operative, a grand jury investigating this leak wanted her to testify and identify her source in the administration.

Ms. Miller spent 85 days in jail in defence of journalistic freedom, and it was not until White House official Lewis "Scooter" Libby confirmed her release of the confidentiality of their communications that she agreed to testify.

CASE IN POINT

Confidential Sources in Canada

R v National Post, [2010] 1 SCR 477

In this case, the Supreme Court of Canada considered whether the Charter has changed the law on reporter–source privilege. The issue in *National Post* was the validity of a search warrant that compelled production of real evidence that would identify a confidential source. The newspaper argued that the warrant contravened section 2(b) of the Charter, which guarantees freedom of the press, and alternatively, that secret sources were protected by common law privilege. The Supreme Court rejected the claim that there was constitutional protection pursuant to section 2(b) of the Charter, on the basis that the right is enjoyed by everyone who chooses to exercise their freedom of expression (at para 40):

> [T]he protection attaching to freedom of expression is not limited to the "traditional media", but is enjoyed by "everyone" (in the words of s. 2(b) of the Charter) who chooses to exercise his or her freedom of expression on

matters of public interest whether by blogging, tweeting, standing on a street corner and shouting the "news" at passing pedestrians or publishing in a national newspaper. To throw a constitutional immunity around the interactions of such a heterogeneous and ill-defined group of writers and speakers and whichever "sources" they deem worthy of a promise of confidentiality and on whatever terms they may choose to offer it (or, as here, choose to amend it with the benefit of hindsight) would blow a giant hole in law enforcement and other constitutionally recognized values such as privacy.

The class would be too large to include under the umbrella of constitutional protection. Instead, the court opted to approach the claim of privilege involving journalists and their sources on a case-by-case basis utilizing Wigmore's four criteria.

Many other relationships are of the sort where one or more of the parties would like to keep the information confidential. However, if the information becomes relevant, whether the information stays confidential will depend on the court's interpretation of the criteria outlined by Wigmore.

CHAPTER SUMMARY

In determining whether a communication is privileged, the court first looks at whether the communication arose within a class of protected relationships. If the court finds that the communication does not attract privilege by class, the court applies Wigmore's four criteria to determine whether the communication is protected on a case-by-case basis. If privilege does not attach and the communication is otherwise admissible, the court will allow the evidence. If the communication is privileged, the court will exclude the evidence unless it falls within one of the exceptions to the privilege rule, such as the public safety exception.

KEY TERMS

confidentiality, 172
in camera hearing, 181
incompetent witness, 183
innocence at stake exception, 174
judges' privilege, 185
litigation privilege, 175
non-compellable witness, 183
potentially injurious information, 181
privilege, 170
privilege by case, 170
privilege by class, 170
public safety exception, 171
sensitive information, 181
solicitor–client privilege, 171
spousal privilege, 183
Wigmore test, 185
without prejudice, 177

NOTES

1   The settlements were in the form of a Pierringer agreement, which permits the plaintiff to continue the action against the non-settling defendants for only the losses they caused and waives any claim of joint liability between settling and non-settling defendants.

2   Section 38 of the *Canada Evidence Act* sets out a comprehensive scheme for the claim and review of this form of privilege.

3   The procedure set out in the *Canada Evidence Act* for dealing with this form of privilege was found to be constitutional by the Supreme Court of Canada in *R v Ahmad*.

4   For example, section 11 of the Ontario *Evidence Act* provides that "a person is not compellable to disclose any communication made to the person by his or her spouse during the marriage."

5   The main feature of this bill is that it provides victims of crime access to and standing in the Canadian justice system. While some features of the bill enhance victims' rights, critics point out that the proposed legislation essentially codifies and standardizes existing good practices that the justice system has long used.

REFERENCES

1522491 Ontario Inc v Stewart et al, 2010 ONSC 727.

A (LL) v B (A), [1995] 4 SCR 536.

Ahmad, R v, 2011 SCC 6, [2011] 1 SCR 110.

Basi, R v, 2009 SCC 52, [2009] 3 SCR 389.

Blank v Canada (Minister of Justice), 2006 SCC 39, [2006] 2 SCR 319.

Canada Evidence Act, RSC 1985, c C-5.

Canadian Charter of Rights and Freedoms, Part I of the *Constitution Act, 1982*, being Schedule B to the *Canada Act 1982* (UK), 1982, c 11.

Canadian Victims Bill of Rights, SC 2015, c 13, s 2.

Carey v Ontario, [1986] 2 SCR 637.

Celanese Canada Inc v Murray Demolition Corp, 2006 SCC 36, [2006] 2 SCR 189.

Chancey v Dharmadi, 2007 CanLII 28332 (Ont SC).

Criminal Code, RSC 1985, c C-46.

Evidence Amendment Act, 1853 (16 & 17 Vict), c 83.

General Accident Assurance Company v Chrusz, 1999 CanLII 7320 (Ont CA).

Gruenke, R v, [1991] 3 SCR 263.

Legge, R v, 2014 ABCA 213.

Lloyd et al v The Queen, [1981] 2 SCR 645.

McClure, R v, 2001 SCC 14, [2001] 1 SCR 445.

McGinty, R v (1986), 52 CR (3d) 161 (YKCA); application for leave to appeal to the SCC discontinued.

Named Person v Vancouver Sun, 2007 SCC 43, [2007] 3 SCR 253.

National Post, R v, 2010 SCC 16, [2010] 1 SCR 477.

Nguyen, R v, 2015 ONCA 278.

O'Connor, R v, [1995] 4 SCR 411.

Ontario, *Apology Act, 2009*, SO 2009, c 3.

Ontario, *Evidence Act*, RSO 1990, c E.23.

Ontario, *Highway Traffic Act*, RSO 1990, c H.8.

Pritchard v Ontario (Human Rights Commission), 2004 SCC 31, [2004] 1 SCR 809.

RJS, R v (1985), 45 CR (3d) 161 (Ont CA).

Rules of Civil Procedure, RRO 1990, reg 194.

Sable Offshore Energy Inc v Ameron International Corp, 2013 SCC 37, [2013] 2 SCR 623.

Salituro, R v, [1991] 3 SCR 654.

Schell, R v, 2004 ABCA 143.

Smith v Jones, [1999] 1 SCR 455.

Tony Wilson, "The Best Legal Advice Is Often an Apology," *The Globe and Mail* (1 February 2011), online: <http://www.theglobeandmail.com>.

Union Carbide Canada Inc v Bombardier Inc, 2014 SCC 35, [2014] 1 SCR 800.

REVIEW QUESTIONS

1. Briefly describe Wigmore's four criteria for assessing claims of privilege.

2. What are the features of spousal privilege?

3. When might a lawyer be required to divulge communications with a client?

4. What are the differences between solicitor–client privilege and litigation privilege?

DISCUSSION QUESTIONS

1. Are communications between a paralegal and her client privileged?

2. Brad is charged with threatening to kill his estranged wife, Janet. His lawyer has objected to the admission of the threat on the basis of spousal privilege under the *Canada Evidence Act*. Is this evidence admissible? Why or why not?

3. Jim and Brock are a married same-sex couple. Jim confided in Brock that while honeymooning in Niagara Falls with Brock, he accidentally ran over a pedestrian while driving his SUV. The Crown has subpoenaed Brock, hoping that he has incriminating evidence against Jim. Is Brock's statement admissible? Why or why not?

4. Tommy Chang is charged with the murder of Dennis Yeung. Tommy is having drinks with his lawyer, Edward Nugent, when, in a drunken stupor, he blurts out, "I killed Dennis because he always got the glory." Lori, the bartender (and a number of other patrons), overhears this conversation. Is Lori's evidence as to what she heard admissible? Why or why not?

5. Sir Oswald Osborne, an eccentric English gentleman, has recently been ordained a Catholic priest. During confession, Deborah Boone confides that she once downloaded a song from the Internet and played it backward to look for hidden messages. Oswald is offended by what he considers theft of protected material and goes to the police. Is the information conveyed by Deborah during the confession privileged? Why or why not?

6. Patrick Ramos coaches high school hockey. He has forged a reputation as a firm but caring person who can be trusted. It is widely known that he has been a father figure for hundreds of troubled youths and is credited with saving dozens from a life of drug abuse. A star player has turned to Patrick for help with his drug problem and confided that he sold drugs to teammates. Is this evidence admissible? Why or why not?

7. Ed consults lawyer Michael Oliverio. Ed tells Michael that he murdered a young girl. Is this evidence admissible? Why or why not?

8. Ed consults lawyer Michael Oliverio. Ed has a severe speech impediment and writes Michael a note indicating that he murdered a young girl. Is this note admissible? Why or why not?

9. Ed consults lawyer Michael Oliverio. Ed has a severe speech impediment and brings in a page from his diary indicating that he murdered a young girl. Is this page admissible? Why or why not?

10. Ed consults lawyer Michael Oliverio. Ed has a severe speech impediment and brings in a short video showing that he murdered a young girl. Is this video admissible? Why or why not?

PART III

Evidence and the Charter

Self-Incrimination

11

LEARNING OUTCOMES

After completing this chapter, you should be able to:

- Demonstrate an understanding of the scope of the right against self-incrimination.

- Demonstrate an understanding of the dimensions of the right against self-incrimination, including the right to remain silent, the right not to be compelled to be a witness against oneself, and the right to testify freely without fear that the testimony will be used in a subsequent proceeding.

- Identify and apply the confession rule and the right to be free from oppressive or unfair police questioning.

- Demonstrate an understanding of the dangers of the Mr. Big technique, and apply the test for determining the admissibility of evidence obtained from it.

Introduction

right against self-
incrimination
a person's right not
to be compelled to
be a witness against
himself in criminal or
quasi-criminal proceedings

The **right against self-incrimination** can be generally described as a person's right not to be compelled to be a witness against himself in criminal or quasi-criminal proceedings. When looking at the issue of self-incrimination, we must be mindful of the context within which the right is claimed. In this chapter, we examine a number of questions relating to the issue of self-incrimination. When we speak of the right against self-incrimination, we are obviously talking about a suspect's right to refuse to speak to police investigating a crime. But what if a suspect confesses to committing a crime to the police? What if the confession is made to a teacher or other private citizen? What if a suspect makes an incriminating statement to a police operative posing as a major crime figure? What happens to the right against self-incrimination after a person has been charged with an offence? What happens if the right is breached?

In the past, persons accused of crimes did not always enjoy the right to silence. In fact, an accused person could be subjected to extreme forms of persuasion, including violence or threats of violence, to induce a statement. However, the information that derived from coerced statements was often unreliable. The authorities who were subjecting the accused to coercion obviously believed that the accused committed the offence, and were unlikely to stop if the accused simply professed his innocence. Often, the accused realized this and would confess to end his pain. In fact, the torturers would often write out the confessions for the accused to sign. In such circumstances, accused persons were known to confess to crimes they could not have committed, simply to avoid the brutality being inflicted upon them. Present-day protection against self-incrimination during the investigative stages of a crime derives from those times when authorities were likely to extract a confession from an accused through violence or threats of violence.

The Right to Silence: Before Trial

Many people find it surprising that the *Canadian Charter of Rights and Freedoms* does not expressly provide the right for an accused to remain silent when dealing with authorities during the investigation of a crime or prior to trial. The Supreme Court of Canada, in *Rothman v The Queen* ([1981] 1 SCR 640), described the source of the right to silence in the following terms (at 683):

> In Canada the right of a suspect not to say anything to the police is not the result of a right of no self-crimination but is merely the exercise by him of the general right enjoyed in this country by anyone to do whatever one pleases, saying what one pleases or choosing not to say certain things, unless obliged to do otherwise by law.

In other words, the right to silence is really the absence (in most cases) of an obligation to provide any information to the police. We have all seen television shows where the arresting officer informs the arrested person of his rights, including the right to remain silent. This means that an individual does not have any obligation to assist the authorities who are trying to build a case against him.

The Charter has been interpreted as reinforcing the pre-trial right to silence in section 7, which provides as follows:

> Everyone has the right to life, liberty and security of the person and the right not to be deprived thereof except in accordance with the principles of fundamental justice.

In *R v Hebert* ([1990] 2 SCR 151), the accused spoke to his lawyer and advised the police that he wished to remain silent. The police placed an undercover officer in the accused's cell and tricked the accused into providing an incriminating statement. The Supreme Court of Canada ruled that this evidence should be excluded because of the interaction of section 7 of the Charter with the general right to remain silent. The court stated (at 181):

> *Charter* provisions related to the right to silence of a detained person under s. 7 suggest that the right must be interpreted in a manner which secures to the detained person the right to make a free and meaningful choice as to whether to speak to the authorities or to remain silent.

The court went on to add (at 181):

> In keeping with the approach inaugurated by the *Charter*, our courts must adopt an approach to pre-trial interrogation which emphasizes the right of the detained person to make a meaningful choice and permits the rejection of statements which have been obtained unfairly in circumstances that violate that right of choice.

As a result, detainees have a constitutionally protected right to silence under section 7 of the Charter, which includes the right to make a free choice to speak to authorities or to remain silent. When an undercover agent actively elicits information from a detained suspect who has exercised the right to remain silent, the suspect's section 7 right to silence has been violated. It follows that where there has been no active elicitation by an undercover officer—for example, where an officer is placed in a cell to merely observe the accused—there is no section 7 violation.

In spite of this interpretation of section 7, we still see the use of jailhouse informants, as opposed to undercover officers, as a method of extracting information from an accused person. Generally, the courts have not treated jailhouse informants as police agents and thus have not subjected them to the same restrictions as police officers. Accordingly, the courts have generally allowed statements made to these informants. However, where such informants are essentially "professionals" who use their ability to gain the confidence of a suspect in order to obtain some information that they can trade for a lesser sentence or parole eligibility, the line between them and a police agent blurs. In addition, the use of jailhouse informants has been strongly criticized as being dangerous and unreliable in various wrongful conviction reviews, including the Sophonow inquiry conducted by Supreme Court of Canada Justice Peter Cory.

CASE IN POINT

Does Persistent Questioning Violate the Right to Silence?

R v Singh, 2007 SCC 48, [2007] 3 SCR 405

It is clear that while a person charged with an offence has a right to remain silent and can refuse to speak to the police, this does not mean that the authorities cannot continue to try to obtain information from the accused. In *R v Singh*, the accused was facing second-degree murder charges in the shooting of an innocent bystander. The accused was advised of his right to counsel and spoke to a lawyer after he was arrested. During two interviews, Mr. Singh told the police 18 times that he did not wish to provide any further information about the incident. The police persisted in questioning Mr. Singh and he eventually made several incriminating statements. The statements were admitted at trial following a voir dire to determine their admissibility, and the accused was convicted.

The Supreme Court of Canada dismissed Mr. Singh's appeal, with the majority of the court explaining that the right to silence does not require the police to refrain from questioning a suspect who has asserted the right to remain silent. The court, however, recognized a need to maintain a balance between individual and societal interests and stated that "the law as it stands does not permit the police to *ignore* the detainee's freedom to choose whether to speak or not" (at para 47).

The court then added (at para 47):

> Under both common law and Charter rules, police persistence in continuing the interview, despite repeated assertions by the detainee that he wishes to remain silent, may well raise a strong argument that any subsequently obtained statement was not the product of a free will to speak to the authorities.

The law sometimes imposes an obligation to provide information to the police in certain circumstances. For example, various provincial statutes require motorists to report collisions and to provide specified information to the police following a motor vehicle accident.[1] The courts have extended the right to silence under section 7 of the Charter to protect people who are statutorily compelled to provide information to the authorities (see *R v White*, [1999] 2 SCR 417 at para 30). Usually, statements made under legislative compulsion "are inadmissible in criminal proceedings against the declarant because their admission would violate the principle against self-incrimination" (at para 30). In order to claim protection under section 7 of the Charter, the person making the statement must establish, on a balance of probabilities, an honest and reasonably held belief that he or she was required by law to provide the information to the authorities (*R v White* at para 75).

It is crucial to note, however, that a finding that there has been a violation of a Charter right does not end the discussion—this topic will be more fully discussed in Chapter 12, Wrongfully Obtained Evidence. The courts then must consider section 24 of the Charter to determine what, if any, remedy is appropriate in the circumstances.

The Charter right to silence is reinforced by section 10, which provides:

> Everyone has the right on arrest or detention …
>
>   b) to retain and instruct counsel without delay and to be informed of that right.

This provision basically ensures that all persons will have access to legal advice if arrested or detained. Even a law student or a properly trained paralegal will have enough legal knowledge to tell an accused that she enjoys a right to silence and suggest that the accused exercise that right. However, it is clear that a person under arrest or detained by the police does not have the right to have a lawyer present during a police interrogation or investigation (see *R v Sinclair*, 2010 SCC 35, [2010] 2 SCR 310).

The Supreme Court of Canada has established three duties that section 10(b) imposes on the police upon the arrest or detention of a suspect (see *R v Bartle*, [1994] 3 SCR 173 at 191-92). They are:

(1) to inform the detainee of his or her right to retain and instruct counsel without delay and of the existence and availability of legal aid and duty counsel;

(2) if a detainee has indicated a desire to exercise this right, to provide the detainee with a reasonable opportunity to exercise the right (except in urgent and dangerous circumstances); and

(3) to refrain from eliciting evidence from the detainee until he or she has had that reasonable opportunity (again, except in cases of urgency or danger).

The first duty is an *informational* one only. It is satisfied upon providing the specified information to a person who has been arrested or detained. The second and third duties are more in the nature of *implementation* duties and are not triggered unless and until a person indicates a desire to exercise his or her right to counsel (*R v Bartle* at 191).

The Right to Silence: During Trial

The right to silence remains with a person charged with an offence as she goes through the court system. The basic right is found in both the *Canada Evidence Act* and the *Canadian Charter of Rights and Freedoms*. Section 11 of the Charter provides:

Any person charged with an offence has the right …

c) not to be compelled to be a witness in proceedings against that person in respect of the offence.

This Charter right applies not just to criminal offences but to all offences, including provincial offences. If either the police or the Crown required the accused to provide information over her objections, this would be grounds for excluding the evidence at a trial.

It should be noted that section 11 does not prevent an accused person from testifying in her own defence; it only prevents the Crown from calling the accused as a witness. However, once the accused has decided to testify, section 11 has no further application and the Crown can freely cross-examine the accused. In other words, an accused person cannot testify selectively, providing only information that helps her defence while avoiding harmful details.

The Accused's Choice Not to Testify

An accused's right to silence would be meaningless if her choice not to speak to the police could be used against her at trial. As a result, the Supreme Court of Canada has made clear that the trier of fact is not permitted to use the silence of an accused either before or during a trial to help establish his or her guilt (see *R v Noble*, [1997] 1 SCR 874 at paras 71, 75). If this was not the case and the trier of fact was permitted to draw an inference of guilt from silence, remaining silent would be tantamount to acknowledging guilt.

In fact, the Crown and the judge are prohibited from even commenting on the accused's choice not to testify (see s 46(6) of the *Canada Evidence Act*). This is often referred to as adverse comment on the accused's *failure* to testify. Note, however, that the language contains a bias that testifying is expected. Testifying or not is a tactical choice, usually arrived at through consultation with counsel, not a "failure." Similarly problematic is what appears to be an exception to the "no comment" rule, which is that if there is already enough evidence before the trier of fact to find the accused guilty beyond a reasonable doubt, it is permissible to comment on her choice not to testify as evidence of an absence of an explanation that could raise a reasonable doubt (see *R v Noble* at para 77). This raises what appears to be a troubling question. If the judge already knows that the accused is guilty, why consider the choice not to testify at all? In other words, why would the judge even think of commenting on the accused's decision not to testify, unless there exists some thought that the evidence did not prove guilt beyond a reasonable doubt? This sort of circular logic serves only to confuse a relatively simple concept—nobody, Crown, judge, or trier of fact, should consider the accused's choice not to testify for any purpose at all.

The rationale for the exception is that this is what is sometimes referred to in civil matters as the "slip rule": the appeal court does not want to throw out an entire trial if, at the very end, someone slips up and mentions "the elephant in the room"—the fact that the accused has not testified. The exception is created to address circumstances where mentioning the lack of testimony would not make any difference to the outcome.

As mentioned above, although an accused person is under no obligation to testify, once a decision has been made that the accused will tell her side of the story to the court, the Crown is free to cross-examine her extensively on her evidence. In that respect, anything that the accused does tell the court can be used against her in the same proceeding. The Charter does, however, protect all witnesses from having incriminating evidence used against them in any other proceeding. Section 13 provides:

> A witness who testifies in any proceedings has the right not to have any incriminating evidence so given used to incriminate that witness in any other proceedings, except in a prosecution for perjury or for the giving of contradictory evidence.

Section 13 has two implications. First, the Crown cannot use in the present proceeding any incriminating evidence that was given by the accused in a prior proceeding. Second, an accused can testify freely without having to worry that her testimony will be used against her in a subsequent proceeding. For example, a person who has been charged with murder can freely testify that it was impossible for her to have committed the offence because she was robbing a bank across town at the same time the victim was shot. The Crown would not be permitted to introduce this testimony if the accused were later charged and tried for robbing the bank.

In addition, section 13 of the Charter would also provide the accused with immunity for any evidence that could not have been obtained but for the compelled testimony. This is referred to as **derivative evidence**. Suppose a witness is compelled to testify at a murder trial and testifies that she was the killer and buried the murder weapon in her backyard. Not only would the witnesses' testimony be inadmissible in a subsequent prosecution against her, but so too would the evidence of the murder weapon found in the backyard. It is now clear that section 13 applies not only to different offences, but also to the same offence. In *Dubois v The Queen* ([1985] 2 SCR 350), the accused was tried twice for the same murder as a result of a successful appeal of the first trial. The accused had testified at the first trial but not at his second. As part of its case, the Crown used the accused's testimony from the first trial. This evidence was admitted by the trial judge, but the Supreme Court of Canada later ruled the evidence inadmissible.

However, the accused is not free to lie to the court without fear of repercussions. There is a stipulation with the section 13 protection that the witness must tell the truth. Her words can be used against her in a prosecution for perjury or to contradict the witness at a subsequent proceeding. Section 13 states that it does not apply if the accused is facing perjury-related charges as a result of providing false evidence in an earlier proceeding. The accused's prior testimony may be introduced notwithstanding the provisions of section 13 when the accused is being tried for lying in the previous proceeding.

> **derivative evidence**
> evidence that derives from a breach of an accused's rights

CASE IN POINT

Cross-Examination on Prior Inconsistent Evidence

R v Nedelcu, 2012 SCC 59, [2012] 3 SCR 311

In this case, the Supreme Court of Canada dealt with the issue of whether the Crown is permitted to cross-examine the accused on any differences between the accused's evidence at trial and evidence given during an earlier civil proceeding. In *Nedelcu*, the accused was charged with dangerous driving causing bodily harm and impaired driving causing bodily harm. During his examination for discovery, the accused testified that he had no recollection of the accident until he woke up later in hospital. At his criminal trial, however, the accused gave detailed evidence of the events leading up to and during the accident. The Crown was granted leave by the trial judge to cross-examine the accused on his discovery evidence. The evidence of the accused at trial was found to be unreliable, and he was found guilty of dangerous driving causing bodily harm.

The Ontario Court of Appeal allowed Mr. Nedelcu's appeal on the basis that the earlier evidence should not have been used, because section 13 of the Charter permits contradictory evidence to be used only in a prosecution for perjury or for the giving of contradictory evidence. In restoring the trial judge's conviction, the Supreme Court held that the evidence given by the accused was not incriminating evidence. In this regard, the court stated (at para 9):

> What then is "incriminating evidence"? The answer, I believe, should be straightforward. In my view, it can only mean evidence given by the witness at the prior proceeding that the Crown could use at the subsequent proceeding, if it were permitted to do so, to prove guilt, i.e., to prove or assist in proving one or more of the essential elements of the offence for which the witness is being tried.

In this case, the discovery evidence standing alone did not incriminate the accused. The discovery evidence was used to test the credibility of the accused and for no other purpose. It was not used as evidence from which the trier of fact could infer guilt.

Confessions

We have seen that persons accused of crimes have a right to remain silent while being investigated and being tried for a crime. They also have a right not to have their own testimony used against them in subsequent proceedings. However, what if an accused does not stand on her rights and confesses to the police? Does the right against self-incrimination extend in any way to confessions made by the accused?

The Problem: False Confessions

conscriptive evidence
evidence obtained as a result of the accused's being compelled to participate in the creation or location of evidence

There are significant dangers associated with admitting **conscriptive evidence**—evidence that has been extracted or conscripted from a suspect by the police. Apart from various societal issues that we may have, this evidence can be extremely unreliable if made under physical or emotional threat. Similarly, if the authorities offer promises of favour or offer other inducements, an arrested person may be much more likely to tell the authorities what he believes they want to hear. After all, if the police tell a suspect that they will release him if he simply admits to the crime, there is no way of knowing whether any confession was made truthfully, or made simply to gain freedom.

Most people would have difficulty believing that someone would confess to a crime that the person did not commit. Yet it has been documented that hundreds of confessions have later been proven to be false (see *R v Oickle*, 2000 SCC 38 at para 35, [2000] 2 SCR 3). Some have even confessed to murder. For example, Romeo Phillion spent over 30 years in prison after confessing to killing an Ottawa firefighter before being cleared of any wrongdoing in 2009. Kyle Unger was exonerated in the same year after having been convicted in 1992 of sexual assault and murder following his confession. Unfortunately, people do confess to crimes that they have not committed.

The Solution: The Confession Rule

As a result, the common law developed a rule that essentially deemed a confession to be inadmissible unless the Crown could prove it to be voluntary. In order to be voluntary, the statement had to be free from threats or promises. Statements not made voluntarily can thus be viewed the same as privileged communications—they are not admissible before the trier of fact. A judge sitting alone may hear a confession to determine whether it was made voluntarily, but once she rules it was made involuntarily, she is then required to "disabuse" her mind of it. If the other evidence falls short of a conviction on its own, the judge would then be required to acquit a person she knew had confessed to the offence he is charged with.

confession rule
rule that a statement made to a person in authority is not admissible unless it was made voluntarily

The **confession rule**, also called the *Ibrahim* rule, can be stated in the following terms:

> A statement made by an accused to a person in authority is a confession and is not admissible against the accused unless the Crown proves beyond a reasonable doubt that the confession was made voluntarily.

This rule was first established at common law in the 1914 case *The King v Ibrahim* ([1914] AC 599 (PC)). *Ibrahim* remained the leading case on the confession rule for three-quarters of a century. In essence, it stated that the Crown was obliged to prove that a statement made to a person in authority was voluntary "in the sense that it has not been obtained from the accused either by fear of prejudice or hope of advantage exercised or held out by a person in authority."

The Modern Confession Rule

The *Ibrahim* rule has been refined over time, and the Charter raised the standard that needed to be met by the state in proving voluntariness. The case of *R v Oickle* set a new standard for admission of statements from an accused to persons in authority. In *Oickle*, the accused was charged with setting a series of eight fires in the Waterville, Nova Scotia area. He was a volunteer fireman and attended each fire. The police questioned Oickle extensively over a period of about eight hours. He had agreed to take a polygraph test along with four or five other individuals to help the police narrow down suspects. Of note is the finding that the police exaggerated the reliability of the polygraph when informing Oickle that he had failed the test. Over a series of interrogations from a number of officers, Oickle progressively incriminated himself to the point where he took the police on a videotaped tour of the scenes, describing how he set each fire. The police gave him "official warnings" at a number of key points in the interview process and informed him that he could leave at any time, but there was some "unfortunate" use of language implying that "it would be better" for him to confess his involvement in setting these fires and the making of offers of psychiatric help to overcome his pyromania.

The Supreme Court of Canada examined the traditional confession rule and whether it continued to be appropriate in the present context. The court felt that the *Ibrahim* rule (which had undergone some modifications at common law) required further modification and clarification and extended the rule to provide a thorough template for assessing the voluntariness of a statement by an accused to a person in authority. The extended rule is known as the **Oickle rule**. What underlies the majority reasoning in *Oickle* is the provision that any choice by a suspect to speak to the authorities must be a meaningful one. The *Oickle* rule may be summarized as follows:

Oickle **rule**
rule requiring that the will of the accused has not been overborne by inducements, oppressive circumstances, or lack of an operating mind, and that police trickery has not unfairly denied the accused the right to silence

1. The rule applies to statements made to persons in authority.
2. The Crown has the obligation to establish beyond a reasonable doubt that any statement to a person in authority is voluntary in the circumstances by showing that the will of the accused has not been overborne by
   a. threats or promises,
   b. oppressive circumstances, or
   c. lack of an operating mind.
3. The Crown has the obligation to establish beyond a reasonable doubt that there has not been any police trickery that *unfairly* takes away the accused's right to silence.

The Test for Voluntariness

The obligation on the Crown to prove, beyond a reasonable doubt, that a statement was made voluntarily has been maintained from the *Ibrahim* approach. This means that the prosecution must show that the confession was made freely without threats or promises to the accused. Before the advent of the Charter, those parts of a confession that were proven to be true could be admitted as evidence even if the confession was made involuntarily. This makes sense if the purpose of the confession rule is only to exclude unreliable evidence. If the evidence was collaterally proven to be reliable, what possible reason can there be for throwing it out of court? There are, of course, other societal reasons for the confession rule. Do we want to sanction police beatings even if an accused confesses the truth? What about the right to remain silent? The Charter has now changed the situation so that involuntary statements are always excluded, whether they are proven to be true or not.

The test for voluntariness is subjective—is the person making the statement voluntarily?—because what would be "oppressive circumstances" to one person would not faze another. For example, a person who is claustrophobic and locked in a tiny interrogation room may do almost anything if she believes that it will get her some more space. Similarly, treatment that would constitute an inducement to a nicotine addict, such as withholding cigarettes until a confession is offered, would not significantly affect a non-smoker. The use of the expression "in the circumstances" assures that the interpretation must be individualized.

What this means is that there cannot be a list of objective factors that can be used to determine voluntariness. In *Oickle*, the Supreme Court of Canada found that "hard and fast rules simply cannot account for the variety of circumstances that vitiate [spoil or invalidate] the voluntariness of a confession." The court recognized that while certain factors such as "imminent threats of torture" will obviously make a confession involuntary, most cases will not be so clear. For example, the use of veiled threats may require close scrutiny, but will not always result in the inadmissibility of a confession. The court also recognized that the police will often offer some inducement to obtain a confession and not every inducement will invalidate a confession. This is only a problem if, after looking at all of the factors, the inducements are strong enough to raise a reasonable doubt about the voluntariness of the confession. One especially important consideration is whether there was a *quid pro quo* offer made— a favour or advantage expected or granted in return for a confession. A confession may not be invalidated simply because a cigarette was offered during the interrogation. However, the court may take a dimmer view if the accused was told that he would get a cigarette after telling the police what had occurred.

To ensure that the statement truly is voluntary, the rule requires a "free" operating mind. That is, the accused must know two things: He must know what he is saying, and he must know that it may be used against him. Thus, a suspect who is mentally ill, intoxicated, high on drugs, or hypnotized might not pass the *Oickle* test. Significantly, the court does not need to determine whether the accused made a wise choice in speaking to the authorities or whether the choice was in the accused's best interest, simply whether the accused had the "limited degree of cognitive ability to understand what he or she is saying and to comprehend that the evidence may be used in proceedings against the accused" (see *R v Whittle*, [1994] 2 SCR 914 at 939).

Police Trickery

Police trickery is not outlawed; indeed, some of the best work that police departments do is by tricking the "bad guys." It has often been said "that the investigation of crime and the detection of criminals is not a game to be governed by the Marquess of Queensbury rules" (see *Rothman v The Queen* at 697). But such trickery cannot be of the unfair kind. In addition to a sense of fair play, the courts have a vested interest in ensuring that the administration of justice not be sullied by the endorsement of unfair police practices. Police trickery is not acceptable where it violates the right to silence, undermines voluntariness as such, or is so appalling as to shock the community (see *R v Oickle* at para 67). If a police officer pretended to be a justice of the peace setting bail for an accused, this would be not only an unfair trick, but one that would cast the justice system in a negative light. Other often-cited examples of dirty tricks would be a police officer posing as a lock-up chaplain to hear a suspect's confession, pretending to be a lawyer eliciting an incriminating statement from a suspect, or injecting truth serum instead of insulin into a diabetic suspect (see *R v Oickle* at para 66).

CASE IN POINT

Dirty Tricks

R v Welsh, 2013 ONCA 190

In this case, the Ontario Court of Appeal dealt with the issue of the admissibility of a statement made by two suspects to an undercover police officer posing as an obeahman. Obeah is a religion based on mysticism and spiritualism and is commonly practised throughout the Caribbean and by many Caribbean Canadians. An obeahman is believed by adherents to have the ability to communicate with the spirit world and to influence events and people in the physical world. In order to gain the trust of the two suspects, the police devised an elaborate ruse involving a ritual where an egg was broken that contained red dye to simulate blood. Later, a dead crow was left at a residence to demonstrate the power of the "obeahman." As part of the ruse, a white handkerchief was provided as a protective device against the police. A police office later feigned illness during a staged traffic stop of a person carrying the handkerchief. Eventually, the suspects made incriminating statements to the undercover officer concerning the death of the victim in order to stop the "evil spirit" from harming them and their family.

The accused were convicted and appealed. There were several grounds raised on appeal, including that the obeah statements should not have been admitted by the trial judge for three reasons. First, the statements were made to a religious adviser and therefore privileged. Second, the statements were obtained in a manner that infringed the appellants' Charter rights to freedom of religion and equality. Third, the police employed "dirty tricks" in obtaining the statements. In dismissing the appeals, the court found that there were no Charter violations and that the communication was not privileged.

The court also found that the obeahman operation did not constitute a "dirty trick." The court provided four reasons for this finding. First, the appellants were not in custody when they made the statements. Second, the undercover officer was not a person in authority, so voluntariness was not an issue. Third, the appellants' corrupt purpose in making the statements undermined any legitimate religious considerations. The appellants made the statements to thwart the police and the justice system, not to fulfill a religious purpose or spiritual need.

The court concluded as follows (at para 105):

> Fourth, this is not a case where admitting the Obeah statements would shock the conscience of the community or bring the administration of justice into disrepute. The standard for finding that a police investigative technique rises to that level is a high one. While many cases speak of the dirty tricks doctrine, few if any apply it to exclude inculpatory statements.

Proving Voluntariness

Sometimes, during a trial, an accused person or his lawyer or legal representative will admit that a confession was made voluntarily because it may be exculpatory or simply because there may not be any chance of its being excluded. Normally, however, if the prosecution wishes to introduce a confession into evidence, it must prove voluntariness on a voir dire. As you may recall from Chapter 1, a voir dire is a trial within a trial to determine the admissibility of a piece of evidence. The evidence on a voir dire does not form part of the case against the accused in the trial. The evidence is used solely to determine whether a confession is admissible. The accused may testify on the voir dire if he wishes, offering his side of the story. However, it is fairly well established in Canada that the Crown can ask the accused whether the confession is true or not because this relates directly to the issue of voluntariness.

Person in Authority

person in authority
person in a position to influence the prosecution against an accused

Not all statements are confessions. Only statements made to a **person in authority** are confessions and therefore subject to the confession rule. The court system is designed to regulate state action and not individual initiatives. Thus, a private vigilante who acquires evidence of child pornography by coercing a confession would not run afoul of these provisions, although the evidence would still fall within a judge's residual discretion to exclude.

The test for determining whether someone is a person in authority is whether the accused reasonably believed that the person was in a position to influence the prosecution against him (see *R v Hodgson*, [1998] 2 SCR 449 at para 34). Clearly, police officers are persons in authority. But so too are prosecutors, jailers, security guards, fire marshals, and even owners of property that has been stolen. Teachers, guidance counsellors, doctors, employers, social workers, and even parents may also be persons in authority if the circumstances warrant. However, an undercover police officer (who is not recognized as such by the accused) is not a person in authority because the accused has no reason to believe that the officer can have any impact in the prosecutorial process.

The accused's belief must not only be honest, but also be reasonable. In other words, the test is partly subjective—what did this person believe?—and partly objective—what would a reasonable person believe? Both parts must be satisfied before someone qualifies as a person in authority.

The Confession Rule and Section 7 of the Charter

As we saw earlier in this chapter, section 7 of the Charter has been interpreted by the courts as providing a pre-trial right to silence. While the two are closely related, it is important to recognize that the Charter right exists independently from the confession rule. The Supreme Court of Canada characterized the similarities between the two in the following terms (*R v Singh*, 2007 SCC 48 at para 37, [2007] 3 SCR 405):

> Therefore, voluntariness, as it is understood today, requires that the court scrutinize whether the accused was denied his or her right to silence. The right to silence is defined in accordance with constitutional principles. A finding of voluntariness

will therefore be determinative of the s. 7 issue. In other words, if the Crown proves voluntariness beyond a reasonable doubt, there can be no finding of a *Charter* violation of the right to silence in respect of the same statement. The converse holds true as well. If the circumstances are such that an accused is able to show on a balance of probabilities a breach of his or her right to silence, the Crown will not be in a position to meet the voluntariness test.

In short, a voluntary confession will not infringe the right to silence contained in section 7 of the Charter, and an infringement of the Charter right will preclude a finding of voluntariness. However, it is wrong to see one doctrine as subsuming the other.

Comparing the Charter Right to Silence with the Confession Rule

The following chart compares the right to silence as defined in the Charter with the confession rule.

Charter Right to Silence	Confession Rule
Applies to any statements made to the police upon arrest or detention.	Applies only to statements made to persons in authority.
Applies only upon arrest and detention.	Applies also to pre-arrest and pre-detention statements.
Applies to all statements, including statutorily compelled statements.	Does not protect voluntary statutorily compelled statements.
Derivative evidence may be excluded under section 24(2) of the Charter.	Does not protect against the use of derivative evidence.[2]
Burden is on the accused to show, on a balance of probabilities, a violation of constitutional rights.	Burden is on the prosecution to show, beyond a reasonable doubt, that the confession was voluntary.
Except for statutorily compelled statements, a statement is excluded under section 24(2) of the Charter only if admitting the evidence would bring the administration of justice into disrepute.	Violation results in automatic exclusion of evidence.

Mr. Big

The Mr. Big operation is a covert investigative technique used in cases involving serious unsolved crime. The technique was developed in Canada and has been used by police more than 350 times. The Mr. Big operation has helped to secure convictions in hundreds of cases (see *R v Hart*, 2014 SCC 52 at paras 56, 61, [2014] 2 SCR 544).

A typical Mr. Big sting involves the use of undercover police officers to gain the trust of a suspect. The suspect is usually befriended by the officer and gradually drawn into an escalating series of fictional crimes. At some point, the suspect meets with the crime boss, known colloquially as "Mr. Big," in an interview-like meeting. The suspect is asked to divulge information about the crime the police are investigating to earn the trust of Mr. Big and gain entry into the fictional criminal organization. Often the suspect initially denies any involvement in the targeted crime, but as the questioning intensifies, it becomes clear to the suspect that acceptance by Mr. Big and membership in the organization are predicated on "confessing" to the crime. The suspect is then arrested and charged.

Because the undercover officers are not persons in authority, any statements made by a suspect would be admissible without the Crown's having to prove that they were made voluntarily. There is also no right to silence because the accused is not detained. As a result, statements made during the course of a Mr. Big operation have been routinely admitted under the party admissions exception to the hearsay rule (*R v Hart* at para 63). But there has been considerable controversy about this technique, and its use is prohibited in many jurisdictions, including the United Kingdom and the United States.

The biggest concern is with reliability (at para 68). Suspects tell Mr. Big what he wants to hear after being exposed to powerful inducements and sometimes veiled threats. The issue is the same as with confessions to persons in authority: Is the suspect really telling the truth, or has the suspect's will been overborne by the inducements or threats?

Another concern with this evidence is that it shows the accused in a bad light. The trier of fact will hear that the accused willingly participated in "simulated" criminal activity and was eager to join a criminal organization. This sullies the accused's character and creates significant prejudice (at para 73). The risks therefore also parallel those associated with introducing bad character evidence against a person who has been charged with a criminal offence.

Finally, there is a societal concern about condoning this type of conduct by the police (at para 78). As part of the scheme, suspects are encouraged to commit crimes and are rewarded, often by cash payments. The police cultivate criminal behaviour and create an aura of violence during the sting operation. The question, simply put, is: should the ends justify the means? In other words, are we prepared to condone such conduct from the police in the pursuit of justice?

As a result of these concerns, the Supreme Court of Canada developed a two-pronged solution in *R v Hart* when dealing with statements made during a Mr. Big operation. The first prong establishes a new common law rule of evidence that addresses reliability concerns, and the second "relies on a more robust conception of the doctrine of abuse of process to deal with the problem of police misconduct" (at para 84).

In setting out the new common law rule for assessing the admissibility of these statements, the court provided as follows (at para 85):

> The first prong recognizes a new common law rule of evidence for assessing the admissibility of these confessions. The rule operates as follows: Where the state recruits an accused into a fictitious criminal organization of its own making and seeks to elicit a confession from him, any confession made by the accused to the state during the operation should be treated as presumptively inadmissible. This

presumption of inadmissibility is overcome where the Crown can establish, on a balance of probabilities, that the probative value of the confession outweighs its prejudicial effect.

The onus is therefore on the Crown to demonstrate that the probative value of the evidence exceeds its prejudicial effect. Probative value is assessed in terms of the reliability of the evidence. This is balanced against the prejudice that flows from the bad character evidence, which is invariably associated with the conduct of the accused during the course of a Mr. Big operation (at para 85).

The second prong deals with the issue of police misconduct. The courts have the right to exclude evidence to prevent an abuse of process when the state manipulates events and people for the purpose of seeking convictions (at para 112). The flip side to this, as we have seen in *Oickle*, is that a certain degree of police trickery is not necessarily a bad thing when dealing with criminals. So where is the line drawn between acceptable and unacceptable police conduct?

The starting point is that the varied nature of these operations makes it impossible to draw an inflexible line that delineates abusive police conduct. In *Hart*, the court indicated that police conduct becomes problematic when it is coercive. As a result, a statement derived from a Mr. Big operation is not admissible if the defence can demonstrate that it would be an abuse of process to admit the evidence (at para 89). Police conduct that overcomes the will of a suspect and coerces a confession would almost certainly be an abuse of process (at para 115). The court identified physical violence and threats of violence as examples of coercive police conduct. Taking advantage of a suspect's vulnerabilities, such as mental health problems, substance addiction, or youthfulness, is similarly problematic. The court further raised the possibility that Mr. Big operations may be abusive in other ways, thus providing trial judges wide latitude in identifying abuses of process (at paras 116-118).

The Mr. Big Rule

A statement made by an accused person during a Mr. Big operation is presumed to be inadmissible. For the statement to be admissible, the Crown must overcome two hurdles:

1. The Crown must demonstrate, on a balance of probabilities, that the probative value of the evidence exceeds its prejudicial effect.

2. Even where the Crown can establish that the probative value of the evidence exceeds its prejudicial effect, the evidence may be excluded to prevent an abuse of the court process.

Compellability in "Related Proceedings"

Because the world we live in is layered and complex, one legal matter often influences or interconnects with another. While an accused has a right to remain silent and not testify in a criminal proceeding, what happens when a related civil proceeding requires his evidence in order to proceed? This sort of situation arises when one unfortunate circumstance leads to both a criminal process and a civil one, such as where a mine collapse results in a public inquiry as well as criminal negligence charges, or where a death results in a coroner's inquest as well as murder charges. Most common is the motor vehicle accident where the driver responsible for causing the accident is both sued by the victim and charged with a driving offence. While the jeopardy that a person faces in these civil proceedings can include damages, fines, public humiliation, and loss of vocation, in criminal matters an accused faces imprisonment. It is because of this serious potential consequence that our system of justice ensures that the accused is afforded the greatest possible protection.

Let's first deal with the situation where a person who has been charged with a criminal offence is also facing a related civil lawsuit. As already discussed in this chapter, the accused (or the defendant in the civil case) would have the protection of section 13 of the Charter, and any incriminating evidence given in the first proceeding would generally not be admissible in the second proceeding. It is well-established practice, however, that the civil action will otherwise proceed normally unless there are extraordinary and exceptional circumstances. In those rare cases, the appropriate remedy would be to stay the civil action pending final determination of the criminal charges (see *Nash v Ontario*, 1995 CanLII 2934 (Ont CA)).

Another situation that may arise is when two people are charged with committing a criminal offence together, but face separate trials. This may occur, for example, because one of the accused is under the age of 18 and faces a trial under the provisions of the *Youth Criminal Justice Act*, while the other is over the age of 18 and is prosecuted under the provisions of the *Criminal Code*. The question is whether one can be compelled to testify against the other, and the answer generally is yes. Neither accused has any special status in terms of non-compellability at the trial of the other accused. One accused's testimony is compellable in a trial against the other accused under the general rule applicable to all witnesses. The principle against self-incrimination is satisfied by the **simple use immunity** provided by section 13 of the Charter, together with a residual derivative use immunity in respect of evidence that could not have been obtained but for the compelled testimony (see *R v S (RJ)* at 566). As previously discussed in this chapter, this means that not only are the accused's words protected, but any evidence that could not have been obtained but for the compelled testimony will also likely be excluded by the trial judge.

simple use immunity immunity that prevents the use of compelled testimony as evidence against a witness

In other situations, procedures such as public inquiries are used to address causes of tragedies that affect scores of people, so it is equally important that they not be frustrated. Take the example of the Walkerton inquiry and the criminal charges arising from the same incident (see Ontario Ministry of the Attorney General, *Walkerton Commission of Inquiry Reports*, online: <http://www.attorneygeneral.jus.gov.on.ca/english/about/pubs/walkerton>). Clearly, the people of Ontario and, to a lesser extent, the people of Canada had a lot at stake in determining what caused seven people to die and 2,300 to become seriously ill. The inquiry commenced, and two primary witnesses were Stan Koebel, the manager of the Walkerton Public Utilities Commission, and his brother Frank, who was a foreman during the relevant time. During the inquiry, the police were in the process of an investigation that could and in fact did result in charges against the brothers. In April 2003, both were charged with endangering the public and various forgery and breach-of-trust offences. The brothers would have been well advised to be concerned that the information they provided to the inquiry would aid the investigators in their job of determining whether any criminal acts led to the disaster. Of course, section 13 of the Charter ensured that their words in the Walkerton inquiry could not be used in evidence against them in a criminal proceeding. However, even though the actual words could not be used, they would be helpful to police investigators.

What determines whether a person can decline to participate in a civil proceeding on the basis that criminal charges are pending? In order to balance an accused's right to silence with the protection of the public and administration of the overall justice system, the courts apply the following principles in determining whether an accused or suspect may be compelled to testify in related civil proceedings:

1. The judge must determine the purpose of the civil proceeding.
2. If the sole purpose is to obtain information from a suspect or accused to aid in prosecuting that person, the subpoena for the civil matter will be quashed.
3. If the purpose includes resolution of a legitimate public interest concern, then, unless the predominant purpose is to conscript the accused's testimony against himself, the suspect or accused will be required to testify.

Balancing the right of an accused to remain silent and the importance of the inquiry to the state can be difficult. If the state were to call a public inquiry into the increase in marijuana grow operations and call as a witness someone whom the police suspect of being a kingpin in the drug trade, the right of the accused might well outweigh the interests of society, particularly where there are less intrusive means of obtaining information on grow-ops. When considering the administration of justice, if the police were routinely to use a public inquiry process to aid their investigations of suspected criminals whom they could not catch through conventional investigative means, then the public's perception of the administration of justice and respect for public inquiries would diminish, causing damage to this legal process.

CHAPTER SUMMARY

The right against self-incrimination is broad and protects a person during the investigative stage right through to trial. It includes the right to remain silent, the right not to be compelled to be a witness against oneself, the right to testify freely without having to worry about authorities using the testimony in a subsequent proceeding, and the right to be free from oppressive or unfair police questioning. The courts are willing to grant relief under the Charter or common law in appropriate cases to protect these important rights.

KEY TERMS

confession rule, 206
conscriptive evidence, 206
derivative evidence, 205
Oickle rule, 207
person in authority, 210
right against self-incrimination, 200
simple use immunity, 214

NOTES

1   For example, see sections 199 and 200 of Ontario's *Highway Traffic Act*.

2   Recall that derivative evidence is evidence that is derived, or comes about, as a result of a breach of an accused's person's rights. The classic example is of the murder weapon being found by the police after a confession was beaten out of the accused. This evidence is sometimes referred to as "the fruit of a poisoned tree."

REFERENCES

Bartle, R v, [1994] 3 SCR 173.

Canada Evidence Act, RSC 1985, c C-5.

Canadian Charter of Rights and Freedoms, Part I of the *Constitution Act, 1982*, being Schedule B to the *Canada Act 1982* (UK), 1982, c 11.

Dubois v The Queen, [1985] 2 SCR 350.

Hart, R v, 2014 SCC 52, [2014] 2 SCR 544.

Hebert, R v, [1990] 2 SCR 151.

Hodgson, R v, [1998] 2 SCR 449.

Ibrahim, The King v, [1914] AC 599 (PC).

Nash v Ontario, 1995 CanLII 2934 (Ont CA).

Nedelcu, R v, 2012 SCC 59, [2012] 3 SCR 311.

Noble, R v, [1997] 1 SCR 874.

Oickle, R v, 2000 SCC 38, [2000] 2 SCR 3.

Ontario, *Highway Traffic Act*, RSO 1990, c H.8.

Ontario Ministry of the Attorney General, *Walkerton Commission of Inquiry Reports*, online: <http://www .attorneygeneral.jus.gov.on.ca/english/about/pubs/ walkerton>.

Rothman v The Queen, [1981] 1 SCR 640.

S (RJ), R v, [1995] 1 SCR 451.

Sinclair, R v, 2010 SCC 35, [2010] 2 SCR 310.

Singh, R v, 2007 SCC 48, [2007] 3 SCR 405.

Thomas Sophonow Inquiry Report. Final report 4 November 2001, online: <http://digitalcollection.gov .mb.ca/awweb/pdfopener?smd=1&did=12713 &md=1>.

Welsh, R v, 2013 ONCA 190.

White, R v, [1999] 2 SCR 417.

Whittle, R v, [1994] 2 SCR 914.

REVIEW QUESTIONS

1. Summarize the Supreme Court of Canada's extension of the confession rule.

2. How is an individual's "right to silence" protected in Canada?

3. What is a person's remedy for a breach of a Charter right? Is this any different in a situation where a confession was not made voluntarily?

4. What three principles do the courts consider in deciding whether to compel a suspect or an accused to testify in a related civil proceeding such as a public inquiry?

DISCUSSION QUESTIONS

1. Patrick MacNamara teaches at a local high school and coaches the school hockey team. He suspects that certain members of his team are smoking marijuana. Patrick calls them into his office individually for a "friendly chat." All of the players initially deny drug use, but Patrick assures them that it is in their best interests to "come clean." He further states that if he finds out that any of his players lied to him, he will kick them off the team. The team captain readily admits to using drugs as well as providing drugs to some of his teammates. Patrick goes to the police with this information, and the player is charged with both possession and trafficking offences. Is the statement made by the player a confession? Is it admissible? Why?

2. The police go door to door after a six-year-old girl is brutally assaulted and murdered. They ask all males who live within two blocks of the girl's home for samples of their DNA. Most comply, but several refuse. The police subsequently follow those who refused, hoping to find some evidence linking them to the deceased. The police remove a pop can from the trash after it is discarded by one of the suspects and recover a sample of his DNA. The police match the suspect's DNA with samples found on the body of the girl. Is the evidence admissible? Why or why not? Do you think that the police have a right to ask all adult males in a certain geographical area to provide samples of their DNA?

3. A police officer investigates a minor traffic accident and asks both drivers to provide the usual documentation and their version of events. One complies but the other refuses to provide any information, including his driver's licence and evidence of insurance, claiming a "right to silence." Do you think that the second driver was justified in his actions? Why or why not?

4. Ravi Singh is a former police officer. As a cop, he was as tough as they come. He is being questioned about $5 million in drug money that has disappeared from the police station. The investigating officers tell Ravi that they have a video of him removing the money. No such video exists. They also tell him that they are sick of bad cops and will put him in a holding cell with other criminals unless he talks. Police officers are known to have short lifespans when placed in the general prison population. Ravi, however, has no fear of being put in a holding cell and relishes the opportunity to knock a few heads. However, he decides that there is ample evidence to convict him based on the video, so he admits to taking the money. Is Ravi's statement a confession? Is it admissible? Why or why not?

Wrongfully Obtained Evidence

12

LEARNING OUTCOMES

After completing this chapter, you should be able to:

▪ Demonstrate an understanding of when a right under the *Canadian Charter of Rights and Freedoms* may be limited.

▪ Identify the two criteria set out in the *Oakes* test that must be met before a Charter right can be limited.

▪ Demonstrate an understanding of the rights set out in sections 8 and 9 of the Charter.

▪ Describe the remedies a court may prescribe when evidence is obtained through a breach of a person's Charter rights.

▪ Identify and apply the five components of an exclusionary remedy.

▪ Identify and apply the test for excluding evidence that was obtained as a result of a violation of a right set out in the Charter.

Introduction

Wrongfully obtained evidence is often referred to as "improperly obtained" evidence. The authors have chosen to use the word "wrongfully" because it has a stronger connotation than "improperly." This is another area of evidence law where the principle that all valuable evidence should be put before the trier of fact may give way to another, more important principle—that the courts cannot be seen to support illegitimate methods of acquiring evidence. The court must balance the interests of putting all relevant evidence before the trier of fact against the importance of preserving individual rights and the reputation of the justice system.

The fact that evidence was obtained through illegitimate avenues does not mean that the evidence is less trustworthy; indeed, evidence that has been wrongfully acquired may, in many respects, be more reliable. For example, if the police break into a private home or a dwelling to surreptitiously place a listening device, the occupants, having no fear of repercussion, will likely speak openly and honestly. Similarly, the police would likely put a large dent in the marijuana grow-op industry if they were permitted to search all private dwellings on mere suspicion. The problem is that illegally obtained evidence infringes the rights of individuals and harms the reputation of the justice system.

Before the *Canadian Charter of Rights and Freedoms* existed, individuals had little recourse when the police obtained evidence against them through illegitimate means. The prevalent view in the court system was that it was appropriate to "set a thief to catch a thief." In other words, the courts believed that people who resorted to criminal means should have no expectation that the state will treat them in anything but a like manner. Evidence that was illegally obtained was not usually excluded and the police were not usually disciplined. However, it was always open to a judge to exclude evidence on the basis that to admit it would undermine the public's faith in the justice system. But judges seldom did, choosing instead to save this remedy for the most extreme abuses. The landscape was significantly and permanently altered when the Charter became part of the Canadian Constitution on April 17, 1982.

Overview of the Charter

The Charter sets out a number of legal rights. Some Charter rights serve to confirm and reinforce previously existing common law rights, but others are entirely new. The rights and freedoms contained in the Charter, however, are not absolute. Section 33 permits governments in Canada to expressly declare any statute valid, notwithstanding the guarantees contained in section 2 and sections 7 to 15 of the Charter. By invoking the notwithstanding clause, a government can trump the rights set out in these sections of the Charter.

Another important factor to keep in mind is that, by virtue of section 32, the Charter applies only to interactions between the state and individuals. More specifically, it applies only to governments in Canada. That is, the Charter does not apply to interactions between individuals and foreign governments.

CASE IN POINT

The Charter and Foreign Government Actions

R v Harrer, [1995] 3 SCR 562

In this case, the accused's boyfriend escaped custody in Vancouver while in the process of being extradited for trial in the United States on drug charges. The accused was detained by US immigration authorities after they learned that she was staying with her mother in Cleveland. Immigration authorities turned her over to US Marshals officers, who questioned her about her boyfriend. During that interrogation, the officers changed their focus from the boyfriend to possible criminal activity by the accused in Canada. They did not re-warn the accused of her rights, as would be required under Canadian law, when the focus of their investigation shifted to her activities.

The question before the Supreme Court of Canada was whether the subsequent statements made by the accused were admissible in her trial in Canada, in light of the fact that the actions of the US authorities would have breached her Charter rights if they had taken place in Canada. The court found that Canadian authorities have no right to control the US investigative process and that the US authorities were not acting as agents of the Canadian authorities. In his analysis, La Forest J, writing for the majority, stated (at para 12):

> What I think is determinative against the argument that the *Charter* applied to the interrogation in the present case is the simple fact that the United States immigration officials and the Marshals were not acting on behalf of any of the governments of Canada, the provinces or the territories, the state actors to which, by virtue of s. 32(1) the application of the *Charter* is confined .... It follows that the *Charter* simply has no direct application to the interrogations in the United States because the governments mentioned in s. 32(1) were not implicated in these activities. The United States authorities involved in the present case can in no way be considered as acting on behalf of those governments, and this was not really contested at the hearing.

Although this chapter deals mainly with the interaction between the Charter and evidence that has been wrongfully obtained, it is noteworthy that the Charter can have other implications to the law of evidence. Section 52(1) of the *Constitution Act, 1982* can be used to strike down or modify laws that are inconsistent with the provisions of the Charter. Section 52(1) provides:

> The Constitution of Canada is the supreme law of Canada, and any law that is inconsistent with the provisions of the Constitution is, to the extent of the inconsistency, of no force or effect.

Because the Charter is part of the Constitution, any law that violates or infringes a Charter right is, to the extent of the inconsistency, of no force or effect. The courts have taken a very broad approach to section 52(1); not only will the offending parts of any law be removed, but in appropriate cases, courts may, in effect, amend the impugned law by **reading into** or adding provisions that would make the law consistent with the provisions of the Charter. Clearly, this can have implications in evidence law. Any law that offends a Charter right is open to a Charter challenge. For example, both spousal privilege at common law and the statutory provisions dealing with spousal privilege require spouses to be married to each other in order for their communications to be privileged. This law discriminates against common law spouses on the basis of their marital status and appears to be contrary to the equality provisions

reading into
a court's adding of language into legislation in order to make it comply with Charter provisions

of section 15 of the Charter. While the law is not yet settled by the Supreme Court of Canada, some courts have extended this form of privilege to unmarried common law spouses, while other courts have not.[1]

However, as mentioned above, the rights and freedoms set out in the Charter are not absolute. The drafters of the Charter recognized that in a democracy a friction exists between the rights of the individual and the will of the majority, and attempted to balance these competing interests by including section 1, which provides:

> The *Canadian Charter of Rights and Freedoms* guarantees the rights and freedoms set out in it subject only to such reasonable limits prescribed by law as can be demonstrably justified in a free and democratic society.

This provision does two things: It guarantees the rights that follow it and, at the same time, it sets out certain limitations on those rights. What this means is that section 1 permits governments to enact legislation that infringes a Charter right where the criteria of section 1 are met.

Once the courts establish that a Charter right has been infringed, the onus shifts to the state to justify the law on a balance of probabilities. As a threshold consideration, the limit must be prescribed by law. In *R v Therens* ([1985] 1 SCR 613), the Supreme Court of Canada found that the prosecution could not rely on the provisions of section 1 to remedy a breach of the accused's section 10(b) right to retain and instruct counsel because the limit on the accused's right to consult counsel was imposed by the conduct of the police officers and not by Parliament.

Oakes **test**
test used by the courts to determine whether a Charter right or freedom can be limited by section 1; the measure limiting the right or freedom must be sufficiently important, and the means chosen must be reasonable and demonstrably justified

The Supreme Court of Canada in *R v Oakes* ([1986] 1 SCR 103) found that two criteria must be satisfied before section 1 can apply. This is known as the ***Oakes* test**. First, the objective of the measures limiting the Charter right must be "of sufficient importance to warrant overriding a constitutionally protected right or freedom." Second, the means chosen must be reasonable and demonstrably justified. This second criterion involves a "proportionality test," which consists of three parts. The first part requires that the measures limiting the Charter right be rationally connected to the objective in question. They must not be arbitrary, unfair, or based on irrational considerations. The second part examines to what degree the measures impair the Charter right. The measures should impair "as little as possible" the right or freedom in question. The third part compares the effects of the measures and their objective. There must be proportionality between the effects of the measures that are responsible for limiting the Charter right or freedom, and the objective that has been identified as being of "sufficient importance." What this means is that the more severe the effects of a measure, the more important the objective must be if the measure is to be saved by section 1.

The Oakes Test

1. **Sufficient Importance**

   The Crown must show that the objective of the statute is sufficiently import-ant to override a Charter right.

2. **Proportionality Test**

   a. **Rational Connection**

      The measures limiting the Charter right must be rationally connected to the objective sought.

   b. **Minimal Impairment**

      The measures must impair the Charter right as little as possible.

   c. **Proportionality**

      There must be proportionality between the effects of the measures limit-ing the Charter right and the objective referred to in the threshold requirement.

Breach of a Charter Right

The Charter contains a number of basic rights that everyone enjoys, and state inter-ference with many of these rights has direct evidentiary implications. We have al-ready looked at some of the rights enshrined in the Charter when we dealt with self-incrimination in Chapter 11. We saw that the Supreme Court of Canada has in-terpreted the section 7 right to life, liberty, and security of the person as including a general right to silence (*R v Hebert*, [1990] 2 SCR 151). Other rights that we looked at were the right under section 10(b) to retain and instruct counsel and to be advised of that right; the right under section 11(c) not to be compelled to be a witness against oneself; and the right under section 13 not to have incriminating evidence given in one proceeding used against the person in another proceeding.

There are several provisions of the Charter that we have not yet discussed that sig-nificantly affect how evidence is gathered and presented in court. These are discussed in the sections below.

Unreasonable Search or Seizure

Section 8 of the Charter expressly protects individuals against unreasonable search or seizure, as follows:

Everyone has the right to be secure against unreasonable search or seizure.

Any protection against unreasonable searches by the state must balance the competing interests of a person's right to privacy against the state's interest in crime prevention. Otherwise, we would have a rule that either outlawed all searches or permitted all searches. In order to reconcile these competing interests, the courts have adopted the concept of a reasonable expectation of privacy. It is only where there is a reasonable expectation of privacy that a search must be conducted in a reasonable manner. In other words, section 8 of the Charter does not apply to those situations where there is no reasonable expectation of privacy. For example, a person who openly consumes alcohol in a car or walks down the street waving a gun cannot have any reasonable expectation of privacy. In fact, the converse is true: That person can be expected to be apprehended by the authorities because of the public manner in which he displayed his actions. On the other hand, a person who consumes narcotics at home may be breaking the law, but is doing so privately and has a reasonable expectation of privacy.

What Factors Determine a Reasonable Expectation of Privacy?

In *R v Belnavis* ([1997] 3 SCR 341), the Supreme Court of Canada, quoting from *R v Edwards* ([1996] 1 SCR 128), summarized the principles applicable to section 8 as follows (at para 20):

> 4. As a general rule, two distinct inquiries must be made in relation to s. 8. First, has the accused a reasonable expectation of privacy. Second, if he has such an expectation, was the search by the police conducted reasonably.
>
> 5. A reasonable expectation of privacy is to be determined on the basis of the totality of the circumstances.
>
> 6. The factors to be considered in assessing the totality of the circumstances may include, but are not restricted to, the following:
>
>> (i)   presence at the time of the search;
>> (ii) possession or control of the property or place searched;
>> (iii) ownership of the property or place;
>> (iv) historical use of the property or item;
>> (v)   the ability to regulate access, including the right to admit or exclude others from the place;
>> (vi) the existence of a subjective expectation of privacy; and
>> (vii) the objective reasonableness of the expectation.
>
> 7. If an accused person establishes a reasonable expectation of privacy, the inquiry must proceed to the second stage to determine whether the search was conducted in a reasonable manner.

We see that the Supreme Court is vague when assessing the circumstances where a reasonable expectation of privacy arises. This is because there is no sure way to predetermine the circumstances where such an expectation exists. Ownership and possession, while important, are not the sole considerations. For example, just because a person happens to own and be in possession of a car does not mean that he has a reasonable expectation of privacy if a gun is openly displayed on the dashboard. Courts refer to this as the **plain view doctrine**. On the other hand, a person may reasonably expect privacy if he places something in the trunk.

The **reasonable expectation of privacy test** as set out in *Belnavis* contains both a subjective and an objective element. The question the court must ask is whether the accused had an actual expectation of privacy that was reasonably held. So, even if a suspect expected to be free from intrusion by the state, section 8 might not apply if that expectation was unreasonably held. For example, in *R v Lauda* ([1998] 2 SCR 683), a trespasser growing marijuana in a private field was found to have no reasonable expectation of privacy even though the accused may have been actively avoiding detection.

Once it has been determined that there is a reasonable expectation of privacy, the inquiry then focuses on whether the search was reasonable. The first point to recognize is that section 8 of the Charter places a limit on state powers to conduct searches or to seize evidence of a crime. It does not confer any additional powers on the state to conduct "reasonable" searches. The Supreme Court of Canada held in *Hunter v Southam Inc* ([1984] 2 SCR 145) that the purpose of section 8 is to prevent unreasonable searches from happening, rather than to determine after the fact whether a search should have been conducted in the first instance. Prevention can be achieved only by a system of "prior authorization" rather than "subsequent validation" (at para 27). The court went on to say that there is a presumption that all searches conducted without the express authority of a search warrant are presumed unreasonable, and that the party seeking to justify a warrantless search has the onus to rebut this presumption (at para 30).

This does not mean that the police must always have a search warrant for a search to be reasonable. There are strict technical and procedural requirements for obtaining a search warrant. An officer must usually first appear before a justice and swear a legal document called an information. The justice must be satisfied that there are reasonable and probable grounds to believe that there is physical evidence related to an offence at the place to be searched before issuing a search warrant. As a practical matter, it is simply not possible for the police to obtain a search warrant every time they wish to conduct a search for evidence. For example, suppose the police have good reason to believe that a suspect has narcotics in his car. By the time the officer has prepared the necessary documentation and obtained a search warrant from a justice, there is a real risk of the vehicle and evidence disappearing, especially if the suspect knows that the police are interested in what is in the trunk or under the seat.

The *Criminal Code* authorizes searches without a warrant in exigent or urgent circumstances where it is either impossible or impractical to obtain a search warrant. So, if the police are chasing a suspect with a gun or some other piece of evidence, they would be permitted to follow the fleeing suspect into a house because there is simply not enough time to obtain a search warrant.

The common law also permits the police to conduct a search without a warrant in those circumstances where the search is incidental to the arrest of a suspect. What this means is that if the police have arrested a person, they are permitted to search the suspect for weapons or for evidence.

Sometimes the police will detain a person without arresting him or her. As we shall soon see in the section dealing with arbitrary detention or imprisonment, the police have the power to conduct **investigative detentions** of suspects in certain

plain view doctrine
rule that a police officer may act without a search warrant if the evidence is in plain view

reasonable expectation of privacy test
test used by the courts to determine whether section 8 of the Charter has any application in the circumstances of a particular case

investigative detention
detention that may occur where there are reasonable grounds to suspect, in all the circumstances, that the individual is connected to a particular crime and that such detention is necessary

situations (see *R v Mann*, 2004 SCC 52, [2004] 3 SCR 59 at para 45). When during an investigative detention a police officer has reasonable grounds to believe that his or her safety or that of others is at risk, the officer may conduct a protective pat-down search of the detained person (at para 45).

The Supreme Court of Canada refined the law as set out in the *Hunter* decision in *R v Collins* ([1987] 1 SCR 265). In that case, the court stated that although a person accused of a crime has the burden to demonstrate that his or her Charter rights have been violated, once it is shown that a search was conducted without benefit of a warrant, the onus shifts to the Crown to show that the search was, on a balance of probabilities, reasonable. According to the **Collins test**, a search is reasonable if

1. it is authorized by law (either common law or statute),
2. the law that authorizes the search is itself reasonable, and
3. the search is conducted in a reasonable manner.

As a result of the second and third parts of the *Collins* test, even searches authorized by law must be reasonable and conducted in a reasonable manner. What is reasonable depends largely on the circumstances. The standard of reasonableness varies depending on the facts in any given situation. One factor that a court considers is the nature of the charge—is it criminal or regulatory? For regulatory offences, which do not carry criminal sanctions, the court usually applies a less rigorous standard than that used for criminal charges. Some other factors are whether it was necessary to infringe on the accused's privacy and whether other, less intrusive alternatives existed. Thus, a border search may be reasonable, but the same search conducted four hours later on a motor vehicle stopped at a service station may be unreasonable. Bodily searches that use more force than required would also be unreasonable because less intrusive searching methods are available.

Collins **test**
test used by the courts to determine whether a police search is reasonable; the search must be authorized by law, the law that authorizes the search must itself be reasonable, and the search must be conducted in a reasonable manner

---

CASE IN POINT

Searches of Mobile Devices

R v Fearon, 2014 SCC 77, [2014] 3 SCR 621

Mobile devices have evolved so much that smartphones are now powerful mini-computers capable of storing vast amounts of digital data. The question of how far the police can go in searching these devices as an incident to arrest was dealt with by the Supreme Court of Canada in *R v Fearon*. Kevin Fearon and Junior Chapman were arrested by the police following an armed jewellery robbery. When Mr. Fearon was arrested, a pat-down search was conducted by the police as an incident to his arrest. A cellphone was found in Fearon's pocket. The police then searched the cellphone and found a text message relating to jewellery with the words "we did it." The police also found a photo on the phone of the handgun used during the robbery. At trial, Fearon argued that the

search of the phone violated section 8 of the Charter and sought to have the evidence excluded. The trial judge admitted the evidence and convicted Fearon of the robbery and other related charges. The issue before the Supreme Court was whether the search of the phone was unreasonable and therefore contrary to section 8 of the Charter.

The Supreme Court found that the pat-down search and seizure of the cellphone was a lawful search incidental to Fearon's arrest for robbery. The real issue was whether the further warrantless search of the cellphone was reasonable. In a 4–3 decision, the Supreme Court decided that it was. Cromwell J, writing for the majority, found that the common law power of the police to search as an incident to a lawful arrest permits the search of cellphones and other similar devices found on suspects. The dissent recognized that searches of personal digital devices risk serious encroachments on privacy and was of the view that warrantless searches of these devices are not normally permitted as a search incidental to arrest.

In recognizing that searches of digital devices have important privacy implications, the majority of the court set out (at para 83) the following four conditions that must be met in order for the search of a digital device incidental to arrest to comply with section 8 of the Charter:

1. The arrest must be lawful;
2. The search must be truly incidental to the arrest in that the police have a reason based on a valid law enforcement purpose to conduct the search, and that reason is objectively reasonable. The valid law enforcement purposes in this context are:
   (a) Protecting the police, the accused, or the public;
   (b) Preserving evidence; or
   (c) Discovering evidence, including locating additional suspects, in situations in which the investigation will be stymied or significantly hampered absent the ability to promptly search the cell phone incident to arrest;
3. The nature and the extent of the search must be tailored to the purpose of the search;[2] and
4. The police must take detailed notes of what they have examined on the device and how it was searched.

Arbitrary Detention or Imprisonment

Section 9 offers broad protection from arbitrary detention or imprisonment with the provision:

> Everyone has the right not to be arbitrarily detained or imprisoned.

We all know that imprisonment means taking people's liberty away by putting them in jail. The meaning of detention is not as clear, but acts that fall short of imprisonment can qualify as detention. The courts have interpreted "detention" in both sections 9 and 10 as meaning a restraint of liberty. Obviously, a physical act of restraint would qualify as a detention, but so too would control over the movement of a person by a police officer by demand or direction. In other words, a person can be detained physically or psychologically (*R v Therens* at para 57).

In *R v Grant* (2009 SCC 32, [2009] 2 SCR 353), the Supreme Court identified the following two forms of psychological detention (at para 30):

> The first is where the subject is legally required to comply with a direction or demand, as in the case of a roadside breath sample. The second is where there is no legal obligation to comply with a restrictive or coercive demand, but a reasonable person in the subject's position would feel so obligated.

The first of these two forms of psychological detention is easily understood. This form of detention occurs whenever a person has a legal obligation to comply with a direction or demand made by the police. There either is or is not a legal obligation. If there is no legal requirement to comply, then a suspect is not detained and is free to go. Of course many people may be intimidated by a demand from the police and feel compelled to cooperate. For example, *Grant* involved a young black man who was stopped by a uniformed police officer while walking down a sidewalk in a high crime area. Soon afterwards, two undercover officers stopped behind Mr. Grant and identified themselves as police officers. Upon further questioning, Grant handed over a small amount of marijuana and a loaded revolver to the police officers.

There was no legal obligation to stop for the police in *Grant*, but the Supreme Court of Canada found that there had been a psychological detention in the circumstances of this case. In so finding, the Supreme Court of Canada used an objective approach and asked the following question (at para 31): Would the police officers' conduct cause a reasonable person to conclude that he or she was not free to go and had to comply with the police direction or demand? The court added that "the focus must be on the state conduct in the context of the surrounding legal and factual situation, and how that conduct would be perceived by a reasonable person in the situation as it develops" (at para 31).

When Is a Person Detained?

The Supreme Court answered this question as follows in *Grant* (at para 44):

1. Detention under ss. 9 and 10 of the *Charter* refers to a suspension of the individual's liberty interest by a significant physical or psychological restraint. Psychological detention is established either where the individual has a legal obligation to comply with the restrictive request or demand, or a reasonable person would conclude by reason of the state conduct that he or she had no choice but to comply.

2. In cases where there is no physical restraint or legal obligation, it may not be clear whether a person has been detained. To determine whether the reasonable person in the individual's circumstances would conclude that he or she had been deprived by the state of the liberty of choice, the court may consider, *inter alia*, the following factors:

   (a) The circumstances giving rise to the encounter as they would reasonably be perceived by the individual: whether the police were providing general assistance; maintaining general order; making general inquiries regarding a particular occurrence; or, singling out the individual for focussed investigation.

   (b) The nature of the police conduct, including the language used; the use of physical contact; the place where the interaction occurred; the presence of others; and the duration of the encounter.

   (c) The particular characteristics or circumstances of the individual where relevant, including age; physical stature; minority status; level of sophistication.

Not all detentions or arrests result in a breach of section 9 of the Charter. Otherwise, the police would not be able to detain or arrest any suspect. In order for a detention or arrest to offend section 9, it must be arbitrary. The courts have used language such as "capricious, despotic or unjustifiable" (see *R v Cayer* (1988), 66 CR (3d) 30 at 43 (Ont CA)) to describe a detention that is arbitrary. Clearly, an arrest or detention under the authority of a warrant or summons is not arbitrary. Similarly, the police may arrest without a warrant anyone found committing an offence or, in some situations, a person whom the officer has reasonable grounds to believe has committed or will commit an indictable offence. The police also have the lawful power to detain suspects in the course of an investigation to determine whether the person is involved in a criminal activity, provided that "there are reasonable grounds to suspect in all the circumstances that the individual is connected to a particular crime and that such a detention is necessary" (see *R v Mann* at para 45). Some trial judges refer to this as "**articulable cause**" for the detention (see, for example, *R v Morris*, 2011 ONSC 5142 at para 34). Articulable cause means that there must be objective facts sufficient to provide the officer with reasonable grounds to suspect that the person has done something criminal. Officers have to be able to articulate an objective basis for detaining an accused. A mere hunch is not sufficient.

articulable cause
the existence of objective facts that give rise to reasonable grounds to suspect that a person has committed a criminal act

In setting out the test for determining whether a detention is arbitrary, the Supreme Court of Canada in *Grant* summarized: "[I]t should now be understood that for a detention to be non-arbitrary, it must be authorized by a law which is itself non-arbitrary" (at para 56). Put another way, a detention is arbitrary where it is not authorized by law, or where the law itself is arbitrary.

It has long been established that stopping motorists entirely at random under statutory authority, such as the *Highway Traffic Act*, will result in an arbitrary detention. The Supreme Court of Canada first dealt with this issue in the 1988 decision of *R v Hufsky* ([1988] 1 SCR 621 at para 13):

> Although authorized by statute and carried out for lawful purposes, the random stop for the purposes of the spot check procedure nevertheless resulted, in my opinion, in an arbitrary detention because there were no criteria for the selection of the drivers to be stopped and subjected to the spot check procedure. The selection was in the absolute discretion of the police officer. A discretion is arbitrary if there are no criteria, express or implied, which govern its exercise. The appellant was therefore arbitrarily detained, within the meaning of s. 9 of the *Charter*.

Even though the random stopping of motorists clearly offends section 9 of the Charter, it is equally clear that the detention will be justified under section 1 of the Charter if the police act within the limited statutory purpose for which the power to stop a motor vehicle was conferred (see *R v Nolet*, 2010 SCC 24 at para 22, [2010] 1 SCR 851). In other words, all Charter rights, including the section 9 prohibition of arbitrary detention, may be limited under section 1 by such measures prescribed by law as can be demonstrably justified in a free and democratic society (see *R v Grant* at para 56). Of course, the police cannot justify an arbitrary detention if the detention is made outside the scope of legislative authority. In *Brown v Regional Municipality of Durham Police Service Board* (1998 CanLII 7198 (Ont CA)), an Ontario police force set up checkpoints to stop all members of a motorcycle gang travelling to a weekend retreat, believing that the club was involved in illegal activities. The Ontario Court of Appeal found that the stops were lawful under certain provisions of the *Highway Traffic Act* that gave police broad powers to stop motor vehicles.

In *Brown*, the court found that the stops were justified on the basis of, among other things, valid highway safety concerns. In recognizing a valid purpose for the stops, the court went on to add (at para 39):

Officers who stop persons intending to conduct unauthorized searches, or who select persons to be stopped based on their sex or colour, or who stop someone to vent their personal animosity toward that person, all act for an improper purpose. They cannot rely on s. 216(1) of the *HTA* even if they also have highway safety concerns when making the stop.

However, highway safety concerns were only one of the reasons motivating the stops in this case, because one of the other purposes was to gather intelligence about suspected gang members. The court permitted a dual-purpose approach, recognizing that police often operate under more than one purpose (at para 31):

> In addition to ensuring that the driver is properly licensed, the police may wish to identify the driver for other purposes. It may be, as in this case, that the police are interested in knowing the identity of all those who are connected with what they believe to be organized criminal activity. The gathering of police intelligence is well within the ongoing police duty to investigate criminal activity. As long as the additional police purpose is not improper and does not entail an infringement on the liberty or security of the detained person beyond that contemplated by the purpose animating s. 216(1) of the *HTA*, I see no reason for declaring that a legitimate police interest beyond highway safety concerns should taint the lawfulness of the stop and detention.

The Supreme Court of Canada adopted the "dual purpose" approach in *R v Nolet*, finding that it is both acceptable and appropriate that the police operate with multiple purposes in mind. In *Nolet*, the initial stop of a tractor-trailer was a random check. The validity of the initial stop was not in dispute. The police then conducted a series of searches of the tractor-trailer and discovered a large amount of cash and marijuana.

In recognizing the validity of the initial stop, the court recognized that "random checks of vehicles for highway purposes must be limited to their intended purpose and cannot be turned into an unfounded general inquisition or an unreasonable search" (at para 3). The court went on to add (at para 4):

> Nevertheless, roadside stops sometimes develop in unpredictable ways. It is necessary for a court to proceed step by step through the interactions of the police and the appellants from the initial stop onwards to determine whether, as the situation developed, the police stayed within their authority, having regard to the information lawfully obtained at each stage of their inquiry.

In *Nolet*, the police had the authority under a provincial statute to make the initial stop of the tractor-trailer. During this stop, it was discovered that the tractor-trailer was not licensed to operate in Saskatchewan. This provided officers with the authority under provincial legislation to conduct a search of the tractor-trailer. During this search, a large amount of cash was discovered in a duffle bag in the cab of the tractor-trailer. The accused was arrested for the possession of the proceeds of crime. Later, the police conducted a further search of the trailer, and a large quantity of marijuana was discovered in a secret compartment. The court found that the marijuana search was lawful as a search incidental to the arrest for possession of the proceeds of crime.

It is therefore clear that in assessing whether a person's Charter rights under sections 8 or 9 have been violated, the courts will look at the transactions individually in making the determination, and not engage in a global assessment of the entire interaction between the person and the police.

Remedies for Breach of a Charter Right

The next issue to look at is what happens once it has been established that there has been a breach of a person's rights by the police. There must be some mechanism to give effect to Charter rights. In other words, there must be a remedy available to anyone whose rights have been infringed. Section 24 of the Charter provides:

> 24(1) Anyone whose rights or freedoms, as guaranteed by this Charter, have been infringed or denied may apply to a court of competent jurisdiction to obtain such remedy as the court considers appropriate and just in the circumstances.
>
> (2) Where, in proceedings under subsection (1), a court concludes that evidence was obtained in a manner that infringed or denied any rights or freedoms guaranteed by this Charter, the evidence shall be excluded if it is established that, having regard to all the circumstances, the admission of it in the proceedings would bring the administration of justice into disrepute.

The first thing to note about section 24 is that subsection (1) provides a remedy that is "appropriate and just" to anyone whose rights or freedoms, as guaranteed by the Charter, have been infringed or denied, while subsection (2) provides a remedy where evidence was obtained in a manner that infringed or denied any rights or freedoms guaranteed by the Charter. Clearly, there are two separate remedies contained in section 24: a general remedy under section 24(1) and a remedy for evidence that was obtained in a manner that infringed on a person's rights.

Section 24(1) provides a broad remedy of what is "appropriate and just" in the circumstances. Although "appropriate and just" remedies might include damages and injunctions, the usual remedy in a criminal or quasi-criminal context is a stay of proceedings, where the accused is not acquitted but where the Crown is prevented from continuing the tainted prosecution. This may be an appropriate remedy where there has been a breach of an accused's right to be tried within a reasonable period of time pursuant to section 11(b) (see *R v Askov*, [1990] 2 SCR 1199) or where the Crown has repeatedly failed to provide complete disclosure to the accused (see *R v Stinchcombe*, [1991] 3 SCR 326).

The words "appropriate and just" provide a wide range of other possible remedies. Clearly, there can be no exhaustive list, and the possibility exists for novel approaches in appropriate cases. For example, section 24(1) has been used to return property seized in violation of section 8 of the Charter to the lawful owner (see *Lagiorgia v Canada*, [1998] 3 FC 28 (CA)).

Although section 24(1) of the Charter is best known in a criminal law context, this section has been applied extensively in civil cases to provide civil relief where an individual's Charter rights have been breached. For example, in *Eldridge v British Columbia (Attorney General)* ([1997] 3 SCR 624), the applicant was successful in obtaining a declaration that the government must provide public funding for medical interpreters. In *Little Sisters Book and Art Emporium v Canada (Minister of Justice)* (2000 SCC 69, [2000] 2 SCR 1120), the Supreme Court of Canada determined that customs officers had breached the store's freedom of expression and equality rights through their seizures of materials destined for the store. Although the court declined to provide injunctive relief, it did note (at para 158) that there was a place for carefully structured relief in the right circumstances. So, from a civil law perspective, an appropriate and just section 24(1) remedy may be in the form of an injunction or declaration, which might provide a limited period of time for the government to rectify the offending practice or legislation before it would be deemed invalid. It may also be possible for a court to award compensatory and punitive damages in appropriate cases (see *Mackin v New Brunswick (Minister of Finance)*, 2002 SCC 13, [2002] 1 SCR 405).

The primary Charter provisions with regard to wrongfully obtained evidence are contained in section 24(2). When the provisions of section 24 are combined with Charter protections such as section 7 (life, liberty, and security of the person), section 8 (unreasonable search or seizure), section 9 (arbitrary detention or imprisonment), and section 10 (rights on arrest or detention), any evidence that is obtained in breach of those rights is subject to exclusion by the court.

Section 24(2) of the Charter provides the exclusionary remedy that allows the court to take away the fruits of the authorities' wrongful acts. Thus, it removes the incentive for committing those wrongful acts and discourages the police from conducting themselves in this manner. So, if the courts rule that strip-searching a person in public is contrary to the individual's right to be secure from unreasonable search or seizure and they exclude the cocaine found in the attendant body cavity search, the police will very quickly stop that practice and conduct such searches in private. The process of excluding evidence is not so much punitive as an attempt to reform substandard practices and educate or retrain law enforcement personnel regarding the proper Charter standard that applies to their dealings with the public.

There are a number of purposes for excluding evidence that is wrongfully obtained. These include the following:

- to restore the aggrieved party to the position they were in before the Charter breach;
- to stop the police from engaging in an improper practice;
- to educate the police and the public;
- to ensure that the courts continue to be held in high regard; and
- to recognize and protect a core group of basic human rights.

The question whether section 24(2) is the only available remedy for excluding evidence was first dealt with by the Supreme Court of Canada in *R v Therens*. In that case, Le Dain J, who dissented in the result, made the following comments, which the majority of the court appeared to approve (at para 64):

> I am satisfied from the words of s. 24 that s. 24(2) was intended to be the sole basis for the exclusion of evidence because of an infringement or a denial of a right or freedom guaranteed by the *Charter*. It is clear, in my opinion, that in making

explicit provision for the remedy of exclusion of evidence in s. 24(2), following the general terms of s. 24(1), the framers of the *Charter* intended that this particular remedy should be governed entirely by the terms of s. 24(2).

The first indication from the Supreme Court of Canada that evidence may also be excluded under section 24(1) came in *R v Harrer* (at para 42), where McLachlin J stated for the minority that although evidence obtained in breach of the Charter may be excluded only under section 24(2),

> [e]vidence not obtained in breach of the *Charter* but the admission of which may undermine the right to a fair trial may be excluded under s. 24(1), which provides for "such remedy as the court considers appropriate and just in the circumstances" for *Charter* breaches.

The law is now clear that section 24(1) can be used to exclude evidence in certain circumstances. The Supreme Court of Canada held in *R v White* ([1999] 2 SCR 417) that section 24(1) "may serve as the mechanism for the exclusion of evidence whose admission at trial would violate the *Charter*" (at para 88). In that case, the issue was whether the admission of a statement would contravene the principle against self-incrimination. The court found that section 24(1) "may appropriately be employed as a discrete source of a court's power" (at para 89) to exclude evidence whose admission would render a trial unfair. The key point is that section 24(1) would apply only when the admission of evidence creates a breach of the Charter or an unfair trial, not where the evidence has been obtained in a manner that has violated a Charter right. In the latter case, section 24(2) would apply.

In Chapter 11, we discussed how the courts have interpreted section 7 of the Charter as including a general right to silence. The reader will recall that a distinction was made between statements made to the police under statutory compulsion and statements made where there is no legislative requirement to speak to the police. It is now well established that the admission of a statutorily compelled statement violates a person's section 7 right, and any statement made under legislative compulsion is protected by simple use immunity and is excluded under section 24(1) of the Charter on the basis that that it would make a trial unfair (*R v White* at para 89).

It is possible to see other situations where evidence might be excluded because its admission would render a trial unfair. In *R v Bjelland* (2009 SCC 38, [2009] 2 SCR 651), the Supreme Court of Canada dealt with the issue of the impact on trial fairness of late disclosure. In that case, the trial judge excluded evidence that was disclosed by the Crown on the eve of trial because its use at trial would be unfair and prejudicial to the accused. The trial judge's decision was reversed on appeal. In upholding the decision of the Alberta Court of Appeal, the Supreme Court set out the circumstances (at para 24) where such evidence would be excluded:

> Thus, a trial judge should only exclude evidence for late disclosure in exceptional cases: (a) where the late disclosure renders the trial process unfair and this unfairness cannot be remedied through an adjournment and disclosure order or (b) where exclusion is necessary to maintain the integrity of the justice system. Because the exclusion of evidence impacts on trial fairness from society's perspective insofar as it impairs the truth-seeking function of trials, where a trial judge can fashion an appropriate remedy for late disclosure that does not deny procedural

fairness to the accused and where admission of the evidence does not otherwise compromise the integrity of the justice system, it will not be appropriate and just to exclude evidence under s. 24(1).

In *Bjelland*, any unfairness or prejudice to the accused could have been cured by an adjournment and a disclosure order. In addition, the lateness of the disclosure was not the result of any deliberate Crown misconduct, nor was there any other reason to believe that the integrity of the justice system was compromised.

The Requirements for an Exclusionary Remedy

It is clear from the wording of the Charter that there is a relationship between the exclusionary remedy contained in section 24(2) and the wording of section 24(1). Before there is even a consideration of whether or not the evidence should be excluded, there has to be a "proceeding" under section 24(1) to determine whether there in fact has been an infringement of an individual's right or freedom. For this reason, it is not possible to ignore the provisions of section 24(1) when looking at the exclusionary remedy under section 24(2).

The components of the exclusionary remedy are therefore as follows:

1. Anyone
2. Whose rights or freedoms, as guaranteed by this Charter, have been infringed or denied
3. May apply to a court of competent jurisdiction ... .
4. Where, in proceedings under subsection (1), a court concludes that evidence was obtained in a manner that infringed or denied any rights or freedoms guaranteed by this Charter,
5. The evidence shall be excluded if it is established that, having regard to all the circumstances, the admission of it in the proceedings would bring the administration of justice into disrepute.

The individual components of the remedy are discussed below.

1. Anyone

It is the person whose rights or freedoms have been infringed who has a remedy.

It is only the individual who has been subjected to an infringement of his or her rights that has a remedy. So, if the police enter your friend's home without a warrant (which they are required to obtain in searching a "dwelling house") and they find you in possession of cocaine, you have no remedy under the Charter to have the cocaine excluded as a result of the warrantless search. However, your friend would have such a remedy if he were charged. At trial, your friend, who was trafficking in cocaine and from whom the police seized three kilograms of the drug, might go free because the evidence against him could be excluded under section 24 of the Charter while you are convicted of possession of cocaine for having the poor judgment to be caught in the apartment when the unlawful raid happened.

It should be noted that the word "anyone" sets out a remedy for all individuals, whether natural persons or artificial persons such as corporations. Accordingly, a corporation charged with an offence would have the same Charter protection as any natural person.

> 2. Whose rights or freedoms, as guaranteed by this Charter, have been infringed or denied
>
> A *Charter right* must have been breached by the authorities in dealing with an accused.

In considering an exclusionary remedy, the court must determine whether a Charter right has been breached. Note that not all poor behaviour on the part of the authorities constitutes a Charter breach. For example, if an accused complains, "The officers were very impolite to me and made me feel like a criminal when they stopped me for impaired driving," she would not have a remedy, barring some more scandalous behaviour by the police.

This is the part of the analysis where the court considers the Charter rights that we dealt with earlier in this chapter—for example, the right to be secure against unreasonable search or seizure and the right not to be arbitrarily detained. The court reviews the conduct of the police to determine whether any of the accused's Charter rights have been breached, what the impact of the breach was, and what would be the appropriate remedy.

Of some interest is the fact that the Supreme Court has determined that, in spite of the retrospective language in section 24(1), courts can grant remedies in anticipation of a Charter breach. In *New Brunswick (Minister of Health and Community Services) v G (J)* (1999 SCC 653, [1999] 3 SCR 46), the Supreme Court of Canada dealt with the issue of whether indigent parents have a constitutional right to be provided with a state-funded lawyer in situations where the state is seeking an order suspending the parents' custody of their children. By the time the case reached the Supreme Court, the constitutional issue was moot because the substantive elements had already been decided and the appellant had pro bono legal representation. Nonetheless, the court decided to approach the constitutional question as though a prospective breach of the Charter were at issue.

> 3. May apply to a court of competent jurisdiction … .
>
> The application must be made to a court of competent jurisdiction.

This provision has been interpreted by the courts as giving authority to the trial judge to deal with applications to exclude evidence. In addition, superior and appellate courts also have the jurisdiction to grant remedies under section 24(1) of the Charter (see *R v Rahey*, [1987] 1 SCR 588). However, judges presiding over preliminary hearings do not have the discretion to exclude evidence using the Charter. The leading case on this point is *Mills v The Queen* ([1986] 1 SCR 863), where the court found that a preliminary-hearing judge is not a court of competent jurisdiction within the meaning of section 24. According to McIntyre J (at para 264), who wrote the majority decision, a preliminary-hearing judge

> is given no jurisdiction which would permit him to hear and determine the question of whether or not a *Charter* right has been infringed or denied. He is, therefore, not a court of competent jurisdiction under s. 24(1) of the *Charter*.

The Supreme Court of Canada followed the *Mills* approach in *R v Hynes* (2001 SCC 82, [2001] 3 SCR 623) where McLachlin CJ defined a court of competent jurisdiction "as one that has: (1) jurisdiction over the person; (2) jurisdiction over the subject matter; and (3) jurisdiction to grant the remedy" (at para 17).

It has long been established that an administrative tribunal may be a court of competent jurisdiction (see *Cuddy Chicks Ltd v Ontario (Labour Relations Board)*, [1991] 2 SCR 5). In *R v Conway* (2010 SCC 22, [2010] 1 SCR 765), Abella J, writing for the unanimous court, stated that "we do not have one *Charter* for the courts and another for administrative tribunals" (at para 20). She then went on to define the test for determining whether an administrative tribunal is a court of competent jurisdiction in the following terms (at para 81):

> [W]hen a remedy is sought from an administrative tribunal under s. 24(1), the proper initial inquiry is whether the tribunal can grant *Charter* remedies generally. To make this determination, the first question is whether the administrative tribunal has jurisdiction, explicit or implied, to decide questions of law. If it does, and unless it is clearly demonstrated that the legislature intended to exclude the *Charter* from the tribunal's jurisdiction, the tribunal is a court of competent jurisdiction and can consider and apply the Charter—and Charter remedies—when resolving the matters properly before it.

Abella J then went on to add (at para 82) that even if a tribunal is a court of competent jurisdiction, consideration must be given to whether the tribunal can grant the remedy that is sought:

> Once the threshold question has been resolved in favour of Charter jurisdiction, the remaining question is whether the tribunal can grant the particular remedy sought, given the relevant statutory scheme. Answering this question is necessarily an exercise in discerning legislative intent. On this approach, what will always be at issue is whether the remedy sought is the kind of remedy that the legislature intended would fit within the statutory framework of the particular tribunal. Relevant considerations in discerning legislative intent will include those that have guided the courts in past cases, such as the tribunal's statutory mandate, structure and function.

Administrative Tribunals and Charter Remedies

There is a two-step process in determining whether an administrative tribunal has the power to grant a Charter remedy:

1. Determine whether the tribunal is a court of competent jurisdiction by determining whether it has the power to decide questions of law.

2. If the answer to the first step is yes, the second step is to determine whether the particular remedy sought can be granted by the tribunal under its enabling legislation.

If the answer to the second step is also in the affirmative, the tribunal has the jurisdiction to grant the specific remedy sought.

In short, there are two distinct questions: Can the tribunal grant Charter remedies? and, Does the tribunal have the authority to grant *this* remedy?

> 4. Where, in proceedings under subsection (1), a court concludes that evidence was obtained in a manner that infringed or denied any rights or freedoms guaranteed by this Charter,
>
> The evidence was obtained in a way that infringed a Charter right.

The threshold requirement of section 24(2) is that the evidence was obtained in a manner that infringed or denied a right or freedom. What this means is that there must be a connection or relationship between the breach and the obtaining of the evidence. If there is a direct causal connection between the infringement of the right or freedom and the evidence, the threshold will be met. So, if an accused is denied her right to speak to a lawyer and makes a confession or has her dwelling house searched for stolen property without a warrant, the connection between any evidence obtained as a result of these breaches will satisfy the threshold requirement. In these cases, the obtaining of the evidence flows directly from the Charter breach.

However, there will be many cases where the connection is not as direct or obvious. For example, assume that a motorist was arrested for impaired driving and read his rights, but the police failed to mention that free and immediate legal advice was available from duty counsel. The accused then indicated that he did not want to call a lawyer and the police administered a Breathalyzer test that the accused failed. Is there any causal connection between the failure to advise the accused of his right to duty counsel and the failed test? Most people would think not, because a lawyer would probably have advised the accused that he would be charged if he failed to take the Breathalyzer test. In other words, the accused would have been charged with either operating a motor vehicle with an excess of alcohol in the blood or failing to comply with an officer's demand, both of which carry the same penalty, regardless of whether any legal advice was received by him.

There is no direct causal connection in the above example between the Charter breach and the impugned evidence. However, the Supreme Court of Canada dealt with these precise facts in *R v Bartle* ([1994] 3 SCR 173) and found (at 208-9) that

> [u]nder the first threshold requirement, there must be some connection or relationship between the infringement of the right or freedom in question and the obtaining of the evidence which is sought to be excluded. However, a strict causal link between the *Charter* infringement and the discovery of the evidence is not required. … Generally speaking, so long as it is not too remotely connected with the violation, all the evidence obtained as part of the "chain of events" involving the *Charter* breach will fall within the scope of s. 24(2). … This means that in the initial inquiry under s. 24(2) as to whether evidence has been "obtained in a manner that infringed or denied" *Charter* rights, courts should take a generous approach.

The "chain of events" test is far broader and easier to meet than the "causal connection" test. Critics charge that the approach the Supreme Court has adopted represents a kind of judicial activism and extends the reach of the court beyond what the Charter envisioned. Defenders of this approach argue that in the era of the Charter, the courts have a supervisory role to ensure that police action in obtaining evidence for use in courts meets a high standard of propriety and does not trample on anyone's rights.

Of course, the determination of whether evidence was obtained in a manner that infringed or denied a right or freedom does not in of itself result in a remedy. The actual test for excluding such evidence is dealt with in the following section.

> 5. The evidence shall be excluded if it is established that, having regard to all the circumstances, the admission of it in the proceedings would bring the administration of justice into disrepute.
>
> The evidence is excluded if the admission of the evidence would harm the reputation of the justice system.

Evidence that meets all of the other components of the exclusionary remedy will still be admissible unless its admission would bring the administration of justice into disrepute. Another way of saying this is that the public would lose respect for the justice system if such evidence were admitted. For example, a confession that was obtained by torture or evidence that was obtained by police officers who searched people because of their skin colour or the way they dressed would cause the public to have less respect for the justice system.

R v Collins was an early Charter case to consider this particular phrase. The *Collins* decision has now been largely overturned by the Supreme Court of Canada's decision in *R v Grant* as it relates to section 24(2) of the Charter. However, *Collins* continues to clarify a number of points. First, the Supreme Court made it clear that the burden is on the party seeking to have the evidence excluded to demonstrate, on a balance of probabilities, that its admission would bring the administration of justice into disrepute. Second, the court noted that the English and French versions of the Charter are very different, with the French version of "would bring the administration of justice into disrepute" translating as "could bring the administration of justice in disrepute."

The Supreme Court therefore found that the test to be applied is whether the admission of the evidence could (not would) bring the administration of justice into disrepute (see *R v Collins* at para 43).

The leading authority on the meaning of this phrase is now the Supreme Court of Canada's 2009 decision in *R v Grant*. This case was first discussed earlier with regard to the section 9 *Charter* right to be free from arbitrary detention or imprisonment. Prior to *Grant*, the test for what would bring the administration of justice into disrepute was spelled out in *R v Collins*. The *Collins* test involved three considerations:

1. Would admission of the evidence affect the fairness of the trial?

2. Is the breach serious or merely technical in nature?

3. What would be the impact on the reputation of the justice system if the evidence were excluded?

Collins had been the authority on this point since 1987 and was criticized for its rigid approach to trial fairness that almost always excluded all conscriptive evidence flowing from a *Charter* violation unless it would have been independently discovered. As a result, conscriptive evidence was routinely excluded under *Collins*, even for minor or technical breaches of the *Charter*, while non-conscriptive evidence was often admitted despite serious *Charter* violations.

This all changed following *Grant*. In laying the foundation for a new approach to section 24(2) of the *Charter*, McLachlin CJ and Charron J, writing for the majority of the court in *Grant*, explained (at paras 67-70):

> The words of s. 24(2) capture its purpose: to maintain the good repute of the administration of justice. The term "administration of justice" is often used to indicate the processes by which those who break the law are investigated, charged and tried. More broadly, however, the term embraces maintaining the rule of law and upholding *Charter* rights in the justice system as a whole.
>
> The phrase "bring the administration of justice into disrepute" must be understood in the long-term sense of maintaining the integrity of, and public confidence in, the justice system. Exclusion of evidence resulting in an acquittal may provoke immediate criticism. But s. 24(2) does not focus on immediate reaction to the individual case. Rather, it looks to whether the overall repute of the justice system, viewed in the long term, will be adversely affected by admission of the evidence. The inquiry is objective. It asks whether a reasonable person, informed of all relevant circumstances and the values underlying the *Charter*, would conclude that the admission of the evidence would bring the administration of justice into disrepute.
>
> Section 24(2)'s focus is not only long-term, but prospective. The fact of the *Charter* breach means damage has already been done to the administration of justice. Section 24(2) starts from that proposition and seeks to ensure that evidence obtained through that breach does not do further damage to the repute of the justice system.
>
> Finally, s. 24(2)'s focus is societal. Section 24(2) is not aimed at punishing the police or providing compensation to the accused, but rather at systemic concerns. The s. 24(2) focus is on the broad impact of admission of the evidence on the long-term repute of the justice system.

The following points emerge from the above passages:

- The court is returning to the original intent of section 24(2) based on its wording.
- The focus is on the factors that serve to maintain the integrity and public confidence in the justice system over the long term.
- The test under section 24(2) is objective. The standard is that of the reasonable person, informed of all relevant circumstances and the values underlying the Charter.
- The focus is prospective. Courts should look at the damage that will be caused by admitting the evidence, not the damage already done by the Charter violation.
- The focus is societal. Section 24(2) not intended to punish the police or compensate the accused. Instead, it is intended to address systemic problems.

The court in *Grant* then went on (at para 71) to establish a revised approach, known as the ***Grant* test**, for excluding wrongfully obtained evidence under the Charter:

Grant **test**
three-part test used by the courts to determine whether the admission of evidence obtained through a Charter violation would bring the administration of justice into disrepute

A review of the authorities suggests that whether the admission of evidence obtained in breach of the *Charter* would bring the administration of justice into disrepute engages three avenues of inquiry, each rooted in the public interests engaged by s. 24(2), viewed in a long-term, forward-looking and societal perspective. When faced with an application for exclusion under s. 24(2), a court must assess and balance the effect of admitting the evidence on society's confidence in the justice system having regard to: (1) the seriousness of the *Charter*-infringing state conduct (admission may send the message the justice system condones serious state misconduct), (2) the impact of the breach on the *Charter*-protected interests of the accused (admission may send the message that individual rights count for little), and (3) society's interest in the adjudication of the case on its merits. The court's role on a s. 24(2) application is to balance the assessments under each of these lines of inquiry to determine whether, considering all the circumstances, admission of the evidence would bring the administration of justice into disrepute. These concerns, while not precisely tracking the categories of considerations set out in *Collins*, capture the factors relevant to the s. 24(2) determination as enunciated in *Collins* and subsequent jurisprudence.

The Grant Test

The following are considered in assessing whether the admission of evidence obtained in breach of the Charter would bring the administration of justice into disrepute:

1. Seriousness of the Charter-infringing state conduct (admission may send the message that the justice system condones serious state misconduct),

2. Impact of the breach on the Charter-protected interests of the accused (admission may send the message that individual rights count for little), and

3. Society's interest in an adjudication on the merits of the case.

The Grant Considerations

The factors set out by the Supreme Court of Canada in *R v Grant* are dealt with in more depth in this section.

1. SERIOUSNESS OF THE CHARTER-INFRINGING STATE CONDUCT

According to *Grant* (at para 72):

> The more severe or deliberate the state conduct that led to the *Charter* violation, the greater the need for the courts to dissociate themselves from that conduct, by excluding evidence linked to that conduct, in order to preserve public confidence in and ensure state adherence to the rule of law.

In assessing the seriousness of the conduct, courts will consider whether the breach of a Charter right was inadvertent or minor. Admission of evidence in these situations will only minimally undermine confidence in the justice system. On the other hand, admitting evidence that was obtained through a wilful or reckless disregard of the Charter "will inevitably have a negative effect on the public confidence in the rule of law, and risk bringing the administration of justice into disrepute" (at para 74).

2. IMPACT OF THE BREACH ON THE CHARTER-PROTECTED INTERESTS OF THE ACCUSED

Here, the focus is on the seriousness of the impact of the Charter breach. The impact may range from fleeting and technical to profoundly intrusive. For example, a situation where a search warrant contains an irregularity is far different than conducting a full body cavity search on a suspect. Both may violate the Charter, but a search that demeans a person's dignity has a far greater impact on the person's Charter-protected right to be free from an unreasonable search. Thus, the more serious the impact, the more likely the evidence will be excluded. In assessing this consideration, that court used the following language (at para 76):

> The more serious the impact on the accused's protected interests, the greater the risk that admission of the evidence may signal to the public that *Charter* rights, however high-sounding, are of little actual avail to the citizen, breeding public cynicism and bringing the administration of justice into disrepute.

3. SOCIETY'S INTEREST IN AN ADJUDICATION ON THE MERITS

It is expected that criminal cases will be judged on their merits. No one wants to see a person who has committed a serious criminal offence go free because a crucial and reliable piece of evidence was kept from the trier of fact. Thus, in assessing how helpful the impugned evidence is to proving the allegations against the accused, courts will consider both the reliability of the evidence and how essential it is to the prosecution. The exclusion of important and reliable evidence may undermine the truth-seeking function of the justice system, thereby bringing the administration of justice into disrepute (at paras 81, 83).

Applying the Grant Considerations

Grant is intended to replace the more rigid approach previously used by judges when dealing with the issue of exclusion of evidence under section 24(2) of the Charter. A general exclusionary rule appears to be contrary to the requirement of section 24(2) that in determining the admissibility of evidence, a court must consider *all the circumstances*. Clearly, any rule that focuses on a single consideration is not giving effect to the words of the Charter. In considering *all the circumstances*, courts must assess and balance the *Grant* factors in determining the effect that the admission of the evidence would have on society's confidence in the justice system. The weighing and the balancing is a matter for the trial judge in each case. As a result, where a trial judge has considered the proper factors and come to a determination on whether the admission of the evidence would bring the administration of justice into disrepute, appellate courts should generally defer to that determination (at para 86).

Specific Types of Evidence Under Grant

One thing that the Supreme Court found troublesome in *Grant* was that the prior jurisprudence made the kind of evidence that was in issue a major factor in determining its admissibility. We have already seen that courts almost always excluded conscriptive evidence flowing from a Charter violation unless it would have been independently discovered. *Grant* has effectively overturned this line of cases, because the test for excluding evidence under section 24(2) of the Charter involves an assessment and balancing of all three *Grant* factors in the circumstances of each case individually. The court, however, recognized that the type of evidence in issue may very well play a role in the assessment and balancing process. The court felt the point was sufficiently important that it warranted further treatment. In particular, the court discussed the impact of *Grant* on the following types of evidence.

1. STATEMENTS BY THE ACCUSED

The first point is that *Grant* does not change the common law confession rule or deal with admissibility of statutorily compelled statements under section 24(1) of the Charter. These matters were fully discussed in Chapter 11, Self-Incrimination. However, the Supreme Court noted that that the assessment and balancing approach would tend to lead to the exclusion of statements under section 24(2) where the procurement of the statement resulted from a Charter violation. The court in *Grant* went as far as to say that "[t]he three lines of inquiry described above support the presumptive general, although not automatic, exclusion of statements obtained in breach of the Charter" (at para 92). The first and second factors, when balanced against the third, normally favour exclusion. Societal concerns about police conduct in taking statements from suspects and the importance of protecting the right to silence to preserve a person's liberty and autonomy usually outweigh the third *Grant* consideration of an adjudication on the merits of the case, especially since this kind of evidence is often unreliable (at para 98).

2. BODILY EVIDENCE

Bodily evidence is evidence taken from the body of a person, such as DNA evidence and breath samples. Section 8 of the Charter protects against the unreasonable search and seizure of bodily evidence. Prior to *Grant*, bodily evidence was seen as a form of conscriptive evidence and, because its admissibility had an impact on trial fairness, it was almost always excluded when it was obtained in violation of the Charter. The Supreme Court pointed out that after *Grant*, judges will conduct an assessment and balancing of the *Grant* considerations in all the circumstances on a case-by-case basis. However, the court went on to add (at para 111):

> While each case must be considered on its own facts, it may be ventured in general that where an intrusion on bodily integrity is deliberately inflicted and the impact on the accused's privacy, bodily integrity and dignity is high, bodily evidence will be excluded, notwithstanding its relevance and reliability. On the other hand, where the violation is less egregious and the intrusion is less severe in terms of privacy, bodily integrity and dignity, reliable evidence obtained from the accused's body may be admitted. For example, this will often be the case with breath sample evidence, whose method of collection is relatively non-intrusive.

As a result, bodily evidence will tend to be excluded when the police conduct is deliberate and the impact on the accused is significant.

3. NON-BODILY PHYSICAL EVIDENCE

This type of evidence would include any physical evidence that was not obtained from a person's body and would include, for example, weapons, drugs, proceeds of crime, digital storage devices, and so forth. The usual assessment and analysis would be conducted on the first two *Grant* considerations in determining the admissibility of this kind of evidence. The third consideration—whether the admission of the evidence would serve society's interest in having the case adjudicated on its merits—would also be resolved on the basis of the facts of the particular case. However, because this evidence is normally reliable, the third consideration tends to weigh in favour of admission (at para 115).

4. DERIVATIVE EVIDENCE

Recall that derivative evidence is physical evidence discovered as a result of an unlawfully obtained statement. The classic example is where a person confesses to committing a crime and tells the police where he hid the gun. The gun is an example of derivative evidence. The common law confession rule does not exclude derivative evidence because this evidence is generally reliable, while an involuntary confession may not be. Section 24(2) of the Charter has modified this approach where there has also been a Charter violation of the right to silence. In those cases, the derivative evidence may be excluded if the admission of the evidence would bring the administration into disrepute.

Prior to *Grant*, the law on derivative physical evidence was dominated by two related concepts—conscription and discoverability. Physical evidence that would not have been discovered by the authorities but for an inadmissible statement was conscriptive and inadmissible. On the other hand, derivative evidence that would inevitably have been discovered would generally be admitted. Now, the determination of admissibility is made in accordance with *Grant*. However, the fact that the impugned evidence is derivative continues to play a role in the second and third branches of the *Grant* analysis.

The second part of the *Grant* analysis focuses on the impact of the breach on the Charter-protected interests of the accused. The discoverability of derivative evidence may be an important factor in this analysis. If the derivative evidence was independently discoverable, the impact of the breach on the accused is lessened and admission of the evidence is more likely (at para 125).

Similarly, under the third part of the *Grant* approach, because derivative evidence is usually reliable, "the public interest in having a trial adjudicated on its merits will usually favour admission of the derivative evidence" (at para 126).

In summing up the discussion on derivative evidence, the court concluded (at para 127):

> The weighing process and balancing of these concerns is one for the trial judge in each case. Provided the judge has considered the correct factors, considerable deference should be accorded to his or her decision. As a general rule, however, it can be ventured that where reliable evidence is discovered as a result of a good faith infringement that did not greatly undermine the accused's protected interests, the trial judge may conclude that it should be admitted under s. 24(2). On the other hand, deliberate and egregious police conduct that severely impacted the accused's protected interests may result in exclusion, notwithstanding that the evidence may be reliable.

CHAPTER SUMMARY

The *Canadian Charter of Rights and Freedoms* has brought about significant changes in how the police deal with suspects and accused persons. Evidence that is wrongfully obtained is often excluded by the courts when police actions have resulted in violations of the Charter. The exclusion of evidence applies equally to the original evidence and to any evidence derived from it. Section 24 of the Charter has been carefully analyzed and applied to maintain a high level of respect for the administration of justice in Canada. Where evidence is obtained as a result of a breach of a suspect's or accused's Charter rights, a court may exclude the evidence if its admission would bring the administration of justice into disrepute.

KEY TERMS

articulable cause, 229
Collins test, 226
Grant test, 240
investigative detention, 225
Oakes test, 222
plain view doctrine, 225
reading into, 221
reasonable expectation of privacy test, 225

NOTES

1   There are conflicting decisions on this point at the time of writing. In *R v Nguyen*, the Ontario Court of Appeal found that the spousal incompetency provisions of the *Canada Evidence Act* infringed the section 15 equality provisions of the Charter. However, the court used section 1 to preserve the impugned provisions. Interestingly, subsequent amendments to the *Canada Evidence Act* revoked the provisions that were challenged in *Nguyen*. However, in *R v Legge*, the Alberta Court of Appeal refused to invoke the saving provisions of section 1 of the Charter in similar circumstances. Both cases refer to a number of contradictory lower court decisions. This area of law is complicated, as the conflicting jurisprudence suggests. It would not be at all surprising to see the Supreme Court of Canada settle this issue at some point in the future.

2   In practice, this will mean that usually only recently sent or drafted emails, texts, photos, and the call log may be examined, although other searches may in some circumstances be justified (see *R v Fearon* at para 76).

REFERENCES

Askov, R v, [1990] 2 SCR 1199.

Bartle, R v, [1994] 3 SCR 173.

Belnavis, R v, [1997] 3 SCR 341.

Bjelland, R v, 2009 SCC 38, [2009] 2 SCR 651.

Brown v Regional Municipality of Durham Police Service Board, 1998 CanLII 7198 (Ont CA).

Canada Evidence Act, RSC 1985, c C-5.

Canadian Charter of Rights and Freedoms, Part I of the *Constitution Act, 1982*, being Schedule B to the *Canada Act 1982* (UK), 1982, c 11.

Cayer, R v (1988), 66 CR (3d) 30 (Ont CA).

Collins, R v, [1987] 1 SCR 265.

Constitution Act, 1982, being Schedule B to the *Canada Act 1982* (UK), 1982, c 11.

Conway, R v, 2010 SCC 22, [2010] 1 SCR 765.

Criminal Code, RSC 1985, c C-46.

Cuddy Chicks Ltd v Ontario (Labour Relations Board), [1991] 2 SCR 5.

Edwards, R v, [1996] 1 SCR 128.

Eldridge v British Columbia (Attorney General), [1997] 3 SCR 624.

Fearon, R v, 2014 SCC 77, [2014] 3 SCR 621.

Grant, R v, 2009 SCC 32, [2009] 2 SCR 353.

Harrer, R v, [1995] 3 SCR 562.

Hebert, R v, [1990] 2 SCR 151.

Hufsky, R v, [1988] 1 SCR 621.

Hunter v Southam Inc, [1984] 2 SCR 145.

Hynes, R v, 2001 SCC 82, [2001] 3 SCR 623.

Lagiorgia v Canada, [1987] 3 FC 28 (CA); leave to appeal to Supreme Court of Canada refused (1988), 43 CCC (3d) vi (note).

Lauda, R v, [1998] 2 SCR 683.

Legge, R v, 2014 ABCA 213.

Little Sisters Book and Art Emporium v Canada (Minister of Justice), 2000 SCC 69, [2000] 2 SCR 1120.

Mackin v New Brunswick (Minister of Finance); Rice v New Brunswick, 2002 SCC 13, [2002] 1 SCR 405.

Mann, R v, 2004 SCC 52, [2004] 3 SCR 59.

Mills v The Queen, [1986] 1 SCR 863.

Morris, R v, 2011 ONSC 5142.

New Brunswick (Minister of Health and Community Services) v G (J), [1999] 3 SCR 46.

Nguyen, R v, 2015 ONCA 278.

Nolet, R v, 2010 SCC 24, [2010] 1 SCR 851.

Oakes, R v, [1986] 1 SCR 103.

Ontario, *Highway Traffic Act*, RSO 1990, c H.8.

Rahey, R v, [1987] 1 SCR 588.

Stinchcombe, R v, 1991 SCC 45, [1991] 3 SCR 326.

Therens, R v, [1985] 1 SCR 613.

White, R v, [1999] 2 SCR 417.

REVIEW QUESTIONS

1. What section of the Charter does the court rely on to exclude evidence that is unconstitutionally obtained?

2. What are the five components of the exclusionary remedy under section 24?

3. What factors do the courts take into account when determining whether the admission of evidence could bring the administration of justice into disrepute?

4. What is derivative evidence?

DISCUSSION QUESTIONS

For each of the following scenarios, identify whether there have been any Charter breaches and if so, the appropriate remedy or remedies.

1. James Horton, a 19-year-old black male, was driving his parents' late-model Audi when he was stopped by police, who indicated that they were investigating a rash of auto thefts in the area. During the stop, the police smelled marijuana and asked James where the smell was coming from. James freely admitted that he was smoking marijuana and turned over a small quantity to the police. James was charged with possession of marijuana. Do you think that the evidence of the marijuana would be admitted?

2. Suppose that, in question 1 above, after James was arrested for possession of marijuana, the police searched his car and discovered high-powered weapons and bomb-making equipment in the trunk of the car. Do you think that this evidence would be excluded?

3. Sally Quick was involved in a motor vehicle accident. After the accident, she was asked by the investigating officer to identify herself and to tell him what had happened. Sally refused, telling the officer, "I know my rights." Was Sally correct in refusing to speak to the officer?

4. Suzanne Evans was stopped by police at a roadside checkpoint designed to reduce impaired driving. She had not consumed any alcohol, but police detected the odour of marijuana and charged Suzanne with impaired driving. The police then searched her car and discovered a small quantity of marijuana in the glove box. Suzanne was charged with possession of marijuana.

5. Scott Kwan was going to a rock concert downtown. Before entering the stadium, he noticed a sign that stated that persons entering the premises must open their bags and empty their pockets. He was asked by arena security to empty his pockets and, while doing so, turned over a small bottle of liquor. The security officer in turn handed the liquor over to police, and Scott was charged with a liquor offence.

PART IV

Methods of Presenting Evidence

Forms of Evidence

13

LEARNING OUTCOMES

After completing this chapter, you should be able to:

- Identify and explain the three forms of evidence.

- Understand when a view may be used.

- Define the best evidence rule and understand how it has evolved.

- Identify the three criteria that judges use in determining whether to admit photographs and videos.

- Understand the role of computers in documentary evidence.

- Understand how the spoliation of evidence undermines the justice system in Canada.

Introduction

Evidence constitutes the building blocks of any party's case in any hearing. Judges and juries are not entitled to make decisions based on emotions or a "gut feeling" about the matter at hand. They are charged with the responsibility for making decisions based on the facts in evidence before them. Evidence can take one of three forms:

1. oral evidence,
2. real evidence, or
3. documentary evidence.

This chapter provides an overview of these three forms of evidence. Chapter 14 discusses oral evidence in detail.

Oral Evidence

oral evidence
evidence given orally by witnesses

By far the most common form of evidence in any hearing is **oral evidence**. Witnesses come to the hearing or trial and are questioned, according to various rules, by the lawyers representing the parties in the case.

The common law at one time required that all evidence be taken under oath. This meant that the witness had to swear on the Bible to tell the truth. The idea behind testimony under oath was to emphasize to the person testifying the solemnity of the occasion and the importance of telling the truth. When the practice of testifying under oath arose, the belief that there were religious consequences for lying was common, so it was quite natural to look at swearing an oath as the means to encourage truth-telling in court. For many years, the process of testifying under oath continued as the proper form for witnesses to testify, but the oath itself was clearly not very meaningful for those persons who did not believe in God or who were not Christians.

oath
promise made on the Bible or other holy book to tell the truth in court

More recently, given both the cultural and religious diversity in Canada, and the diminishing influence of religion in the lives of many, both statute law and the common law have evolved to the point where giving evidence under oath no longer plays the same role in determining truth-telling. Although **oaths** are still regularly used in courtrooms, now a person may instead give a **solemn affirmation** to tell the truth. A solemn affirmation, often referred to as simply an affirmation, is a promise to tell the truth. Evidence given under oath and evidence given under affirmation both carry the same weight, and no legal differentiation is made between the two methods. The *Canada Evidence Act* and the provincial evidence acts or similar legislation make an affirmation equivalent to an oath. There is no difference between an oath and an affirmation in relation to the criminal offence of perjury (giving false testimony).

solemn affirmation
promise to tell the truth in court that has the same value as an oath

Real Evidence

real evidence
tangible evidence that is put before the trier of fact

Real evidence is any tangible evidence put before the trier of fact. Tangible evidence is evidence that can be touched. (This category of evidence technically includes documents, but because there are some issues that pertain specifically to documentary evidence, we deal with documents as a separate category under the heading "Documentary Evidence.") Real evidence is unique because the trier of fact experiences it first-hand rather than having it interpreted by a witness. The trier of fact is entitled to draw its own conclusions about the evidence, even to draw from it information unnoticed by those presenting the evidence.

Real evidence is typically created in the course of the events that gave rise to the charge or dispute—for example, a knife stained with the blood of the victim or, in a manufacturer's liability case, a defective product that caused injury and is brought into the courtroom. Real evidence may also take the form of demonstration devices such as diagrams, maps, models of body parts, and PowerPoint presentations that aid the trier of fact in understanding evidence. Forensic evidence, such as blood, fingerprints, or hair samples, is a specific type of real evidence that courts today greatly rely on.

For real evidence to be admissible, the judge must determine that it does not distort the facts or create a biased perspective. Real evidence may be excluded if the court determines that its potential for prejudice outweighs its probative value.

Views

Usually, real evidence is brought into the courtroom and entered into evidence as an exhibit, but this is not always possible. The tangible object may be too large, or there may be a valid reason for the trier of fact to see the scene of the alleged offence. In such cases, the court may order a **view**, whereby the courtroom is relocated to a particular place so that the jury will have the opportunity to see the real evidence first-hand. The judge, court staff, jury, accused, and sheriffs all attend the view, and one of the parties, or perhaps both, makes a presentation at the site. The presentation could take the form of expert explanation in relation to the scene or object being viewed by the fact-finder, or simply a request by counsel to have the fact-finder personally examine the scene or object so that this personal observation will aid its understanding when hearing evidence at a later date. Views are an interesting aspect of evidence law but are rarely used because they usually involve substantial arrangements and expense. However, in some cases, views are deemed necessary by the court.

In one anecdotal account of a view that took place years ago, an accused struck a pedestrian who was walking alone at night on a dark road. The driver continued home, switched cars, and returned to the scene of the accident. When he noticed police there, he left again, but ultimately turned himself in to the police, accompanied by his lawyer. The driver, charged with dangerous driving and leaving the scene of an accident, stated that he did not know he had hit anyone until he got home. He claimed that while he was fiddling with something in the car, the wheels left the road and moved onto the soft shoulder. The bump that he felt, he initially concluded, was the wheels bumping up onto the road again. By attending the scene, the jurors were in a position to weigh this evidence more effectively and compare it with the Crown's theory. They convicted the accused, likely based on Crown evidence that showed that the body bounced up onto the hood of the car and struck the windshield, as well as other evidence from the damage to the vehicle that undermined the accused's claim that he did not realize he had hit a person. Section 652 of the *Criminal Code* sets out the procedure for the court to direct a view in a criminal case.

view
relocation of the court to the site where the evidence is located; a judge may order a view when the evidence is too large to bring into the courtroom or when there is a valid reason for the trier of fact to see the site

Taking a View

In the Air India trial, which concerned the bombing of Air India flight 182 on June 22, 1985, the jury was taken to view the warehouse where the wreckage had been partially rebuilt and where experts had viewed it to develop their theories about the site of the explosion on the plane. The Crown expert testified that the bag that exploded was in a location on the plane indicating that it was loaded in Vancouver, whereas the defence expert testified that the location of the explosion confirmed that it was loaded in Toronto. Presumably, by viewing the wreckage laid out in its original configuration, the jury would be better able to determine which of these theories deserved more merit.

Documentary Evidence

documentary evidence
any document, including text, film, video and audio recordings, and photographs, presented in court for reference by the trier of fact

Most people, if asked to define a document, would describe some sort of text, written or printed on a piece of paper. Certainly, that is a document, but **documentary evidence** includes many more types of evidence. For instance, section 30.01(1) of the Ontario *Rules of Civil Procedure* for the Ontario Superior Court of Justice provide that the word "document" includes a sound recording, videotape, film, photograph, chart, graph, map, plan, survey, book of account, and data and information in electronic form. In British Columbia, rule 1-1(1) of the *Supreme Court Civil Rules* provides that "document" includes a photograph, film, recording of sound, any record of a permanent or semi-permanent character, and any information recorded or stored by means of any device.

In criminal law, the definition of document is also fairly broad. For example, section 321 of the *Criminal Code* defines "document" for the purposes of part IX as "any paper, parchment or other material on which is recorded or marked anything that is capable of being read or understood by a person, computer system or other device, and includes a credit card, but does not include trade-marks on articles of commerce or inscriptions on stone or metal or other like material."

Documents are regularly relied on as evidence in both civil and criminal cases, as well as in hearings before administrative tribunals. In order to be admitted into evidence, a document of any type must first be authenticated, or validated. This process has become particularly important with the advent of sophisticated copying techniques and computer records, which can be used to alter documents. Authentication requires establishing that a document is truly what it purports to be. Very often, the opposing party does not challenge the validity of a document and agrees to have it admitted on consent. For example, in a contract dispute, both parties may agree that the document presented is in fact the contract on which the case is focused.

However, if there is no agreement as to the authenticity of a document, a witness must be called to identify and validate it. The witness may have written or created the document, or may have been present when the document was created or signed. If the document is a photograph, the photographer is usually called to identify it and to provide some evidence of how and when it was taken. Sometimes, an expert witness is called to help verify a document. In some cases, a document may be presumed to be authentic if there is no indication of fraud and the document has been properly preserved, or if there are a series of documents—for example, a set of email messages in which a message could only be a response to an earlier message.

Best Evidence Rule

The **best evidence rule** was designed to ensure that only original documents would be presented in evidence. With present-day technology, it is frequently almost impossible to tell an original from a copy. In order to combat potential adulteration of documents, the rule developed that the original, or "best evidence," must be provided to the court, the point being that any careful inspection of an original document is much more likely to uncover a forgery than an examination of a photocopy.

best evidence rule
a largely outdated rule that requires the original document to be presented in evidence if it is available

A Clue to a Forgery

An example of how close examination may reveal a forgery is the alleged memo from the supervising colonel of the Texas Air National Guard that called into question George W. Bush's military service during the war in Vietnam. The problem with this particular forgery was that the type of font used in the memo was not available, or at least not in common use, in the 1970s, but rather was a product of computers and Microsoft word processing.

The best evidence rule has historically been used to stop a party from entering a copy of a document as evidence. Where the original could not be located or produced, the party might not be able to prove the contents of the document, which might contain information crucial to its position. Today, this approach is much more relaxed. An original is preferred—in fact, if the original is available, the court likely would require the party to produce it—but if it is not available because it is lost, has been destroyed, or is out of the reach of the court (in another jurisdiction), a copy may be admitted. The trier of fact gives the copy whatever weight it would deserve in the circumstances. For example, if there is no good reason why the original is not available and one party provides two witnesses who insist that some wording on a contract was scratched out and initialled on the original, the trier of fact could conclude that the copy was of no assistance to them as evidence of the wording of the contract. But in many other instances, copies are admitted. In fact, the *Canada Evidence Act* has substantially modified the best evidence rule to facilitate the entry into evidence of copies with respect to government and public documents, police and court documents, and some types of business documents (s 30(3)). Copies of these documents may be admitted without the need for producing the original. However, the copy must be certified to be a true copy of the original by the person responsible for keeping the record or document. The certification, stating that "This is a true copy of the original," must be printed or stamped on the copy and signed by the record-keeper.

Photographs and Videos as Documentary Evidence

It is not unusual in a criminal case for the Crown to attempt to introduce photographs of the crime scene or, in a murder case, photographs of the autopsy. Often, the evidence is admitted, even when it is graphic, as in photos of a dismembered body. Critics have charged that such graphic documentary evidence has little evidentiary value and has a high potential to prejudice a jury.

Photographs of crime scenes can also present problems. Consider the following scenario. A couple are having a heated argument in their bedroom and the man grabs the woman by the throat and chokes her. She reaches from the bed over to the dresser, grabs a metal nail file, and stabs him. The woman is charged with attempted murder and pleads self-defence. The Crown wants to enter into evidence photos of the room where the stabbing took place. The photos show the bed and the dresser where the nail file was. The problem is that in the pictures the dresser looks like it is a considerable distance from the bed. The photos therefore imply that the accused got up, walked a number of steps back to the bed, and stabbed the victim. In reality, the dresser is within arm's reach of the bed, making it possible that the accused was still in the man's grasp when she reached over for the nail file and stabbed him with it. The photographer acknowledges that the photos make the distance between the dresser and the bed appear greater than it is because of the type of lens that he used. The court decides to admit these pictures, but their impact is lessened by the photographer's testimony about the distorting effect of the photos.

Judges assess the admissibility of photographs and videos using the following criteria, as set out in the case of *R v Creemer and Cormier* ([1968] 1 CCC 14):

1. their accuracy,
2. their fairness and absence of potential to mislead, and
3. verification on the oath of a witness that they are what they purport to be.

In *R v Maloney (No 2)* ((1976), 29 CCC (2d) 431 (Ont Co Ct)), the court rejected videotaped footage of a hockey assault because of the distorting effect of slow-motion taping. Periodically, particularly gruesome photos of corpses are not admitted because, although they obviously relate to the issues to be decided, they have no value in determining the issues before the trier of fact. However, videotape evidence has even been used by the court to identify a person charged with robbing a convenience store where the witnesses at the scene could not identify the accused. In *R v Nikolovski* ([1996] 3 SCR 1197), the trial judge was prepared to make that identification using the surveillance video from the store. On appeal to the Supreme Court of Canada, the court upheld the judge's use of the video.

Video evidence is becoming much more common as more people carry cellphones with video-recording capability. Courts are now regularly faced with the admissibility of videotapes as evidence.

Robert Dziekański: Video Justice

On the afternoon of October 13, 2007, Robert Dziekański arrived at Vancouver International Airport on a flight from Poland that was two hours late in arriving. He was in the process of immigrating to Canada to live with his mother, Zofia Cisowski, who lived in Kamloops, British Columbia. He spoke no English.

His mother told him she would meet him in the baggage claim area. Neither she nor her son were very experienced air travellers, and neither realized that this was a secure area of the airport that she would be unable to enter. Dziekański apparently waited for his mother for about seven and a half hours, at which time he attempted to leave the secure area. He was redirected back to immigration because he needed further processing on his entry visa. After processing, the immigration authorities took him back to the international arrivals area, where they left him.

Meanwhile, Mrs. Cisowski had been making inquiries at the airport for hours and was repeatedly told her son was not there. After many hours of waiting, she returned to Kamloops thinking her son must have missed his flight.

Shortly after being left in the arrivals area by immigration staff, Dziekański became agitated. He had now been at the airport for approximately 10 hours and could not find his way about. Because he spoke no English, he was unable to ask for assistance or directions. In apparent frustration at his situation, he began pacing and at one point, threw a chair and a computer to the floor. The Royal Canadian Mounted Police were called to deal with the situation.

Four officers—constables Gerry Rundel, Bill Bently, Kwesi Millington, and supervisor Corporal Benjamin (Monty) Robinson—arrived on the scene. Within 25 seconds of their arrival, Dziekański was tasered and fell to the ground, where he lay convulsing and screaming. He was tasered four more times while he was on the ground and then handcuffed. By this time, the multiple taserings had resulted in his heart failing, and he was declared dead at the scene.

Paul Pritchard, a witness to the police interaction with Dziekański at the airport, made a video of the incident which, he said, contradicted the police version. The RCMP then seized the video, and Pritchard had to go to court to get it back, at which time he released it to the media. The video played a major role in the subsequent public inquiry, during which it was determined that the police were not justified in tasering Dziekański and that the officers had purposely misrepresented their actions to the investigators.

Although no charges were ever laid against any of the officers in direct relation to Dziekański's death, all four were charged with the very serious offence of perjury, in that they allegedly lied to the inquiry. Two of the officers, Kwesi Millington and Benjamin (Monty) Robinson, were convicted of the offence in early 2015, seven and half years after Dziekański's death. Without the video, the police officers' conduct would not likely have been called into question.

Computer-Generated Records

Computer-generated records is an area of evidence law that will likely see increased attention in the future. Where the evidence was input by humans, the rules dealing with hearsay exceptions can determine admissibility. But with some computer-generated evidence, the work is done by the computer. For example, where a computer stores and retrieves data automatically in creating telephone usage records, approving credit card transactions, or tracking websites visited, no person has input the information, yet it will be invaluable in answering many questions that arise in both civil and criminal trials. This sort of evidence is not hearsay; it is more like a snapshot in time and should be treated like a photograph. In other words, it should be authenticated and, based on the authentication, given weight by the trier of fact.

Another area where computers are valuable, although potentially dangerous, is recreations or models to assist a party in visually demonstrating a fact. Triers of fact will have a much clearer understanding, particularly of a complex matter, when they can be led through it by watching an animated program. The dangerous aspect is that the animation will show whatever it is programmed to show. What the triers of fact are viewing is not "reality" or a historical replay, but just what the party presenting it wants them to see. Like evidence from any novel science, computer-generated information should be treated with caution and scrutinized for reliability and bias.

Spoliation of Evidence

spoliation
the destruction, mutilation, alteration, or concealment of evidence

Spoliation refers to the destruction, mutilation, alteration, or concealment of evidence. This occurs, for example, when emails are deleted or documents are shredded. Deleted emails, in particular, are a common source of spoliated evidence because they can be retrieved by skilled computer technicians. When deleted emails are recovered, they can form even more damning evidence in light of the effort that was put into hiding the information. Lawyers are warned that when they forward correspondence to the opposing counsel electronically, the communication will contain metadata, which includes electronic instructions contained in the document that are not visible unless one has the expertise to display them. This means that earlier versions of the same document that contain rejected drafts will be recoverable in an electronic communication. This can have implications in a civil suit if sensitive information, such as a less favourable offer or position, was considered in the earlier version—for example, "I'd take $100,000 but let's try for $150,000 first."

The concern with the spoliation of evidence is that courts are left with a harder job if relevant evidence is destroyed and may be forced to render decisions based on even more imperfect evidence. Various jurisdictions in Canada are currently working on how to remedy the problem presented by after-the-fact coverups, and we can expect that this will be an active area for proactive responses to a problem that undermines the Canadian system of justice.

CHAPTER SUMMARY

There are three forms for presenting evidence: oral evidence, real evidence, and documentary evidence. Oral evidence is presented by witnesses who are called to give testimony under oath or solemn affirmation. Real evidence is tangible evidence that can be put before the trier of fact by physically bringing the item into court or by taking the trier of fact to the location of the evidence for a view. Documentary evidence is evidence in a recorded form, and includes written words, film, video, audio recordings, photographs, charts, graphs, maps, plans, books of account, and information recorded in electronic form.

The best evidence rule is a largely outdated rule that requires the original document to be presented into evidence if it is available. Today, this approach is far more relaxed. An original is preferred, but if it is not available, a copy can be admitted by the court.

Judges assess the admissibility of photographs and videos using three criteria: their accuracy, their fairness and absence of potential to mislead, and their verification by a witness under oath. Computer-generated records may be of great value to the trier of fact, but they also carry the potential to mislead and must be scrutinized for reliability and bias.

The spoliation of evidence refers to the destruction, mutilation, alteration, or concealment of evidence.

KEY TERMS

best evidence rule, 253
documentary evidence, 252
oath, 250
oral evidence, 250
real evidence, 250
solemn affirmation, 250
spoliation, 256
view, 251

REFERENCES

British Columbia, *Supreme Court Civil Rules*, BC reg 168/2009.

Canada Evidence Act, RSC 1985, c C-5.

Creemer and Cormier, R v, [1968] 1 CCC 14.

Criminal Code, RSC 1985, c C-46.

Maloney (No 2), R v (1976), 29 CCC (2d) 431 (Ont Co Ct).

Nikolovski, R v, [1996] 3 SCR 1197.

Ontario, *Rules of Civil Procedure*, RRO 1990, reg 194, rule 30.01(1)(a).

REVIEW QUESTIONS

1. Name the three forms in which evidence may be presented and admitted.

2. What is the difference between an oath and a solemn affirmation?

3. What is a "view," and when might it be used? Give an example.

4. What types of information can be grouped under the heading of "documentary evidence"?

5. What is the best evidence rule? How is it applied by the courts today?

6. What criteria will the judge use in determining the admissibility of videos and photographs?

DISCUSSION QUESTIONS

1. Discuss how the development of information stored on computers has affected the manner in which evidence is recorded and presented. What are the benefits of computers in gathering and presenting evidence? What are some of the concerns that this type of evidence-gathering and presentation has generated?

2. It is often said that "seeing is believing." Discuss this saying in relation to video and photographic evidence. Is seeing always believing? What are some of the benefits of, and problems with, video and photographic evidence?

Oral Evidence

LEARNING OUTCOMES

After completing this chapter, you should be able to:

- Describe the two facets of the test for competence of a witness.

- Understand the federal and provincial rules governing the testimony of child witnesses.

- Understand who can be compelled to testify and who cannot.

- Understand the purpose of examination-in-chief; cross-examination, including the limits on cross-examination; and re-examination.

- Describe the ways in which the testimony of witnesses can be undermined by opposing counsel.

- Understand when a judge may issue a discretionary warning regarding corroborating evidence.

Introduction

One of the most common ways to introduce evidence is by calling or requiring witnesses to come to court to give oral evidence, or testimony. The witnesses are examined through questions asked by all the parties to the proceeding. This chapter deals with the rules and procedures that apply specifically to oral evidence.

Calling Witnesses

We say that a witness is "called" to testify. This may be done by simply arranging with a willing witness for her to testify, but the best practice is to subpoena or summon a witness, even if the witness is a good friend or a family member of the party who is relying on her testimony. A **subpoena** or a **summons** is a formal, legal document requiring the witness to appear or to suffer legal consequences for failing to do so. Generally speaking, "subpoena" is the term used for the document calling a witness in a criminal case, and "summons" is the term used in civil or non-criminal matters. If a witness has been formally called to give evidence and does not appear, the court will likely grant an adjournment. Should a subpoenaed or summoned witness fail to appear at a hearing, a warrant may be issued for her arrest.

However, not all witnesses who attend a hearing are permitted to testify. In order to give testimony at a hearing, a witness must be both competent and compellable.

Competency and Compellability

Competence

Competence is the legal ability to give oral evidence in a hearing. Whether or not a witness is competent is a matter to be determined by the judge. The test for competence of a witness has two facets. The first facet is **capacity**. The witness must have an acceptable capacity to observe, then to correctly recall his observations or experiences, and an acceptable ability to communicate these observations or experiences to the trier of fact.

The second facet requires that the witness be able to comprehend the necessity of truth-telling and the consequences should he not tell the truth. This facet of the test for competency is referred to as **responsibility**.

Historically at common law, the parties to the proceedings were regarded as **incompetent**, or not permitted to give evidence in matters they were litigating, to testify in their own case. The courts believed that the parties' personal interest in the outcome of the case severely compromised their ability to give an objective account of their experiences or observations. It was thought that, at best, they would tend to slant their testimony and, at worst, they would lie outright.

In addition to the parties themselves, the spouses of the parties were also considered incompetent. The assumption was that spouses are just as likely to slant their observations or to lie as the parties were. Because the courts believed that any potential evidence was tainted by this close association, such evidence was avoided entirely. This approach certainly prevented the admission of possibly unreliable evidence,

subpoena
formal, legal document requiring a witness to appear at a hearing in a criminal case

summons
formal, legal document requiring a witness to appear at a hearing in a civil case

competence
the legal ability to give oral evidence in a hearing

capacity
an acceptable ability to observe and then correctly recall observations or experiences, and an acceptable ability to communicate these observations to the trier of fact

responsibility
the ability to comprehend the necessity of being truthful and the consequences of not telling the truth

incompetent
not permitted to give evidence

but it also had the effect of reducing the amount of information that the trier of fact could rely on in reaching a conclusion.

Other persons historically considered to be legally incompetent were persons disqualified through infamy—that is, persons with a criminal history. The courts believed that persons who had shown disregard for society's rules could provide no credible information. Today, a criminal history does not make a witness incompetent, but it may lessen the impact of that witness's testimony because of a possible lack of credibility. Being a child was another basis for disqualification as a witness. Vestiges of this approach remain today in the qualification of child witnesses in some provincial jurisdictions, discussed below under the heading "Competency of Child Witnesses." Mental incapacity was another disqualification, and one that persists to this day, although it has been criticized for contributing to the vulnerability of a group that is already the target of physical, sexual, and economic abuse. Critics charge that the abuse of mentally incompetent persons is more likely to occur if abusers feel that they can abuse members of this group without fear that their victims will testify against them.

One aspect of incompetence that has fallen by the wayside is the exclusion of persons who do not profess a belief in a supreme being. Taking an oath in order to testify was initially based on the belief that persons would be loath to lie if they had promised in God's name to tell the truth and feared divine punishment for breaking their oath. With the increasingly secular nature of our society, one would be hard pressed to find persons who truly believe that they will be struck by lightning for lying under oath, and it is exceedingly rare for anyone with an interest in litigation to "tell the whole truth and nothing but the truth." The fact-finder's job is more often to sort through the evidence to find the version of the truth that is the most reliable version or likely the most accurate.

Competency of Child Witnesses

Historically at common law, there was a rebuttable presumption that children over the age of 14 were competent to give evidence. This means that children under 14 had to be qualified to testify. The process of qualifying required the judge to question the witness to determine whether the child understood the nature of an oath and to verify that he or she comprehended the religious aspects of taking an oath. If the judge determined that the witness did not understand an oath—that is, the concept of divine consequences for the failure to tell the truth—the child would be found incompetent and would be unable to testify.

Statute has changed the common law, largely in an attempt to discourage those who believe they can abuse children without fear that the children will testify against them. The first legislative changes permitted child witnesses to give unsworn evidence if the judge determined that they could understand the necessity of telling the truth. However, no one could be convicted of an offence, or found liable in a civil court, on the uncorroborated evidence of a child. This meant that there had to be other evidence that supported the child's testimony—for example, forensic evidence or evidence from an adult witness.

The corroboration requirement has been removed from the *Canada Evidence Act*. In addition, more recent changes to the Act in sections 16 and 16.1 provide that a child under 14 years of age is presumed to have the capacity to testify. To determine the admissibility of a child's testimony, section 16.1 requires that the test to be applied by the judge is that the child is capable of understanding and responding to questions. No child under the age of 14 will be permitted to take an oath or make a solemn declaration, but the evidence given by the child shall have the same effect as if it were taken under oath or affirmation. Instead of taking an oath or affirmation, a child will be required to promise to tell the truth. However, changes to the *Canada Evidence Act*, section 16.1(7) prohibit asking questions regarding the witness's "understanding of the nature of the promise to tell the truth."

There is no uniformity on this issue among the evidence statutes of the common law provinces. We find a number of different approaches. British Columbia, Saskatchewan, and Manitoba use the previous wording of the *Canada Evidence Act* in their evidence acts (in ss 5, 12, and 24, respectively).

Under the evidence acts of Alberta and Nova Scotia (ss 19 and 63, respectively), a young child may give unsworn evidence at the discretion of the judge if the child does not understand the nature of an oath; however, the unsworn testimony must be corroborated by other material evidence.

Under the evidence acts of New Brunswick and Ontario (in ss 24(1) and 18.1(1), respectively), the court must determine whether or not a child understands the nature of an oath (or solemn affirmation in Ontario). If the court determines that the child does not, the child may give unsworn evidence without the need for corroboration (see Ontario's *Evidence Act*, ss 2-3). The evidence act for Newfoundland and Labrador (in s 18(1)(b)) does not require that a child comprehend the nature of an oath; rather, the child must demonstrate that he understands what it means to tell the truth and is capable of communicating the evidence. Even if the child does not promise to tell the truth or is unable to understand what it means to tell the truth, the court may still admit the evidence if it is thought to be reliable (s 18(3)). There is no requirement for corroboration in either event.

Finally, Prince Edward Island has no statute dealing with child evidence, and therefore the common law applies. A child must understand the nature of an oath or she will be found incompetent and will be unable to give evidence.

Most of the evidence statutes either directly require or imply that the court must conduct an inquiry into a child's competence. That said, in some jurisdictions, judges may leave this task to the lawyers for the parties, who will question the child. The ability to perceive and recollect is a general one and not tied to the specific facts before the court, and the test for competency of a child witness is not a very high hurdle for the child to clear. If she can string together coherent sentences, that is usually enough to satisfy the court.

Section 16 of the *Canada Evidence Act* applies to all persons over 14 whose capacity to give evidence is in question. This would include an adult who has developmental delays or mental health issues. The statue provides that if the witness's mental capacity is challenged, the court shall conduct an inquiry to determine mental capacity before permitting the person to give evidence. The test is twofold:

1. Whether the person understands the nature of an oath or solemn affirmation; and

2. Whether the person is able to communicate the evidence.

If the person understands the nature of the oath or affirmation, and is able to communicate the evidence, the witness shall testify under oath or affirmation. A person who does not understand an oath or affirmation, but is able to communicate the evidence, may testify on promising to tell the truth, but the witness may not be questioned on his understanding of the nature of the promise to tell the truth.

Competency of Spouses

As we noted earlier, historically at common law, neither a party to the litigation nor his or her spouse could give evidence in a proceeding. Spouses were regarded as incompetent to testify in either a criminal or a civil proceeding on the basis that it was unlikely they would tell the truth given their interest in the case's outcome.

This common law rule no longer applies in civil matters, and parties and their spouses are regarded as competent and compellable witnesses. They can be called to give testimony by any party, including the opposing litigant. They may also choose voluntarily to give evidence against their spouses.

In criminal matters, the competency and compellability of accused persons and their spouses are no longer determined by common law but by section 4(1) of the *Canada Evidence Act*, which provides that

> [e]very person charged with an offence, and, except as otherwise provided in this section, the wife or husband, as the case may be, of the person so charged, is a competent witness for the defence, whether the person so charged is charged solely or jointly with any other person.

Pursuant to this subsection, both the accused and his or her spouse are competent to give evidence for the defence. Recent amendments to the *Canada Evidence Act*, section 4(2) (the *Victims Bill of Rights*) now provide that a spouse is not incompetent or uncompellable by the prosecution solely because they are married to the accused. However, a spouse may still claim spousal privilege related to communications of the accused to the spouse that took place during the course of the marriage (see Chapter 10, Privilege).

Both the statutory provisions and the common law rule have applied only to persons who are legally married and not to couples who are living together. The marriage must also be a functioning marriage at the time of the proceeding. If the marriage has broken down, the spouse may be called to give evidence. There has been some case law that addresses the issue of applying spousal privilege to common law relationships, but the law across the country is not consistent at this time (see *R v Nguyen*, 2015 ONCA 278). It is likely that this issue will be dealt with by the Supreme Court of Canada in the near future.

Compellability

In addition to being competent to testify in a proceeding, a witness must also be **compellable**. The general rule is that a witness who is competent is also compellable. This means that the witness can be compelled, or forced, to give evidence, and her failure or refusal to do so will result in legal consequences. A witness's refusal to testify in the face of a court order to do so will result in a finding of contempt of court, which can easily lead to incarceration.

compellable
legally required to give evidence at a hearing

There are some exceptions and limitations to the rule that a competent witness is compellable. Under the *Canadian Charter of Rights and Freedoms*, a person charged with an offence cannot be compelled to give evidence against himself in a criminal or quasi-criminal proceeding. Therefore, an accused person cannot be forced to give evidence for the prosecution.

Accused persons did not always enjoy the right to silence. Indeed, in the 15th and 16th centuries, the court of Star Chamber in England used various methods to compel accused persons to provide evidence in the proceedings against them. Torture was a common interrogation technique, and failure to take an oath in the Star Chamber was tantamount to a confession of guilt.

The current approach to an accused's right to silence owes its existence in part to the excesses of the Star Chamber, which ultimately led to sweeping changes to protect the rights of an accused. By the 18th century, an accused could, by right, refuse to answer any question put to him at trial where the answer would tend to incriminate him. Initially, this privilege applied only to statements made by an accused at trial and did not preclude the questioning of a witness prior to trial. This approach was extended to pre-trial questioning by the Jervis Acts of 1848.

Ultimately, a common law right developed for the accused not to cooperate with the authorities in their efforts to obtain a conviction, as well as a right not to take the stand and subject himself to cross-examination. So, the accused is protected from answering questions either before the trial or during the trial. The right not to incriminate oneself is enshrined in the *Canadian Charter of Rights and Freedoms*. However, if an accused decides to take the stand, he becomes a witness, almost like any other, and he can be cross-examined thoroughly about the events leading to the charge.

In Canada, the tradition of being able to compel incriminating testimony from a witness who is not an accused continues and shows a distinct difference from the approach in the United States. Section 5 of the *Canada Evidence Act* requires a reluctant witness to testify. Prior to the Charter, where an objection was made, the witness was protected from having that specific evidence used against him in a subsequent proceeding. The Charter extended the protection to all testimony.

The right against self-incrimination as set out in the Charter applies to all dealings with authorities, both pre-trial and during a trial, and places a heavy onus on the authorities to play by the book. In *R v Hebert* ([1990] 2 SCR 151), the Supreme Court of Canada determined that a statement made by Hebert to his cellmate (who was an undercover officer) after he had expressly refused to give a statement to the authorities breached his right to silence. In excluding the statement, the court effectively put an end to that sort of police trickery. (For more on this topic, see Chapter 11, Self-Incrimination.)

Examination-in-Chief

examination-in-chief
questioning of a witness by the party who called the witness; its object is to bring out information that will establish facts that the litigant must prove to win the case

Typically, in a civil trial, the lawyer for the party who calls the witness asks the witness a series of questions aimed at eliciting information that will help to establish facts that this litigant must prove to win the case. This questioning is known as **examination-in-chief**, or direct examination.

The questions during examination-in-chief must not be leading questions. Instead, they must allow the witness to tell her story for the trier of fact. A general guideline provided by the courts is that a question that requires a yes or no answer, without elaboration, is a leading question. However, a question such as, "Did you kill her?," although a yes or no question, is not leading because it does not imply that a certain answer is sought or preferred. Perhaps the best guide is that a question that contains the answer without elaboration is a leading question. Thus, "You didn't want to hurt her, did you?" is leading because we can expect the answer to be "No, I didn't want to hurt her." The court requires that the witness give her evidence with the least amount of direction from counsel as is possible. If counsel seems to be "putting words into the witness's mouth," the evidence from the witness is much diminished in value, even worthless, to the trier of fact.

Another example of the use of leading questions is obtaining information from a witness by asking questions that contain the answer being sought:

"You saw the car that hit yours travelling at a high rate of speed, isn't that right?"
"You always travel down Georgia Street when you visit your sister, don't you?"
"You hadn't consumed any alcohol that night, had you?"
"When you struck Mr. Jones, you thought that he had a weapon, didn't you?"

In examination-in-chief, asking leading questions can give the witness a clue as to what the "right" answer, or the expected answer, is. It is much like a marionette show, where the questioner pulls the strings and the puppet-witness responds accordingly. Thus, with the question, "You hadn't consumed any alcohol that night, had you?," the witness easily gets the point that it would be a good thing if he had not and will be strongly tempted to answer accordingly. Similarly, with the question, "When you struck Mr. Jones, you thought that he had a weapon, didn't you?," the witness is likely to give the anticipated answer designed to shore up a self-defence strategy. The answers to these questions should not be given much weight, if any, by the trier of fact. On the other hand, a question such as, "What was going through your mind when you struck Mr. Jones?" is much more instructive and valuable to the trier of fact.

Leading questions also include questions that presume a fact that has not been proved, thus tricking the unwary witness into agreeing with a proposition that she might not accept:

"What speed were you going when you ran into my client's car?"
"So, you made the decision because you are the head of your household?"
"You felt sorry that Mr. Jones was injured in your attack, didn't you?"

In the first question, if the witness answers, "The speed limit," he has been tricked into acknowledging that he ran into the other driver. In the second question, if the witness answers yes, it is unclear whether he is agreeing to the fact that he is the head of the household or that he made the decision, or both. In the third question, if the witness answers yes, he has expressed his regret but also admitted to the attack on poor Mr. Jones.

Not all leading questions asked in examination-in-chief are objectionable. In fact, it would be very awkward indeed to conduct a trial without permitting counsel to ask some leading questions of its own witness. There are guidelines for when leading questions are permissible, and in some instances the judge will allow opposing counsel to alert the examiner to avoid leading the witness.

The most frequent use of leading questions in examination-in-chief is in relation to introductory or non-contentious matters, as in the following exchange between counsel and witness:

> "Your name is Frank Olson?"
> "Yes."
> "And you live at 132 West 19th Avenue?"
> "Yes, that's correct."
> "You were at home on the night of March 12, 2014?"
> "I was."

At this point, opposing counsel would likely interject:

> "Your honour, my friend appears to be about to get into the actual incident that took place. I would like to remind him to avoid leading the witness on disputed matters."

There is nothing objectionable about this sort of introductory questioning as long as it does not tread upon matters that the parties are disputing. Probably nobody questions that the witness's name is Frank Olson, or that he lives next door to the plaintiff, or that he was at home on the evening the incident in dispute took place. But it may be very crucial to hear from the witness exactly what he saw and did on that occasion. His credibility and reliability as a witness may be in dispute, and the defence may want to make sure he gets no help from the plaintiff's counsel in "remembering" the events as they unfolded.

The court may also allow leading questions for the following purposes:

- to jog the memory of a witness, or give a witness a "jump start";
- to aid the witness in communicating complex, scientific, or technical matters;
- to question a witness about statements made by other witnesses for the purpose of contradicting those statements;
- to allow the witness to identify objects in evidence or related persons; and
- to facilitate the testimony of nervous, confused, young, or old witnesses.

The main concept here is that, in many instances, leading will aid in the flow of the litigation and will not have any contaminating effect on the information that results. Leading questions may also be permitted where a witness has been declared hostile or adverse, discussed more fully under the heading "Cross-Examining Your Own Witness," below. This is a special provision designed to help counsel get at the truth even where a witness has no intention of helping that lawyer's client.

Cross-Examination

cross-examination
questioning of a witness by opposing counsel after examination-in-chief

Cross-examination is mostly reserved for questioning an opponent's witness. After the lawyer who called the witness has questioned him or her in examination-in-chief, it is the opposing party's turn to ask questions. The method of questioning will usually differ from that used in examination-in-chief. Unlike examination-in-chief, cross-examination affords an opportunity for opposing counsel to ask leading questions and to suggest answers to the witness. It is thought that by permitting the examiner to test the evidence that the witness has brought in the crucible of cross-examination, the truth will emerge.

Cross-examination is generally considered the most effective method of challenging or diminishing the impact of an opponent's testimony. Remember that most witnesses are inexperienced in giving evidence, whereas examining counsel will have examined witnesses numerous times.

One danger of cross-examination is that the witness may contradict herself in spite of her efforts to be honest and forthcoming with the trier of fact. The only safeguard in that situation is the trier of fact's ability to discern wilful dishonesty from honest mistake. For example, when cross-examining a witness, lawyers look for contradictions between what the witness says and previous statements by that person. The prior statements may have been made in an earlier hearing, such as a preliminary inquiry, or to the police or other entities. Jurors tend to think of the truth as immutable and therefore expect the statements by a witness to be consistent over time. When counsel uncovers a contradiction in a witness's statements, this can be very effective in undermining that witness's credibility or, at the very least, her reliability.

Judges, being experienced triers of fact, know that not all contradictions imply dishonesty or even unreliability in a witness. A witness who tells the police that an event took place at about 6:00 p.m. but later in court places the time at closer to 7:00 p.m. is not necessarily dishonest. She may have had the opportunity to think through the day in question more carefully and be more precise in her time estimate. Similarly, a witness who initially indicates that a fight she saw took place on December 19, 2013 may correct herself and say it was December 18, 2013 without calling her credibility into question. Typically, there would be no dispute that the fight under discussion in the litigation was the same fight the witness observed. The trier of fact must look at the contradiction and determine whether it is significant given the issues in the litigation, or whether it is simply an indication of the witness's nervousness. If the key issue is who the aggressor was, the witness may have given excellent evidence describing the way in which the parties conducted themselves. Being uncertain of the exact date is of no consequence to the value of that evidence and should have no impact on it. Nevertheless, opposing counsel may try to trap witnesses in silly contradictions, and it is important for the trier of fact to assess whether the contradiction is significant before determining what impact those contradictions will have. It is also within the purview of the trial judge to stop counsel from pursuing picayune or irrelevant contradictions because of the potential to confuse the jury.

Leading questions are often used extensively in cross-examination. Lawyers sometimes refer to this as "leading the witness down the garden path." The questioning is not hostile or threatening to the witness, a tactic that would tend only to make the witness more wary and careful with her responses, but gradually works the witness into a corner, forcing her to divulge the desired information. The examiner begins by asking the witness a series of inoffensive questions, which cause her to relax. She lets her defences down, developing a false confidence in her ability to deal with what she anticipated would be an onslaught from opposing counsel.

Consider the following exchange between defence counsel and a witness who has testified that he saw the accused strike the victim at a house party:

"Now, you were at the party on Halloween night last year?"

"Yes, I was."

"And you had been to Bert's Halloween parties before, right?"

"That's correct."

"And Bert throws a good party, doesn't he?"

"Yes, he does."

"So you were looking forward to having a good time that night?"

"I was."

"And there were a lot of your friends there having a good time, weren't there?"

"Quite a few, yes."

"People were drinking alcohol at the party, your friends were consuming alcohol, weren't they?"

"Yes, most people were drinking."

"Well, it's quite natural, quite expected to drink at a Halloween party, I take it?"

"Yes, it's common."

"And you were drinking too, weren't you?"

"Well, I guess so, yes."

"You arrived at the party at 9:00 p.m. or so?"

"Yes."

"Had you had anything to drink before going to Bert's?"

"A few beers, I guess."

"A few beers, would that be more than two?"

"Well, a bit more, I guess."

"So, four or five beers?"

"Probably, I wasn't counting."

"Okay, and you had your first drink at the party around 9:00 p.m.?"

"I suppose."

"People were drinking shooters at the party, kind of a loosen-up-and-get-to-know-ya thing?"

"Yeah, Bert had shooters lined up at the door to welcome us."

"And you had a few of those when you arrived?"

"I expect that I did."

"And a few being four or five?"

"Could be."

"And the fight in question took place at 4:30 the next morning?"

"About that time, yes."

"So you'd been drinking and partying that whole time, I take it?"

"Pretty much so, I guess."

As you can see, counsel has slowly worked the witness into a corner where he acknowledges that he consumed a huge quantity of alcohol that night. At the very least, the trier of fact will have to give his testimony less weight, if not discount the testimony entirely, because of his level of impairment.

Cross-examination has another role to play in relation to evidentiary matters: to gain information from the opponent's witness that is helpful to your case. This can be as valuable to a party as attacking a witness's credibility. However, the witness usually does not want to divulge helpful information. In such cases, examining counsel may use very specific leading questions that force the witness to give very short answers. Consider the following exchange between defence counsel and a crime scene investigator who has testified against the accused:

> "You examined the body at the scene?"
> "I did."
> "And you saw my client, Frank Getty, there?"
> "I did."
> "Did you observe any blood on his hands, clothing, or any other part of his body?"
> "I did not."
> "Yet there was blood all over the room where the victim was found, wasn't there?"
> "There was."

Through this tightly scripted questioning, the examiner has controlled a non-supportive witness and obtained valuable concessions and information. Note that the last question is meant to imply that if the accused had killed the victim, he would have gotten blood on his clothes, given that there was blood all over the room. The examiner might have asked this question outright: "So, can you explain how my client could have killed the victim and gotten no blood on himself?" However, this strategy carries a risk: if the witness replies, "No," the gamble has paid off, but if the witness offers a credible explanation, it can be devastating to the examiner's case. For example, the witness might well say:

> "Yes, counsel, I can. I noticed that your client's hair was wet, as if he had recently showered. I then examined the downstairs shower, which was also wet, and in the drain we recovered traces of blood, which we matched to the victim. If you want my opinion, I think your client killed the victim, then went downstairs and showered before calling the police."

As long as this answer responds to the question, counsel is powerless to stop it. It is like letting a genie out of a bottle.

Limitations on Cross-Examination

We sometimes get the impression from watching television shows that cross-examination is a matter of shouting at and badgering a witness to the point that he or she breaks down and admits everything. This is not the sort of cross-examination that is permitted in Canadian courts of law. Yes, counsel is entitled to "test" witnesses, to challenge them and point out discrepancies and logical gaps, but witnesses are entitled to a certain degree of respect. This means that lawyers, when questioning a witness, must not be insulting, aggressive, or hostile in either tone or manner. The judge has the right and obligation to restrict cross-examination that is irrelevant, prolix, or insulting. Prolix cross-examination occurs when the examiner is unnecessarily lengthy in questioning or pursues a topic in excessively minute detail. Counsel must avoid wearing witnesses down to the point where they will say anything just to get off the stand. In addition, counsel are not permitted to suggest or imply facts that are not in evidence or that counsel are not in a position to prove, or the judge may order that such conversation be struck from the record, as in the following example:

> Examining counsel: "Witness, how often do you get stoned?"
>
> Witness: "I don't do drugs."
>
> Examining counsel: "Come, come, witness, you're a teenager. You expect the jury to believe that you don't do *any* drugs?"
>
> Witness: "No, I don't."
>
> Examining counsel: "So, you are really trying to assert that you have never smoked marijuana?"
>
> Witness: "No, I haven't."
>
> Examining counsel: "How about on the May long weekend when you went to the beach with your friends?"
>
> Witness: "None of them smoke marijuana."
>
> Examining counsel: "So a bunch of teenagers go to the beach for a wild weekend and sit around playing poker?"
>
> Opposing counsel: "I object to this line of questioning."
>
> Judge: "Finally. What about it, counsel, do you have any evidence to support these allegations?"
>
> Examining counsel: "Well, no, Your Honour. I was sort of hoping that he might just admit to it. I thought all young kids did drugs."
>
> Judge: "Well, you're way out of line, counsel. You can't go around making negative allegations without any evidence to back them up. I'm going to strike that entire conversation, and you had better be a lot more careful in the future or I'll cite you for contempt."

A related issue arose in *R v Ellard* (2003 BCCA 68), in which a young woman in British Columbia was charged, and eventually convicted, of the bullying murder of a female classmate, Reena Virk (see the Case in Point in Chapter 6, Traditional Exceptions to the Hearsay Rule). Crown counsel cross-examined Ms. Ellard and repeatedly asked her to explain why the Crown witnesses would lie in their testimony. The Court of Appeal, in reviewing the Crown's questioning, stated (at para 22):

> The potential prejudice arising from this form of questioning is that it tends to shift the burden of proof from the Crown to the accused. It could induce a jury to analyze the case on the reasoning that if an accused cannot say why a witness would give false evidence against her, the witness's testimony may be true. The risk of such a course of reasoning undermines the presumption of innocence and the doctrine of reasonable doubt. The mind of the trier of fact must remain firmly fixed on whether the Crown proved its case on the requisite standard and not be diverted by the question whether the accused provided a motive for a witness to lie.

The courts impose these limits on cross-examination, not only in the interest of a fair trial, but because the behaviour of counsel affects the public's perception of the justice system. If the judicial process is seen as unfair and witnesses are permitted to be bullied, the public may view the justice system as hostile and avoid the courts, leading to greater lawlessness in society.

Cross-Examining Your Own Witness

By calling a witness to testify, counsel is taken to be "vouching" for the witness's credibility. It stands to reason that counsel would not call someone to testify whom she thinks is unreliable or untruthful. Therefore, counsel are not usually permitted to cross-examine their own witnesses. To do so would be to attack the very witness being offered up to the court as trustworthy. However, sometimes witnesses turn out to be neither trustworthy nor cooperative. In such cases, counsel may want to cross-examine the witness. If counsel wish to engage in cross-examination of their own witnesses, they must seek the court's permission to do so.

There are two ways that counsel can get permission from a judge to challenge their own witness. The first is to ask that the witness be declared hostile. A **hostile witness** is just what it sounds like—a witness who responds with hostility to the lawyer's questioning. The exchange might go something like this:

> "Do you know the accused person, Randolph Small?"
> "What if I do?"
> "Can you tell me how long you have known Mr. Small?"
> "Long enough."
> "I'm not very clear about how long 'long enough' is."
> "Well, that's your problem then, isn't it?"
> "Your Honour, I'd ask that the witness be declared hostile."

hostile witness
witness who has been called by a party to give evidence but is uncooperative and responds with hostility to the questions posed by counsel

If the judge declares the witness hostile, counsel can shift into cross-examination to more closely control the witness and to attempt to corner him into being truthful.

The second approach is to ask the court to declare the witness to be "adverse." Unlike a hostile witness, an **adverse witness** may be polite and forthcoming in her evidence, yet it is clear that the witness's interests are aligned with those of the opponent and that she is likely to colour her evidence in favour of the opponent. This may be the situation when one party is suing another and calls the opposing party's spouse to testify because she is uniquely positioned to provide the information required to win the case. The spouse may be honest and of good character, yet the information she provides can be expected to be unfavourable because she is biased in favour of her spouse. In practice, counsel would likely call such a witness only where counsel has in hand a statement from the witness confirming the information that counsel wishes to place before the trier of fact. Because the statement would be considered inadmissible as hearsay, counsel must have the person testify if the information is to get before the trier of fact. When the spouse reluctantly testifies and "disappoints" by testifying differently about the events she had described in her earlier statement, counsel can apply to the court under section 9 of the *Canada Evidence Act* to have the witness declared adverse:

adverse witness
witness whose testimony shows her interests to be aligned with those of the opponent and who is therefore likely to colour her evidence in favour of the opponent

> 9(1) A party producing a witness shall not be allowed to impeach his credit by general evidence of bad character, but if the witness, in the opinion of the court, proves adverse, the party may contradict him by other evidence, or, by leave of the court, may prove that the witness made at other times a statement inconsistent with his present testimony, but before the last mentioned proof can be given the

circumstances of the supposed statement, sufficient to designate the particular occasion, shall be mentioned to the witness, and he shall be asked whether or not he did make the statement.

9(2) Where the party producing a witness alleges that the witness made at other times a statement in writing, reduced to writing, or recorded on audio tape or video tape or otherwise, inconsistent with the witness's present testimony, the court may, without proof that the witness is adverse, grant leave to that party to cross-examine the witness as to the statement and the court may consider the cross-examination in determining whether in the opinion of the court the witness is adverse.

It may be possible to establish this adversity by showing an inconsistency between what the witness says on the stand and an earlier statement made by that witness. However, the cross-examination must be restricted to the inconsistencies evident in the witness's testimony and cannot expand to a general attack on the witness's character, because the party calling the witness still imparts an aura of credibility to the witness by presenting him or her to the court. At the same time, the cross-examination can extend beyond "impeaching" the specific testimony of the witness and can permit an exploration of the underlying circumstances to attempt to ascertain other relevant information.

To what use can the evidence derived from this cross-examination be put? If a witness acknowledges that her earlier statement is in fact correct, then the trier of fact may adopt that evidence as a proven fact in the case. If, however, the witness sticks to her guns and denies making the earlier statement or says that it must have been wrong, the trier of fact cannot rely on that earlier statement to prove the fact in issue. The statement, can, however, be used to establish that the witness cannot be relied on in relation to the "new" evidence. Thus, a witness who says he saw Alex stab the deceased and later says Alex wasn't even there is a less believable witness. While the trier of fact may not be able to rely on the earlier evidence of stabbing to convict Alex, they can disregard the part about Alex not being there as equally unreliable.

The Supreme Court of Canada, in the cases of *R v B (KG)* ([1993] 1 SCR 740) and *R v U (FJ)* ([1995] 3 SCR 764), extended the use of prior inconsistent statements. The court ruled that in very limited circumstances in which there were adequate substitutes for testing reliability, the prior statement could be admitted into evidence for the truth of its contents, not just to challenge the credibility of the recanting witness. In both of these cases, the witness was present in court and could be cross-examined on the differences in the statements he made. (See "Prior Inconsistent Statements," below.)

CASE IN POINT

Air Amnesia

R v Malik and Bagri, 2003 BCSC 1428; 2005 BCSC 350

On June 23, 1985, Air India flight 182, en route from Montreal to Delhi, India, was destroyed by an on-board bomb as it flew over the Atlantic Ocean off the coast of Ireland. The bombing killed 329 people, 286 of whom were Canadians. On the same day, a piece of luggage that had come from Vancouver en route to an Air India flight to Bangkok exploded at the New Tokyo (Narita) International Airport, killing two baggage handlers and injuring four others. The suspects in both incidents were a militant group in Canada who were seeking retaliation against the government of India for what they viewed as prior injustices. A number of individual suspects were eventually arrested, charged, and tried in Vancouver. Only one person, Inderjit Singh Reyat, was convicted.

The trial provides an example of how sections 9(1) and 9(2) of the *Canada Evidence Act* provisions may come into effect. As seen in this example, a hostile witness may be nothing more than a frightened witness who succumbs to threats or anticipated reprisals and develops circumstantial amnesia about the issues before the court. We will refer to the witness as Ms. X, because she is in the witness protection program and cannot be named. Although the accused clearly knew who she was, she had some concerns that publication of her identity would put her in danger from militant members of the suspect group.

When called to testify, Ms. X claimed to have no memory of statements she made to the RCMP in which she stated that Ajaib Singh Bagri confessed his involvement in the Air India bombing to her and subsequently threatened her life if she revealed this to anyone. She made the statements over a considerable period of time in a series of 17 interviews.

Crown counsel sought to have Ms. X declared hostile to permit cross-examination of her in relation to her earlier statements, pointing out to the court how unlikely it was that she would forget these conversations given her discussions with the police, the fact that her life had been threatened, and the fact that she lost relatives on the Air India flight. Ms. X had always told the police that she would never testify against Bagri, and her "forgetfulness" appears to be the embodiment of this promise.

The judge rejected the Crown's argument in a ruling where he stated that although he did not believe that the witness did not remember these events, he was not convinced that the inconsistencies in her testimony about Bagri were enough to have her declared hostile.

The court had earlier ruled against the Crown's request to have their witness, Inderjit Singh Reyat, declared hostile. After pleading guilty to his role in the bombing and receiving a five-year sentence, Reyat also developed significant memory loss, which limited any usefulness of his testimony.

Failure to Cross-Examine a Witness

When cross-examining an opponent's witness, counsel must give the witness a chance to explain any contradictions or inconsistencies in her testimony that counsel intends to rely on by calling later evidence, such as a contradicting witness. This rule ensures fairness in the proceeding and prevents the confusion that could result if this approach were not taken. Failure to cross-examine a witness on a point on which counsel wishes to later contradict her could result in the judge's directing that the earlier witness be recalled so that she can comment on the discrepancy between her testimony and the later evidence. Not only can this process be confusing and disruptive, but the witness may be unavailable. If the witness cannot be recalled, the judge may reject the contradictory evidence entirely or minimize the contradiction to the point where it loses its impact.

The judge is charged with ensuring that the trier of fact has helpful and reliable evidence before it. If counsel pursues evidence late in a trial that contradicts earlier testimony that was not cross-examined, the trier of fact is left with an evidentiary imbalance. It unfairly advantages one party by denying the earlier witness the opportunity to explain the apparent contradiction, which has the effect of misleading the trier of fact.

Fairness mandates that when counsel contradicts the witness with a prior inconsistent statement, counsel must alert the witness to the inconsistency and give her an opportunity to explain it. Alerting the witness to a contradiction in an earlier statement is referred to as "laying the foundation" for this particular attack on credibility.

Counsel can even be held to the requirement to cross-examine a witness on a particular fact or else be seen to have accepted this evidence without challenging its veracity. This could be a fatal decision. It sometimes seems pointless to cross-examine because counsel will expect to hear a series of denials, but the trier of fact can be aided by hearing those denials in order to assess the demeanour of the witness and weigh that evidence against the opponent's.

Re-examination

Once a witness has gone through examination-in-chief and cross-examination, the original examining counsel will often wish to ask further questions. This can be problematic if the re-examination raises issues that opposing counsel want to re-cross-examine on, which could lead to a potentially endless cycle. To avoid this situation, the courts have developed rules governing re-examination.

Re-examination is restricted to asking questions on topics that were not dealt with in examination-in-chief and that the examiner could not have anticipated would be dealt with in cross-examination. In other words, re-examination cannot be used to get the last word in and re-emphasize the key points brought out in direct examination. It is also not appropriate to "split your case" by bringing out some of your key points in examination-in-chief, saving some additional ones until after the cross-examination.

If something new and unanticipated arises in cross-examination, counsel can, with leave of the court, ask a few additional questions in that area. Opposing counsel may even be permitted to ask a few questions arising from the re-examination. It is entirely a factor of the patience and flexibility of the judge.

One instance where re-examination will generally be permitted is where the witness's credibility has been attacked in cross-examination. The court usually permits some questions designed to "rehabilitate" the credibility of the witness. If the attack has been with regard to the witness's general credibility, counsel may even be permitted to call additional witnesses, including possibly expert witnesses, to provide evidence to reinforce the general credibility of the witness or undermine this attack on general credibility.

Credibility and Reliability

By calling a witness, a party vouches for that witness's credibility, in effect saying to the court, this is a person worthy of being believed. Typically, that witness dutifully recites the expected evidence that supports the party that called her to testify. The opponent, in cross-examination, tries to limit or minimize the harmful impact of this witness's evidence. This can be done by attacking the witness's credibility or by undermining her reliability. These concepts differ because attacks on credibility imply that the witness is trying to deceive the trier of fact, whereas attacks on reliability suggest only that the witness got it wrong, and apply equally to deceitful and to honest witnesses.

Credibility

Typically, counsel attacks the credibility of a witness by attempting to show that she is biased and therefore has a motive for lying. The relationship that the witness has with the party on whose behalf she has testified will imply motive or lack of motive. For example, it is presumed that a spouse, child, parent, or other close relative will shade her evidence to support her relative. "Blood is thicker than water" is an expression that will resonate with most triers of fact. Another way to reveal bias is to show that the witness and the party share a common interest, such as where the two are business partners or the witness stands to benefit from a successful verdict by the party. In some cases, counsel may attempt to prove that the witness has been induced to change or fabricate her story, such as where counsel has evidence of an exchange of cash or benefits—for example, a promotion that could be linked to the witness's testimony.

Bias can be more general. The witness may think all young people are troublemakers or have religious or racial views that favour the party on whose behalf she is testifying, and discriminate against the opponent. Where bias can be shown, the trier of fact is entitled to discount the evidence of that witness on the basis that her bias may colour her perspective and cause her to either intentionally or unintentionally make misleading statements.

Counsel may also attack a witness's credibility by attempting to show that she has a history of dishonesty and is of poor character. Thus, a witness, other than the accused in a criminal case, may be subject to broad-ranging questions about her criminal past, reputation in the community, and general character. Recall that different rules apply to questioning an accused in a criminal case about her character (see Chapter 8, Character Evidence).

The following techniques, then, are commonly used to challenge a witness in cross-examination:

- showing that the witness has a bias that would taint her evidence;
- showing that the witness has interests that are aligned with those of the opponent;
- establishing that the witness may have succumbed to inducements to alter or fabricate a story;
- showing that the witness is prejudiced against a party, either because of personal beliefs or just because of who the party is;
- attacking the character of the witness by showing a criminal record or other bad acts; and
- attacking the witness's reputation.

Reliability

Opposing counsel may attempt to undermine the confidence that the trier of fact has in the witness's reliability so that the evidence will not compare well in the final analysis with the evidence they intend to call. Attacks on the reliability of the witness are primarily focused on the witness's capacity to observe, remember, and communicate.

For example, counsel may attempt to discredit the testimony of a witness who claims to have seen the accused stab the victim by establishing that the incident occurred at night and the witness was 20 metres away, behind some bushes, and not wearing her prescription glasses. Counsel may also try to reduce the impact of testimony given in examination-in-chief by testing the witness's ability to recall details of the event. If the witness does not recall whether the accident happened at night or during the day, whether it was raining or sunny, whether the accused's car was white or black, or whether anyone else was at the scene, her claim to have a complete memory of other specific points may be called into question by the trier of fact. Finally, counsel may attempt to show that the witness's testimony is imprecise or misleading and therefore unreliable. For example, a witness who describes the accused as "completely blotto," and then concedes under cross-examination that she really meant she smelled alcohol on his breath, is unreliable. Or if she says that the assailant was a "giant, hulking man," but later agrees that he was about the same build as the prosecutor, who is 1.7 metres tall (5 feet, 8 inches) and 63 kilograms (140 pounds), she shows her testimony to be unreliable.

Impeaching Testimony

There are several methods that may be used to "impeach" the evidence of a witness—that is, limit the impact of the evidence on the trier of fact or convince the trier of fact to ignore the evidence entirely. The most common method is cross-examination, where the statements of the witness are challenged directly. Lack of consistency, or pointing out where the witness has said different things during the course of her testimony, is another tactic of impeachment. In addition, a witness can be challenged with regard to previous statements that are inconsistent with what she has stated under oath on the witness stand. Further, other witnesses, including on occasion expert witnesses, can be called to contradict what a witness has said, thus eliminating or reducing the impact of her statements.

Prior Inconsistent Statements

A first step in attempting to impeach a witness through prior inconsistent statements requires confirming the evidence that the witness has given in the proceeding. Next, the witness is alerted that there is a prior statement that counsel believe is contradictory. The witness is given an opportunity to read the prior statement, and then asked whether the statement was truthful. In so doing, the examiner hopes to trick the witness into saying that two contradictory statements are both true, thus destroying the witness's credibility. Occasionally, the witness will be cooperative enough to adopt the former statements, aiding the examining opponent. If the statement is adopted, it forms part of that witness's evidence and may be weighed by the trier of fact. If the prior statement is not adopted, it can be used only to challenge the truthfulness of that witness, but is not evidence of its contents. The rare exception to this is where there are **circumstantial guarantees of reliability** that allow the statement to fit into the principled approach to hearsay exceptions, such as in *R v B (KG)* and *R v U (FJ)*,

circumstantial guarantees of reliability aspects of the circumstances surrounding the formation of the evidence that enhance its reliability

referred to above. In these circumstances, the prior statement may be admitted for the truth of its contents.

Bolstering the Credibility of Your Own Witness

Because all witnesses are presumed to be truthful unless shown to be otherwise, a party is prohibited from calling evidence that is designed to enhance or shore up the credibility of one of its witnesses. For example, Robert testifies that he bought a car privately, thinking that it was brand new because the odometer showed only 23 kilometres, but discovered a year later that it had 30,000 kilometres on it and had been in an accident. The defendant claims that he told Robert there were 30,000 kilometres on the car, and explained that the odometer said 23 kilometres because the mechanism had to be repaired after the accident. Robert wishes to call Father Michael, who has known him as a former choir boy and parishioner for the past 18 years. Father Michael, the court is told, will testify that Robert is honest, that he handled church moneys for years, and that he was polite and kind to the older parishioners. Is this evidence relevant? Would it help the trier of fact? Should the judge admit it?

The evidence will not be admitted because it is offered simply to enhance Robert's credibility. Father Michael knows nothing of the parties' transaction but is prepared to support his longtime parishioner from a sense of duty. We also recognize that in many instances, otherwise honest and reliable people have been known to be untruthful. (See Chapter 8, Character Evidence.)

Collateral Facts Rule

This is a trial court management rule for the benefit of the court. In order to conduct a trial that does not spin out of control, judges will restrict the calling of evidence in a number of ways. Sometimes they may limit the number of witnesses that can be called. Where one witness has testified in relation to a fact, does it add much to have 10, 20, or 30 witnesses say the same thing? Many litigants feel that "more is better," so it is a matter of self-protection for the courts to place a limit on the number of witnesses who will be permitted on one particular issue. In addition, if the courts permit one side to engage in unlimited calling of witnesses, the issues may blur and the trier of fact may lose its focus regarding what it should be determining. In order to provide a protection against the unlimited calling of evidence, courts have developed the **collateral facts rule**. This basically states that where an opponent's witness provides contradictory evidence on matters that are not material issues, counsel are not permitted to call other evidence in response. Cross-examination on the point is still permitted, but no additional witnesses may be called to disprove the collateral facts.

collateral facts rule rule that limits the calling of additional evidence on immaterial issues between the parties

Let's say that a witness to a car accident, introduced as a chartered accountant for the past 10 years, testifies that the defendant ran a red light. The defendant happens to know that the witness graduated from high school less than five years ago, so he could not have been a chartered accountant for the last 10 years. He wants to call evidence from the Chartered Professional Accountants of Canada to prove that the witness lied. The collateral facts rule would stop the defendant from calling this witness. He could cross-examine the original witness and try to prove him wrong, but if the witness stuck to his guns, the defendant would have no recourse and would be essentially "stuck" with that answer. The trier of fact may choose not to believe the evidence of the witness regarding his profession, but because it does not relate to an issue between the parties, valuable court time will not be spent in proving this collateral fact. If the witness's evidence is not believed, there will be an absence of evidence on the point, as if nothing were ever said about it.

The rule comes into play often on issues of whether a witness had consumed drugs or was drinking—facts that the witness may not wish to share. If the witness denies these allegations, whether counsel will be permitted to call any witnesses to contradict the claims will depend on whether the court feels that the evidence of substance abuse is collateral. Some would argue that matters of credibility or reliability are always substantive, while others claim they are collateral. It seems that in Canada, the courts lean toward finding general credibility matters to be more collateral than substantive. Even so, the courts have shown an inclination to find exceptions, including where the credibility issue goes toward showing

1. bias or interest in the litigation,
2. past convictions or untruthfulness, or
3. expert evidence that undermines the reliability of the witness.

Some argue strongly in favour of a more flexible approach to this matter, suggesting that the judge should have considerable discretion to weigh the probative value of the evidence and to admit it when the probative value exceeds the prejudice. In weighing the probative value, the judge could determine, in the context of the matter before her, what significance the contradictory evidence would have and not be bound by a fixed and inflexible rule to reject evidence that would be useful for the trier of fact.

Although there is some indication that courts are gradually moving toward a more flexible approach to the rule, leaving it to the trial judge's discretion on a case-by-case basis, to date the Supreme Court of Canada has not provided direction on the issue.

Refreshing Memory

With certain witnesses or at certain points in examination-in-chief or cross-examination, a witness's memory may fail him. This is not necessarily an attempt by the witness to lie or distort evidence, but could be merely an indication of nervousness or even forgetfulness with the passage of time since the incident being described. In these circumstances, it is permissible (subject to the judge's discretion) for counsel to jog the witness's memory in various ways. Typically, counsel will show the witness a previous statement. This will often spur a memory, and the witness can then continue to testify about the incident from this revived memory. If the witness's previous statement does not revive a memory, he may still be permitted to adopt the earlier statement as a truthful statement at the time that it was made. This statement would be hearsay even though it is that witness's own statement, but it may be sufficiently reliable to deserve some weight.

Other methods can be used to jog a witness's memory, including showing him a photograph; playing an audiotape, videotape, or other sound or video recording; taking the witness to the scene of an incident; permitting the witness to examine an exhibit; or using any other strategy that a judge deems is a legitimate effort to access a witness's memory.

Therefore, refreshing a witness's memory can generate evidence in two ways. One is described as **present memory revived**, which implies that the technique of refreshing the memory caused the witness to revive actual memories and details of the incident. Implicit in this is that the revived memories are more complete than the information that was used to jog the memory. On the other hand, if the witness remembers only the words in the statement and not the incident itself, the witness is probably relying on the statement and not having an original memory. In this circumstance, we refer to the process as **past recollection recorded**. With this, the effort at revival does not jog an original memory but the witness acknowledges making the statement and its "truthfulness at the time." Such a statement may be admitted. Its weight may be less than testimony that derives from an actual memory of the events, particularly where detail is important or effective cross-examination is thwarted by the witness's reliance on the statement for all of his "recollection."

present memory revived
process whereby the witness revives actual memories and details of an incident; cf. past recollection recorded

past recollection recorded
process whereby the witness recalls the words he made in a statement but not the incident itself

Corroboration

Corroborating evidence has not always worked to support just outcomes in criminal proceedings. The term **corroboration** describes evidence that supports or confirms other evidence. So, if you allege that your neighbour dented your car, another neighbour who also saw it happen would corroborate your testimony. As the laws of evidence developed, certain kinds of evidence were thought to be unreliable on their own and so rules were put in place requiring independent evidence to confirm the substance of the "unsafe" evidence. The difficulty was that evidence considered to be unsafe included the evidence of children (because of their age) and, in some instances, women (because of their sex). It therefore became difficult to obtain a conviction in cases of sexual crimes against children and women where no corroborating evidence existed. Accomplices to a crime were another group where warnings to the jury were required. This is because an accomplice who implicated his partner was almost certainly buying some lesser penalty by cooperating with the authorities. The selfish motive made the allegations against the partner suspect.

In Canada, these rules have changed and, as in many areas of evidence law, the courts have largely moved toward a "principled approach" to the issue of corroboration, moving away from mandatory and arbitrary corroboration warnings to discretionary warnings. With discretionary warnings, the judge warns the trier of fact about the danger of the evidence only if the circumstances warrant such a warning. In adopting the new approach, the courts have acknowledged that the rules surrounding corroboration had become extremely rigid and formulaic, often ignoring

corroboration
evidence that supports or confirms other evidence

rather than considering the facts of the case. For corroboration to exist, it was not good enough for it simply to support the allegation; it also had to

- be independent,
- confirm the testimony corroborated in a "material particular" (a particular fact that is specific to the matter before the court), and
- implicate the accused.

Under this formula, a child's evidence that she was sexually assaulted by a neighbour could not proceed based only on the evidence of the child, even with confirmation that there had been injuries consistent with a sexual assault. The medical evidence would need to be independent and even confirm the likelihood of a sexual assault. Without DNA, regardless of the clarity and credibility of the child's testimony, no conviction could occur. This approach to the evidence of a child is now considered to be outmoded thinking. Today, a child's evidence may deserve special scrutiny but will not need corroboration for a conviction.

Corroboration and Jailhouse Informants

Some evidence still cries out for corroboration because of the inherently "dangerous" circumstances surrounding it. For example, Douglas Martin, a jailhouse informant in the Shannon Murrin murder trial, who shared a cell with Murrin, claimed that Murrin confessed to him that he killed Mindy Tran. His evidence was thoroughly undermined by defence counsel, however, who established that Martin had 109 criminal convictions that included one for perjury. He was known in the cells as "Father Confession" because of the nine times that he claimed to have been the recipient of jailhouse murder confessions. Martin was also involved in the conviction of Thomas Sophonow, who was later released after being exonerated by DNA evidence despite Martin's obtaining his "confession." The experience with Douglas Martin and Thomas Sophonow has gone a long way toward proving just how dangerous evidence from jailhouse informants can be. In addition to jailhouse informants, witnesses of "unsavoury character" will also attract warnings.

Currently, the only situation in which the evidence of a witness attracts a mandatory warning is where the accused has been charged with one of the following historical offences: offences of high treason, perjury, or procuring a feigned marriage. All of these *Criminal Code* offences specify that no person shall be convicted of the offence on the evidence of only one witness, unless the evidence of that witness is corroborated in a material particular by evidence that implicates the accused person. For other classes of precautionary witnesses such as accomplices, jailhouse informants, unsavoury characters, and children, warnings are discretionary for the judge. Note that these warnings are now

- no longer mandatory for specific categories of witnesses,
- no longer limited to specific categories of witnesses, and
- not limited to a formulistic warning that includes implication of the accused.

The Supreme Court of Canada case dealing with the discretionary nature of these warnings is *Vetrovec v The Queen* ([1982] 1 SCR 811). In a later Supreme Court decision, the court dealt with the discretion of a judge to provide a **Vetrovec warning** about the testimony of jailhouse informants in the case of *R v Brooks* (2000 SCC 11, [2000] 1 SCR 237). Brooks was charged with murdering his girlfriend's 19-month-old daughter. The disturbing facts of the case are set out below (at paras 32-36):

> Around 10:30 p.m. on December 13, 1992, 19-month-old Samantha Johnings stirred in her sleep when her aunt checked on her before leaving the apartment. The next day at 11:00 a.m., Samantha's mother Norma Jean Johnings found her dead in her crib. She had been murdered. Rigor mortis was setting in. There was blood and vomit on her face. Her left eye was swollen shut and she had three bruises on her head caused by blunt force trauma. The body was wrapped in a green comforter. Her mother attempted in vain to revive her. She then called 911.
>
> Only two persons had access to Samantha on the night of her murder—her mother and the respondent. The respondent had been living in the apartment with Norma Jean since the previous October. He was not the father of Samantha, nor of her newborn brother, Anthony.
>
> At autopsy, it was noted that Samantha's genital area had a well-demarcated area of bruising and redness, which was inconsistent with a diaper rash but consistent with a rubbing action, or the use of a blunt object. Trace amounts of semen were found on vaginal and anal swabs taken from her body. The cause of death was acute brain injury. The head injuries could have but did not necessarily precede the injuries to the vagina and anus. A healing lesion of one centimetre in diameter was also noted on the right buttock.
>
> DNA testing of the sperm proved inconclusive, likely due to contamination of the sample. No one could be included or excluded as the source.
>
> The respondent's grey track pants were found in the apartment and seized on January 27, 1993. Those pants contained blood stains of the same blood type as Samantha's. An expert witness for the Crown testified that the blood's DNA signature matched Samantha's and that the frequency of that profile in Caucasians is one in 80 million. The track pants had semen on them, as well as a juice substance, similar to what was found in Samantha's bottle.

At trial, the Crown led evidence from two jailhouse informants, King and Balogh, who testified that the accused had admitted to them that he had killed the child because she was crying. The trial judge did not provide a *Vetrovec* warning to the jury. The accused was found guilty and appealed, ultimately going to the Supreme Court of Canada. There, although the court was divided on whether the trial judge should have given a *Vetrovec* warning in relation to the evidence of these jailhouse informants, the justices did agree (at para 2) that the decision to give a *Vetrovec* warning is properly at the discretion of the judge:

> In *Vetrovec*, Dickson J (as he then was) held that a trial judge has the discretion, and not the duty, to give a clear and sharp warning to the jury with respect to the testimony of certain "unsavoury" witnesses. Dickson J followed what he referred to as the "common sense" approach, moving away from "blind and empty formalism" and "ritualistic incantations" ... .

Vetrovec warning
warning to the jury given where the judge determines that the evidence of a particular witness is called into question and requires special scrutiny; jurors are cautioned that they may accept the evidence without corroboration but it is dangerous to do so without independent confirmation of material parts of that evidence

The court identified (at para 4) two factors to be considered in determining whether to give the warning—the credibility of the witness and the importance of the witness to the Crown's case:

> In exercising his or her discretion to warn the jury regarding certain evidence, the trial judge may consider, *inter alia*, the credibility of the witness and the importance of the evidence to the Crown's case. These factors affect whether the *Vetrovec* warning is required. In other words, the greater the concern over the credibility of the witness and the more important the evidence, the more likely the *Vetrovec* caution will be mandatory. Where the evidence of so called "unsavoury witnesses" represents the whole of the evidence against the accused, a "clear and sharp" *Vetrovec* warning may be warranted. Where, however, there is strong evidence to support the conviction in the absence of the potentially "unsavoury" evidence, and less reason to doubt the witness's credibility, the *Vetrovec* warning would not be required, and a lesser instruction would be justified.

The majority, in determining that a "clear and sharp" warning was not required in the circumstances, quoted (at para 10) from the Crown's factum in noting that there was substantial corroborating evidence to support the credibility of the informants' information:

> There was a richness of detail concerning the circumstances of the event as opposed to a simple allegation or a bald admission by the accused. King and Balogh's evidence contained details as to the location of the injuries, the prior hitting of Samantha by the Respondent, the detail that the mother had also hit the child on occasion to discipline her, that Samantha was always crying and that she was crying on the night she died and that she choked.
>
> *Many of the facts in the accused's admissions to King and Balogh were confirmed by independent evidence.* The fact that the baby's mother's name was Norma, that she was the Respondent's girlfriend, that they lived in the apartment building near the Centre, and that the mother was going to testify against the Respondent were all accurate. *The evidence that the Respondent told King and Balogh that he had struck … Samantha repeatedly in the head was consistent with the medical and forensic evidence as to the location of the injuries. The fact that Samantha choked was confirmed by the vomit on … her face. The fact that the [Respondent] would hit Samantha when she cried was confirmed by the evidence of witnesses at the trial. The fact that Samantha was crying on the night she was killed was confirmed by the mother.*

Judges, therefore, are to assess the evidence objectively and to warn where the evidence of the witness is a significant part of the Crown's case and the credibility of the witness is objectively questionable. Now that the rigid formula is gone, judges can give a range of warnings tailor-made to the degree of danger inherent in that witness's testimony.

Objections

We have all seen television shows and movies where a lawyer jumps to her feet and shouts "Objection!" in response to a question from her opponent or an answer given by a witness. Sometimes the lawyer may go on to provide further details about the objection, while other times only a word or two is said. While perhaps overly dramatic, this is one aspect of the trial process that is fairly accurately represented in popular culture.

What Are Objections?

If we think back to the roles served by the different parties in the courtroom, we recall that one function of the judge is to serve as the trier of law. In this capacity, the judge will interpret and apply the law. As part of this function, the judge determines what is admitted as evidence during the trial. However, remember that judges in the adversarial system are not expected to take an active role in the trial process. It is the litigants, often through their legal representatives, who are expected to marshal and present the evidence that best supports the theory of their case. As a result, judges do not usually make their decisions about the admissibility of evidence until the opposing party objects to the admission on the basis that it violates a rule of evidence.

As an example, during the course of a trial, if one party's witness was about to say something in the witness box that the opposing party believes is hearsay, counsel for the opposing party would rise to his feet and say, "Objection, Your Honour. That is hearsay." The judge would then make a ruling as to whether the objection would be dismissed and the statement admitted or rule that the objection was substantiated, meaning that the statement is hearsay and will not be admitted.

If the objection is going to require legal argument before the judge makes a decision, there will usually be a voir dire, a mini-hearing within the trial, in which the lawyers for the parties submit their legal arguments to the judge. In the case of a jury trial, the jury would be sent out of the courtroom while the voir dire takes place.

An objection can apply not only to oral evidence but also to any other form of evidence, such as documentary and real evidence.

CHAPTER SUMMARY

In order to testify at a hearing, a witness must be competent and compellable. Children may give evidence if they are deemed competent under the evidence act of the province in which the trial is held.

Witnesses are questioned during examination-in-chief, cross-examination, and re-examination.

Counsel are not permitted to ask leading questions during examination-in-chief unless the questions are in relation to introductory or non-contentious matters, or if counsel are questioning a witness about statements made by other witnesses for the purpose of contradicting those statements.

Counsel may ask an opponent's witness leading questions during cross-examination in an attempt to challenge or diminish the impact of the witness's testimony by showing that the witness is dishonest or unreliable, or to obtain information that is helpful to its case. However, the judge may restrict cross-examination that is irrelevant, prolix, or insulting, or that could prejudice the jury.

Generally, counsel are not allowed to cross-examine their own witnesses. However, if a judge declares a witness hostile or adverse, counsel may engage in cross-examination to elicit truthful information from the witness for the benefit of the trier of fact.

The court imposes rules to ensure that witnesses are treated fairly and that the information that is put before the trier of fact is reliable and not misleading, including the rule that counsel must give the witness a chance to explain any contradictions or inconsistencies that counsel intends to later rely on.

If one of the parties is of the view that a particular piece of evidence should not be admitted because it violates the rules, she may make an objection. The judge will then decide if the objection should be sustained and the evidence ruled inadmissible or whether it should be dismissed and the evidence be admitted. The objection procedure may take place in a voir dire, a hearing within a hearing, in which the judge will hear legal argument on behalf of all parties and then make a decision on the admissibility of the evidence.

KEY TERMS

adverse witness, 271
capacity, 260
circumstantial guarantees of reliability, 276
collateral facts rule, 277
compellable, 263
competence, 260
corroboration, 279
cross-examination, 266
examination-in-chief, 264
hostile witness, 271
incompetent, 260
past recollection recorded, 279
present memory revived, 279
responsibility, 260
subpoena, 260
summons, 260
Vetrovec warning, 281

REFERENCES

Alberta Evidence Act, RSA 2000, c A-18.

B (KG), R v, [1993] 1 SCR 740.

British Columbia, *Evidence Act*, RSBC 1996, c 124.

Brooks, R v, 2000 SCC 11, [2000] 1 SCR 237.

Canada Evidence Act, RSC 1985, c C-5.

Canadian Charter of Rights and Freedoms, Part I of the Constitution Act, 1982, being Schedule B to the Canada Act 1982 (UK), 1982, c 11.

Criminal Code, RSC 1985, c C-46.

Ellard, R v, 2003 BCCA 68.

Hebert, R v, [1990] 2 SCR 151.

Malik and Bagri, R v, 2003 BCSC 1428.

Malik and Bagri, R v, 2005 BCSC 350.

Manitoba Evidence Act, CCSM, c E150.

New Brunswick, *Evidence Act*, RSNB 1973, c E-11.

Newfoundland and Labrador, *Evidence Act*, RSNL 1990, c E-16.

Nguyen, R v, 2015 ONCA 278.

Nova Scotia, *Evidence Act*, RSNS 1989, c 154.

Ontario, *Evidence Act*, RSO 1990, c E.23.

Saskatchewan, *Evidence Act*, SS 2006, c E-11.2.

U (FJ), R v, [1995] 3 SCR 764.

Vetrovec v The Queen, [1982] 1 SCR 811.

Victims' Bill of Rights, CCSM c V55.

REVIEW QUESTIONS

1. What do we mean when we say that a witness is "called to give evidence," and how is this accomplished?

2. What are the two facets of the judicial test for competence of a witness?

3. Under the *Canada Evidence Act*, what must the judge determine before a child under the age of 14 is allowed to testify?

4. Is there any difference between criminal and non-criminal law in relation to whether a spouse may give evidence against the other spouse?

5. What does section 5 of the *Canada Evidence Act* state?

6. What is the purpose of examination-in-chief?

7. What is a leading question? Give an example of this type of question.

8. Can a leading question ever be asked during examination-in-chief? Explain your answer.

9. What are the two major roles that cross-examination plays in a hearing?

10. What sorts of limits are placed on the cross-examination of witnesses?

11. In what circumstances are counsel not permitted to cross-examine their own witness?

12. In what circumstances might counsel be able to cross-examine their own witness?

13. What are some of the problems that can arise should counsel fail to cross-examine an opponent's witness?

14. What are the limits placed on re-examination of a witness?

15. What are some of the techniques that may be used to challenge the credibility of a witness?

16. What does it mean to "impeach the evidence" of a witness?

17. How do counsel use prior inconsistent statements to challenge a witness?

18. Why is there a court rule against bolstering the credibility of your own witness?

19. What is the collateral facts rule?

20. What are the two major methods of refreshing a witness's memory? Explain each method.

21. What is corroboration evidence?

DISCUSSION QUESTIONS

1. Because mentally incompetent persons are not permitted to give evidence, they are more vulnerable to people who feel they can abuse them without fear that they will testify against them. Can you think of any ways that evidence law might deal with this problem?

2. Your client, George, offers his best friend, Armen, as an alibi witness. Armen is giving this evidence voluntarily. He promises that he will be at court at the date and time you have told him that his evidence is required. You decide not to subpoena him because you want to save George a few bucks and you don't want to antagonize Armen by making him think you find him unreliable. Discuss the problems that may arise with this approach.

3. What problems would arise if leading questions were allowed in examination-in-chief? Can you think of any benefits to allowing such questions in examination-in-chief?

4. The rules governing corroborating evidence, such as the evidence of a child, have changed drastically in recent times. Discuss these changes. What do you think of this new approach to corroboration?

Glossary

A

administrative tribunals: decision-making bodies, similar to courts, that rule on regulatory disputes

admissible evidence: evidence that may be considered by the trier of fact

admission by action: meaning or intention conveyed by an act or gesture

admission of a party: anything said by a party by way of word or conduct that the other party wishes to introduce against that party

adversarial system: judicial process in which parties present evidence before an impartial decision-maker, who then makes a decision in the case

adverse witness: witness whose testimony shows her interests to be aligned with those of the opponent and who is therefore likely to colour her evidence in favour of the opponent

air of reality test: test of whether the defence to a charge is reasonable in light of the evidence

articulable cause: the existence of objective facts that give rise to reasonable grounds to suspect that a person has committed a criminal act

B

balance of probabilities: standard of proof in civil matters, determined on the basis of more likely than not

best evidence rule: a largely outdated rule that requires the original document to be presented in evidence if it is available

beyond a reasonable doubt: very high standard of proof in criminal matters

burden of proof: a party's obligation to prove certain facts or matters in issue

business record: record made in the ordinary course of business by an individual performing the duties of employment who has no motive to fabricate

C

capacity: an acceptable ability to observe and then correctly recall observations or experiences, and an acceptable ability to communicate these observations to the trier of fact

character evidence: evidence of past acts to prove that a person acted in a certain way

charge to the jury: judge's instructions to the jury, before the jury begins deliberations, regarding the applicable law, the standard of proof, and the available defences

circumstantial evidence: indirect evidence from which the trier of fact can logically infer the existence of a material fact

circumstantial guarantees of reliability: aspects of the circumstances surrounding the formation of the evidence that enhance its reliability

co-conspirator exception: rule allowing evidence against one member of a conspiracy as evidence against all other members

collateral facts rule: rule that limits the calling of additional evidence on immaterial issues between the parties

***Collins* test:** test used by the courts to determine whether a police search is reasonable; the search must be authorized by law, the law that authorizes the search must itself be reasonable, and the search must be conducted in a reasonable manner

compellable: legally required to give evidence at a hearing

compendious mode of expressing facts: testimony in which the witness mixes opinion into his narrative in order to express himself; permitted by the court where it is difficult for the witness to express the information without stating an opinion

competence: the legal ability to give oral evidence in a hearing

conditional relevance: term describing evidence that may not initially appear relevant but is admitted on condition that its relevance will be established

conditionally admissible: term describing evidence that is admitted for a specific purpose but that is not at that stage admissible on the larger issue

confession rule: rule that a statement made to a person in authority is not admissible unless it was made voluntarily

confidentiality: the ethical duty of a law professional not to disclose information related to the representation of a client

conscriptive evidence: evidence obtained as a result of the accused's being compelled to participate in the creation or location of evidence

conspiracy: a common design or plan by two or more persons to commit a criminal act or omission

corroboration: evidence that supports or confirms other evidence

court martial: formal military justice process in which civilian rules of evidence apply

cross-examination: questioning of a witness by opposing counsel after examination-in-chief

D

declaration against interest: a statement made by a party that is against the party's legal interest

derivative evidence: evidence that derives from a breach of an accused's rights

direct evidence: evidence given by a witness about a material fact that the witness experienced

directed verdict: order from the judge to acquit the accused because the Crown has not made a *prima facie* case

disclosure: the requirement that the Crown produce to the defence, before the trial begins, all the evidence that has been gathered in a criminal case

discovery: the process in a non-criminal case through which every party to the case has an opportunity to examine the evidence

documentary evidence: any document, including text, film, video and audio recordings, and photographs, presented in court for reference by the trier of fact

dying declaration: statement made by a person who is certain he or she is about to die

E

examination-in-chief: questioning of a witness by the party who called the witness; its object is to bring out information that will establish facts that the litigant must prove to win the case

excited utterance: statement made while the speaker's mind is still dominated by a startling event

excluded evidence: evidence that cannot be considered by the trier of fact

expert opinion: testimony given by a properly qualified person with specific expertise in an area that is in issue before the court; permitted in order to assist the trier of fact in coming to conclusions of fact in that area

G

***Grant* test:** three-part test used by the courts to determine whether the admission of evidence obtained through a Charter violation would bring the administration of justice into disrepute

H

hearsay: statement, originally made out of court, that is repeated in court for the truth of its contents

hearsay evidence: evidence given by a witness that is based on information received from others rather than personal knowledge; generally considered inadmissible

hostile witness: witness who has been called by a party to give evidence but is uncooperative and responds with hostility to the questions posed by counsel

I

implied statement: action, behaviour, or course of conduct that conveys information to observers

in camera **hearing:** a private hearing, often in a judge's chambers, that is closed to the public

incompetent: not permitted to give evidence

incompetent witness: an incompetent witness is one who is *legally unable* to give evidence in a proceeding

innocence at stake exception: an exception to solicitor–client privilege when the otherwise protected communication is necessary to establish a person's innocence

investigative detention: detention that may occur where there are reasonable grounds to suspect, in all the circumstances, that the individual is connected to a particular crime and that such detention is necessary

J

judges' privilege: privilege that protects judges and administrative tribunal members against disclosing information behind their decisions

judicial discretion: a judge's freedom to apply rules or decide issues in the context of a case

judicial notice: a judge's recognition of a fact without requiring a party to prove it

L

layperson's opinion: opinion given by an ordinary witness on a matter of ordinary experience; permitted where the opinion does not unnecessarily encroach on the trier of fact's role

litigation privilege: privilege that protects communications between a client's lawyer or law firm and third parties

M

material fact: a fact that relates to any matter in dispute between parties

moral prejudice: prejudice that results from the admission of evidence of bad character showing the accused to be a morally bad person and leading the trier of fact to conclude that he is guilty

N

natural justice: fundamental legal principle entitling a person to a fair and unbiased hearing

non-compellable witness: a non-compellable witness is one who *cannot be legally required* to give evidence in a proceeding

non-suit: order from the judge dismissing the case because the plaintiff has failed to meet a *prima facie* case

notorious fact: a fact that is so generally known and accepted that it may not reasonably be disputed

O

Oakes **test:** test used by the courts to determine whether a Charter right or freedom can be limited by section 1; the measure limiting the right or freedom must be sufficiently important, and the means chosen must be reasonable and demonstrably justified

oath: promise made on the Bible or other holy book to tell the truth in court

Oickle **rule:** rule requiring that the will of the accused has not been overborne by inducements, oppressive circumstances, or lack of an operating mind, and that police trickery has not unfairly denied the accused the right to silence

opinion evidence: evidence given by a witness that is based on conclusions or inferences drawn from facts or observations; generally, the witness is not permitted to state the conclusions or inferences themselves, only the observations

oral evidence: evidence given orally by witnesses

P

past recollection recorded: process whereby the witness recalls the words he made in a statement but not the incident itself

pecuniary or proprietary interest: concerned with financial or ownership matters

penal interest: matter that could result in the person's being incarcerated

person in authority: person in a position to influence the prosecution against an accused

plain view doctrine: rule that a police officer may act without a search warrant if the evidence is in plain view

potential prejudice: the potential for a piece of proposed evidence to be misused (usually, given too much weight) by the trier of fact

potentially injurious information: information of a type that, if it were disclosed to the public, could injure international relations, national defence, or national security

prejudice: the potential for a trier of fact to give evidence more weight than it deserves

present impression: statement regarding a person's perception of their immediate physical surroundings or actions

present memory revived: process whereby the witness revives actual memories and details of an incident; cf. past recollection recorded

presumption: a fact that is taken to be true without the requirement of formal proof

***prima facie* case:** case in which there is sufficient evidence on its face that no further proof is required for a party to succeed

principled approach: method of applying rules of evidence by reference to the policy underlying the rules

principled exception: exception to the hearsay rule based on the principles of necessity and reliability

privilege: status accorded communicated information that makes the information unavailable to the trier of fact

privilege by case: privilege extended to communication on a case-by-case basis

privilege by class: privilege based on the relationship between the communicator of information and the recipient

probative value: the degree to which a potential piece of evidence helps prove a proposition; the value or strength of a fact in proving what the party seeks to establish

propensity or disposition evidence: evidence of an accused person's psychiatric tendency to act a certain way

public safety exception: an exception to privilege when the otherwise protected communication poses a threat to public safety

R

reasonable expectation of privacy test: test used by the courts to determine whether section 8 of the Charter has any application in the circumstances of a particular case

reasoning prejudice: applies to evidence that, if admitted, may confuse the trier of fact or distract it from the issue it must decide

rebut: to present opposing evidence or arguments

relevant fact: a fact that logically supports a proposition

***res gestae* or spontaneous statement:** statement made in an excited state or expressing an existing physical, mental, or emotional state

responsibility: the ability to comprehend the necessity of being truthful and the consequences of not telling the truth

reverse onus: situation where the obligation to prove a fact is shifted from the Crown to the accused

right against self-incrimination: a person's right not to be compelled to be a witness against himself in criminal or quasi-criminal proceedings

S

sensitive information: information relating to international relations, national defence, or national security that is in the possession of the Government of Canada, whether originating from inside or outside Canada, and is of a type that the Government of Canada takes measures to safeguard

similar fact evidence: evidence that shows that an accused committed similar offences in the past, which may be admitted provided that it is relevant in establishing an important matter other than the accused's predisposition to commit that type of offence

simple use immunity: immunity that prevents the use of compelled testimony as evidence against a witness

solemn affirmation: promise to tell the truth in court that has the same value as an oath

solicitor–client privilege: privilege that protects communications between lawyer and client made for the purpose of obtaining legal advice

spoliation: the destruction, mutilation, alteration, or concealment of evidence

spousal privilege: privilege based on the spousal relationship that prevents one spouse from testifying against the other

subpoena: formal, legal document requiring a witness to appear at a hearing in a criminal case

summons: formal, legal document requiring a witness to appear at a hearing in a civil case

T

trier of fact: person in a trial who assesses the evidence and renders a verdict; in a jury trial, the jury

trier of law: person in a trial who controls the trial process, determines the admissibility of evidence, and instructs the trier of fact on the applicable law; in a jury trial, the judge

U

ultimate issue opinion: opinion on the ultimate issue that is before the trier of fact; generally, witnesses are not permitted to give an ultimate issue opinion because the trier of fact could be swayed by it

V

***Vetrovec* warning:** warning to the jury given where the judge determines that the evidence of a particular witness is called into question and requires special scrutiny; jurors are cautioned that they may accept the evidence without corroboration but it is dangerous to do so without independent confirmation of material parts of that evidence

vicarious admission: admission made by an authorized speaker for a party

view: relocation of the court to the site where the evidence is located; a judge may order a view when the evidence is too large to bring into the courtroom or when there is a valid reason for the trier of fact to see the site

voir dire: mini-trial, or trial within a trial, that is designed to determine the admissibility of evidence in the absence of the trier of fact

W

Wigmore test: four criteria for assessing case-by-case claims of privilege

without prejudice: protection claimed for information provided by a party that prevents the information from being used in court

Index

J

judges' privilege, 185
judicial discretion, 21
judicial notice
    administrative tribunals, and, 48
    defined, 46
    examples of, 47-48
    social framework facts, 48-50
junk science, 163-64

L

layperson's opinion, 149-50
litigation privilege, 175-77
litigation process, 4-6

M

material fact, 55
military justice, 32
Mohan factors
    absence, exclusionary rule, 152
    necessity, 152
    relevance, 151-52
    qualifications, 152
moral prejudice, 137
Mr. Big, 211-13

N

national security matters, 181
natural justice, 28
non-compellable witness, 183
non-suit, 42
notorious fact, 46
novel science, 160-63

O

Oakes test, 222-23
oath, 250
oath helping, 159-60
objections, 283
Oickle rule, 207
opinion evidence
    defined, 148-49
    expert
        bias, 154-55
        defined, 150
        hired gun syndrome, 154

        limits, 154, 155-65
        Mohan factors, 151-53
        provincial/territorial rules, 155
        qualification process, 153
        rule, 150-51
    layperson, 149-50
    rule against, 148
oral evidence
    collateral facts rule, 277-78
    corroboration, 279-82
    defined, 250
    objections, 283
    witnesses
        bolstering credibility, 277
        calling to testify, 260
        competence, 260-64
        credibility, 275
        cross-examination, 266-73
        examination-in-chief, 264-66
        failure to cross-examine, 273-74
        impeaching testimony, 276
        re-examination, 274
        refreshing memory, 278-79
        reliability, 275-76
oral histories, 106-7, 118
out-of-court statements, 73-74

P

paralegal–client privilege, 188
past recollection recorded, 105, 118, 279
pecuniary or proprietary interest, 90
penal interest, 92-94
person in authority, 210
plain view doctrine, 225
potential prejudice, 126
potentially injurious information, 181
prejudice, 59-60
present impression, 96
present memory revived, 279
presumption
    civil cases, 45-46
    criminal cases, 43-45
    defined, 42
prima facie case, 41-42
principled approach, 21
principled exception to hearsay rule
    application of, 120-22
    defined, 119
    development of, 119-20